D0108390

Flying High

ALSO BY EUGENE RODGERS
Beyond the Barrier:
The Story of Byrd's First Expedition to Antarctica

Flying High

*The Story of Boeing and the
Rise of the Jetliner Industry*

Eugene Rodgers

The Atlantic Monthly Press
New York

Published simultaneously in Canada
Printed in the United States of America

FIRST EDITION

Library of Congress Cataloging-in-Publication Data

Rodgers, Eugene.
   Flying high: the story of Boeing and the rise of the jetliner
industry / Eugene Rodgers. — 1st ed.
       p.   cm.
   Includes bibliographical references and index.
   ISBN 0-87113-655-4
   1. Boeing Company.   2. Aircraft industry—United States—History.
3. Aeronautics, Commercial—United States—History.   I. Title.
HD9711.U63B6365   1996
338.7'62913'0973—dc20   96-24453

Design by Laura Hammond Hough

The Atlantic Monthly Press
841 Broadway
New York, NY 10003

10 9 8 7 6 5 4 3 2 1

*Dedicated to the memory of my father, Thomas A. Rodgers,
an engineer like those whose story I tell here, and to
my children, Eric and Cathy Rodgers, who will learn
from this book what life with a corporation is like.*

Contents

Part I

Building the Foundation

1 || Flying High

O ne day in 1989, a United Airlines DC-10 jetliner flying over western Washington state turned south and began its approach to the Seattle-Tacoma Airport, better known as SeaTac. On board was Jim Guyette, then executive vice president–operations for Chicago-based United Airlines, the country's largest air carrier. Guyette was on his way to see Dean Thornton, then president of the Boeing Commercial Airplane Group, the biggest division of the Boeing Company and the world's preeminent maker of jetliners. Guyette wanted to persuade Thornton to allow him to cooperate in setting the specifications for the 777, which would be the first new model Boeing airplane to go into airline service in over twelve years and would represent a new jetliner generation.

It would replace the big, wide-body, Douglas DC-10s such as the one carrying him, and the DC-10's only direct competitor, the similar Lockheed L-1011. The Douglas and Lockheed models would both be twenty-five years old and nearing senility in 1995, when the 777 would be ready for delivery. United Airlines would need a couple dozen or more new jetliners beginning that year. Guyette wanted to see a model on the market that would have almost exactly the features and performance he wanted. He couldn't guarantee a sale to Boeing—that would take place years down the road and would depend on price, financing, and other parts of a deal besides features and performance. He could, however, offer Boeing advice that would make the jetliner attractive to all airlines and obviously give Boeing a leg up in the future bid for United's order.

Whatever make United ordered, the purchase would be a major investment, more akin to a family's acquiring an expensive house than buying a car. Airplanes in the 777 class would probably sell for over $100 million each. Only two other manufacturers in the world made large and medium-sized jetliners, and both would offer appealing models competing with the 777: the venerable Douglas division of the McDonnell Douglas Corporation in the United States, and the feisty European consortium, Airbus Industrie. Guyette knew all three companies and their top executives well. Boeing was the last of the three to begin development of its new generation, and therefore the only one whose design United could then influence heavily. Guyette wasn't displeased by any means; he told people, "I have the highest degree of respect" for Boeing and "I enjoy doing business with them."

Over the years, through personal contacts, presentations, and reading, he had been thoroughly exposed to reams of information and statistics about the company he was visiting. Guyette knew that Boeing, which had its headquarters in Seattle and made most of its products in the Seattle area, was a corporation that other companies looked up to. It was usually included when one magazine or another published its list of most-admired companies in America.

Boeing was king of the jet makers. The company had built the world's first successful jetliner, the 707, which had begun carrying passengers in 1958. Almost by itself, the trailblazing 707 had turned ocean liners and passenger trains into quaint means of transportation, and started the jet revolution that made long-distance travel common. Boeing had discontinued the old 707, but sold four later models, more than any other firm. Its offerings included the world's largest jetliner, the 747. Airlines shopping for jets could choose just the right model for a route depending on its length and the number of passengers served. Boeing then commanded an extraordinary worldwide market share of over 60 percent, and had made more than half of all jetliners that ever flew. All its jetliners had made money or were well on their way to being profitable. The large majority of other companies' jetliners—including the DC-10 and L-1011—had lost money for their makers, most of whom, like Lockheed, were no longer competing with the seemingly indomitable Boeing ("Economic failure is the norm in the civil aviation business," Wolfgang Demisch, a leading aerospace industry analyst, has observed.)

Boeing excelled in virtually every aspect of its business—engineering, manufacturing, financing, marketing, after-sale support—and enjoyed a reputation for being exceptionally imaginative and innovative. No other aircraft maker could match its productivity. Boeing's products were first-class, famed among airlines as the Cadillacs of jetliners. Customers depended on Boeing to sell them high-quality airplanes that satisfied them, to provide high-quality service, and to charge reasonable prices. Again and again, airline executives declared that they found in Boeing just what people tried to find in merchants who sold them cars and clothing—someone who wouldn't subject you to the hard sell and, most of all, someone you could trust. In a twist on the business world's saying about IBM, airline executives assured each other that no one ever got fired for buying Boeing. (In the mid-1990s, travelers driving downtown from SeaTac passed a billboard that proudly proclaimed Southwest Airlines as 100% BOEING.)

Boeing was big. With well over a hundred thousand employees, the company delivered a new airplane about every day on average, and grossed billions of dollars and netted hundreds of millions every year. Boeing made its 747 jumbo jets in the world's largest factory, a gigantic plant covering sixty-three acres. The busy company usually ended each year as the nation's largest exporter, with over 60 percent of its sales being made outside the United States; no matter where in the world a jetliner was waiting at an airport gate, no matter what country's colors it bore, chances were that it was made in America by Boeing. Boeing alone was responsible for a significant part of the U.S. balance of payments. In 1993, *Fortune* magazine observed that Boeing was "arguably, the flagship of America's global competitiveness." With staff continually flying all over the planet to hawk or maintain its widely scattered products, Boeing was the airlines' single biggest customer, buying tens of millions of dollars in tickets every year.

Making Boeing's airplanes was a worldwide effort. Boeing actually spawned fewer than half the components in its own plants. Thousands of suppliers made parts, systems, and aircraft sections in every state and dozens of foreign countries, and shipped them to Seattle for assembly. Engines, accounting for up to a third of a jetliner's total cost, were made by two other companies in the United States and one in England. Many heavy expenditures had nothing directly to do with aircraft—Boeing bought tens of millions of dollars of printing and publishing services, for instance.

The Boeing corporation was one of the country's leading defense and space contractors, this work comprising a fifth to a quarter of its business. During World War II, the company's phenomenal production of bombers, the B-17 "Flying Fortress" and B-29 "Superfortress," had helped significantly to defeat the Axis; the company's effort to develop the B-29 was second in America's war priorities only to the Manhattan Project that developed the atomic bomb (and a Boeing B-29 , the *Enola Gay*, dropped the first A-bomb). At the beginning of the cold war, *Business Week* magazine had asserted, "No manufacturer . . . is more important to the freedom of the free world than Boeing." In 1987, when takeover specialist T. Boone Pickens tried to grab Boeing, Gary Reich, first vice president of the E. F. Hutton & Company brokerage, decried the raider's effrontery, stating, "Boeing is a national asset. For anybody to do that to make a fast buck would be scandalous and morally corrupt."

Boeing was among the most prominent companies in the world. Its stock was one of thirty blue chips used to calculate the influential stock-market yardstick, the Dow-Jones industrial average. Boeing had twice been the subject of *Time* magazine cover stories (one of which had declared, in 1980, that Boeing jetliners "are the best, safest, most efficient aircraft anywhere. . . . Boeing is on its way to becoming as synonymous with passenger jets as is Kleenex with facial tissue"). A popular French farce about flight attendants on 707s was titled *Boeing! Boeing!* A magazine writer described how jet setters "Boeing" their way around the globe. The world's most prestigious airplane, Air Force One, which carried the president of the United States and his staff, was a Boeing 707.

The word that distinguished jetliner manufacturers from most other large corporations, and that characterized Boeing most of all, was "daring." The bold companies gambled enormous amounts of money in development and start-up costs for new jetliner models that might flop in the marketplace. The business world uses the phrase "betting the company" when a corporation makes a risky investment that exceeds the firm's net worth. It means looking bankruptcy in the face and staring it down. Boeing had thrived by betting the company on several new models—although it came within the thickness of a dollar bill of losing everything on one occasion. The ante for the 777 deal would be several billion dollars. Dean Thornton and Frank Shrontz, the chairman of Boeing, would be long retired or dead by the time the aircraft just broke even. Retired Executive Vice President Joe Sutter, designer of the 747 (said to be financed by the greatest wager ever made on a business project), told colleagues he had found a theme song for Boeing when he turned on his car radio coming home from work one day and heard Kenny Rogers singing "The Gambler," which compares life to a card game.

The stakes had risen so high in the jetliner industry's "sporty game," as author John Newhouse called it, that Boeing and Douglas were the only completely private companies still sitting at the table where wagers for large and medium-sized jetliners were placed (Airbus Industrie being a joint venture subsidized by the governments of the participating companies). Wall Street financier George Ball pointed out, "There are no historic precedents or current parallels for the magnitude of financial exposure risked by an American airframe company." Although the industry had only three participants, they produced goods relatively low in quantity and high in price, so no oligopoly existed; in fact, the three rivals fought intensely—some would say viciously—for sales.

From the assembly lines to the boardroom, people who worked for Boeing were proud of the strong character and conspicuous achievements of their company. (A Boeing employee walking—one might almost say "strutting"—through a plant called the attention

of a visitor to a banner hanging on a wall that proclaimed WE BUILD
LEGENDS.) A magazine writer reported that Chairman Frank Shrontz
"clearly feels atop the best company selling the best damn product
the world has ever seen." Dean Thornton, talking about the excitement of careers at Boeing, asserted that "there's not one [of us] who
doesn't get goose bumps when he sees a 747 in the air. This isn't
like making toothpaste."

Looking out the windows on the right side of the DC-10, Jim
Guyette took in the picturesque sight of the coastal range, the Olympic Mountains, and—closer—Everett, the small city with the colossal
plant high on a bluff where Boeing made today's biggest airplanes,
747s and 767s, and would make the 777. Passengers on the left could
see the inland range, the Cascade Mountains. Tall evergreens
stretched up toward Guyette as the airplane descended to an altitude of a few hundred feet. The craft winged over Lake Union at
the northern end of Seattle and followed the eastern edge of the city.
Lake Washington, a long body of water running north and south
that bordered Seattle to the east, could be seen from the left side of
the airplane. Out of the right side, Guyette caught sight of the famous Space Needle marking the site of the 1962 World's Fair, whose
buildings were still used for cultural and sporting events. Then came
the tall buildings of downtown Seattle and, just after them, the huge
round roof of the Kingdome, the city's enclosed stadium (named
for King County, which includes Seattle and its immediate sur-
roundings). The waters of Puget Sound's Elliott Bay glistened in
the sun on the other side of the buildings. Only a few seconds later
Boeing's sprawling corporate headquarters complex, including
offices, plants, and Boeing Field, passed just under the airplane.
Within moments the DC-10 touched down at SeaTac.

A driver from Boeing met Guyette at the United baggage claim
area and carried his bags to a van. Taking state Route 518 east and
Interstate 405 north through the outskirts of greater Seattle, they
drove seven miles to the city of Renton at the foot of Lake Washington. Here they arrived at the headquarters of Boeing's Commer-

cial Airplane Group, next to the plants that made Boeing's smallest airplanes, 737s and 757s. Dean Thornton met Guyette in the lobby, handed him a security badge with the words ESCORT REQUIRED in big red block letters, and took his valued customer up to his office.

Thornton was hesitant about the idea of United's getting deeply involved in designing the 777. Boeing had linked with airlines on other designs, but those carriers had paid for the privilege by placing predevelopment orders. There was a danger, too. Historically in the aircraft industry, designs too oriented to one customer had sometimes turned off other customers. Thornton would need the flexibility to make the 777 universally attractive. After a while, they adjourned for lunch. During the meal, Guyette challenged Thornton: "Do you trust us or not?" Thornton reflected that the advantages of bringing in United outweighed the disadvantages, and he shook hands with Guyette. Back at the office, they wrote and signed a memorandum of understanding formalizing the arrangement.

Guyette left to pay a courtesy call on Frank Shrontz. The van drove him five miles northwest along the Martin Luther King Jr. Highway to a short cutoff going due west and ending at the Duwamish River, the waterway that wends down the middle of the land sandwiched between Puget Sound and the southern half of Lake Washington. They turned right on Boeing's street, East Marginal Way, a main road lined with industrial buildings. (A left turn would have taken them back to SeaTac, past bars with signs such as HOT NAKED GIRLS ON STAGE! DISCOUNT WITH BOEING I.D.) Boeing Field and the Museum of Flight appeared on the right. The airfield extended a couple of miles up the road. The small wooden building called the "red barn" that had been Boeing's original headquarters and plant combined stood next to the museum, transported from its working location right on the Duwamish. The buildings on the left belonged mostly to Boeing, many of them defense and space facilities.

Also on the left, about a mile up the road from the museum, just after crossing the city line into Seattle proper, Guyette came to the long, three-story Boeing headquarters building, of pre–World War II vintage. The imposing main entrance in the middle, with a clean, streamlined look, had long been closed. The limousine drove over railroad tracks between headquarters and the road, and dropped Guyette off at the reception area on the right side of the building. The fine edifices of downtown Seattle, where most of the city's executives worked in elegance, lay twelve miles ahead. Microsoft, the area's other celebrity corporation, resided on a pleasant "campus," as that company styled it, on the other side of Lake Washington.

As Guyette walked inside to greet a smiling Frank Shrontz, he might have thought, like other visitors who knew the company, that the preference of Boeing executives for this nothing-fancy, industrial neighborhood adjoining an airfield typified the corporation and its people. Clipping on his security badge, he followed Shrontz up to the chairman's big third-floor office. Guyette looked forward to working at the side of Shrontz, Thornton, and company during what would be a lengthy, arduous task to create the latest marvel of the airways.

A jetliner is a small, compact hotel with wings and engines. The guests occupy seats that can double as beds, lamps radiate light, air circulates at a desirable temperature, storage space accepts coats and luggage, fire protection systems stand guard, entertainment systems provide distraction, "room service" offers meals and drinks, lavatories are handy, all within a sturdy structure with windows. Airplane technology has been maturing for almost a century, jetliner technology for four decades. Why shouldn't designing a new jet passenger airplane be as easy as designing a new hotel? It might seem a simple matter of getting a few engineers in the right specialties together, supplying them with a hundred thousand dollars or so, and giving them several weeks with their computers and drafting tools. Why, then, do new jetliners like the 777 demand thousands of engineers, billions of dollars, and several years of work? The answer lies in the incredible complexity of jetliners, and the need to keep passengers comfortable and as safe as humanly possible while the airplane shoots them along close to the speed of sound, five or six miles above the earth.

The surfaces of the wings that lift the hotel-like cabin into the air must be subtly curved according to principles of physics to provide the maximum upward force as the air strikes their undersides and flows over their tops. The wing structure must be strong enough to hold up the weight of the cabin with all its passengers and amenities. And the engines must put out sufficient power to lift the entire airplane, accelerate it up to the sound barrier, and push it through the air for thousands of miles.

Two primary tasks of jetliner designers are aimed at helping engines do their jobs: keeping weight as low as they can so the engines don't have to lift as much, and making the jetliner's shape as sleek as possible so the engines don't have to spend more fuel than necessary pushing the craft through the air. This helps the airplane to fly far at a cost that's reasonable—and even, airlines hope, cheap. These requirements force designers to go to great lengths to make everything extremely light and compact, which are not considerations at all for hotel designers.

In reality, of course, a jetliner is much more than a hotel with a few aerodynamic things bolted on. Designers also give it sophisticated systems such as those to control flight, navigate, talk by radio, see by radar, and take off and land. Although other companies design and make the engines, Boeing engineers have to develop engine mountings and fuel and control systems—Boeing employs more power-plant specialists than any engine manufacturer.

One overriding consideration rules engineers who design jetliners, a constraint that most differentiates their work from hotel design and consumes much of the vast amounts of time, money, and labor they expend: the imperative to keep passengers snug and out of harm's way in a situation that wants badly to kill them. A jetliner at cruising altitude is assailed by winds twice those of the most destructive tornadoes, exposed to temperatures low enough to freeze an unprotected person to death in minutes, surrounded by air without enough oxygen to keep an unprepared person alive, pressurized so highly relative to its environment that without built-in precautions it would explode like an overinflated balloon (windows, for instance, withstand hundreds of pounds of pressure), and hanging from nothing but air molecules at a height that would splatter a fallen person like an egg smashed against concrete. The jetliner cannot stay up unless it keeps moving fast; if serious trouble occurs, the pilot can't pull over and shift into PARK while he fixes it. Every part of the jetliner related to safety—and most parts are so related—must work right during all the hours the airplane is jetting through the air.

The criteria of lightness, compactness, and safety and comfort in a hostile setting strain technology to its limit. Jetliner design draws on the latest advances in metallurgy and materials, such as new alloys and composites; electronics; computers and software; and other science-based technologies. The voracious appetite of the aircraft industry for innovation impels progress in several fields of high technology, and helps to make the industry a keystone of the national economy.

"An airplane is probably the biggest assembly of intricate parts in any independently operational unit," retired Boeing engineering executive Bill Cook wrote in his book. Engineers carefully and skillfully design each small part, keeping in mind everything that might happen to the part during both flight and airport operations. Lavatory engineers, for instance, have to remember that, in some countries, facilities will often be cleaned by illiterate workers, so cleaning must be foolproof. The engineers design—and then redesign repeatedly as requirements continually change. Jetliners are so finely engineered that the parts are interdependent; engineers have to try new approaches as interactions or potential interactions with other parts reveal themselves in the elaborate "ecology" of developing aircraft systems. Then engineering managers inevitably decree modifications to the overall airplane design. Short deadlines place the engineers under heavy pressure, and most of them work long days and weeks. They find the process something like going through drafts of chapters for a group writing project. Flight testing and government certification trials burn millions of dollars more and generate additional changes.

Daryl Banks, lead engineer for passenger door design on the 777, explained what he went through. Doors—elementary parts of land-based hotels—become complicated organs of 560 parts when they go on jetliners. Current door technology dates back to propeller days, when a Boeing door accidentally flew open in the air and sucked a flight attendant out to her death, initiating an overhaul in door design.

Banks and the engineers in his group had to design the doors to stringent specifications covering both normal and exceptional operations. The doors must always open when they're supposed to, and never open when they're not supposed to. Although they're big and heavy, they must be easy for small people to open and close. If one way of opening, shutting, or locking the door should fail, an alternative way must be activated. If the door is pounded, as if a deranged passenger tried to kick it open, it should lock tighter. If the jetliner should suffer a minor crash landing that warps the doors and frames slightly, surviving passengers should still be able to open them—even if the accident occurs in a storm that coats the fuselage with a thick layer of ice. A person outside the cabin must be able to open the door in an emergency. Maintenance and repair should be easy to perform, preferably without having to remove the door. The door could not weigh more than a specified number of pounds.

Banks was given the rough "first draft" design of the entire jetliner as a starting point for his work, and ordered to fit the doors into it. The outside of the doors form parts of the fuselage surface, for example, and Banks had to know the curvature of the surface at each door location. Banks estimated that his project would take fifteen man-years of work—before changes.

While Banks was designing the doors, the shape of the fuselage changed twice and its size changed several times. Experts in other specialized fields, such as stress analysis, reviewed his designs and usually suggested changes. In one major alteration, the size of the inflatable emergency slides, which are built into the doors, grew from three to nine cubic feet, requiring wholesale changes in the door. Banks had a test door built, and deployed the slide five hundred times to perfect it.

As usual, some things didn't work well on the test door. One big headache was the outside handle, which was supposed to fold all the way into a housing when the door was locked from the outside. It didn't, and would interfere with streamlining if left uncorrected. Banks put three men on the problem, one of whom logged fifty-six hours of overtime. Banks never worried that this or any other problem might prove insoluble. "Almost any engineering problem can be solved with enough time, people, and money," he declared.

At the peak of door development, Banks had forty engineers working with him. He's proud of what they accomplished, noting particularly that they saved eighty pounds over initial specifications. Some of them are still at it, incorporating changes as the need shows up in service. There's more water in the 777 than Banks knew about, for instance, especially in the galley areas, so he had to fine-tune the design to allow for a possibly greater threat of frosting up.

Another example dramatizes the time that designers must devote to fulfilling exacting standards for every part, illustrating that no part is minor. Dean Wilkinson, an avionics (aircraft electronics) engineer, devoted five months of equivalent full-time work—he toiled on several projects at once—to develop the first master brightness control for the displays on a flight deck (as cockpits came to be called when crews could walk around in them). His one knob increases or decreases the brightness of all displays at once, supplementing individual controls on about thirty displays. Again, safety was paramount; Wilkinson had to be sure, for instance, that on a dark night all the lit displays couldn't go out at once. He won the President's Award of the Commercial Airplane Group (a congratulatory message and a watch) for his achievement.

Flight controls engineer Doug May talked about all the "running around" and nontechnical activities that take place during development, consuming resources. He investigated whether adding a guard around a certain rod inside the wings would increase safety; it would definitely add a little weight and cost, so it had to be researched thoroughly. He talked with, or exchanged memos with, people who worked on flight characteristics, structures, and hydraulic and electrical systems. He presented his findings and recommendations in meetings, reports, and presentations up through increasingly higher levels of review—several times having to make changes and restart the tedious process. May commented plaintively on the many weeks he spent dealing with others in the human and bureaucratic side of development: "Sometimes people are too busy, sometimes on vacation, and, in a high-stress environment, sometimes very aggravated. It can be very frustrating and tense, as when you find your document buried in someone's in-box an hour before your scheduled big presentation. The job is twenty-five percent engineering and seventy-five percent coordination, paper shuffling, and clerical work." (On his recommendation, Boeing added the guard.)

While jetliner development is under way, other engineers pursue a parallel and equally demanding and expensive effort to design and build the manufacturing tools, which must be created individually for each airplane model. "Tools" in the aircraft industry are often really giant, sophisticated machines, such as the one that holds and rotates the entire 777 fuselage.

Historically, by the time new jetliners have started flying away from Seattle painted in airline colors, Boeing's treasury has been down to a thin layer of coins on the floor, the gamble that its engineers could succeed has ended, and the gamble that its salesmen could sell enough products to refill the coffers has just begun.

Boeing derives importance not only from its own activities but from the high stature of its industry. Boeing is classified as an airframe manufacturer—it constructs entire airplanes but doesn't build the engines (these days, nobody makes both). The company is a member of the aircraft industry, which includes Boeing's two commercial competitors, plus producers of military aircraft, which Boeing also makes, and others. The aircraft industry, in turn, is a member of the aerospace industry, which further includes manufacturers of missile and space products, both of which Boeing makes, and their suppliers. Beginning with World War II, the aerospace industry has always been the largest or among the largest industries in the United States.

In a study of the nonmilitary portion of the aircraft industry, the National Academy of Engineering stated, "Few other industries combine in as large a measure a crucial role in national security, a major contribution to national economic health and foreign trade, and a flagship role in the global posture of technological leadership accorded the United States." Other studies have shown that air transportation has made the second greatest contribution to economic development, exceeded only by education. English social historian Walter H. G. Armytage wrote, "It is not too much to say that aviation has had a more comprehensive and far-reaching effect on all fields of material endeavor embarked on by humans than any other previous single development." Because a strong aircraft industry is a keystone of economic and military might in every country that participates in it, aircraft manufacturing may be the most important business politically all over the world.

In 1992, the Congressional Research Service reported to the House and Senate on the tremendous economic impact of the entire aircraft industry. The report showed that, for every additional dollar of shipments of aircraft, output of the economy increased by about $2.30; when the industry shipped a dollar less in value, the economy contracted by $2.30. Others pointed out that because jetliners comprise a significant market for other high-technology industries, a decline in U.S. competitiveness in the jetliner sector would adversely affect other important industries such as electronics and materials. Militarily, the aircraft industry is vital to the nation, and the Pentagon views a vigorous jetliner business as a way of keeping the industry healthy and ready for potential wartime production.

While other industries that arose early in the century are dying or stagnating, the aircraft industry remains vibrant. Prominent economist Lester Thurow, dean of the Sloan School of Management at MIT, in 1992 listed civil aviation among the key industries of the next few decades. The next year, the investors' publication *Barron's* wondered editorially if Boeing was up to the modern challenges: "Boeing . . . appears to have reached the pinnacle of its corporate might. Decay often follows, bred by resistance to change and complacency. Could it be that Boeing is fated to wither like so many other once-world-class US manufacturers?" To this, Boeing's executives by their actions shout "Baloney!" They're fighting vigorously for their corporate lives, battling not merely other corporations, but also the political and economic might of the European countries backing the awesome Airbus Industrie consortium. And they're struggling to overhaul their octogenarian company to serve a changing market that newly emphasizes fast production of jetliners and low sticker prices.

Most of Boeing's plants and offices are in the Seattle area, and the great majority of Boeing's people live there. The company's facilities in the Puget Sound region lie roughly on a north-south line, paralleling the sound, beginning at Everett in the north and ending at Auburn, some forty miles south, the site of a components manufacturing plant. Kent, about five miles north of Auburn, hosts a large complex devoted mostly to military and space work. The Renton jetliner operation is another five miles north of Kent. The plants are nondescript factory complexes, clean and smoke-free but architecturally undistinguished. A legion of guards keeps the plants safe and secure. The two other main plants are in Wichita, Kansas, where a factory that formerly made bombers now makes the nose sections of jetliners, and suburban Philadelphia, home of the helicopter division.

Boeing's Seattle-area employees enjoy living in a city widely considered one of the most beautiful and desirable locations in the country; Seattle and other Puget Sound cities are frequently identified as the best places in the United States to live and do business. Boeing regards its superlative locale as a key asset for attracting and keeping the best white-collar employees (and, its engineers' union claims, paying them less money than they'd get elsewhere). A disadvantage is Seattle's seclusion way up in the top left-hand corner of the country. John Borger, who was an official of the now-defunct Pan American Airlines, has blamed the isolation for a certain provincialism in business dealings that he termed Boeing's "Pacific Northwest psychology." On the other hand, Wolfgang Demisch, the industry analyst, postulates that the remote location isolates Boeing from pressures to follow the latest industry "fad du jour" that sometimes overcomes good sense in the megalopolises.

Seattle began as a lumber town and seaport, and remains a key shipping center, the fifth largest container port in the United States. In appearance, ambiance, and livability, Seattle is much like San Francisco. The city is bordered on the west by Puget Sound, really an inlet of the Pacific that makes a dogleg turn to the south above Seattle, and on the east by Lake Washington. Steep hills descend from midtown to the sound. Many of Boeing's current and retired high-level executives live in the expensive homes on or with a good view of the sound or lake. The waters are easily navigable, and many residents like to sail and fish: one out of every five persons in the region owns some kind of boat, the country's highest proportion of boat owners. The mountain ranges that flank the area are snow-covered most of the year, and skiing is another popular activity. Mount Rainier, the huge dormant volcano, has come to symbolize Seattle. Although about sixty miles away in the Cascades to the southeast, it's so immense that it looms over the area, a sentinel easily visible on clear days from many parts of the city.

To head downtown from Boeing's headquarters, one would get on Interstate 5, the main highway on the west side of Lake Washington. The traffic is always terrible, almost bumper to bumper at sixty miles per hour at any time of day, and made worse by inadequate highway signs. There are so few highways that all the main arteries in the area are chronically clogged; geography and the protests of ubiquitous environmentalists block new highway construction. Authorities plead with little success for drivers to form car pools. A few minutes into the trip, a magnificent view of Seattle's skyline appears ahead and to the left. The closest buildings are the low, white structures of old Seattle. Towering behind them are the dark skyscrapers of "new"—post-1962 World's Fair—Seattle, like huge black monsters advancing on the old city.

I-5 skirts downtown's eastern edge, plunging under the convention center. Continuing north, the freeway leaves downtown on a bridge that crosses Lake Union, which—with canals extending east and west—links Puget Sound and Lake Washington. Houseboats line sections of Lake Union's shore; one of them served in the 1994 hit movie *Sleepless in Seattle* as the home of the widower and his son.

At the other end of the bridge is the exit for the state-supported University of Washington, whose large campus spreads over the countryside to the right. (The university is Boeing's largest single source of professional employees, and engineering professors have done important research for Boeing in the school's wind tunnel.) White lettering on green highway signs announces that travelers are heading toward Everett and, farther on, Vancouver, British Columbia, some 130 miles distant. Vancouver is the closest major city, and much visiting takes place between the two metropolises.

Seattle and environs are clean, and stands of fir trees color the area a rich green; Seattle has nicknamed itself the "Emerald City." The cause of the cleanliness and lush growth, however, is widely regarded as Seattle's biggest drawback: frequent rains that wash the city and water the plants. Clouds cover the skies on two out of three days, often sprinkling the ground below with drizzle. The steady drip rarely becomes torrential; a cats-and-dogs rain is sufficiently unusual to draw people to their windows. The telling slogan of the roofed Kingdome stadium is "We Keep You Covered," although residents are so inured to the light rain that for brief excursions they usually don't bother with raincoats or umbrellas. Because drenching downpours are infrequent, rain gauges at the airport seldom collect much; Seattle's boosters are quick to point out that New York, Boston, and Washington, D.C., record higher annual rainfalls.

The steady if not driving rain is worst in winter, a gloomy, dark season with sunlight made scarce by the overcast and nights made long by Seattle's high latitude; it takes a map to convince many skeptics that Seattle is farther north than the upper tip of Maine, and even farther north than Québec City. One Boeing engineer advises friends to ward off depression by leaving all the lights in the house on all the time in winter. The rain, darkness, and heavy traffic combine to make winter driving a nightmare. A consolation is that, with winter temperatures commonly in the forties, Seattle seldom gets bitterly cold or snowy. Residents look forward to the glorious months of summer and early fall, with their mild temperatures, relatively dry weather, and long, bright days, when the citizens can enjoy their magnificent outdoors to the utmost and actually see Mount Rainier most of the time.

In the mid-1990s, over half a million souls lived in the city of Seattle, and some three million persons inhabited the entire Puget Sound area. The population includes more Scandinavian-Americans (descendants of Norse fishermen attracted to Seattle early in its history) and Asian-Americans, but fewer African-Americans, than the average in most big cities. The natives call themselves by a nick-name that's awkward but has a space-age ring to it: Seattleites. They speak in clipped cadences, as if they were swallowing their tongues, and pronounce "Boeing" in two distinct syllables as "Bo-wing." Typical of the West Coast, they tend to be affable and insouciant. Compared to people in other cities, more of them work in white-collar jobs. They're highly educated. Almost 40 percent have gradu-ated from college, the second highest level among cities nationwide, and a higher proportion have graduated from high school than in any other city.

Seattleites like coffee: Every corner seems to have its coffee stand, and every block its Starbucks coffeehouse, vending espresso, latte, and other specialized brews. They like fish, especially the salmon yanked in great numbers from nearby waters. They like sports as both participants and spectators. Seattle has been identi-fied as the best city in the country for bicycling, and *Places Rated Almanac* has several times named it the best city for recreation. Major-league baseball, basketball, and football teams play in Seattle. Residents, or the younger ones at least, like rock music; many Seattle bands have achieved national prominence, and in the mid-1990s rock fans all over the country tuned in to the "Seattle sound." Seattle audiences like stage productions. The city claims to have more the-atrical performances annually than any place outside New York, and more professional theater companies than any other city its size in the nation. The Seattle Opera Association bills itself as the leading Wagnerian opera company in the United States. A symphony, bal-let company, and numerous museums round out the cultural scene. Seattle's consumers don't like the state sales tax, a whopping 8 percent, although they enjoy not having to pay state income taxes.

Readers in Seattle enjoy both morning and evening newspapers, a luxury unavailable to most other people these days. There's some mention of Boeing almost every day in the local media, and important company news merits front-page or lead-story placement. Seattleites know airplanes. A Microsoft programmer and his wife on a Northwest Airlines flight out of SeaTac were overheard comparing the Airbus A320 they were on with the similar Boeing 757. Many work at the area's large employers, which include Price Costco discount warehouses, Weyerhauser pulp and paper products manufacturers, Nordstrom department stores, and Microsoft. Some fifteen hundred computer-related development firms operate in the area. But more of Seattle's workers go to Boeing in the morning than to any other private organization.

Boeing exerts a major force on the lives of the people of Seattle and Washington state. A reporter for the *Economist* magazine wrote in 1991 that "Boeing . . . has come to influence daily life in its home state of Washington—economically, politically, culturally— on a scale unmatched by any other firm in America."

In many other cities and states dominated by a strong corporation, especially one like an aircraft company that frequently lays off thousands of workers, the populace resents and resists its muscle. Amazingly, Boeing enjoys mostly good relations with the people in its domain. Some of the employees' pride in Boeing's accomplishments rubs off on their friends and neighbors. One fall Saturday in 1994, for example, Boeing held a public exhibit at Boeing Field of a B-2 Stealth bomber, the black, strange-looking aircraft for which it's the major subcontractor to Northrop; a second B-2 flew dramatically in a low pass over the crowd. Boeing had announced the event in the media, and throngs of employees and nonemployees alike came from all over the area with their families to see the once-top secret airplane. In a festive atmosphere, they listened to speeches, bought refreshments, waited in line at the pilot's autograph booth, and had as good a time as they might have had at a state fair.

Visitors to Seattle sense the special nature of the company when they peruse the area-attractions racks at their hotels and pull from them the flyers of a commercial bus touring company advertising jaunts to the biggest factory in the world. There, tourists can see airplanes being formed in Boeing's womb, the fetal aircraft giving off a light green shine from the coating that protects them during production. The company conducts several tours daily, ending at the inevitable souvenir shop dedicated to exorbitantly priced caps, T-shirts, mugs, toys, puzzles, books, et cetera, all with an aviation theme.

Seattleites tend to view Boeing as "our" company, and unabashedly take the attitude that what's good for Boeing is good for Seattle and therefore good for them. Most of them accept that layoffs are in the nature of Boeing's business. The public's toleration undoubtedly owes much to Boeing's character. While the company is sometimes unheeding, stupid, or hardhearted, it doesn't exhibit the gratuitous, large-scale ruthlessness of many near-omnipotent corporations. And the Boeing culture values integrity. A group of cynical aerospace reporters, gathered for the unveiling of the 777 in April 1994, were discussing industry scandals. They laughed at the mention of Boeing's most grievous offenses, made to seem ridiculous by the magnitude of sins committed by competitors. The people who live around Puget Sound sometimes get angry at Boeing when disputes arise, and even battle the company fiercely on labor and other issues, but they don't feel the deep-seated antagonism that poisons the atmosphere in some other company towns.

Boeing revolutionized society when it introduced jetliners, and grew into one of the greatest corporations on earth: the best in its business, large and powerful, daring and exciting, vital to the nation's defense and balance of trade, a pillar of American technological leadership, influential worldwide. Much of the company's phenomenal success is due to the contributions and continuing influence of its founder, a businessman who had an inkling that an aircraft company could make it big when airplanes were just wood-and-canvas toys, a Seattle timber baron who founded both Boeing and United Airlines on the side, one of the most remarkable yet least recognized figures in American history, Bill Boeing.

2 || Bill Boeing

In 1881, Detroit, Michigan, was a city of immigrants: more than a third of the population had come from Europe, mostly from Germany. The Detroit area was rich in natural resources, and one of the immigrant couples, the Boeings—he from a town in Germany, she from Vienna—had fulfilled the American dream by amassing a fortune in the timber and iron-ore businesses. On October 1, 1881, Mrs. Boeing gave birth to a son whom they christened Wilhelm Edward.

When Wilhelm was only eight years old he suffered the tragedy of his father's death. Nothing else is known about Boeing as a boy except that he was sent to Switzerland for part of his education. At some point, he Anglicized his first name to William and asked friends to call him Bill. Eventually he entered Yale University to study engineering, apparently intending a career in industry. After his junior year, Boeing learned of a fabulous opportunity to make money in the timber business in the Pacific Northwest, likely on a tip from the family's connections in the business. At the age of twenty-two, wanting to go off on his own anyway because of contention with his stepfather, he left Yale and, like his natural father, journeyed to a land of promise to seek his own fortune in lumber.

Fair-haired, light-skinned, still boyishly freckled, young Boeing settled in a small city in the tall-tree country near the Washington

coast southwest of Puget Sound. There's no record of Boeing's timber business, but by 1914, at the age of thirty-three, he had become
a multi-millionaire through some combination of his own earnings
and inherited wealth. Six years before, he had moved to Seattle, a
small but rapidly growing lumber town. A friendly but dignified man
with a touch of Yale arrogance, a bit taller than average with a spare,
athletic figure, Boeing lived in style as one of Seattle's most eligible
bachelors. He was building a thirty-room mansion in the ultra-
exclusive Highlands enclave on the sound just north of the city
(a location that would become home to several of his company's
senior executives over the years). The Highlands was a fenced-in,
well-guarded, 308–acre community of fewer than one hundred families—some with old money, some with earned fortunes, but all
well-to-do—living in splendor on large, terraced, heavily treed lots
connected by narrow, winding roads. The homes had nothing so
vulgar as street addresses, so mail would be addressed simply to
MR. WILLIAM E. BOEING, THE HIGHLANDS, SEATTLE, WASHINGTON. A private Episcopal church served the spiritual needs of those who
dwelled there. The Highlands had only recently been formed, and
Boeing had the honor of giving his name to the creek that ran by his
estate. (The Highlands is so secluded and purposely kept so little
known that even today many Seattle residents don't realize it exists.)

In the mid-1950s, Bill Boeing told the story of his life and career
to the Boeing Company's public relations chief, Harold Mansfield,
who also interviewed many other current and retired executives.
Mansfield's anecdotal book based on these talks, *Vision*, remains
the standard history for Boeing's early days. According to Mansfield,
the Boeing Company began as a holiday lark on a hot Saturday, the
Fourth of July, 1914. Bill and his best friend, a Navy lieutenant and
also a former engineering student named G. Conrad Westervelt,
celebrated that Independence Day by going to Lake Washington
to ride in a seaplane flown by a barnstorming pilot who was selling
rides. Flying machines were a sensational novelty. Although the
Wright brothers had flown for the first time over ten years before,
airplanes still had virtually no practical applications. Archduke Franz
Ferdinand had been assassinated only days before; the world was

on the threshold of a war in which airplanes would fly to kill and destroy—but they hadn't flown in battle yet. Nor were they carrying mail, cargo, or travelers. Intrepid barnstormers roamed the country, amazing crowds with their daring exhibitions and selling rides to the brave, and a few air meets had been held featuring various competitions for sporting pilots, but few people had ever seen an airplane; some skeptics didn't even believe they were for real. Boeing and Westervelt had gone to air meets and become excited about flying, and had jumped at this chance to go up in the air themselves.

Anybody planning to take one of the flights that bright day might have had second thoughts on beholding the flimsy airplane. It wasn't much advanced over the contraption in which the Wright brothers had risked their lives in 1903. The biplane was made of fabric stretched over a wooden frame, and a backward-facing pusher propeller was hung between the wings. Spindly struts mounted the puny airplane to twin pontoons. The pilot and one passenger sat on the front edge of the lower wing in front of the propeller. The passenger gripped the edge of the wing and braced his feet against footrests to keep his place; there were no seat belts.

The pilot handed Boeing a pair of goggles. Westervelt watched as his friend took off his rimless eyeglasses and slipped the goggles over his big rectangular face with its small mouth topped by a small mustache. Eyes properly protected, undoubtedly feeling butterflies in his stomach, Boeing clambered onto the airplane to take the first trip. The frail craft raced across the lake, faster and faster, then lifted off the water. Up, up, up it went, turning toward shore and leveling off at about a thousand feet, then disappearing over trees and houses. Minutes later the airplane soared back into sight and settled down gracefully on the lake like a great water bird. No one documented Boeing's reaction, but others who made their first flights in those primitive planes wrote of their incredible euphoria, having fulfilled mankind's age-old wish to fly. Thrilled by the experience, Boeing and Westervelt went up again and again that day—which says something about Boeing's willingness to take risks when they seemed worthwhile, a trait that would carry him and his company to the heights of the business world.

Both friends having technical backgrounds, they closely examined the construction of the rickety airplane. Unimpressed, they agreed that they could design a better craft, and that it would be fun to build and fly an airplane of their own. Most conversations never lead anywhere when they begin with the oft-spoken phrase, "Wouldn't it be great if we could . . ." But Boeing was different from most people: He was wealthy enough to follow through on his whims. He'd already done so. A few years before he'd wanted a yacht but hadn't liked any that were for sale, so, couseled by Westervelt, he nonchalantly bought a shipyard to build one. Boeing loved sailing his custom-built yacht. Now, captivated by the thought of doing the same kind of thing with an aircraft, he decided to go ahead as casually as another man might undertake a home workshop project.

He and Westervelt first had to learn the principles of aircraft design, so Westervelt wrote to the leading experts in the new field of aeronautical engineering for information and advice. Boeing went down to Los Angeles to buy a ten-thousand-dollar seaplane and take flying lessons from Glenn Martin, a noted aviation pioneer and manufacturer. Flying the Martin airplane would give him and Westervelt invaluable practical experience. The friends pursued their joint hobby leisurely. As time went by, historic developments transformed aviation. Four weeks after the memorable Lake Washington flights, a world war broke out in Europe. Both sides used aircraft for observation and reconnaissance. That autumn, English pilots winged over Germany and dropped the war's first airborne bombs. On Christmas day, English pilots fired on German pilots who had flown across the Channel—history's first air combat.

Aviation burgeoned in the hellish war, producing a huge demand in Europe for the rapid development and production of fighters, bombers, scout planes, and trainers. America, clearly about to be drawn into the conflict, would soon have to buy thousands of airplanes. In previous wars, the U.S. government had manufactured most of its armaments, but in the next conflict would turn this job over to private enterprise; this has been called the start of the military-industrial complex. The smell of money attracted many businessmen, who rushed into aviation to serve this market and position themselves for the civilian market that would likely follow from expected wartime progress in aeronautics. At some point—it's not clear when—Boeing decided to turn his rich man's dalliance into a profit-making business. He hired Herb Munter, a talented Seattle mechanic who built his own airplanes and flew them in barnstorming shows, and Westervelt enlisted the help of a marine architect who worked with him, Jim Foley. Boeing and some friends formed a branch of the Aero Club of America to promote aviation and defend it against the legion of antiwar protestors who opposed American development of aircraft that could then be used only for fighting. In an Aero Club campaign to influence public opinion, Bill Boeing and Herb Munter staged a dramatic, attention-getting event. They flew the Martin airplane just over the building tops of downtown Seattle and dropped red propaganda leaflets shaped like artillery shells. The leaflets warned that sleeping America was critically short of airplanes and was unprepared to defend herself. Equating private interest with public need in a way that was common and raised no eyebrows then, one message pleaded in part, "For national defense, encourage aviation . . . our country needs more airplanes."

Westervelt did most of the design work for the new airplane. He drew plans for a seaplane that borrowed heavily from the Martin airplane. (Seaplanes were popular because few runways existed.) The proud partners named their creation after themselves, shortening Boeing and Westervelt to B&W. Boeing bought an engine from an automobile motor manufacturer who also built aircraft engines, purchased manufacturing space on Lake Union, assigned his shipyard to make the wings and pontoons, and hired others to make the rest of the airplane and assemble the finished aircraft. Seattle was a good location for making airplanes. Nearby water accommodated seaplane takeoffs and landings, and never froze. Airplanes were made mostly of wood, and the city had abundant, cheap supplies of wood and skilled woodworkers; Boeing would adopt the advertising slogan "Built Where the Spruce Grows."

Boeing established standards of quality that would contribute to defining the character of the company and maintaining its reputation long after he departed. He seemed always aware that people's lives depended on the good work of his company, something his associates (and other airplane makers) sometimes forgot. Visiting the shop one day, he noted that a workman sawing wing ribs had nicked some of them. He told the man that this was unsatisfactory. The worker responded haughtily that the ribs were good enough. Saying nothing more, Boeing picked up the nicked ribs, ran them through the whirring saw, and threw the pieces on the floor.

The Navy unintentionally dealt the fledgling enterprise a blow when Lieutenant Westervelt got orders transferring him from his assignment of overseeing construction of destroyers in Seattle to another job on the East Coast. Believing the airplane business held great promise for his future, he tried to resign but was refused. He doggedly appealed all the way to Secretary of the Navy Josephus Daniels but, with the world unsettled and the Navy needing to retain experienced officers, he had to leave Seattle and abandon his role in the business.

Work on the B&W continued. The biplane was completed and ready for flight test on June 16, 1916. Made of white Irish linen stretched over a wooden frame, it weighed thirty-two hundred pounds but looked fragile as it bobbed on Lake Union. The 125-horsepower engine gave the craft a potential top speed of only seventy-eight miles per hour. The airplane was much advanced over the one in which Boeing had made his first flight, however. The pilot sat on a seat in the fuselage, and the propeller was mounted on the nose to pull the airplane through the air. Boeing christened the prototype *Bluebill*, after a type of duck.

Munter was to be the test pilot but, when he hadn't appeared by flight time, Boeing impatiently took the airplane out himself. He skimmed across the lake, gathering speed until the noise of the pontoons slapping waves ceased and he rose into the air. He leveled off quickly and darted just above the water for a quarter-mile without incident, then set the airplane gently back on the water. Succeeding trials were just as gratifying.

Surely feeling ebullient, Boeing converted his shipyard on the west bank of the Duwamish River into an aircraft manufacturing facility, started production of a second B&W, began efforts to sell the airplanes, ordered design work to begin on the next-generation aircraft, and incorporated his firm. (The Boeing Company today celebrates the incorporation date of July 15, 1916, as its birthday.) The corporate officers were Boeing, president; his cousin, chemical engineer Edgar N. Gott, vice president; and Jim Foley, who had helped to design the B&W, secretary and general manager. They bossed sixteen hourly employees. Boeing invested one hundred thousand dollars in the firm to capitalize it, and took money out of his own pocket to meet his weekly payroll of seven hundred dollars. Reflecting his vision and ambition, the corporation—then called the Pacific Aero Products Company—was chartered to do business in just about every aspect of the aviation industry, current and predicted, from making airplanes to flying passengers and freight to operating flying schools. Boeing may have had dreams of an aviation empire like the automotive empire being established by his fellow Detroit native, Henry Ford. He was clearly getting in on the ground floor: In the whole country, only about four hundred aircraft were built in 1916.

Boeing had already hired a new designer, an improbable choice considering the time and place: a Chinese man named Tsu Wong, here on a visa. A brilliant engineer, Wong had been the student of Professor Jerome C. Hunsaker, who had designed America's first successful wind tunnel and formed an aeronautical curriculum at MIT. Hunsaker had been one of the helpful experts who had corresponded with Westervelt on the B&W design.

Boeing was disappointed not to find a customer, military or civilian, for the B&Ws. (He would finally sell them abroad three years later to the small organization that eventually became Air New Zealand.) He remained optimistic, nevertheless. He thought he had a good chance to sell the next model to the Navy as a trainer; trainers had two seats with dual controls and were designed for safety rather than performance. Boeing called the new airplane the "Model C" for obscure reasons. Leaning heavily on Professor Hunsaker for advice, Wong introduced several radical design ideas into the Model C involving wing angle and placement, and reductions in control surface areas.

On the Model C's first test flight, Herb Munter rose some two hundred feet over Lake Union. He turned the airplane and then tried to straighten out, but the prototype only went into a tighter turn. The stiff controls resisted his attempts to move out of the turn. Down, down, down spiraled Wong's airplane, threatening to corkscrew Munter into a watery grave. With all his strength, Munter slowly forced the stubborn airplane out of the spiral barely in time to land safely. Shaken, he refused to fly the oddly configured aircraft again until it had been redesigned. Back to the drawing board, literally. Wong moderated his approach and made the product somewhat more conventional.

Boeing talked with the Navy about the Model C. In January 1917, he received an electrifying telegram from Navy Secretary Daniels saying the service would consider the trainer, and urging speedy completion of the prototype. The United States declared war on Germany on April 6, 1917. Three days later, Munter tensely lifted off on the first flight of the second prototype—and it flew beautifully. The airplane vindicated Wong's basic ideas and began Boeing's vaunted tradition of technological innovation. Bill Boeing exuberantly ordered his staff to build five more of the airplanes for testing by the military services. (Boeing people then tended—and still do—respectfully to call the craft providing their livelihood by the full name "airplane," and not by the somewhat slangy "plane" contraction.)

On April 18, Boeing scrapped the Pacific Aero Products designation and gave the company the name under which it would become famous—the Boeing Airplane Company. This brought the firm in line with the many other aircraft manufacturers named after their founders. Bill Boeing may also have considered the marketing value of the name. He was about to go to Washington, D.C., to line up business personally and would make a greater impression as Mr. Boeing of the Boeing Company.

While in the nation's capital, Boeing was handed a wire from Seattle bearing bad news: Wong had resigned to go back to China. The resignation wouldn't affect Model C business, but Boeing would have to find yet another designer. (When last heard from, in

1934, Wong was head of an aircraft manufacturing company in China.)

The Navy needed fifty trainers. The contract would go to the winner of a competition to be held that summer at the new naval air station in Pensacola, Florida. Boeing sent Munter and the mandated two airplanes to Florida and awaited the decision that could help to make the dream of an aviation empire come true or end it. The Navy announced its choice on a now-forgotten date that autumn: Boeing. The thrilling victory was worth $575,000—not bad for a first sale. The good news put the infant company in business for keeps.

Setbacks soon turned Bill Boeing's elation to gloom, however. The Army tested two Model Cs configured as land airplanes and turned them down because conservative Army experts didn't trust the unconventional features. An even bigger shock came when Boeing delivered the first production Model C to the San Diego naval facility. The commanding officer didn't like the pioneering design, either, and felt his unit was being used as a guinea pig for unproven technology. As a result, the Navy ordered retesting of the airplane. Worried that his victory was about to be snatched away, Bill Boeing himself was on hand for the additional tests at the Hampton Roads, Virginia, naval facility. He watched anxiously as inspectors first went over the airplane carefully. His heart sank as one of them pointed to a cable so badly frayed that it was about to part; it severed when the inspector yanked it. The pilot and anybody in the second seat might have been killed had they taken off with the failing cable.

Boeing angrily fired off a letter about the embarrassing incident to Gott, who was in charge of the company's day-to-day affairs. He ended the message severely: "A fine state of affairs. What is the matter with our inspection? If I were judging the machine, I would condemn it for all time. I want a complete report made. For the good of the company, the person responsible has to go. Any such laxity is unpardonable, and I for one will close up shop rather than send out work of this kind." Tough words, but they helped to establish the company's much admired concern with quality and safety. Boeing was surely relieved when the flight tests proved the Model

C a superior product and persuaded the Navy to accept it despite the misfortunes.

Boeing was hit by the loss of another key person when Jim Foley, an officer of the corporation, resigned to head his own company. Foley had recently been serving as Boeing's representative in Washington, primarily to seek new business. Fortunately, Boeing landed another plum despite Foley's departure—a Navy contract to build fifty Curtiss flying boats (airplanes whose fuselages rest in the water, unlike seaplanes, which float on pontoons). Boeing would make the three-seater patrol planes under license from Curtiss, which didn't have the capacity to make all the flying boats of its design needed for the war. Boeing hired more workers, bringing employment to 337 by mid-1918. The company won its first commendation for excellence, a Navy citation for turning out the best flying-boat hulls and producing them for a remarkably low price. Plainly helped by his experience running his shipyard, Boeing made the hulls for a cost little more than a third that of any other plant doing the same work. More than that, however, Boeing's twenty-four-year-old production chief, Phil Johnson, was proving wonderfully skilled at finding the cheapest way to make high-quality items. Boeing had his eye on him.

November 11, 1918, was a great day for the bloodied world but a bad day for Boeing's business: The great war in Europe ended. Boeing had completed production of Model Cs but was only partway through the flying-boat run. The Navy soon cut the order in half. With no replacement business in sight, Bill Boeing reluctantly laid off half his workers, beginning what was to become a familiar boom-or-bust pattern for the company. He ordered design work to begin on a new seaplane for civilians, but he had to find something to hold the skeleton workforce together until the airplane was ready for production. He decided to take advantage of the company's woodworking skills and diversify into wood products.

One line the company got into was a type of large, fast speedboat called a sea sled, made under license to a Boston firm. Boeing sold just ten of them. The first three sold slowly but, according to one account, the last seven went quickly and shifty customers paid cash when Prohibition went into effect, opening a market for boats that could outrun Coast Guard cutters. The other new make-work lines were wooden interiors for restaurants and retail stores—including a Pig 'N Whistle eatery, and corset, glove, and confectionery shops—and furniture. Thus it happened that people who prowl antique shops in Washington state today can buy Boeing Queen Anne bedsteads—the company's principal furniture product—and Boeing dressers, phonograph cabinets, tables, stools, hat racks, umbrella stands, and other furniture pieces. The furniture cost more to make than Boeing could charge for it, however. An employee asked Phil Johnson if he could buy a bedroom set at cost. Johnson is supposed to have replied, "Cost? Why pay the cost? Buy it at retail and save money."

Worse, the prospects for the civilian seaplane evaporated, killed by the military. The government had not yet learned the strategic importance of maintaining a strong aircraft industry. The Army and Navy were dumping thousands of surplus airplanes on the market at a fraction of cost, and no one was buying new models from manufacturers. By fall of 1919, Boeing was anticipating a loss of nearly one hundred thousand dollars for the year, and several times that for 1920. The company had laid off all but thirty employees. With no aircraft manufacturers selling anything to speak of, 90 percent of them had already gone out of business since the war.

Bill Boeing in no way depended on the business. He was still a timberman and spent most of his time at an office in downtown Seattle running his lumber business and tending his investments. Aviation was just a sideline for him; he rarely visited the aircraft building on the outskirts of the city. But lumber was in a downturn, too, so he couldn't afford to be cavalier about aircraft losses. Regretfully, he took the prudent course: He put his dying if not already dead aviation business up for sale. He had no takers. Friends urged him to cut his losses and abandon the failed enterprise, but, for reasons he never explained, he couldn't or wouldn't do it.

Boeing got a couple of small Army contracts to refurbish observation planes and build a few ground-attack planes of Army design, but nevertheless in 1920 the company lost a staggering three hundred thousand dollars. By hanging on, however, Boeing was ready to grab his big chance when it came.

Boeing learned that the Army planned only one aircraft order in the near future, but it would be the biggest since the war—construction of two hundred Thomas-Morse pursuit planes, the Air Service's principal fighters, to be bid in April 1921. Although Thomas-Morse had designed the airplane, Army policy then was to bid construction separately. Six companies submitted bids. When the envelopes were opened, Thomas-Morse itself had bid $1.9 million and four of the other companies had bid close to that figure; the highest was $2.2 million. Boeing's bid was way down at $1.4 million, the lowest by far—and the winner.

Ed Gott, who attended the bid opening, couldn't feel happy; in fact, he seemed to have a sinking feeling in the pit of his stomach. Thomas-Morse not only had designed the airplane but was making fifty of them as winner of an earlier construction order. That company knew its costs far more precisely than Boeing. With a bid so much lower than Thomas-Morse's and everyone else's, Boeing had made a calamitous error in its figuring and would lose more money than ever, Gott feared. The bid wouldn't take effect until accepted some weeks later. Until then, Boeing could withdraw. Gott discussed this option with Phil Johnson and Bill Boeing, but they could find nothing wrong with their estimate. They kept their bargain-basement bid in, and it was officially accepted.

Boeing's employees celebrated, their jobs saved by the contract award, but Boeing, Gott, and Johnson wouldn't sleep well until the first airplanes were out and firm cost data were in. Then they rejoiced: They were making a profit, a good profit; in fact, Bill Boeing awarded himself a bonus of $6,050 out of the earnings. Johnson grew in stature as a manufacturing wizard. Boeing's reputation as the most productive, most cost-efficient producer goes way back to this era—the Curtiss flying boats and Thomas-Morse fighters made under Johnson's direction. (Significantly, of the six bidders for the Thomas-Morse contract, only Boeing has survived as an independent company.)

In 1922, Bill Boeing stepped up to become chairman of the board and promoted Ed Gott to president. Boeing may have wanted to pass more of his time-consuming duties to Gott. He had reason to. His main business demanded most of his attention, and the year before, he had taken on a new responsibility—marriage and family. He had wed Bertha Potter Paschall, who had two sons by a previous marriage. Bill and Bertha produced another son they named William E. Boeing Jr.

As the military's fleet of primitive wartime aircraft grew old, and rapid developments in aeronautics made wartime technology obsolete, the Army and Navy increased orders to the aircraft industry for newer and better airplanes. As an established supplier, Boeing got its share of business and then some, including major contracts to produce Boeing-designed Army and Navy fighters and a Navy trainer. A tally of contracts awarded from 1919 to 1925 showed that Boeing had won the highest total dollar value, $3,945,547. Curtiss was next with some $600,000 less, and no other company was even close. Bill Boeing's wealth nevertheless remained a great asset for his company. The heavy initial costs of designing and making aircraft are recovered slowly as airplanes are delivered and paid for, so he was still pouring in his personal funds to sustain the firm's cash flow well into the 1920s.

Everything seemed to be going well in January 1925 when the company was rocked by a high-level resignation. Ed Gott, president and second in command, quit to become a vice president of rival Fokker Aircraft. His resignation was apparently forced. Bill Boeing reportedly caught him lying on a business matter and fired him. Boeing never forgave him; Boeing's associates learned never to mention the name of Gott in his presence.

Boeing resumed the duties of president. He had a talented young employee whom he wanted to groom to succeed Gott, however: Phil Johnson. A mechanical engineer who had joined Boeing in 1917 when he graduated from the University of Washington, Philip Gustav Johnson was the son of Swedish immigrants, a plump, dimpled little man with small, narrow but friendly light-blue eyes.

Boeing immediately promoted Johnson to first vice president and general manager. Johnson proved himself over the next year, and in February 1926, when Johnson was only thirty-one years old, Boeing happily named him president.

In February 1925, the U.S. House of Representatives had passed a bill sponsored by a Pennsylvania congressman that would profoundly affect Boeing and the entire aviation industry. Known informally as the Kelly bill and officially as the Airmail Act, it ordered the Post Office Department (later the U.S. Postal Service) to turn its airmail routes over to private enterprise. The Post Office had begun airmail on May 15, 1918, with flights between New York City, Philadelphia, and Washington, D.C. Using its own airplanes and pilots, the Post Office had built up an airmail system based on a trunk route from New York to San Francisco and a network of regional routes connected to the trunk. Airmail was the only significant civilian application of aircraft. By establishing airfields and installing navigational beacons along its routes for its own purposes, however, the Post Office had begun to establish an infrastructure that would allow commercial aviation to expand. Congress hoped to speed up development of passenger and freight service by providing a large, steady airmail business for private airlines. The Post Office privatized airmail gradually, putting its regional groups up for bid a few at a time, and planning to spin off the trunk line last.

Certainly, Boeing stood to benefit from the growth of civilian aviation by selling more airplanes. In fact, Bill Boeing had promoted airmail and his company's airplanes right after the war by agreeing to carry airmail from Vancouver, British Columbia, to Seattle as part of a Canadian exhibition—the first airmail flown between Canada and the United States. Boeing and company test pilot Eddie Hubbard (Herb Munter had left to form his own air charter service) had made the 125-mile flight in a Model C on March 3, 1919. Boeing saw that commercial aviation offered him more than bigger airplane sales, however. He had farsightedly incorporated his company not only to make airplanes but also to fly passengers and freight. But the time had not yet been ripe to set up an airline. Boeing had not even bid on a regional airmail route, believing that he couldn't turn an adequate, steady profit; the additional risks were greater than he cared to take on while he was building his risky manufacturing business. There was no more telling statistic about the danger in airmail or other airline operations than this gruesome fact: Of the original forty airmail pilots, thirty-one had been killed in crashes by 1925.

In 1926, nevertheless, Boeing felt the time had come to test the passenger business in a limited way. He resolved to establish a Puget Sound airline to fly between Seattle and the British Columbia cities of Vancouver and Victoria. He wanted Eddie Hubbard to run the operation. After the airmail promotional flight, Hubbard had struck out on his own as an airmail contractor, dropped out of business after a few years, and gone to work for Ed Gott at Fokker. Boeing enticed him back.

Hubbard arrived pushing a more ambitious idea than flying around Puget Sound. The Post Office had announced that on November 15 it would put the trunk airmail route up for bid in two segments: New York–Chicago and Chicago–San Francisco. On the basis of his experience, Hubbard was sure Boeing could handily run the western segment at a good profit. The pilot didn't want to go directly to Bill Boeing with his idea, without support from someone else in authority, but Phil Johnson was out of town. Hubbard approached Claire Egtvedt, chief engineer and third most powerful man in the company, and quickly persuaded Egtvedt that the company should submit a bid. Egtvedt even strengthened the argument they'd present to Bill Boeing. The engineer had designed an airplane for the Post Office that had the bad luck to make its first flight just as the government was ceasing to fly the mail itself. Egtvedt thought they could update the design and produce an airplane with exceptionally low flying costs—meaning they could submit a low bid with an excellent chance of winning and still make good money.

Egtvedt and Hubbard quickly worked up a presentation and eagerly went to see Bill Boeing. They told him he'd need a fleet of twenty-five airplanes by July 1, 1927; outlined the costs, including an initial investment of $750,000; and pointed out that their airplane could be designed to carry one or two passengers and some freight for extra revenue. Boeing heard them out and questioned them closely on the risks: the vast expanse to cover (at almost two thousand miles, it was the country's longest airmail route), the high mountain ranges to cross, the winter blizzards, the new kind of engine Egtvedt wanted that used lightweight—and therefore low-cost—air cooling instead of conventional, proven water cooling. The decision was a major personal as well as corporate choice for Boeing; as always, he'd bankroll the capital requirements himself. (Later, describing Bill Boeing's support of his company then, Egtvedt pointed out, "Usually the main item on the agenda at board meetings was to pass a resolution accepting another contribution from Mr. Boeing.") He was noncommittal, and Egtvedt and Hubbard left with the impression that he didn't like their grandiose idea.

When Egtvedt and Hubbard came to work the next morning, they found messages from Bill Boeing asking them to come back to his downtown office to go over the airmail proposal again. Arriving there, they found that the idea had intrigued him and he'd been turning it over in his mind, but he was worried about the risks and unknowns. They pored over the idea again in detail and Boeing asked more questions. By the time they'd exhausted the subject, Bill Boeing had determined to seize the opportunity: he'd submit a bid.

When the Post Office unsealed all the bids, Boeing's was the lowest by a third—half what the route had been costing the government, and even less than the cost of the short, easy New York–Boston regional route. Postmaster General Harry New thought the bid was unrealistic and considered tossing it out: a carrier couldn't deliver the mail if it went broke. Bill Boeing responded with a political move, getting Washington state's U.S. Senator Wesley Jones to intercede with New. The postmaster general approved the bid, but only on the condition that Boeing post the maximum performance bond— eight hundred thousand dollars. Confident now of his company's ability to do business at spectacularly lower costs than other firms, Bill Boeing personally underwrote the bond. He told Egtvedt to get busy on the redesign of the mail plane, which would be produced in Boeing's "red barn" factory on the Duwamish, by then the largest aircraft plant in the country. According to the system Boeing had adopted for naming design projects, the airplane would be designated the Model 40A, meaning it was a variation on Boeing's fortieth seriously considered design (but not the fortieth airplane—not all designs got off the drafting table). Boeing set up his airline as a subsidiary, Boeing Air Transport Company, incorporating it on February 17, 1927. (This was the beginning of what would become and remain a dominant carrier, later renamed United Airlines.) Perhaps Bill Boeing was lucky, perhaps he sensed undercurrents in the country, but the timing of his entry into the airline business was just right. A great boom in aviation was ignited at 5:22 P.M. Eastern Standard Time on May 21, 1927: Lindbergh landed in Paris after flying nonstop from New York.

No American before or since was idolized like Charles Lindbergh. His flight, like no other, awakened Americans to the progress made in aviation since the war. People who had once pictured airplanes as mainly abhorrent military weapons now believed they could do much good for peaceful purposes. Travelers seriously considered airplanes and began to seek passenger flights. Businesses thought of airplanes for express freight service and sought out air freight carriers. Financiers felt more inclined to lend or invest money for aviation ventures. Voters and politicians became more willing to approve measures to foster aviation. It seemed that the entire populace had become aviation-minded; no advertising or public relations campaign has ever been as effective as this unstaged happening. Largely due to the Lindbergh boom, the value of aircraft sales would more than triple between 1927: and 1929.

Newspapers and magazines contributed to the boom by increasing coverage of aviation. The *Chicago Herald and Examiner* assigned a twenty-eight-year-old reporter, Jane Eads, to be the first passenger on Boeing's airmail route, flying in the new Model 40A; people at the time believed that if a woman—a girl!—could fly in safety and reasonable comfort, then aviation must indeed have matured. Thus history was given an account of the first time a passenger flew in a Boeing airplane on a commercial flight (which was also the very first United Airlines flight). Cloche hat firmly on her head, Eads flew from Chicago to San Francisco on a journey that began over an hour late at 9:42 P.M. on Friday, July 2, the second day of operations, leaving at night to cross the perilous mountains in daylight. The flight included several stops to switch to fresh airplanes, which usually flew at about 95 miles per hour. After covering 1,950 miles in twenty-four hours and eighteen minutes, the flight ended almost three hours late—but about thirty-seven hours faster than trains—at 7:20 P.M. Pacific time.

The sub-headline GIRL REPORTER TELLS STORY topped Eads's front-page account. She described her accomodations: "I clambered into the luxurious passenger cabin, comfortable and spacious enough. . . . Here I am, sitting at ease in a reclining leather cushioned seat. The walls of my exclusive compartment are sea green. There's a little glazed ceiling light by which I can read and write. I can open and close the windows on both sides of me. I'm thrilled. . . .

Eads recounted her historic journey:

The light in my cabin is not working, so I'm using a flashlight. . . . I feel giddy and my ears are ringing with the sound of the motors. . . . I'd enjoy a cup of black coffee. . . . I curled up in a heap on the seat and tried not to think of dropping to earth. . . . It's cool and fresh and glorious. . . . I'm becoming unbearably weary with the altitude and the rough riding. [The pilot] was surprised that I didn't become ill. . . . Before landing [at Iowa City] I was too frightened to write. The plane tipped and tilted and dropped. I just threw down my pencil and hung on. . . . It was the most exhilarating feeling I've experienced in all my life. . . . Beacon lights here and there along the route are leading us on. . . . Deserts and mountains are now intermingled in a confused set of recollections, through it all running two dominant impressions—intense heat and utter loneliness. . . . Although we flew at an altitude of 10,000 feet [over Nevada], clouds of sand drove at us, stinging hands and face. . . . We winged through a pass in the Coast Range. . . . And then the plane pointed downward, its wheels touched, and my adventure was ended.

Eads subsequently became a nationally syndicated Washington columnist.

The record of Boeing Air Transport justified Bill Boeing's backing of the Hubbard-Egtvedt scheme: the airline consistently generated healthy profits; only one of the other nine existing airlines made a decent profit. Bill Boeing explained that the main reason he could fly the mail so cheaply was his advanced-technology, air-cooled engines, enabling his airplanes to carry "mail over those mountains instead of radiators and water." Another large factor in the airline's profitability was its success in attracting passengers; in the first six months it carried 525 paying riders—near capacity, with only four seats available each flying day. Boeing ordered a design change in the mail plane to double its passenger capacity from two to four.

Other manufacturers were producing large airliners designed primarily for passengers. Ford, trying to gain a foothold in the aviation business, and Fokker had introduced closed-cockpit trimotors, with an engine at the nose and two on the wings, in the mid-1920s. To meet the demands of the Lindbergh boom in passenger traffic, Boeing launched a project to create a trimotor with all the comforts of a Pullman railroad car. The Boeing trimotor, designated the Model 80, entered service in August 1928.

It soon became apparent that Boeing had made his first big mistake. The problems weren't in airworthiness or comfort. The airplane was aerodynamically sound, and its interior was plush, with more passenger amenities than any airliner ever built: plenty of headroom (a person over six feet tall could stand up straight); leather-covered seats three abreast; large, curtained windows for each row; shaded lamps extending from the walls over each window; forced ventilation and heating; an insulated, soundproofed passenger compartment; and a spacious restroom with hot and cold running water. Only the aisle was cramped, with passengers having to squeeze sideways through narrow gaps between the first and second seats in each row.

The Model 80 was a hybrid of wood, fabric, and metal, however, when aggressively designed airplanes such as the Ford trimotor were all metal. The aircraft was a biplane, moreover, when monoplanes such as the Ford and Fokker trimotors, which flew faster for the same horsepower, were taking over. Boeing had agreed to Egtvedt's argument for a biplane because of its slower and therefore safer landing speed (landing speed is about as slow as an airplane can fly safely—much slower and it loses lift, dropping like a stone), and its advantages for flying into and out of the high-altitude airports where Boeing's own airline operated. Boeing might also have expected that the conservative, lower-risk design would appeal to passengers and potential buyers at other airlines; the Army and Navy may have influenced him by sticking with the older tried-and-true approach for their aircraft. Nevertheless, the design proved too old-fashioned for the commercial market. In the fast-changing young airline industry, Boeing's trimotor looked as outdated as propeller-driven airliners look today. Bill Boeing had put his first big passenger airplane on the market too late and too timidly. (Over at Fokker, Gott must have been beaming.) The Boeing Airplane Company sold only one Model 80 outside its corporate family, and built only a dozen others for Boeing Air Transport.

Boeing was much more successful with military aircraft. The company designed and built best-selling fighters that were favorites with the Army and Navy well into the 1930s. Employment had grown steadily since the company nearly folded after the war, and by 1928 had reached nearly one thousand men and women, including an engineering staff of sixty-five. Boeing had expanded into one of the largest aircraft manufacturers in the country and the largest manufacturer of any kind in Seattle. Since its founding, the company had sold more than one thousand aircraft and carried some fifteen hundred passengers on its airline. It was transporting about a quarter of the country's airmail by weight, and did a booming business—half its sales—in spare parts. In 1927, Boeing grossed almost two million dollars. Overall, Bill Boeing was doing very well, and he was on the verge of sensational success.

On October 31, 1928, Boeing made his first acquisition, an airline that operated in California. The very next day, he took a momentous step, a move he couldn't have made until the Lindbergh boom made aviation attractive to investors. He took his burgeoning company public, listing its stock on the New York Stock Exchange, to raise funds for further acquisitions. Bill Allen, Boeing's legal counsel, remarked, "Until Lindbergh, you couldn't get investors to touch Boeing stock with a 10-foot pole."

Events moved fast. Bill Boeing had grown close to Fred Rentschler, the owner of Boeing's chief supplier—the Pratt & Whitney company, which made aircraft engines; Boeing then used Pratt & Whitney power plants exclusively. Boeing and Rentschler became taken with the idea of forming a huge aviation trust that would combine airlines and manufacturers of airframes, engines, and propellers all under one umbrella. Trusts were then in vogue. Airlines were beginning to merge into large carriers, whose size would threaten Boeing Air Transport, which then commanded 30 percent of the airmail and passenger market. The two men agreed to join their companies into a publicly held trust and acquire smaller companies to fill out their empire. Rentschler's brother was an officer of National City Bank of New York (now Citicorp, and still Boeing's main bank), which would help to finance the acquisitions.

Boeing and Rentschler merged their companies on February 1, 1929, forming United Aircraft & Transport Corporation. Bill Boeing became chairman and Fred Rentschler was named president of the conglomerate, headquartered in New York City. UATC quickly bought several other companies, including Stearman Aircraft, which manufactured small biplanes in Wichita, Kansas (and would later become an important part of Boeing). After acquiring three more airlines over the next two years, UATC brought all its air operations together in one airline, the largest in the country, and named it United Airlines. (The legal proceedings leading to the merger revealed that Johnson, Egtvedt, Hubbard, and a few other Boeing executives had become millionaires from appreciation of stock received as bonuses.)

The stock market crash on Black Thursday, October 24, 1929, began the Great Depression that devastated people and businesses the world over. The momentum of the aviation boom carried UATC through the Depression's first years, however, and the trust enjoyed exceptional success. While other businessmen were jumping from windows, Bill Boeing was making millions.

In his position atop the bureaucracy of the sprawling conglomerate, Boeing was much less involved in the details of running his old company than he had been before the creation of UATC. He had overall responsibility for other subsidiaries besides the airplane company, and several layers of management separated him from his namesake organization: Rentschler; Johnson, who was president of both Boeing and United Airlines; and Claire Egtvedt, vice president and manager of day-to-day operations. Bill Boeing, moreover, had set a personal goal of retiring to enjoy his millions when he reached the age of fifty in 1931. He didn't leave then, as it turned out—even though his relationship with Rentschler had soured—but he did begin assigning more of his responsibilities to others and gradually selling his UATC stock. For all practical purposes, Boeing Airplane Company was run by the two Scandinavian-American college classmates, Johnson and Egtvedt, who had been among the first engineers Bill Boeing hired when they joined him in May 1917.

An early challenge facing Johnson and Egtvedt was developing the subsidiary's next transport airplane. Clearly, it would have to be an all-metal monoplane to compete for market leadership. They tried out new design ideas on a mail plane and a bomber that both failed to sell. Feeling that the concepts were sound, however, the engineers launched design of a streamlined, twin-engine monoplane airliner. Designated the Model 247, the prototype first flew on February 8, 1933. Touted as the world's first three-mile-a-minute airliner, it was by far the country's fastest, most advanced passenger carrier, incorporating most of the innovations developed during the renascent twenties. A gleaming, sleek, all-metal aluminum monoplane with wings attached low on the fuselage, it was the first airplane to look like a modern airliner, and the first to have deicing equipment and an automatic pilot. It also maintained the Boeing tradition of luxurious passenger accommodations. So fast and fuel-efficient was this miracle of modern technology that it flew from New York to Los Angeles in "only" nineteen hours and forty-five minutes, with seven stops. Airlines could buy it for around sixty thousand dollars. They charged passengers $160 one way for a flight between coasts, equivalent to two thousand dollars in the mid-1990s.

It so impressed Jack Frye, president of TWA, that he ordered twenty of them. Johnson turned him down, however. The Boeing chief had allocated the first sixty production models to his own United Airlines, and didn't want to give up the competitive advantage the airplane would give him. This was a major, shortsighted mistake. TWA couldn't afford to fall far behind United Airlines, so Frye looked for some manufacturer to produce a similar airplane for him. Donald Douglas, the unknown owner of a small aircraft maker, agreed to take on the challenging project. He borrowed freely from the Boeing design. One stream of information used by his Los Angeles company was said to be data spirited to the firm by a contact who worked at the wind tunnels of the California Institute of Technology, where Boeing tested wooden models of the 247. Donald Douglas went further than Boeing, however, by installing a larger engine and including virtually all the era's aeronautic innovations. With wing flaps, moreover, he could make the airplane bigger and still land safely, so his airplane could fly sixteen passengers. Reportedly, a poster on the wall of Douglas's engineering office pictured a 247 with the caption DON'T COPY IT! DO IT BETTER!

Johnson and Egtvedt gave Douglas plenty of room to do better. Pushed by the conservative pilots of United Airlines, they committed other myopic errors, making the airplane too small, able to carry only ten passengers, and not going far enough in the design; wing flaps to slow the airplane down on landing had been developed but weren't included, for example. (Overly cautious pilots and leapfrogging designs—waiting for competitors to move first and then improving on their concepts—would be recurring themes in Boeing's history.)

Travelers and airlines loved the roomy, economical, technologically superior Douglas airplane, which made the Model 247 obsolete less than a year after its first flight. Boeing sold only fifteen Model 247s to outside airlines. (One of only four 247s surviving in the mid-1990s hangs in the Air Transportation Gallery by the main entrance to the Smithsonian Institution's popular National Air and

Space Museum.) Furthermore, Douglas quickly improved his airplane, creating the legendary DC-3. Boeing fell far behind Douglas in the airliner business and would never even get close to the leader again in the propeller era. (The defeat left many people in Boeing with a bad taste for the airliner business, spawning a strong anti-commercial, pro-military aircraft faction that would remain and grow for decades.)

The financial failure of its streamlined aircraft was a substantial blow to Boeing, but it was nothing compared to the political calamity that was about to befall UATC. Before that disaster, Bill Boeing moved into semiretirement. In August 1933, he relinquished most of his remaining responsibilities. He stayed on as chairman but took no compensation. Rentschler became vice chairman and effectively took over UATC. Seattle native Phil Johnson moved into Rentschler's old slot as UATC president, and the quiet, studious designer, Claire Egtvedt, originally a midwesterner (from Wisconsin—for some reason, Boeing has always employed many midwesterners), replaced Johnson as president of the Boeing Airplane subsidiary.

The disaster began when a tiny airline, one of a mishmash of forty-four airlines then operating in the United States, told reporter Fulton Lewis Jr. (later a controversial radio commentator) that it was low bidder on an airmail contract that went to a much larger and more powerful airline, Eastern, whose bid cost taxpayers three times as much. Lewis discovered that the postmaster general not only had ignored the bids of small carriers, but had conducted a twelve-day meeting of the large airlines—American, TWA, Eastern, and United—to apportion all the airmail routes among them, leaving out the small companies. Lewis tipped off U.S. Senator Hugo Black of Alabama (later a U.S. Supreme Court justice). Black instigated Senate hearings into the situation in January and February of 1934.

The facts ascertained by the Senate committee showed that the actions of the postmaster general and the large airlines had been entirely legal. They had been authorized by the McNary-Watres Act of 1930, and had been directed toward improving the effectiveness of the airmail system and boosting passenger service. The whole idea had been that of Postmaster General Walter Brown, moreover; he had imperiously summoned the large airlines to the meeting and virtually dictated the routes they'd receive.

Brown was a Republican, however, a Hoover appointee, and the administration had changed hands in the election of 1932. With the onset of the Depression in 1929, the public's attitude toward big business and rich businessmen had also changed, from admiration to hatred. In 1934, moreover, antiwar sentiment stood at its peak; a book titled *The Merchants of Death* made the best-seller lists. The citizenry reviled companies that made airplanes, which, as an industry, were making 40 percent of their sales and more of their profits in countries gearing up for war (although Boeing had hardly any export business).

For Bill Boeing, any chance of impartial treatment vanished, and his appearance before the committee became a lynching when, during the hearings, a Boeing fighter with an open cockpit nosed over while landing and the pilot broke his neck; a poor design failed to protect the pilot's head when the airplane accidentally turned over. Trying to picture the UATC chairman as a monster whose insatiable greed led him to value money above human life and the good of his country, Black focused his questioning of Boeing on the huge return he had made from his investment in a particular issue of his company's preferred stock.

To no avail, Boeing tried to show that his profit from his total investments in the company had been reasonable. He highlighted all the money he'd invested in the firm. He described the mammoth risks he'd taken, including his first bid on an airmail contract, testifying, "When we took over the Transcontinental [route], everyone predicted we would go broke." Boeing pointed to the fortune in bonds that he'd endorsed. He declared that his corporation gave the government good value for its money: "In 1932, we carried 45.04 percent of all [air mail] poundage and in compensation received 36.14 percent; in other words, we are carrying the air mail cheaper than the others." Black interrogated him on that point: "You still think that was a fair contract for the government, when you reaped those large profits out of a small industry?" Boeing responded, "As

against the risk and hazard that we took, yes." Defending his profits further, he exclaimed, "I feel that the men that have gone into
[aviation] and have hazarded what they have and contributed what
they have to the development are entitled to remuneration." In a
summation, Boeing implored Black to look at more than one isolated transaction: "Mr. Chairman, you must remember that this
aircraft thing is a life work with me, it has gone over the whole of
my life. I went through all the hazards, periods when everyone
thought I was a fool. . . . I risked a good, big part of my personal
fortune at that time and I stayed with it. This may be a reward for
my life's work—I don't know."

Black and the Democrats were interested only in making political hay, however. Bill Boeing couldn't get support even from his
own state's representatives in Congress. Incredibly, Democratic
Senator Homer T. Bone of Washington state led an assault on the
aircraft industry after the hearings. "The people of this country are
weary of the spectacle of the government being looted, literally
looted, by private airplane companies," he orated. He urged steps
to free taxpayers from "the absolute mercy of private manufacturers of airplanes." President Roosevelt (no friend to Boeing after the
company denied his campaign access to workers during his 1932
run) was easily persuaded by the ambitious Black to cancel all airmail contracts. Black also won a decree from the new postmaster
general that the large airlines could regain airmail business only by
reorganizing, changing their names (United Airlines became United
Air Lines Transport for a while), and firing all officers and directors who had participated in Brown's meeting. Airmail revenue was
so vital that the beaten companies had to comply.

Phil Johnson had represented United Airlines at Brown's meeting. United, which by the time of the meeting was already running
the whole transcontinental trunk line from New York to San Francisco, had nothing to gain from the affair. Brown had asked United
to take over a small, inconsequential regional route in a nonbid
arrangement, and Johnson had agreed. No matter—Johnson had to
go. Theoretically, he could have transferred from UATC back down
to the Boeing subsidiary, but he and Boeing would then have been

on the government's blacklist. Disheartened and disillusioned by politicians, he left, his meteoric career apparently destroyed when he was only forty.

Bill Boeing was bitter about being used by Black and about the government's unfair treatment of his company and employees. Like most industrialists, moreover, he was probably angry at New Deal intrusions into his business. Having achieved his personal goals and wanting to enjoy his fortune, he had no compelling reason to hang on any longer and many reasons to quit. He sold the rest of his UATC stock and retired from the company he'd built, the classic American rugged individualist disappearing into the sunset. (True to his resolve, he spent most of the rest of his life as a country gentleman, breeding cattle and horses in rural Washington, overseeing his investments, and sailing his yacht on Puget Sound.)

The government wasn't finished with UATC. It dealt the trust a crippling blow when Congress passed a law that no airline could be associated with a company that made aircraft or aircraft equipment. The highly successful conglomerate had to break up. Crushed, the board of directors separated United Airlines and split the remainder of the trust into its two original companies, Pratt & Whitney and Boeing. Each company took a share of UATC's acquisitions; Boeing got Stearman Aircraft Company in Wichita. The dissolution formally took place on September 28, 1934. (The federal actions had little effect on the airline industry that Brown had autocratically cobbled together: For the most part, the same large carriers continued to fly the same routes, and the small operators got little business.)

Boeing was launched on its own again into a sea of financial trouble. The company inherited only $582,000 in cash from UATC. Without Bill Boeing as a sugar daddy, the corporation had become a poor orphan. (With the eponym's exit, however, no one owned a controlling interest, or even as much as 10 percent of the stock, an independence that would prove advantageous in the long run.) The bottom had fallen out of the business. Employment had peaked at 2,275 workers in May 1933, when Boeing started to lay off employees. The trickle of employees being turned out soon became a gusher. By the time of the breakup, the company had let go three out of every four workers; employment was down to only 600 people, and most of them were sharing jobs, working two weeks on and two weeks off.

Hoping to turn the company around, Egtvedt had already declared a new strategy, one that eventually would lead Boeing to greatness.

3 || Big Bombers

Claire Egtvedt made his first major strategic decision before the
UATC breakup. History would show that it was a watershed
for Boeing, a great decision that established the company's destiny.
Egtvedt believed that the best future business for Boeing would be
in big airplanes—big passenger airplanes and big bombers, not
smaller models or fighters or other aircraft of unremarkable size. The
large airplanes he envisioned weren't yet commonplace, but he
thought the trend was in that direction. If Boeing could take the lead,
the company could dominate the market when it developed. He
decreed that Boeing would emphasize big airplanes, and ordered
his engineers to begin preliminary design work on two large twin-
engine airplanes, an airliner and a bomber. These two types shared
many design features, and one could benefit from thinking on the
other. His conviction growing that bigness was the key to the future,
Egtvedt soon ordered that the airplanes be equipped with four
engines and made even larger.

His foresight quickly proved excellent. In May 1934, he was
invited to a secret meeting with the chief of the Air Corps Matériel
Division at Wright Field in Dayton, Ohio. When he arrived, he found
that a competitor, the president of the Martin Company, had also
been invited. The Air Corps official explained that he wanted to fund
design and construction of the biggest bomber possible for experi-

mentation. He wanted to learn the flight and control characteristics of an extremely large airplane to find out what might be possible in future production bombers. Boeing and Martin had been judged the manufacturers most capable of making the test bed. He invited both of them to bid on the design in a month.

Egtvedt eagerly got his engineers busy working up an estimate. Bids were accepted on June 15. On June 28, Egtvedt was delighted to learn that Boeing had won the design contract. The paper design was due in a year, and then the Air Corps would decide whether to build the giant airplane. In a project paid for by the taxpayers, Boeing would learn much that would help Egtvedt achieve his ambitions.

Only a few weeks later, the Air Corps announced yet another big-bomber competition. This time the award would be not for an experiment but for production of the next generation of operational bombers. The Air Corps announced that manufacturers who wanted to compete for the contract would have to design and build an airplane on their own and submit it for testing in one year.

Boeing had a head start with the four-engine bomber the company was already working on, and would benefit from studies for the huge experimental bomber. Egtvedt envisioned a flying dreadnought: rugged, armored, bedecked with guns, able to defend itself instead of relying on fighter escorts. Four engines was so big for operational bombers, however, such a radical departure from existing models, that Egtvedt personally went to the Air Corps for assurance that the venturesome Boeing concept would be eligible.

The board of directors of the newly independent Boeing Airplane Company voted $275,000 for the operational bomber, to be called the B-17. Already deep in Depression red, the company borrowed to the limit to raise the funds; Bill Boeing's deep pockets were sorely missed. Egtvedt put almost all the engineers in the company to work on the two promising Air Corps bomber projects. Early in 1935, he ran out of money for the B-17 and begged the directors for more. Eyes fixed on the future, they obliged, appropriating an additional $150,000, although the company was still losing money. The risks were mounting, making this the first of what would be many high-stakes gambles for Boeing.

A partition was put up to wall off a small space for engineers to design the B-17 in secret. Among the many innovations was replacement of hydraulically powered landing gear and flaps with electrically powered mechanisms. (Boeing legend has it that Seattle's geography contributed to this decision when the hydraulic brakes on an engineer's car failed on one of the city's steep hills.) The company completed the airplane on time. It emerged from the plant as a gleaming, aluminum-skinned behemoth, bristling with five machine-gun turrets, its tail three feet wider than the wingspan of Boeing fighters. Impressed after the first test flight by the warplane's expanse, armament, and guns, Dick Williams, a rewrite man for Seattle's afternoon newspaper, the *Times*, described the aircraft as a "flying fortress." The alliterative name caught on, and Boeing copyrighted "Flying Fortress" as the trade name for the B-17.

On August 20, having passed Boeing's own flight tests, the B-17 was flown to Wright Field in Dayton, Ohio, for the Air Corps competition. When the airplane landed, the crew members were surprised that the expected delegation of Air Corps officials wasn't there to meet them. They learned that the greeting party didn't expect them for another two or three hours; the bomber had flown the 2000 miles at the then-incredible speed of 233 miles an hour. Boeing's prospects looked excellent.

The Boeing bomber was competing against smaller, twin-engine contenders from Martin and Douglas, and, as testing progressed, it was leaving them in the dust. The Seattle-made airplane exceeded ambitious government specifications in all major categories. On its last test flight, the bomber rolled down the runway and roared skyward. It climbed steeply, then steeper still until it was going straight up. This wasn't part of the test, nor was it a maneuver the airplane was designed for. When the airplane reached several hundred feet high, horrified spectators saw it tilt sideways and plummet to earth like a felled bird. Two of the men aboard died as a result of the awful crash.

Investigation showed that, before takeoff, the Army crew had failed to operate a new device that released locks preventing the vast horizontal tail surfaces on the parked aircraft from flapping in the wind. The pilot couldn't control his angle of ascent.

After absorbing the impact of the tragic loss of life, Boeing had to face the harsh consequences of the crash on the competition. Although Boeing's airplane was by far the superior entrant, and the crash had been due to an error by the Air Corps's own test pilot, the bomber hadn't passed all the required tests and therefore finished last. Douglas's poorly performing B-18, considerably slower and dangerously vulnerable to enemy fire, snatched the first production orders, for 350 airplanes—orders that would have put Boeing in the black for years. As it was, Boeing was in the hole for half a million dollars and about to go bankrupt. Fortunately, the Air Corps saved the company from going under. Frustrated by the technicality that defeated the better airplane, Air Corps officers used an allotment for "field test airplanes" that could be spent without a competition. The officers special-ordered 14 B-17s, keeping Boeing's hopes alive for future major production orders.

Boeing got the contract to build the monstrous experimental bomber the company had designed for the Air Corps, the XB-15, and first flew it in 1937. In 1939, the giant (over twice as heavy as a B-17) set a world weight-lifting record for aircraft, carrying almost thirty-six tons into the sky. The project taught Boeing and the Air Corps much about design, construction, and performance of large aircraft.

The practice of piggybacking airliner development on publicly funded projects began when Juan Trippe, the dynamic head of Pan Am (whose name belied his Yankee lineage), announced he wanted a manufacturer to design and build a long-range flying boat that could meet the performance specifications he wanted for transatlantic flights. Boeing at first declined to bid because its finances and other resources were strained by existing projects. One engineer was convinced the flying-boat project was worthwhile, however. He was Wellwood Beall, a portly, dapper man with a wisp of a mustache. Destined to be Boeing's most colorful executive, he was far from the stereotypical nerdy engineer or austere corporation man: he savored good food, good wine, and good company, and found fun in partying, drinking, and gambling. He'd been a salesman, selling Boeing fighters in China, and was then heading Boeing's service department. Strictly speaking, the Pan Am project was none of his business, but he felt strongly that Boeing should do it—so strongly that he resolved to show the company that it could complete the project within its resources. Working on his dining room table at home on nights and weekends, surely eager to impress his superiors, he designed a Pan Am flying boat himself, borrowing wholesale from the XB-15's tail and immense wings. The wings spanned 152 feet, over half the length of a football field; they even had a tunnel so a crew member could crawl out into them during flight to make minor engine repairs.

Beall's strategy worked. His rough design persuaded Egtvedt to try for the Pan Am job and assign Beall full-time to head a small team developing a formal, finished design. The final concept was a hulking, four-engine airplane that could carry up to seventy-four passengers and, depending on load, fly as far as 4,275 miles at 150 miles per hour. Each propeller blade, at almost seven feet in length, was taller than a man; the airplane would be the largest in regular service. The cavernous airliner featured an upper flight deck, like today's 747 jumbo jet, where a ten-man crew could work and sleep, and a lower passenger deck that Beall, the bon vivant, delighted in fashioning as the most luxurious passenger space ever seen on an airplane, rivaling that of ocean liners. Advised by his wife, Jeanne, a commercial artist, he laid out a nicely carpeted lower deck, divided into five compartments plus cocktail lounge, dining salon with seating for fifteen, and honeymoon suite. Deluxe cabin appointments were to become virtually a Boeing trademark.

Boeing turned out to be the only applicant for the contract; most other manufacturers thought the project too ambitious, and the Martin and Sikorsky companies, which had built flying boats for Pan Am's Pacific routes, wanted nothing more to do with the calculating Trippe. The Pan Am head wouldn't automatically order more airplanes from Martin and Sikorsky in return for price breaks they'd given him on the earlier orders. (The phrase "business is business" was virtually a motto for Trippe, who would figure prominently, for better or worse, at several critical junctures of Boeing's history.) The famed Charles Lindbergh, a Pan Am consultant, cautioned against the brash Boeing proposal because Boeing was a maker of military airplanes without much of a record in airliners. Trippe liked Boeing's inventive ideas, however, and so signed a contract.

Trippe was acquiring the airplanes, which he called the "Atlantic Clippers," for the first scheduled passenger service to Europe. Only about thirty aircraft had ever crossed the Atlantic. The development of the gigantic airliners was such big news nationwide that the launch of the prototype at Puget Sound on May 31, 1938, for taxiing trials was covered live by network radio and reporters from the East Coast. The craft flew for the first time on June 7. The tests were bad, bad news for Boeing: They showed that the company had to perform major redesign work. Egtvedt, taking a gamble on nothing going significantly wrong, had already begun construction of the six airplanes Pan Am had ordered. The unexpected changes meant Boeing would lose money despite the record price of $512,000 per airplane, the highest any U.S. airline had ever paid. (DC-3s were selling for only $115,000.)

Boeing delivered the first pricey Clipper to Pan Am on January 29, 1939. It was flown to Washington, D.C., for christening by the First Lady, Eleanor Roosevelt. Flights from New York, which began June 28, took slightly over a day to reach Lisbon, Portugal. After taking delivery of the initial six aircraft, and enthralled by their capabilities, Pan Am ordered an additional six. The life of the airplanes as airliners was bright but brief; within four months, the onset of World War II ended Pan Am's regular service to Europe. The Clippers were drafted, requisitioned by the Army and Navy. They carried high-priority cargo and passengers, notably FDR. To decide Allied strategy after victory in North Africa, he traveled to the Casablanca conference to meet with Winston Churchill in January 1943—the first time a president flew. (After the war, airfields proliferated so rapidly that flying boats were made obsolete.)

Shortly after Boeing had begun work on the Clipper, with its XB-15 wing and tail, the company started on another airliner, a four-engine land plane called the Stratoliner, with a B-17 wing and tail.

It would be the largest land airplane then flying in the United States. The major airlines were cooperating in a special arrangement to support Douglas's development of the four-engine DC-4. Boeing hoped to wrest the passenger business from Douglas with the Stratoliner and leapfrog to the head of the airliner industry, which also included Lockheed and Curtiss-Wright. Egtvedt crowed to Trippe of Pan Am and Jack Frye of TWA that his airliner would fly faster and farther than Douglas's, and he could develop it quicker than Douglas could develop its entrant because of Boeing's bomber experience. He persuaded the two airlines to place advance orders; TWA contracted for six aircraft and Pan Am ordered four.

The cockpit and passenger compartment would feature a land-mark innovation—equipment to keep the air at nearly sea-level temperature and pressure, featuring a Boeing-invented pressurization gauge. The higher an airliner flew, the thinner the air became. This usually meant that airliners couldn't fly above storms or choppy air, which, in turn, meant that airlines had to provide bags for wretched passengers to use when they threw up. (Aviation historian Roger E. Bilstein quoted a DC-3 pilot about the roller-coaster passenger flights in the unpressurized aircraft of the 1930s: "The airplanes smell of hot oil and simmering aluminum, disinfectant, feces, leather, and puke. . . . The stewardesses, short-tempered and reeking of vomit, come forward as often as they can for what is a breath of comparatively fresh air.")

The ingenious pressurization system would add six thousand feet to the Stratoliner's ceiling. The system would make flying much more comfortable and faster, too (airplanes travel faster in thin air); the airplane would have a top speed of 250 miles per hour and cruise at 200 miles per hour. That would help to make the Stratoliner exceptionally fast for its day; it would make a coast-to-coast trip in twelve hours and eighteen minutes—two and a half hours faster than a DC-3. Charles Lindbergh especially liked the ability to fly over the weather and approved of this Boeing airplane despite his reservations about the company's capabilities to make airliners.

The prototype made its first flight on the last day of 1938. The Stratoliner's attractions drew KLM, the Dutch airline, close to placing an order. Two KLM representatives traveled to Seattle to test-fly the airplane. On March 18, 1939, the KLM men and eight Boeing people went up in one of Pan Am's airplanes that was being checked out. The KLM shoppers wanted to see how the airplane responded to an unusual emergency condition involving engines cutting out while the airplane was in a sharp turn. Boeing's test pilot carefully put the airplane into the situation KLM had dreamed up, confident he could easily recover. But the Stratoliner did the unexpected: It rolled over and went into a spinning dive. The pilot, perhaps with the husky KLM copilot helping, pulled hard to take the airplane out of the deadly dive—too hard. The severe stress snapped off the wings and tail, and the mutilated fuselage, with no flight capability whatsoever, plunged to earth like a meteorite. All ten people aboard were killed, including Boeing's chief engineer and chief aerodynamicist. (A postcrash analysis reconstructed the events leading to the crack-up.)

Shaken but undeterred by the horrible accident, Boeing corrected the design flaw that caused the accident and went on with its business. Stratoliners entered service on TWA's transcontinental route on July 8, 1940. The airline equipped them with posh interiors, designed by noted industrial designer Raymond Loewy, having wood paneling and indirect lighting. Pan Am placed its Stratoliners in service on its Miami–Latin America routes. No other Stratoliners were ever ordered, however, because of lingering doubts about the Boeing airplane's stability and strength, and because its operating costs were higher than those of its competitors. Boeing lost heavily on the star-crossed Stratoliners. The flying public liked them, nevertheless, and flights were heavily booked. Unfortunately, like Boeing's Clippers, the civilian careers of TWA's Stratoliners were cut short by the war, and they were requisitioned by the Army.

Boeing lost money on the Air Corps's special order for fourteen B-17s. Egtvedt had committed to a price based on an expectation of winning the competition for the next bomber generation and gaining a contract for a large number of airplanes; the cost of making each airplane for the small production volume was greater than the selling price per airplane. Hoping for an eventual mass production sale, Egtvedt also accepted an order for an additional fifteen B-17s at a loss.

Because of the large number of airplanes being built and the large size of the craft, the company had to construct another plant. Giuseppe Desimone, a truck farmer who owned forty acres on the Duwamish across from Boeing's factory, heard that California had offered Boeing land rent-free for ten years to locate a plant in that state. A man of strong civic pride, Desimone offered his parcel to Boeing if the company would build the new factory on it. Boeing took him up, and constructed the facility that would always be known as Plant II. At the time, it was one of the world's largest industrial facilities under one roof.

Boeing had abundant products under way in the 1930s: At one point, work was proceeding on B-17s, the XB-15, Clippers, and Stratoliners simultaneously. Except for a small profit from the XB-15, however, none of the aircraft was making money; in fact, the company was losing staggering amounts: Boeing had lost hundreds of thousands of dollars each year but two since UATC had broken up, and was on its way to losing over three million dollars in 1939. Boeing was living on hope alone.

On top of his financial woes, Egtvedt had to contend with upsetting news from the Air Corps. Boeing was slow in producing the additional B-17s, modified to include superchargers, which would force air into the engines so they could operate at higher altitudes. The Air Corps didn't believe the excuse of problems with the modifications as the reason for the slowdown; the officers thought Boeing's production capabilities had slipped. The Air Corps asked Boeing to license B-17 production rights to Consolidated Aircraft Corporation so Boeing's rival could make the airplanes when high volumes were needed. That was the first blow of a one-two punch. The second blow fell when the opportunistic Consolidated persuaded the Air Force that, instead of producing B-17s, Consolidated should develop and build a similar but better bomber. The Air Corps still wanted B-17s, nevertheless—but made somewhere besides at sluggish Boeing.

Egtvedt must have feared for his job. No airplanes developed under his leadership had done well in the marketplace. Boeing's fighter business, once the biggest in the industry, the pride of the company, and a steady source of income, had vanished as Egtvedt concentrated on big airplanes, and the large orders for big bombers that Egtvedt had been counting on seemed about to disappear. The company's production capabilities, highly regarded before Egtvedt took office, were now held in contempt. From 1936 to 1938, the industry as a whole had exported aircraft worth $147 million, but Boeing had taken an almost nonexistent share of that booming market, with foreign sales of only $104,000. In 1938, Boeing had dropped to tenth in total sales in the industry, at only $2,006,000; Douglas had taken in $28,347,000. The financial press criticized the floundering firm. *Barron's* carped in 1938: "Boeing is known as a brilliant engineering company. It is constantly in the forefront in plane development. But it has not yet learned how to put the business on a basis of reasonable profits." Boeing had lost money in three of the five years since Egtvedt had been president, and by 1939 was hemorrhaging at a fatal rate. Boeing was several million dollars in debt ($4 million or $5 million, according to one executive's later recollection), its credit was exhausted, and the company's nervous banks were conferring with the government's Reconstruction Finance Corporation about emergency assistance for their faltering client. Egtvedt had no obvious major accomplishments to counterbalance the shortfalls.

One day in 1939, Bill Allen asked to see Egtvedt. Allen was the attorney who handled the Boeing account for the company's law firm. Respected for his business acumen, he had also been a general adviser to Bill Boeing, Phil Johnson, and Egtvedt, and was an outside (nonemployee) member of the board of directors. Allen was concerned about the way Egtvedt was running the company. The Air Corps, too, was unhappy about Egtvedt's effectiveness, and had gotten word to Boeing's board of directors that they'd like to have the immensely capable Phil Johnson back as president, especially if the impending war demanded huge fleets of aircraft. After being forced from UATC, Johnson had taken two years off, then become president and controlling owner of Kenworth Motors, a failing Seattle truck manufacturer that he rescued from oblivion; he finally became vice president of operations for the newly established Trans Canada Airlines. He had been a member of Boeing's board of directors since 1936. His fellow members, feeling that his five years in exile from Boeing's executive ranks would have appeased the government, especially with the Air Corps wanting him, had approached him about replacing Egtvedt. Multi-millionaire Johnson had replied that he didn't want the job, didn't need the money, and his wife was opposed. He'd agreed to take over again only if it was essential to Boeing and if he were given complete authority.

Allen later confided to a colleague, "Egtvedt is not a driver. . . . Phil was always a decisive person, and he was a leader, and he liked people, and Claire was just the opposite. And Claire was not cut out, if you want to face up to it, to be in that spot." Allen gave an example of Egtvedt's lack of business sense: "Egtvedt himself determined the Clipper price. He always had the price too damned low. I'm pretty sure Pan Am would have paid for them. We would have been better off if he'd stayed in engineering." Actually, Allen told associates, "We had no damn business" building the money-losing Clipper in the first place.

Allen diplomatically suggested to Egtvedt that he'd be happier devoting his time to design and engineering while Johnson handled the crushing responsibilities of running the corporation. Allen revealed that he and the other members of the board of directors would be glad to create the post of chairman for Egtvedt if he'd step aside and let Johnson become president. Allen later recounted that Egtvedt was "torn" when presented with the idea. He wanted to retain substantial authority, and Allen had to exercise all his tact to get Egtvedt to agree to give up command entirely. Egtvedt, dispirited but having no real choice, finally consented to the plan. Publicly, he announced that he wanted to return to his first love, engineering. In statesmanlike fashion, he proclaimed that the company would be better off in the years ahead with a production man as president. He wouldn't admit to any failing, insisting in one interview, "There were intimations that I was not a good businessman, but this was not the case."

Johnson, called "P. G." as often as "Phil," took over as president and general manager on September 9, 1939. Moving fast, Johnson issued stock to raise more money. He then snagged a multimillion-dollar order for dive bombers from France (England bought the airplanes when France fell), to be made under a design license from Douglas. The Air Corps, willing to give Johnson a chance to solve Boeing's production problems, kept reordering B-17s in increasing numbers; the volume of airplanes ordered passed the break-even point and began making money. In 1940, Johnson's first full year as president again, Boeing made its biggest profit since being spun off from UATC—only $374,655, but better than red ink.

On the day that will live in infamy, December 7, 1941, it was an attack by aircraft that pushed America into the war, as Japanese warplanes bombed Pearl Harbor and destroyed most of America's Pacific Fleet. Shortly after, the Army Air Forces urged Johnson to start making all the B-17s he could as fast as he could—it was impossible to make too many.

Bill Boeing surprisingly reappeared shortly after Pearl Harbor. He offered to forsake his peaceful farm and yacht to do anything he could, gratis, for the war effort; Johnson took his former mentor on as an adviser. Old-timers remember the founder dutifully attending meetings on strategy and important technical decisions.

Some early B-17s went to the Pacific, but Consolidated's version of the big bomber, the B-24 Liberator, had a longer range better suited to the vast distances in that theater. Most B-17s went to Europe, where they gained a reputation for effectiveness and toughness. The aptly named *Flaming Jenny*, for example, returned from a mission in 1942 aflame from nose to tail, missing an engine and a large part of one wing, and riddled with two thousand bullet holes (thought to have inspired the 1943 hit song, "Comin' In on a Wing and a Prayer," which entered the language as a colorful description).

The idea of strategic bombing—crippling the enemy's war machine by knocking out his industrial capabilities—became firmly established with the B-17.

Boeing and military planners had been thinking about the next generation of bombers, which would fly farther and faster and carry more bombs than B-17s—the "superbomber," they called it. On February 5, 1940, Boeing had received in the mail an Army Air Forces (AAF) circular asking companies to submit in one month detailed proposals, with drawings, for a long-distance, high-altitude, high-speed bomber. The winner would be required to complete a full mock-up by August 5 and deliver the first airplane by July 1, 1941. Johnson confidently tendered a bid.

The key stage of the competition was the testing of wind tunnel models from each of the contenders. Consolidated was scheduled first, and its model performed poorly. George Schairer, Boeing's new chief aerodynamicist, who had come over from Consolidated, noticed something that escaped both Consolidated and the AAF: The design wasn't at fault—the model was simply too big and not configured correctly for the tunnel, so it gave the wrong results. The Martin company made the same mistake. Schairer cagily kept his mouth shut and, on Boeing's day in the tunnel, handed over a model that was correctly sized and configured. Boeing's sound whipping of its competitors in the tunnel played a major role in producing the greatest news Boeing had heard in years: The company won the contract to design and produce the superbomber, to be called the B-29 (and later to be nicknamed the Superfortress). Not wanting America's enemies to know about the advanced airplane, the AAF ordered Boeing to develop it in secret.

The concentration of bomber production plants in the Seattle area made the Army Air Forces nervous, especially since the possibility of a Japanese attack on the West Coast couldn't be discounted. The service wanted better test-flying weather and an expanded labor supply, moreover, and so decreed that B-29s be produced in

Wichita, Kansas, as well as Seattle. Wichita was the site of the Stearman Company, the manufacturer of light planes that Boeing had inherited from UATC; Egtvedt had dedicated it to production of military trainers. Boeing built a new plant in Wichita and rented an empty military aircraft manufacturing plant in Renton, Washington, to make the Superforts; the Navy had built the plant for Boeing to make flying boats but decided not to acquire more airplanes of that type after Boeing had produced only one.

After the atomic bomb project, the B-29 program was the costliest weapons project of the war—three billion dollars (not all of it went to Boeing). It soon became a crash project and a great gamble, with the Army Air Forces committing to production a year and four months before the prototype flew. The B-29 had become vital to the Pacific war; no other aircraft could operate effectively over the vast distances. The pressured AAF was taking a huge chance by making plans based on the availability of the airplanes and ordering their production before the first test flight, however. Early flights of the Model 80, the Clipper, the Stratoliner, and even the B-17 had shown that major redesigns were often necessary; wind tunnel testing was not as sophisticated as it would one day become, and big surprises were common in initial flights. The B-29 program presented many opportunities for surprises—requirements kept changing as the airplane was being designed, calling for it to fly much faster, farther, and with a much heavier load than first envisioned. The airplane would have untried, high-power Wright Cyclone engines. It would embody radical new airframe technologies, notably a new approach to controls, and a long, narrow, low-wind-resistance wing with less area than those used on smaller airplanes but that had to provide much greater lift and withstand much greater stress. Yet the AAF couldn't afford surprises with the B-29: the design had to be right on the first try.

Boeing completed the first prototype in September 1942. Because of changing requirements, the program was far behind schedule. The chief test pilot, Eddie Allen, spent some time on taxiing trials testing as much of the airplane as he could without leaving the safety of the ground. Then he lifted up a foot or two, then ten feet, then fifteen feet. Finally, on September 21, he sped down the runway, lifted up, held the airplane just off the ground a moment, then climbed on up. The airplane flew well, and taut nerves in Seattle, Wichita, and Washington relaxed a little.

But later flights revealed a problem—a big problem. The new Wright Cyclone engines often broke down and even caught fire. On one flight, the engine fire spread to the wing, which contained fuel tanks, and the airplane barely landed before the wing disintegrated. Then on February 18, 1943, shortly before 11 A.M., Eddie Allen took the second prototype up with an eleven-man crew. Twenty minutes into the flight, fire started in an engine, but the crew brought it under control and Allen continued the flight. An hour later, while they were over Tacoma, south of Seattle, the engine flared up again. Allen radioed the field to report that they were returning to Boeing Field, thirty miles to the north. He said the trouble wasn't serious but asked that crash equipment stand by. Allen flew past Seattle and then turned around to land into the southerly wind. The airplane was at fifteen hundred feet and several miles from the field when a crew member shouted, loudly enough to be heard through the open mike by people at Boeing Field, "Allen, better get this thing down in a hurry—the wing spar's burning badly!" Allen struggled to make the field but began losing control. All crew members had parachutes; two men jumped, but the airplane was too close to the ground for their chutes to open and they plunged to their deaths. The fire had consumed most of the left wing by the time the airplane reached the vicinity of the Boeing complex. Allen was headed over a five-story, brick meat-packing plant next to the field when he lost all control. The airplane fell onto the structure's roof, killing all crew members and nineteen people in the building. It was Boeing's worst calamity to date.

Alarmed by the delays and problems, the Army Air Forces tightened its control over the vital B-29 program. An Army pilot made the next test flight—successfully—after Boeing tried to fix the problem of wing fires. The company delivered the first operational airplanes to the AAF in July. They performed well, although beset by gremlins because of the rushed production. The B-29s were produced too late in the war to be deployed in Europe, but they were ideally suited to the war in the expansive Pacific. They were the largest airplanes routinely flown by either side in the war.

B-17s and B-29s constituted only 17 percent of all U.S. bombers during the war, but they carried 46 percent of the bombs America dropped in Europe and 95 percent of the bombs the United States dropped in the Pacific. In Europe, B-17 guns accounted for two-thirds of the enemy fighters shot down. Boeing produced 7,000 B-17s, and Douglas and Lockheed built an additional 5,000. For six weeks in 1944, at the peak of production, Boeing's big Seattle plant turned out an incredible 16 B-17s every day. Boeing made 2,766 B-29s, and Bell and Martin produced an additional 1,204. (After the war, Bill Allen complained to a colleague, "It used to burn the hell out of me" that others built B-17s and B-29s and made a lot of money, but gave Boeing next to nothing for the design rights.) Employment hit a peak of forty-six thousand during the war. (While the Flying Fortress was zooming into immortality, the bomber that had won the Army Air Forces competition on a technicality, Douglas's long-forgotten B-18, was relegated to antisubmarine patrol and training duties.)

Johnson had worked his manufacturing magic once again. Boeing's aircraft production per month and production per man-hour both far exceeded industry averages. Boeing was the first airframe manufacturer to receive the military's "E" award for excellence. The war proved immensely profitable for Boeing. Earnings jumped from near zero in 1940 to an incredible $6,113,143 in 1941. In the five years that the United States was in the war, 1941–1945, the company made an astounding profit of $27,579,864, an average of over $5.5 million per year. (In 1946, the first full year of peace, Boeing would lose money again.) Boeing played a conspicuous part in the growth of "big military" during the war to form a trinity with the "big business" and "big government" that had emerged earlier.

The war also earned Boeing favorable publicity of a kind and extent that it never experienced before and wasn't likely ever to know again. Encouraged by the government's wartime propaganda mill, magazines, newspapers, and even comic books extolled the heroic deeds of Boeing's (and other manufacturers') engineers and executives. America's Air Ace Comics told the Flying Fortress story, for example, picturing a grim Egtvedt declaring, "We're going to build an air battleship!"

Boeing suffered an incalculable loss in September 1944. Phil Johnson traveled to Washington, D.C., for an aircraft industry meeting and on the way home stopped in Wichita to visit the Boeing plant. On September 12, he called the plant from his hotel to say he'd be delayed because he wasn't feeling well. When he wasn't heard from again, Boeing executives went looking for him. They found him unconscious in his hotel room, felled by what doctors diagnosed as a stroke. Bill Allen kept a diary that gives a terse description of what followed:

9/12/44   Hear that Phil stricken in Wichita.
9/13/44   Spend most of day at plant getting bulletins on Phil.
9/14/44   Phil died about noon, Wichita time.

Sorrowfully, Claire Egtvedt resumed the presidency, and the board of directors appointed a committee to find the best person possible to lead Boeing after the war, when its booming military business would disappear.

=

One way of looking at a company is to view the big picture, like gazing through a telescope that reveals whole galaxies at a glance. Another way is to scrutinize a detail that promotes understanding of the whole, like peering through a microscope at a single crystal in a moon rock. Putting just the right bit of Boeing under the microscope on Monday, May 15, 1939, would have shown a tall, blond, slender, green-eyed young man entering the engineering offices on East Marginal Way, looking slightly bewildered. He was Dick Henning from Minneapolis, a handsome twenty-four-year-old engineer, a bachelor, who was starting his first day with the company. Dick could imagine, looking out ahead, an exciting career at the frontier of aviation technology and a fulfilling life with a pioneering company in a beautiful city.

Richard Albert Henning was born into a God-fearing family in Brainerd, Minnesota, on January 15, 1915, the sixth of seven children of English, Irish, and German stock. His father had been a machinist for the Northern Pacific Railroad, and later became business agent for a lodge of the International Association of Machinists, the union that happened to represent production workers at Boeing. The Hennings moved to Minneapolis when Dick was two years old.

Dick still vividly remembers the year 1927, when he was twelve. An older sister, Lucille, won the national speed-skating championships in the five-hundred meter and thousand-meter races. And Lindbergh flew the Atlantic, inflaming Dick and a legion of other boys with the desire to become a great pilot. He pinned Lindbergh clippings all over his bedroom walls. Two years later, on entering high school, he decided he wanted to be not only an aviator but an engineer, too. Looking back a lifetime later, he remembered his feelings then: "I began to mold my life to become an engineer, which I desired with all my heart and being, and to be a flyer someday, an innovator, and a man in favor with God and my fellow man in a Christian manner."

Graduating from high school, he went off to the University of Minnesota to study mechanical engineering. He bought his first car, a Model T. In 1935, at the end of his junior year, when the Great Depression was at its worst, hard times caught up with Dick and his family. They ran out of college funds, and Dick had to leave school for a year to replenish his bank account. He found a job at a paper company, which gave him the means to return to school. Continuing his job part-time, and earning money as a YMCA counselor, Dick finished his senior year and received his degree in June 1938.

Having served in an Army ROTC unit, Dick was sent to Randolph Field in San Antonio, Texas, to satisfy the second part of his ambition: He began training as an Air Corps pilot. He soloed in August, but his dream was shattered when his superiors realized that his ROTC ordnance training should have disqualified him from flight training, and he was discharged. He served the remainder of his military obligation in the reserves.

Dick couldn't find an engineering job—the Depression was still raging—so he traveled to Portland, Oregon, to work for a relative's film processing business, developing film for $105 a month. On Christmas day 1938, he had dinner with the family of a coworker, whose brother was down from Seattle, where he worked as a buyer for Boeing. The brother volunteered that Boeing was hiring, and Dick asked him to send a job application. When the form arrived, Dick filled it in and mailed it off. His background in engineering, flying, and military activities was a natural for Boeing. The company offered him a job engineering military airplanes at $120 a month. Joyful at the opportunity to fulfill his ambition, Dick accepted and moved to a room at the Seattle YMCA. He was only the 125th engineer to be hired by the company.

Boeing assigned the newcomer to about the lowest engineering jobs it had—redoing design drawings to make them readable, and helping to count and describe all the rivets on the B-17 prototype. Afterward, he was taken off military aircraft for a spell and given a slightly more challenging task, designing waterproof floor fittings for an advanced Clipper model. At work, Dick lived the unexciting life of a beginning engineer for a couple of years.

At home, Dick's social life was hardly more thrilling. He moved out of the Y to share an apartment with two other guys in West Seattle, but "felt very lonesome." Working the lonely Seattle singles scene, Dick was at a dance downtown at the Drift Inn when he met June Larson. She was also from the Midwest, a Wisconsin native, and he struck up a conversation. They danced—both were good dancers—and enjoyed each other's company. They began to date, and he and his roommates invited June over a few times to fix dinner so Dick could "scout her cooking." He found the dinners "very tasty," and proposed, appropriately, in June 1939. The whirlwind courtship ended with their marriage July 22 in a Methodist church.

The newlyweds held their reception at the Cotton Club in the Maple Valley, where they danced to one of the year's most popular songs, the "Beer Barrel Polka." They moved into an apartment on the aptly named Hill Street in West Seattle. In November, rock faults under the city put them through their West Coast baptism: a twenty-second earthquake that shook their apartment enough to make the venetian blinds sway violently. Not long after, they rented another apartment for thirty-five dollars a month in Wallingford, on the north side of Lake Union.

A year later, Boeing transferred Dick to the group that designed aircraft electrical systems for what was supposed to be a two-week stint (and turned out to be two decades). Boeing had few electrical engineers then, and relied on mechanical engineers like Dick to learn electricity.

In 1941, realizing that war was coming and cars would soon be hard to get, Dick and four friends went as a group to the Stan Sayres Chrysler-Plymouth dealership downtown, where they negotiated a group deal on five cars. Dick bought a maroon '41 Plymouth Business Coupe for $941, tax and Washington state license plate included.

When America did enter the fight, Dick began working tenhour days as Boeing went all out for the war effort. In 1942, his dedication and talent earned him a promotion to lead designer on B-29 electrical and radio systems. Twice he was called up for active duty in the Army, and both times Boeing got the orders canceled because of the high priority of aircraft production. One day while he was working at his drafting table, his boss approached with a proposition: Would Dick like to take leave from Boeing, sign a sixmonth contract with the Lockheed Overseas Corporation, travel to Northern Ireland for half a year with eleven other Boeing employees on leave, and work there on B-17s for the American Eighth Air Force under Lockheed supervision? For two and a half times his regular salary, plus travel expenses, he'd put together and test dismantled and crated B-17s, install equipment and make modifications, and repair battle damage. His time in the job would count toward his Boeing service. Given several days to respond, he talked over the idea with June, thought about it, and gave his reply: yes. He left on June 12, 1942.

When Dick got to Ireland, he found that part of his job involved B-17s of the Royal Air Force, installing a secret new British invention called radar. He put the first-ever bomber radars into the aircraft. Asked to sign up for another six months, Dick stayed a year, coming home in June 1943. Before he left, Lockheed tried to recruit him and the other Boeing employees for salaries much larger than Boeing had been paying, breaking an agreement with Boeing and angering Wellwood Beall, who had been promoted to engineering vice president.

In his new assignment in Seattle, Dick would be the angry one, and the target of his wrath would be Boeing managers who disillusioned him and undermined his unequivocal trust in the company.

4 ‖ The Lawyer

Boeing's board of directors had its toughest job ever in the last year of the war: finding a successor to the talented P. G. Johnson. The board craved someone who was primarily a good businessman. William Boeing himself and Phil Johnson, although trained as engineers, had succeeded because they had good heads for business. Claire Egtvedt, although a good engineer, had failed because he had little sense of how to run a company. The fundamental challenge facing the new president would be one of management rather than technology: how to stay in business. Boeing was then a one-product company, making nothing but B-29s. When the Allies would win the war, considered inevitable although the fighting in the Pacific might be protracted, demand for the product would drop to zero. In all probability, the government wouldn't be ordering airplanes of any kind in substantial numbers for years. The commercial field was equally bleak. Unlike other aircraft companies, Boeing had no successful airliners in its product inventory. There was a good chance that selling airplanes might become such a small business at Boeing that the company could survive only by getting into some other enterprise.

The directors found no one suitable within the company to replace Johnson; most of the corporate officers had declined when allowed to nominate themselves. The board appointed four of its members to a committee to search for a new company leader: Egtvedt, the only inside, or employee, director on the committee, and three outside directors. The nonemployee committee members were Darrah Corbet, Dietrich Schmitz, and Boeing's legal counsel, Bill Allen.

Egtvedt, Corbet, and Schmitz agreed on the person they'd like for the job. He knew the company and its business thoroughly; had been a business adviser to all Boeing's chairmen and presidents; was adept at financing, a particularly critical factor in aircraft manufacturing; and had worked closely and well with the Army Air Forces, Boeing's sole customer at the moment, in arranging contracts—he had formulated the cost-plus-fixed-fee contract that the government used widely during the war. Bill Allen didn't think this man was right for the job, however, and his opinion prevailed—because the favorite of the committee majority was none other than Allen himself. Allen had been a lawyer with a legal firm for his entire career and had never been a manager of any kind, let alone head of a business. "I was amazed, and laughed at their suggestion. I felt that I was completely unqualified for the position and told them so," Allen recollected. He favored Ralph Damon, a vice president of American Airlines, for the position. Damon had been head of Curtiss-Wright, the engine manufacturer, and was second in command at American. Since Damon was the alternate choice of the other directors, the search committee flew to meet him in a B-17 the company used for air travel and offered him the job. Damon turned them down. Disappointed, the searchers sought other possibilities. Over several months, the committee sounded out the head of Boeing's main bank, National City Bank of New York; the heads of engine makers Pratt & Whitney and Curtiss-Wright; and others. They all said "no." Apparently, any man qualified for the job could do better—or thought he could do better—elsewhere (and no woman was considered for the presidency, the idea seeming laughable in 1945). The prospect of taking over a company facing the certain loss of its entire market wasn't enticing.

Boeing experienced a crisis of leadership. Egtvedt was doing no better as acting head of the company than he had done as per-

manent head before the war. He thought he should put major decisions on hold, moreover, until the new man, whoever he might be,
arrived. As bad as the prospects for Boeing were, they were going
to be even worse if the situation continued. The country could suffer as well as the company, since Boeing's B-29s were critical to the
war effort and the end of the struggle wasn't in sight. Corbet and
Schmitz implored Allen to reconsider. Agreeing to think it over,
Allen wrote out the pros and cons of taking the job in his diary:

> Against—1) I do not feel that I have the qualifications. That's the
> all-compelling reason. 2) Trouble lies ahead. 3) Lack of seniority;
> if I don't make a success of it, I would resign, and then where would
> I be? 4) Worry—could I physically stand it. 5) Less time with the
> children. Heaven knows it is little enough now.
>
> For—1) A little greater material return. [At $50,000 annually,
> the president's salary wasn't much better than his current income.]
> 2) It would be a new challenge.

Allen could have added a third point, a factor that might have
weighed heavily on his unconscious mind: "A new job would help
me forget." Allen had suffered a personal tragedy that rocked his
life, and the chance to dull painful memories with a career switch
may have appealed to him.

William McPherson Allen was a brown-eyed, brown-haired,
slender man of Scottish ancestry, slightly jug-eared, ruddy, and
balding. He had a smooth, pleasing voice of medium pitch, with such
well-modulated tones that he sounded like an actor playing an
executive. Only forty-four years old, he'd been born September 1,
1900, in Lolo, Montana, population two hundred, a true town of
the "Wild West." (Lolo, which lies in the foothills of the Bitterroot
Mountains, came into the public eye in 1993 as the site of the gambling den and murder in the movie *A River Runs through It.*) His
family soon moved to nearby Missoula. His father was a well-to-do
mining engineer who designed, built, and managed smelters for the
powerful Anaconda Mining Company. His mother was a strong-
willed temperance champion who closed three saloons and led a

drive to build a church. The Allens were Methodists and exceed-ingly proper. An old photo exists showing the family on a picnic out in a field. They've set up a table and chairs. Mr. Allen has on a black hat, a stiff collar, a vest, and a white shirt. In a concession to the casual nature of the event, he's taken off his jacket, unbuttoned a shirt cuff, and jauntily rolled it up one turn.

Young Allen, no scholar, barely scraped through Montana State University in economics. ("I spent a lot of time sitting around sorority houses," he told an interviewer.) He then traveled east to Harvard Law School, where he earned his degree with average grades. He admitted he wasn't brilliant, explaining that he had to work hard to succeed. In 1925, he looked for a job back west and landed a position with a law firm in Seattle. The city offered views of mountains and great fishing opportunities such as he'd enjoyed growing up, and was a reasonable train ride away from his family and girlfriend in Montana.

Among his assignments at the firm was the Boeing account. Boeing, then a small company trying to make it big in the high-tech industry of its day, had the law firm on retainer for fifty dollars a month. Two years later Allen took the train home and married his high school sweetheart, Dorothy Dixon, daughter of a former Republican governor of Montana. In 1930, Allen was named to Boeing's board of directors. At the time, he also handled the legal affairs of Boeing's sister company, United Airlines.

Bill and Dorothy started a family in 1935 when she gave birth to a daughter, Nancy. A year later, by then financially well-off, the couple built a large, roomy house on four acres in the Highlands, the luxurious hideaway where Bill Boeing had lived. They decorated it with the paintings of Charles Russell, the famous American West-ern artist from Butte, Montana. In 1939, Allen achieved a major professional ambition when the partners in his law firm tapped him to be one of them and renamed the firm Todd, Holman, Sprague & Allen. His second child, another daughter and named Dorothy after his wife, was born in 1940.

Allen's dour personality reflected his upbringing. Thin-lipped, rarely smiling, judging the world through rimless glasses, seemingly born in black shoes and a dark blue three-piece suit, he was a stereotypical archconservative Republican. (His diary entry on election day in November 1944: "Voted in afternoon. Came home and listened to returns. A Democratic landslide. Went to bed pretty discouraged.") As expected of a resident of the Highlands, his main avocation was golf. Usually playing in the privacy of the splendid Highlands course, he shot a respectable game, normally in the eighties. Despite his mother's example and his own astringent outlook, he conformed exuberantly to another Highlands tradition, the cocktail hour. He enjoyed ritual drinks after work, and while getting boorishly drunk at parties was unthinkable, he would often get a glow on. He feared depending on alcohol, and frequently throughout his life rationed his intake or quit entirely for brief periods to discipline himself. Moderate drinking, smoking a pipe at home, and eating crackers at his desk were his only known vices. His cultural interests were heavily in classical music, especially by the German composers. He had a large record collection, and played music constantly at home.

Bill Allen entered 1943 happy at home with his family and successful at work. But darkness fell that year, and his happiness ended. His beloved wife Dorothy found she had cancer, and died before the year was over. She left him with eight-year-old and three-year-old daughters and a shattered life. He started a diary shortly after Dorothy died, perhaps as a way to deal with his loneliness. Allen was reserved even in his private writing, making his diary entries all the more poignant when feelings seeped through his pen onto the pages. In January 1944, he scrawled: "How should I live my life during the coming year? Necessarily it will be a period of adjustment. With Dorothy gone I must re-make my life. I must give the children a great deal of time and thought. To the extent possible, I must take their mother's place." Three weeks later, having stopped off at Missoula on a train ride east, he wrote: "Missoula always does things to me emotionally. All the memories of my happy days there come flowing back mixed with the realization that all of that is gone. And now with Dorothy resting there. . . ." The entry trailed off, as if unendurable emotions had short-circuited Allen's thoughts. A sparkling Sunday that May only made his loss more vivid: "Mother's Day. A beautiful day. If only our sweet Dorothy could be here." Likewise, on another visit to Missoula he visited Dorothy's grave and went to a lake where he had gone swimming with her, then confided to his diary: "Such a beautiful lake, but the memories hurt." He began calling his five-year-old "Poo," after the hero of her favorite storybook, *Winnie-the-Pooh*. He mentioned her in a diary entry, early in 1945, alluding to his grief: "Had dinner with Poo—looking at sunset. Afterwards looked at old snapshots. They bring back poignant memories." In calling her by a preppy nickname (which became her permanent name to family and friends), he avoided having to speak or write her real name, Dorothy. Not long after he'd buried Dorothy, an entry he'd made shows that he regarded his occupation as an antidote to his grief: "I must concentrate on my work—that is one of the best ways to get back on an even keel." He may have been ready for a change; leaving the work he had done with Dorothy at his side and starting anew would make his job even more effective as a healing agent.

This was the Bill Allen in March 1945 who pondered the entreaties from his colleagues to take over Boeing. The "Againsts" seemed to outweigh the "Fors," but on March 22 he informed the directors nevertheless of the decision they wanted to hear: Yes, he'd take the job that nobody wanted.

Allen had discussed his decision with close friends and colleagues. A confidant he talked with frequently was Jim Prince, a lawyer in his firm. Allen, a bit chastened by one of Prince's remarks, told his diary about it: "The other night Prince told me that I was cantankerous as hell. Said he, 'If you were president of Boeing, you'd have them all on your neck, because of your disposition.' He observed that I was unnecessarily curt with secretaries. Well, how about reforming—who am I to act that way?" Continuing in a reflective mood on the night he accepted the Boeing presidency, Allen set down in his diary a list of resolutions for his new career. For his personal life, he promised himself to keep regular hours; limit his evening drinks to two; do sit-up exercises every day and play golf at least one afternoon a week; and minimize his purely fun evenings at home to have more time for business and social obligations, reading, adequate rest, and seeing his children. He penned brief self-admonitions about the administration of his duties at Boeing:

> Must keep temper always, never get mad.
> Be considerate of my associates' views.
> Deal through department heads.
> Don't talk too much, let others talk.
> Don't be afraid to admit that you don't know.
> Don't get immersed in detail, concentrate on the big objectives.
> Make contacts with other people in the industry, and keep them.
> Try to improve feeling around Seattle toward Boeing.
> Make a sincere effort to understand labor's viewpoint.
> Be definite—don't vacillate.
> Act—get things done—move forward.
> Develop a postwar future for Boeing.
> Try hard, but don't let obstacles get you down, take things in stride.
> Above all else be human—keep your sense of humor—learn to relax.
> Be just, straightforward, invite criticism and learn to take it.
> Be confident, having once made the move. Make the most of it. Bring to task great enthusiasm—unlimited energy.
> Make Boeing even greater than it is.

Allen was running his law firm, many of whose attorneys had gone to war, and told Egtvedt that he couldn't start his new job until someone who could take charge came back. When months passed and no one qualified came home, Egtvedt boldly phoned Secretary of the Navy James Forrestal and got a key member of the firm discharged. The sudden surrender of Japan on August 14 after the atomic bomb attacks, ending the war and heralding the imminent collapse of Boeing, may have precipitated Egtvedt's action. Boeing's board of directors formally elected Allen president at a special meeting on September 5, 1945. He started work immediately at his new office.

One of the first problems Allen had to confront was also one of the most unpleasant. When Johnson had died, the second-highest ranking man in the company was Executive Vice President H. Oliver West, head of production. He had overcome a disabling handicap in his rise to power: Small and slight, West was crippled by severe arthritis. He roamed Boeing's factories in a special car tiny enough to fit into elevators. A longtime associate of Johnson, West had left Boeing to accompany him to Canada and returned with him. West ran the company day to day during the war; Johnson spent all his time maintaining relations with the military, companies that worked with Boeing, and other outside organizations, and was frequently away from the office. Like Johnson, West was a manufacturing expert, which was just what the war effort required. West was no Johnson when it came to dealing with people, however. He ran production with an iron fist, treating everyone ruthlessly and alienating both management and labor. The engineers felt he often arbitrarily sacrificed design features, no matter how beneficial, to production expediencies. Johnson seems to have been his only admirer; his enemies were legion.

The company's bylaws had automatically made Chairman Egtvedt CEO again when Johnson died. West had assumed that, as the number two man, he'd immediately be elected president and CEO. West's fellow members on the board of directors, however, had agreed that he wasn't suitable. Egtvedt had asked Bill Allen to give the word to West, even as Allen had given the word to Egtvedt himself before the war. Allen had done so, "and not to Oliver's pleasure, I can assure you," Allen told a Boeing executive. West, apparently unaware of the overwhelming opposition to him, was so shocked and demoralized that he lost interest in his job, often not even coming to work. Wellwood Beall told colleagues that at a board of directors' meeting when West wasn't present, the board members were holding up decisions because they knew West would disapprove. Allen had pointed out that the bylaws permitted the board to expel a member, and suggested that this be done so they could get on with business, which they did.

Still, West didn't resign his executive position with the company. When Allen became president he found the situation intolerable. Firing West could not have been easy, especially given West's affliction, his brother's death in the service of Boeing (killed in the Stratoliner test-flight crash), and his accomplishments in setting fantastic production records to help the country win the war and make millions for Boeing. One wonders if Allen could have treated West humanely, perhaps given him a special position that shunted him aside while allowing him to be productive. Power struggles in the corporate world rarely end so nicely, however. As it happened, Allen asked for and got West's resignation.

When Allen had been named president, friends gave him a present that they said symbolized Boeing. He kept it in his office for years—a scrawny, stunted, and thorny potted prickly pear cactus that could survive the worst conditions. The simile was apt. Japan had signed the official surrender documents on September 2. The day before Allen took office, the AAF canceled some of its B-29 production contracts with Boeing, and then canceled the rest of them the next day, when he was installed in the presidency. Boeing's employment in the Seattle area plunged from thirty-five thousand to six thousand, and at Wichita dropped from sixteen thousand to fifteen hundred. Later, Allen commented ruefully, "The company was, with the exception of a few minor jobs, out of business." Boeing's situation was worse than that of any other aircraft manufacturer. Boeing had been the only manufacturer engaged in maximum war production until the very end, devoting more of its attention and resources to that effort than any other company not by choice but by government fiat. Other companies had had a chance to wind down slowly, and gradually build up other business. Boeing had not had nearly as much spare time or resources to devote to efforts that would pay off in peacetime. The impact was hard on Boeing's workers and the people of the Seattle area, where one in six residents had been getting a Boeing paycheck. Labor wasn't hit quite as hard as the raw figures suggest, however, because many employees, like the immortal "Rosie the Riveter," had signed on only for the duration of the war and didn't want to stay. Most employees and the company itself, however, were catapulted almost in an instant back to the miserable economic depression they had been suffering before the long war.

When Boeing had been in the same position after World War I, the company had turned to making furniture to survive. Starting up a new business was again a serious option. Within days of assuming the presidency, Allen told employees it was likely that Boeing would engage in some form of nonaircraft production. With the important military aircraft business at rock bottom after the war, most aircraft manufacturers tried or at least considered diversification. Several of the companies attempted shipbuilding or general construction, thinking their skills would transfer readily to these industries. Some outfits entered the small private-airplane field. Allen elected to bypass both these attractive ventures, and a good thing. Almost all the companies that went into shipbuilding and construction found they didn't know what they were doing, and had to pull out. The private airplane industry never took off as expected, and the newcomers had to withdraw from the crowded field.

Boeing played it smart and devoted much time to finding appropriate businesses. The company made a serious study of the possibilities, beginning long before the war was over, when Boeing executives realized the fix they were getting into. They established a group to develop new business opportunities, locating the unit in rented space in downtown Seattle known as "the cave." Wellwood Beall and chief engineer Ed Wells gave the project a high priority and devoted Monday mornings to working with the group. The cave dwellers came up with many ideas, some as way-out as making an eggbeater with a pistol grip adjustable for use by left-handers. They patented and even made money on a few products, such as a prefabricated kitchen-bathroom module whose patent was sold to a company that placed them in Alaskan housing projects. They designed a roomy car with an aisle like today's vans, although Boeing soon recognized the folly of trying to compete with Detroit. The only idea that led to a new product line was that of making small gas turbines for specialized military applications, but the business never made much money.

Boeing and the other aircraft makers much preferred to capitalize on the strength they had gained during the war and stay in their traditional business if they could. All the American companies collectively had metamorphosed into the mightiest aircraft industry the world had ever known; if aircraft engine and components manufacturers were considered part of the industry, then it had become the biggest industry of any kind on earth. The firms had increased their assets manyfold—Boeing's had multiplied twenty times—making them the largest companies in the worldwide industry. They had grown from small and medium-sized firms to large corporations. Their plants had evolved from what were essentially job shops almost to mass production factories. (Unlike automobiles, aircraft didn't lend themselves to true mass production.) The magnitude of the change over ten years was striking. In the mid-1930s, British aircraft manufacturers had been the biggest, and the British industry had been twice as large as the American.

Boeing had emerged from the war as the leading producer of large bombers, but that did it little good in what had become a civilian economy. The Pentagon kept the company alive in the aircraft business—barely—with a small order for advanced B-29s and some development funds for the C-97, a troop and cargo carrier based on the B-29, and the B-47, an experimental bomber. None of them seemed promising enough to save the company in the long run. Boeing continued to limp through the postwar period, losing money each year through 1947, glad to have survived but not knowing where it was headed. All the aircraft firms were hurting, even those with airliners to sell, because the commercial business hadn't revived yet, either. An economist called the condition of the aircraft industry in 1947 "appalling."

In 1948, the politicians tried to move in, when Congress considered a bill ostensibly to revive the commercial aircraft industry. The bill was a Trojan horse for a government takeover, however. It gave the government control of the industry, reserving major business decisions for Washington, D.C., and almost nationalizing the industry. Alarmed, Allen and his colleagues fought the treacherous bill and it died.

Allen and the other industry leaders still expected the commercial side to take off, especially with the advancements and opportunities generated by the war. Inexpensive high-octane gasoline had been perfected to vastly increase the efficiency of airplane engines. Military training had created a pool of personnel skilled in flying and maintaining aircraft. Over-ocean flights by land-based planes (as opposed to prewar flying boats like the Boeing Clippers) had become routine during the fighting. Many people had flown in the service and were receptive to commercial flying. Business opportunities in a recovering Europe would stimulate traffic on transatlantic air routes.

Allen thought that Boeing might fill a niche in the commercial market by producing a commuter airliner. Boeing engineers spent over half a year and a couple of million dollars developing a twenty-passenger, two-engine transport for short, regional flights. Unfortunately, Lockheed, Convair, and Martin also entered the market, and Allen discovered that Boeing wouldn't be able to sell its model at a competitive price. Calling the project a "guaranteed loss," he killed it before the designers had built a prototype. Boeing sold the design to Fokker, which used elements of it in the company's popular F-27. Yet another potential moneymaking idea had come to nothing.

The aircraft industry knew that, when the airliner business finally got going again, the companies would make most of their money in the "heavyweight" division: large, long-range airplanes for the trunk airlines. By war's end, all the contenders were developing airliners patterned after America's highly successful four-engine bombers. Boeing was far behind, its time and resources having been limited by B-29 production, but the company's designers had a well-formed idea to present to Allen as soon as he came aboard. Wellwood Beall had had his engineers working on his latest idea, a land-based counterpart to his famous luxury flying boats, the Pan Am Clippers. Beall based the airplane on Boeing's new C-97 military transport. He had already bestowed the name

"Stratocruiser" on it. His strategy for the airliner was twofold. First, he'd follow the C-97 design closely and use the same tooling so that he'd spend much less time and money than usual on developing and tooling up for the Stratocruiser. Adhering so tightly to the military design would limit the airplane to only seventy-five passengers. This payload was so much less than competitive models, planned to be much different from their bomber predecessors, that airlines would lose money if they charged standard fares. This led to the second part of the Beall plan: sell the Stratocruiser as a luxury airliner and speed champion that would command premium fares high enough to allow the airlines to buy the airplanes and make a profit. He figured that Boeing would break even at only fifty sales, much less than the three hundred or so sales it would take to pay for the major redesigns that other companies were undertaking.

Allen had known all this in his capacity as counsel and board member. He was also aware that Boeing, as a marginal player in the commercial game and offering an unusual, bomberlike airliner, might not be able to sell even fifty. Beall's low-cost scheme would minimize losses, however. The project offered substantial benefits even if it should lose money, moreover. It would keep Boeing in the commercial arena, ready to compete again as an established player in the future when the company would, Allen hoped, be in better shape. Even more important, it would avoid the layoff of engineers and loss of experienced talent that would have to take place if Boeing didn't mount another development project. Allen contacted other board members to see if they'd support the project. They would. His second day on the job, Allen ordered full-scale development of the Stratocruiser to begin.

Developers made the airplane speedier than its major competitors: twenty-five miles per hour faster than Douglas's DC-6, and an amazing one hundred miles per hour faster than Lockheed's first Constellations. Beall was at his sybaritic best in choosing the plush layout and appointments for the Stratocruiser. He made it roomier, quieter, and much more comfortable than any rival airliner, paying special attention to providing sumptuous seats. He hired one of the country's leading industrial design consultants, Walter Dorwin

Teague and Associates of New York, to create an atmosphere of unmatched elegance in the cabin (beginning a long-term, fertile relationship between Boeing and the design firm). Beall's pièce de résistance was a spiral staircase that led passengers to a lower deck where they could enjoy a softly lighted cocktail lounge.

Allen secured a launch customer that Boeing knew well a month after okaying the Stratocruiser project—Pan Am. The airline bought twenty of the airliners at $1.3 million each, understanding that the first airplane would be delivered in a year. Allen quickly sold twelve more to other customers. Then he began to meet resistance. Many airlines didn't want to buy a warmed-over bomber, preferring an airliner more refined for their needs and whims. Allen responded by forming Boeing's first separate sales department, placing it under Beall and expanding his job to vice president of engineering and sales.

Turning the rough and ready C-97 military aircraft into a classy airliner proved much more challenging than Beall had anticipated, so Stratocruiser development wasn't as quick and painless as hoped. The aircraft didn't make its first flight until July 8, 1947. It was the last of the competitors up in the air, to the displeasure of the new sales department. Ground and flight testing dragged on. Initial production was so flawed and inefficient that Allen replaced the head of manufacturing, admonishing his employees that they were no longer mass-producing airplanes on a government budget and needed to be more economical.

While Boeing worked on the Stratocruiser, the company was also engaged in a secret military project that would turn out to be one of the most important undertakings in its history.

When Dick Henning returned from the war, Boeing assigned him to serve as a consultant to the Army Air Forces on B-17 and B-29 maintenance at various bases in the United States. His stay at Pratt Air Base near Wichita, Kansas, turned out to be lengthy, but after ninety days the per diem expense pay allowed by Boeing's contract with the AAF dropped to only four dollars a day. That wasn't nearly enough to pay for his hotel, meals, and other expenses while he was on the road, so he asked Boeing to make up the shortfall. The company refused. Dick couldn't find any way to lower his expenses, but he didn't want to quit Boeing, so he had to eat the sizable difference. He was broke by the time the war ended, and had to borrow a hundred dollars to get home in December 1945.

Dick's tribulations continued in Seattle. Despite all he had been through in Europe and Kansas, his bosses had forgotten him. People in his old work group had progressed in the way normal to the Seattle offices, and he had not. They treated him as an outsider, giving him the boring job of writing mundane bulletins on fixing problems with B-17s and B-29s. Sensing that the group didn't want him anymore, he looked for a Boeing unit that needed someone like him.

The electrical design group invited him in, and in February 1946 he arranged a transfer to the more hospitable organization. A promotion came with the move: He was made lead engineer, as engineering coordinators are called, for design of electrical equipment on the C-97 transport. Allowed to be creative and use his engineering skills in his new job, Dick solved a big problem in aircraft electrical circuits. Dust would get into key components known as relays and cause them to spark, sometimes triggering explosions or setting fires. Dick designed the first dust-tight relay enclosure for AAF airplanes. Later that year, the group needed him more in wiring design, and he was transferred to that function.

The next year, Dick was made the electrical group's lead design engineer for all lighting systems on the Stratocruiser. When working on cabin lighting, he cooperated closely with the Walter Dorwin Teague group, Boeing's interior design consultant. Collaborating on lights for the cocktail lounge on the lower deck, Dick's practical nature clashed with Teague's aesthetic thinking. Dick wanted bright lights so that lounge patrons could read; Teague recommended subdued lighting as more appropriate for the lounge atmosphere. Dick had to swallow his disgust when Teague won.

Probably the single proudest moment of Dick's life at this time occurred on November 28, 1946, when June gave birth to their first child, a son. The Hennings chose his name for reasons that bespoke their midwestern values. As Dick explained, they named their boy "after the book about a young college boy named Larry, who had good moral and ethical characteristics, and loved his mother dearly." An expanded family made a bigger residence desirable, so the Hennings also bought their first home. They paid $13,500 ($2,700 down, 5 percent mortgage) for a brick house on a corner lot on Gatewood Hill at the south end of West Seattle. So many of Dick's coworkers attended the housewarming that, he commented, he was "surrounded by loving, caring engineer buddies."

Most of Dick's friends worked with him at Boeing. His favorite recreation was camping and fishing with the guys. Beginning in 1946, he began going on outdoor trips with his buddies as often as he could find the time. Their favorite haunts were a spot on the isolated Icicle River in the Wenatchee National Forest east of Seattle, reachable only by riding horseback and hiking over thirteen rugged miles, and Lake Hi-HI-Hiume (Native American for "Lake of Plenty," referring to the abundant fish) in British Columbia. From 1948 on, he drove to the campsites in his new Chrysler Windsor sedan with a luggage rack on top.

At work, Dick received some assignments whose government entanglements proved insanely frustrating, and other jobs that filled him with the elation he had sought in an engineering career.

Part II

Creating the Jet Age

5 ‖ The Jet Age Begins

A mysterious summons came to Wellwood Beall and Ed Wells in March 1943. The Army Air Forces asked them to attend a meeting at a place called Muroc Air Base, a new facility (since renamed Edwards Air Force Base) that few people had heard of in California's Mojave Desert 150 miles northeast of Los Angeles. The meeting was so secret that Beall and Wells weren't even told what it was about.

When they arrived, the Boeing executives found that their counterparts from all the other major aircraft manufacturers had also been invited. The purpose of the meeting was announced dramatically when the conference participants gathered by the runway and watched a small new fighter on a takeoff run. Modern eyes would have seen nothing remarkable about the aircraft, made by the Bell corporation. The onlookers of half a century ago thought it a spectacular sight, however—the airplane gathering speed on the sunny field in front of them had no visible means of propulsion. No propellers! It rose into the air, turned, and zoomed low overhead, roaring its proclamation that a new age in aviation had begun: the era of jet-propelled airplanes.

Army Air Forces officials briefed their guests on developments. The jet engine they displayed had been invented by an English engineer, Frank Whittle, shortly before the war. The first airplane to use his invention made its historic flight in May 1941. The Royal Air Force kept U.S. Army Air Forces commander General Hap Arnold informed, shipping a jet engine and drawings to America a few months after the first flight. Arnold passed these on to General Electric so GE could develop jet engines. (GE, although not an engine manufacturer, had two key qualifications: The company made both turbosuperchargers for aircraft and turbines to generate electricity. These work like jet engines. Preparing for America's likely entry into the war, moreover, the AAF wanted existing aircraft engine manufacturers to focus totally on production of conventional piston engines to drive propellers.) Bell Aircraft had incorporated two of the GE engines in its experimental jet fighter.

The engineers invited to Muroc knew generally about jet propulsion theory, which had long been discussed in technical circles. Beall confessed, however, that he was much surprised that practical engines had become a reality so soon. Comparing jet engines with piston engines, the AAF briefing team pointed out that the simplicity of jets was the source of many of their virtues. They had no rubbing parts. Combustion energy was converted directly into thrust, instead of driving pistons that turned cranks that spun propellers that pulled airplanes through the air. Speed, not limited by how fast pistons pumped and propellers turned, could be incredible, approaching and possibly even surpassing the speed of sound. Jets could be much more powerful per pound of engine than pistons, and could operate continuously at maximum power with no danger of flying apart or burning out. Sleek jet tubes would present less drag (wind resistance) than propellers and bulky piston engines, with their elaborate cooling systems. Without whirling blades to limit placement, jets could be arranged in many configurations, opening new vistas in aircraft design. They wouldn't create the tremendous vibrations generated by pistons and propellers, which wore down aircraft equipment, the engines themselves, and passengers. Maintenance costs, heavy for pistons, should be much less for jets.

The outstanding characteristics of this seemingly perfect engine were counterbalanced by one huge flaw: heavy fuel consumption. Although in theory jets should get markedly many more miles to the gallon than pistons, in practice they got less; jets were fuel hogs, gulping the propellant 65 percent faster than piston engines, limiting their range and rendering debatable their usefulness for anything other than fighters. What's more, cautious AAF officials were far from certain that the jet's theoretical virtues would hold up over the long haul, and they worried that some fatal flaw might eventually show up. They wanted to know if the aircraft manufacturers thought jet bombers were feasible.

Beall, Wells, and their colleagues returned to their companies to study the matter. By the end of the summer, the corporations had reached the consensus that they could develop practical jet bombers. With the United States then deeply enmeshed in wars on two fronts, and money for defense essentially no object, the AAF decided to fund development of different prototypes by each of the five interested manufacturers. In fall 1943, the service gave contracts to Boeing to produce the B-47, Douglas for the B-43, North American for the B-45, Convair for the B-46, and Martin for the B-48. (The remaining major player, Lockheed, chose to develop a jet fighter.)

At that point, although Boeing realized it only dimly if at all, and the government, military, and other manufacturers hadn't a clue, the race was on for supremacy in the business of making commercial jet airplanes. Right at the start, Boeing jumped out to a lead that it never relinquished, using revolutionary development techniques and producing a design that was radically different from the designs of its competitors. This occurrence had originated in a hotly debated, fateful decision that Phil Johnson and his staff made two years before.

As aircraft design became more sophisticated during the 1930s, Boeing and other aircraft manufacturers felt the need for greater access to wind tunnels, most of them at universities. With the increasing demand for testing hours, it was difficult to make timely bookings at the few existing tunnels. Shortly before the war began, companies began to make cooperative arrangements with universities to build and operate tunnels patterned after those already built, such as the one at the University of Washington (donated by Bill Boeing in 1919). Planning to go along with the trend, Boeing hired as consultants two of the world's leading wind-tunnel experts, Theodore Von Karman and John Markham. Von Karman and Markham pointed out an advantage that Boeing had over its competitors: cheap operating power. Wind tunnels drew vast amounts of current, and the cost of electricity to run them was a major consideration. Because of the newly built Grand Coulee Dam, power in the Pacific Northwest was cheap. Von Karman and Markham argued that Boeing could build its own tunnel and make it much more powerful than the others that were under way for an affordable lifetime cost. The initial cost would be high, however: a million dollars, about four times the cost of a conventional tunnel.

The advantages of having a tunnel all to themselves were clear to Boeing executives, particularly since Douglas had apparently gotten confidential data about the Model 247 from security leaks at Cal Tech's wind tunnel. The need for a mightier wind tunnel wasn't obvious, however. Von Karman and Markham urged an eighteen-thousand-horsepower tunnel that could generate wind speeds of 0.975 Mach—just a few miles per hour short of the speed of sound. No aircraft then existing or even postulated could get anywhere close to that speed. Von Karman insisted that progress would provide the technology to reach the speed of sound, and that breakthroughs would happen sooner rather than later. (As an adviser to the Army Air Forces, he may have known about the top secret jet engine developments then taking place in England.) The consultants successfully pressed their viewpoint on Eddie Allen, the chief test pilot who was also in charge of wind-tunnel testing. (More than a pilot, Allen had written technical papers and a book on the role of flight testing in development.) Allen had a harder time selling the idea to Johnson and the others who had control of the corporate purse. Allen's request for the initial expenditure, twenty-five thousand dollars for a working scale model of the tunnel, aroused controversy but he prevailed. The Muroc conference was held while the tunnel was under construction, allowing all concerned with the tunnel to congratulate themselves on their foresight. The big, totally private tunnel, featuring a fan twenty-four feet in diameter, went into operation in February 1944.

Boeing engineers immediately put the tunnel to use in designing the B-47, running it night and day. With the tunnel at their complete disposal and dedicated totally to the one project, the designers used it to gather experimental data on the effects of jet speeds—which were sparse to nonexistent in the technical literature—and to explore ideas. Even with expanded access to tunnels, Boeing's competitors had only enough test time to validate or reject design decisions already made; unlike Boeing, they could not use tunnels as an integral, continuing part of the design process.

Like the other manufacturers, Boeing started with the idea that designers could more or less use existing airframe concepts and simply replace the piston engines with jets; Boeing planned to base the B-47 on the B-29. Before long, however, Boeing engineers came to an unsettling conclusion: aircraft behaved differently enough at jet speeds that they'd have to design the airplane from scratch to obtain acceptable performance. Boeing's competitors never realized this, since they had no way to find out, which was good for Boeing from the business standpoint. Unfortunately, however, the Army Air Forces couldn't fully appreciate the discovery, either. Although Boeing engineers explained their findings to the military, the pressures for quick development and the competitors' belief that no new approaches were necessary made the B-47 sponsors uneasy. As the other manufacturers moved quickly to prototype construction while the Seattle company moved slowly and proclaimed the need for more study, Boeing was in constant danger of losing its contract. Then there occurred an incident that not only strengthened Boeing's case, but became a landmark in the history of aviation.

Early in 1945, with the Allies marching to certain victory in Germany, the U.S. Army Air Forces planned an intelligence operation to learn Germany's aeronautical secrets before key documents were taken and dispersed by fleeing scientists and engineers. The Nazis obviously had advanced research and development programs, evidenced by the rockets that had terrorized Britain and—to the great surprise of England and the other Allies—jet fighters that had flown circles around Allied aircraft in the last months of the war. Neither England nor the United States had flown jets in battle. U.S. military strategists concluded that if Germany had introduced jets just a little earlier, before the war was all but lost, Hitler could have achieved air supremacy and changed the course of the conflict. The AAF would send teams of aeronautical experts behind the front lines to ransack Germany's aviation facilities as soon as the Nazis surrendered.

One team was drawn from the Army Air Forces Scientific Advisory Board, a group of civilians assigned to the Pentagon for the duration of the war to make sure that America's air arm could take immediate advantage of the latest technical developments. This group was pegged to examine the records and interrogate the staff of the Hermann Goering Aeronautical Research Center in a forest outside Braunschweig in central Germany. Within just an hour or two of surrender, the group swarmed over the center. One member of the party, who at the young age of thirty-two had already become one of America's top aerodynamicists (an authority on the interactions between aircraft and air), was George Schairer ("SHY-rer"). He was the chief aerodynamicist for Boeing whose wing and wind-tunnel expertise had helped the company to garner the B-29 contract. Schairer and teammate Hugh Dryden, who would later head the National Aeronautics and Space Administration, went straight to the library.

They beheld a bonanza. The methodical Germans, planning to carry their documents back to the universities, companies, and agencies they had come from in their peacetime occupations, had carefully prioritized their records and stacked them in piles according to importance. The Americans had descended on them before they could get away. Schairer, who could read German, started plowing through the pile labeled "most important." Soon he came to a drawing, an outline of a jet airplane, that riveted his attention. The shape was startlingly different from any airplane then flying. The wings and horizontal tail surfaces, instead of sticking straight out at ninety degrees from the fuselage in the normal fashion, were angled back—"swept-back" would become the accepted term—about forty-five degrees. The drawing had jolted Schairer because he and another member of his team had spent most of the long flight to Europe making drawings like that and discussing the potential advantages of swept-back wings to jet-powered flight. As far as they knew, the idea had been the recent brainchild of an American government scientist, Robert Jones of the National Advisory Committee on Aeronautics (which later became NASA), who had told them his ideas.

Paging through the material in the pile, Schairer saw that the Germans had run wind-tunnel tests showing that sweepback would significantly reduce drag and improve performance at jet speeds. Like the Americans, the Germans in their first approach had merely installed jets on essentially conventional airframes. The jet fighters they had flown in the war had straight wings. The Messerschmitt company was completing a jet fighter with forty-five degrees of sweep, however. The next day Schairer and the other members of the intelligence team interrogated the staff of the Goering Center, including Adolf Busemann, who had independently conceived the idea of swept wings. Before Schairer had read the Goering Center documents and talked with Busemann, swept wings had been just one of many ideas to explore for possible use in the B-47 project. His experience at the Goering Center persuaded him that swept wings were vital to the success of the project.

Another AAF intelligence group visited the Goering Center briefly on the day Schairer talked with Busemann. That group included another Boeing engineer, an aircraft structural specialist named George Martin. Schairer enthusiastically gave Martin the news about swept wings. Martin was impressed and became an even stronger convert to the swept-wing philosophy when his group visited the Messerschmitt factory, where he saw the nearly completed swept-wing fighter.

With the B-47 already far along, Schairer thought he'd better get word about swept wings to Seattle as soon as he could and not wait until he returned. On his third day at the German research center, May 10, he wrote a letter to Benny Cohn, his second in command at Boeing's aerodynamics unit. The letter (preserved in Boeing's archives) is a charming mixture of the homey and the profound. Schairer twice expressed his delight at being able to use his electric razor on the trip. Stating that "[the Germans] are ahead of us in a few items," the heart of the letter is a serious exposition of the swept-wing notion. Using mathematics and a little sketch, Schairer outlined what he had learned. He didn't mention the top secret B-47, but the implication was clear. Knowing that his letter had to pass Army censors, Schairer tried a little deception to help the swept-wing information get through undeleted. He wrote CENSORED on the envelope and signed his name beneath the word. (The letter has the status of a sacred relic at Boeing. Both the archives and Schairer himself, long retired, proudly pass out copies to visitors.)

When Cohn got the letter—untouched by censors—he was smart enough to get the message. He immediately started making swept-wing B-47 models and testing them in the wind tunnel. The theory was borne out by excellent test results. As might be expected, there was some initial resistance within Boeing's bureaucracy to such a radical change so late in the design process. The opposition disappeared, however, when George Martin returned and was appointed head of the B-47 project. The flight characteristics of swept-wing airplanes are so different from those of straight-wing airplanes that Boeing had to start afresh. The AAF, while not ardent about swept wings, agreed that they looked worth pursuing, and agreed to be patient while Boeing took yet more time on B-47 development. Boeing pursued a risky strategy: The company allowed the other manufacturers to open a wide lead in developing prototypes, counting on reaching a design so superior that the AAF would have no choice but to ignore all the jet bombers available early and order the late-arriving model from Boeing.

In his letter from the Goering Center, Schairer had instructed Cohn to forward the information on swept wings to men he named at the other leading aircraft companies; after all, the information had come to him as a government agent and not as a Boeing employee. All the other groups making bomber prototypes ignored the intelligence, however—regretably for them. Apparently they either did not appreciate its significance or considered the bomber projects too far along to change directions.

Information from the German files helped Boeing to make another audacious decision. The designers' natural inclination was to place the jet engines in the wings, following the pattern set by piston engines. Boeing decided that the danger of fires that could spread to the wings from jets was great enough that perhaps the engines should be in pods hung from the wings on struts. Boeing designers had been impressed by Lockheed's decision to use pods on a jet fighter. The decision was clinched when Schairer found German studies showing the desirability of pods. This had major design ramifications, the most significant being that the wings were made flexible, and they flapped up and down and twisted slightly in response to forces from atmospheric turbulence and pilot maneuvers. All the other manufacturers buried their jets in the wings in the usual way, and built essentially rigid wings.

The technical challenges of the B-47 excited Boeing's engineers, so the company's senior executives, including Bill Allen when he took over in the fall of 1945, gave the B-47 all the support the project needed. Few executives, nevertheless, thought the innovative airplane had much of a chance to go into production. People viewed it as a kind of "plane of the future," a flying test bed of the emerging technologies of jet flight, serving the same function as the single supergiant bomber Boeing had built in the 1930s to investigate the design problems of large airplanes. The AAF felt the same way. While the B-47 project was under way, the military funded Boeing to develop the B-50 and B-54—advanced, propeller-driven versions of the B-29. George Schairer, seconded by Ed Wells, declared ruefully that the B-54 would undoubtedly be Boeing's bread and butter product for many years. The AAF also had Boeing establish a parallel effort to develop a turboprop B-47. Turboprops are halfway between conventional propeller-driven aircraft and pure jets, using jet turbines instead of pistons to power propellers. Many people in the military (and on airline staffs, when they came to consider the possibility of jetliners) thought that aviation would go through a turboprop era before pure jets took over. The logic seemed compelling, even at Boeing before the B-47 flew. The company designed the turboprop B-47, but dropped the project when it became clear that the airplane had nothing to recommend it over piston airplanes.

The B-47 had a size advantage over its competitors that had nothing to do with Boeing's technical astuteness but that came about because of bureaucratic bumbling. After the A-bomb was dropped on Japan, the B-47's mission was defined as carrying just one nuclear bomb to a target. In one of the absurd situations that develop in military and government bureaucracies, however, the officers at Wright Field in charge of bomber development gave the manufacturers the wrong measurements for the bomb; the dimensions were a top secret, and the goof may have had something to do with the restricted flow of such information. As a result, bomb bays in all the prototypes were too small—except for Boeing's. As a member of the Army Air Forces Scientific Advisory Board, George Schairer had learned the bomb's true dimensions. Consequently, Boeing sized the B-47 just right, which became an important consideration in maintaining the AAF's interest in the airplane.

All Boeing's eager competitors had put jet bombers into the air by spring of 1947. Boeing didn't finish the much-different B-47 until September 12 of that year. On that day, the first of two prototypes rolled out of the hangar. Normally rollout day is an occasion for ceremonies and celebrations, but the B-47 (designated XB-47 while in the experimental stage) was still supposedly a secret project (although widely known), so only a few people witnessed the event. One onlooker was Bill Allen, who recorded the occasion the next day in one of his few diary entries that betray any kind of feeling: "Yesterday was a big day in Boeing history. The XB-47 (six-engined jet bomber) . . . was a great sight with its swept back wings and sleek body."

On completion of ground tests, and after several weather delays, the first flight took place on December 17, by coincidence the forty-fourth anniversary of the Wright brothers' first flight. Bob Robbins would pilot the B-47, with copilot Scott Osler sitting behind him in the narrow cockpit. Unusual anxiety gripped everyone at Boeing Field that day. The B-47's design was so revolutionary, the airframe and the engines so new, that there were far many more unknowns than on most test flights. People feared for the lives and safety of the men who would fly the novel machine and worried about the continuation of the project. Bill Cook, an engineer on the B-47 project, recalled later, "To those of us on the ground, the first lift-off was a very tense, dramatic event."

Shortly after 1:30 P.M., the bomber sped down the runway. At about one hundred miles per hour, a red light flashed on the fire-warning panel, indicating an engine on fire. Robbins, his adrenalin spurting, killed the power and tromped on the brakes. Only moments after the aircraft halted, Osler discovered that the light was a false alarm from a fault in the detection system. Robbins bravely decided to try the takeoff again right away, even though the hot brakes might not work if they had to be used on the next run. Again the B-47 raced down the runway. Robbins resolutely kept going when the same defective warning light flashed on. Just after 135 miles per hour the aircraft lifted off and rose quickly. Robbins was relieved to find that the airplane was stable and responsive to the controls. The flaps used at takeoff wouldn't retract immediately, however; an alternative retraction system had to be employed. High in the air, Robbins headed over the Cascade Mountains toward Moses Lake 120 miles away. This first flight would be short and would end at the airfield at Moses Lake Air Base, a wartime training facility, which would be the base of operations for the test flight program; empty airspace and better weather had recommended the site to Boeing. Robbins tested the basic characteristics of the airplane and discovered the expected little glitches here and there, but found nothing that couldn't be fixed quickly, nothing wrong with the fundamental design. The airplane landed safely, to the joy of everybody connected with it.

Subsequent test flights experienced two major misfortunes. Aircraft are supposed to be stable in flight; the pilot should be able to let go of the controls for brief periods, like a cyclist riding no-hands, without affecting the course of the airplane. Robbins found, however, that when he abandoned the controls, the B-47 yawed or fishtailed and banked a bit, then yawed and banked a little more in the other direction and continued the pattern, making S-turns with increasingly larger swirls and steeper banks. Boeing's aerodynamicists recognized this as a classic instability known as "Dutch roll," supposedly named after an ice-skating technique used on Holland's canals. If unchecked, the roll would eventually turn the airplane on its back and throw it out of control. Once started, it was difficult to correct; pilots who didn't know what steps to take or who couldn't improvise quickly enough couldn't get out of it in time to avoid crashing.

The B-47's designers had known that swept-wing airplanes would be prone to Dutch roll, but they thought they had designed it out. Even if they redesigned the plane—and it was too late for that—there was no assurance they'd succeed in eliminating the pernicious instability on their second try. They developed an ingenious solution, a relatively simple control that automatically sensed and stopped the oscillations leading to Dutch roll. For reasons lost to history, they named the control "Little Herbie." This was a notable event in the history of aviation technology, the first time that a design had been accepted despite inherent instability. (Dutch roll is so tough to avoid in swept-wing airplanes that Little Herbie became standard equipment on jets.)

Test pilots say it's usually not the big things that will kill you, but the little things. That's what happened on the fateful flight piloted by Scott Osler and copiloted by Jim Frazier. During the flight, a latch on the canopy failed and the covering flew off. Tragically, it took Osler's head with it. Frazier fought through his horror and landed the airplane, but refused to fly the B-47 ever again.

The B-47 was hard to fly. For one thing, the engines were slow to respond to the controls, like hesitation in an automobile engine but worse. When the pilot called for full power, it could take the engines the better part of a minute to react. The landing gear was so arranged that pilots had to take off and land almost flat, not nose-up as usual, or they'd drag the tail—they couldn't raise the nose of the airplane unless the craft was well clear of the ground. Close to the speed of sound, the nose tended to pitch up sharply and could, if not controlled, toss the airplane into a spin. The sweep and flexibility of the wings, combined with speed and power unprecedented in such a large airplane, made handling much different from what pilots were used to. Boeing paid test pilots a bonus to fly the B-47, but it didn't compensate for the sense of impending catastrophe they felt on every flight. With the pilots' supercautious approach toward probing the limits of the airplane, the test program crawled along and fell far behind schedule. Disgusted with Boeing's timidity, the Air Force—which had become an autonomous service in 1947— assigned its own pilot, Major Guy Townsend, to take over B-47 testing. Townsend (who later become a Boeing executive) sped up the testing and got it back on track before he was reassigned. On the recommendation of the Air Force, Boeing hired one of the country's top civilian test pilots, Tex Johnston, to finish the flight trials. Johnston, who averred that he found the B-47 fun to fly, concluded the testing uneventfully.

Despite Dutch roll, the tricky flying qualities of the prototypes, and the grisly accident, the B-47 did better than expected in its tests. Most impressively, it exhibited a whopping 15 percent less drag than expected, which meant much better speed, range, and fuel economy than predicted—it flew faster than the new F-86 jet fighter. Bill Allen, sparing with praise in his diary, recorded meaningfully on May 27, 1948: "Jet bomber performs beautifully." Of greatest importance to Boeing's business, the swept-wing bomber was so successful technically that the era of straight-wing jet bombers ended only a few months after it began; the jet bombers being flown by Boeing's competitors had become instant fossils. Boeing's nerve in letting the others get ahead while the company pioneered the technology of large jet planes, and the Air Force's patience in sticking with Boeing despite grave doubts, had been rewarded. The B-47 skeptics at Boeing became enthusiasts. Boeing's executives began to believe that a production model could be built that could attract a large Air Force order.

Despite the success of the prototypes, however, it was still an experimental airplane and faced the same resistance to change that retards the adoption of any new technology. Consolidated had designed the B-36, a propeller-driven airplane that could perform the same mission as the B-47. The Air Force was reluctant to go to

B-47s, no matter how exciting, when it had a familiar, comfortable technology in B-36s. The problem was primarily psychological: When it came to ordering aircraft for routine use by the Air Force, no amount of superb B-47 performance figures and favorable reports would persuade the piston-engine Air Force generals to go for something so far-out as the B-47.

Bill Allen seized an opportunity to attack the problem with a psychological solution. In July 1948, General K. B. Wolfe, procurement director of the Air Force's Matériel Command, came to Seattle on business concerning the airplanes Boeing was already producing. Convinced that making Wolfe a fan of the B-47 would be as good as an order in the pocket, a wily Allen determined to get the general to fly in the jet. As Wolfe prepared to leave Seattle, Allen suggested that he stop at Moses Lake, not far out of his way, and watch a B-47 demonstration. Citing his busy schedule, Wolfe declined to take the time. Allen pointed out that Wolfe could fly to Moses Lake in a fast B-50 while the slow B-17 in which he was returning to Wright Field followed, so he could watch a quick demonstration and be ready to leave when his B-17 got there, losing him little time. Wolfe reluctantly agreed.

Allen had quietly arranged for two of his Air Force allies on B-47 promotion to meet Wolfe at Moses Lake: Colonel Pete Warden, who was on Wolfe's staff, and Major Guy Townsend, the test pilot. When Wolfe arrived, Warden and Townsend suggested that instead of just watching a flight, he go along for the ride. Wolfe demurred, but Warden and Townsend, knowing that the old flier would really love to go up in a jet, pointed out that everything was ready and his participation would take no extra time. Wolfe consented. He got into a flying suit, climbed in the copilot's seat behind Townsend, and took off. Townsend made the flight as impressive as humanly and technically possible. He swooped and swerved, turned and rolled, dived and buzzed the runway at fifty feet so Wolfe could watch it whiz by and sense the airplane's great speed, and shot almost straight up, leaving the airfield far below in little more than an instant. Wolfe took the controls awhile. After a sensational flight of twenty minutes, Wolfe climbed out, discarded his flying suit, and immediately boarded his homeward-bound B-17 with no comment.

On a Saturday about a week later, George Schairer was at home when he got a call from the operator at Boeing headquarters. General Wolfe had phoned, trying to reach Allen. With Allen out of contact, Wolfe gave her the names of others he knew and said he wanted to speak with someone immediately; Schairer was the first of his acquaintances the operator could reach. She put him on the line with the general. Wolfe explained that he wanted to order B-47s right away and needed to find somebody with authority to accept the order. Schairer knew that Ed Wells, who had the necessary authority as the recently appointed vice president of engineering, was at his summertime cottage at Lake Meridien, a little south of Seattle. Schairer gave Wolfe the phone number at the cottage. In one of Boeing's more unusual sales transactions, Wolfe connected with Wells and placed a rush order for ten of the jet bombers.

The production contract surely delighted the inhabitants of Boeing's executive suites and B-47 design offices. With the foot in the door provided by this initial order, they were sure of large orders to come. Bill Allen's joy was heavily dampened by an onerous condition that Wolfe imposed, however: The B-47s must be made at the Wichita plant. The government claimed that Seattle was too vulnerable to enemy attack by sea, too close to Russia by great-circle air routes, and—because of the size and importance of the metropolitan area—likely to be a target for nuclear attack in any future conflict. The Air Force had adopted the recommendation, made by a presidential commission in a postwar study of airpower, that future aircraft be produced far inland and away from major cities whenever possible. Obviously susceptible to political influences, the recommendation had been vigorously promoted by the Midcontinent Industrial Council, representing Kansas and seven other central states, and unsuccessfully opposed by the All-America Defense Council, representing most of the rest of the country. Economic factors may have been unspoken considerations. The high-priced B-47—at about three million dollars, the most expensive airplane Boeing had ever sold—would be cheaper to produce in Kansas. The government owned Boeing's Wichita facility and leased it to the company (until Boeing bought it thirty years later), and labor rates were substantially lower in Kansas.

Bill Allen wanted to make the bomber in Seattle, however. He argued forcefully that since the B-47 was a pioneering technological venture, and the Air Force wanted the bombers produced quickly, Boeing should make them in Seattle, where the B-47 design team was located. Design engineers and manufacturing people would have to work closely on airplanes in the first order, and once the tooling was established, it would be prohibitively expensive to move it for subsequent orders. Allen undoubtedly also weighed unspoken considerations. From the standpoint of Boeing's overall business, B-47 production in the Puget Sound area would better balance the workloads between Seattle and Wichita, particularly since it was becoming clear that production runs of all military propeller-driven airplanes would probably be cut short by the advent of jets.

More crucial were the long-term implications. Military aircraft production was the only significant part of Boeing's business. Indeed, it looked as if it could well be Boeing's only business forever. If the government's policy to produce at Wichita continued for all orders to come, then in a few years all Boeing's production could be in Kansas, and Boeing's engineering and administrative groups would have to follow. If that scenario were to play out, the Air Force's decree was tantamount to moving the Boeing company from Seattle to Wichita. Allen thought that would devastate Boeing, primarily because he considered both the blue-collar and white-collar labor pools in Seattle superior to those in Wichita; the quality and quantity of labor were the most important factors in siting facilities in the aircraft industry. He was sure B-47 production in Wichita would be more expensive than in Seattle over the long run. Allen himself seems not to have liked Wichita as a place. He recognized, furthermore, that Boeing's location in the lovely, green Pacific Northwest, with all its attractions, was a magnet for professional talent. He thought he'd lose good people if he tried to relocate them to the flat, dusty, weather-plagued plains of Kansas, and would have trouble recruiting new people. As he commented to a colleague who took notes, "You have to do this job with people. And certain kinds of people have their own ideas of where they want to live. And you just can't do it by fiat."

General Wolfe was unmoved when Allen brought up his objections. Allen couldn't leave Seattle to plead the case face-to-face because a major strike was going on, so he sent a delegation headed by Wellwood Beall to Wright Air Force Base in Dayton, Ohio. Beall came back crestfallen, reporting that Wolfe had refused to listen to them, had insisted that the B-47 be manufactured in Wichita and nowhere else, and "had gotten madder than hell and slapped the table and said, 'That's the way it's going to be and I don't want to hear any more about it.'" Allen felt he had no choice but to leave his post and beard the general himself. He later told a colleague, "I flew there and asked Wolfe, 'Aren't you interested in where we think we can do the best job?' And he said, 'No!' I said, 'That's a hell of a state of affairs.'"

Designing the production model of the B-47, incorporating slight modifications dictated by the results of flight testing the pro totypes, would take time; production wouldn't begin until January 1950. In the meantime, as the consequences of the Air Force decision for Wichita sank in, business and labor groups in Seattle became alarmed. The local controversy quickly escalated into a national issue. Boeing was then supporting one of every seven families in Seattle, and one of every twenty-five nonfarm workers in Washington state worked for Boeing. In mid-August 1949, the Seattle Chamber of Commerce sent emissaries to petition the Pentagon to keep the B-47 and Boeing in Seattle. They returned no more successful than Beall and Allen. Aroused by the real threat of losing the area's largest employer, the scared chamber drew up blueprints for an all-out counterattack against the Air Force, and announced plans to raise a special fund of one hundred thousand dollars to finance the effort. The chamber established a group called the "Keep Boeing & Defend Seattle" committee, and prompted chambers in ten other western states to organize support for Seattle. Governor Arthur Langlie of Washington asked the governors of Oregon and California to help him keep Boeing in Seattle. Since the government's logic would affect the defense industry in the other West Coast states, Governor Langlie suggested that Oregon and California would help themselves by helping Washington state in this first test of the government's new anti-Pacific-Coast policy. Harold Gibson, president of International Association of Machinists (IAM) District Lodge 751, the big union at Boeing, conducted a speaking tour through the Seattle area imploring the government to keep Boeing in the city. The lodge, although impoverished by the big strike, contributed a thousand dollars to the chamber of commerce campaign and mounted its own twenty-five-thousand-dollar advertising crusade to save the company that paid its members' wages. The rival aeronautical union, which was trying to unseat the IAM, put three thousand dollars in the chamber's kitty. In Washington, D.C., the presidents of the IAM International and the American Federation of Labor pledged their support of Seattle's campaign. President Truman promised to look into the matter.

On September 7, 1949, during a trip to Seattle, Air Force Secretary Stuart Symington (later a prominent senator) was besieged by an angry local citizenry. *Time* magazine, reporting on the confrontation, stated melodramatically that, as Boeing's current projects ran out, "the Boeing factories would probably become ghost shops." The magazine reported that a dozen of Seattle's leading citizens took Symington to a private dinner "and banged the table until the china rattled. Then he was led to an Olympic Hotel ballroom to face 75 more inquisitors." *Time* noted that Symington was harried and flustered. A local newspaper observed that the meetings were "tense" and harrumphed that the Air Force secretary "did not make a satisfactory reply to a single point raised by the Keep Boeing committee." Symington did tell a Seattle-area congressman weakly that the Air Force would continue to give some work to Boeing in the city and that he saw "no reason why Boeing should not retain its management and engineering offices in Seattle." Three days after Symington's bruising encounter, he and Allen jointly announced that "arrangements have been made to put additional work at Boeing in Seattle." Neither Boeing nor the Air Force would explain the nature of the additional work, however. Reporters wrote that the fight to keep Boeing would continue.

After the vague, seemingly unsatisfactory joint announcement, nevertheless, stories about the dire threat to Seattle's welfare abruptly dropped off the pages of newspapers and magazines. The issue simply evaporated, and little more was heard of it. A clue about what killed it off may have been uncovered by nationally syndicated business columnist Merryle Rukeyser, who reported a month after Symington entered the lion's den, "The Pentagon brass has been disappointed that Boeing's management did not tell Seattle citizens to lay off." Boeing had kept out of the whole brouhaha, saying nothing publicly and taking no part in any of the committees or campaigns. The war was Seattle—not Boeing—versus the Air Force. Dependent as it was on the good will of Air Force officials, the company would have been foolish to do otherwise. Symington was reported to have been upset nonetheless because of his suspicions (one surmises well-founded) that Boeing acted behind the scenes. The Air Force secretary may well have told Allen to "lay off" in return for a pledge, acceptable to Allen but not reflected in the wishy-washy public statement, to provide significant work for Seattle. We can imagine Allen discreetly passing the assurances on to the chamber of commerce, politicians, labor leaders, and others with thanks and a request to back down. Five years later Allen, musing with a coworker about the affair, observed, "Subsequent to that time, Symington was very friendly with the company—with me. I don't think there's any hard feeling."

Despite the worst fears of Boeing and its home community, the company of course never had to leave Seattle and didn't suffer greatly from the Air Force's oppressive dictate. The B-47 went to Wichita, but the next new Boeing airplane, the B-52, was split between the two cities. The Korean War broke out a year after the flap, and military aircraft production in both places was expanded and extended, providing all the work they could handle. Then the introduction of intercontinental missiles made Wichita also vulnerable to attack and obsoleted the government policy favoring inland locations.

Allen could have taunted Wolfe and Symington with "I told you so" when the separation of engineering from production between Seattle and Wichita proved a major obstacle to efficient B-47 manufacture. Allen had to transfer a squad from Seattle to Wichita to get the program on schedule. Then the Korean War, which began in June 1950, put B-47 production into overdrive. The military needed so many of the bombers so soon for U.S. and NATO forces that Boeing couldn't make them fast enough. The Pentagon ordered Boeing to help Douglas and Lockheed make the airplanes and provide the other manufacturers with all the necessary plans and technical assistance. Boeing made a profit on the arrangement, but had to yield more confidential information on designing and manufacturing large jet airplanes than its competitors could have gotten from legions of industrial spies.

Colonel Pete Warden admitted that the Korean War frightened the Pentagon into building many more B-47s than turned out to be needed: Boeing and the other manufacturers produced 2,040 of the jet bombers, representing an expenditure of some six billion dollars, the most the Pentagon had ever spent on a single weapons system. B-47s served until 1969 but obviously never carried out their primary mission of nuclear bombing. Although adapted for reconnaissance, missile carrying, and other missions, they never flew in battle. They became vital to America's striking power, however. The argument can be made that the B-47 was enormously successful in its strategic mission as a deterrent.

T. A. Wilson, who became Boeing's chairman, asserted that the B-47's demonstration of the value of swept wings and its role as the forerunner of commercial jet airplanes were more important than its military contributions. He declared that Boeing, in acquiring information useful for developing jetliners, learned more from the B-47 than from all the commercial airplanes it had ever built.

While engaged in B-47 bomber development, Boeing also helped to create a new class of aircraft that would boost its business. The British had originated aerial refueling and invented the flexible refueling device for fighters. Refueling was an even greater imperative for the first jet bombers, which had limited range, but the British device wasn't suitable for the bigger aircraft. In 1948, Boeing engineers at Wichita developed the flying boom refueling device for bombers. This created an instant need for a fleet of big aerial tankers that Boeing, with its expertise in building large aircraft, was ready to provide. Boeing modified the C-97 cargo plane to create the KC-97 tanker, which entered service in 1951 and became the primary refueler of its day.

It was military products that pulled Boeing out of the black pit of despair that it had fallen into after World War II. On July 24, 1948, the Soviet Union blockaded Berlin; the next day, the massive Berlin airlift started. The cold war intensified, and the United States began to build up its defenses. It was probably not coincidental that the vacationing Ed Wells received the urgent order for B-47s from General Wolfe at the start of the airlift. On September 29, 1949, President Truman announced dramatically, "We have evidence that in recent weeks an atomic explosion occurred in the U.S.S.R." The news that the Russians had the bomb further accelerated the cold war. On June 25, 1950, North Korean forces crossed the thirty-eighth parallel and invaded South Korea, igniting a major war. The defense business skyrocketed. Bill Allen inscribed in his diary only a month after the war began that he went to Washington, D.C., with other manufacturers to be briefed on the large government purchasing program engendered by the war. The war continued the upturn that Boeing had been experiencing in 1950. Two months into the war, Allen exulted to his diary, "This year operations have improved greatly. . . . Out of debt with money in the bank. Now have large backlog of orders. Authorized substantial capital improvements." The unexpected success of the B-47 and, in the periodic irony of the defense business, the new life breathed into Boeing by the Korean War ended the post–World War II crisis about the company's future—at least until peace should break out again.

Boeing cherishes its company legends, and retelling these tales is part of the corporation's culture. The greatest Boeing legend of all concerns an event in 1948 that's recounted in every book about the company, and told or referred to in almost every article that goes into the history of the company. Boeing made a videotape of the participants in the event sitting around and swapping reminiscences of the affair. The incident has a relic, copies of which Boeing bestows on people seriously interested in the company's past. The story begins back in April 1945:

Once upon a time, in the last days of World War II and before airplanes had jets and swept-back wings, the U.S. Army Air Forces notified aircraft makers that it would fund development of the best design it received for a long-range, heavy-duty bomber to be called the B-52. In June 1946, it awarded the development contract to Boeing. Not trusting yet in pure jets for an airplane twice the size of the B-47, and smitten by the allure that turbine-powered propellers then held for many aircraft buyers, the AAF specified turboprop engines. Boeing worked diligently on the design, and in July 1948 was given a contract to produce two prototypes.

Boeing found itself in a predicament. Now that it was time to build the airplane, the company had to face a hard reality: there was no good propulsion system for it. The demands of the B-52 strained and perhaps exceeded the limits of propeller technology. Development of turboprop engines was lagging far behind the expectations of their devotees. To Boeing, the solution was obvious in principle. B-47 test flights had shown that airplanes powered by pure jets exceeded the expectations of their proponents; General Wolfe had just taken the B-47 prototype flight that persuaded him to order operational versions. Pratt & Whitney had announced development of a new jet engine that could handle an airframe of B-52 size. Aerial refueling of bombers was under development and looking good, and the Air Force had accepted the technique as the way to overcome range limitations of jets. Changing the B-52 from a turboprop to a jet seemed the way to go. The Air Force, too, considered this a possibility, and expediently ordered Boeing to do the groundwork for a jet B-52 while the company worked on the turboprop. If the B-52 should become a jet, however, the design process would have to start afresh after more than three years of costly labor. Allen was afraid that, if such a complete turnabout occurred, the Air Force might consider a jet B-52 to be a different model entirely, and so cancel Boeing's contract and hold a new competition. Since the B-52 project was the most lucrative contract on the Air Force's books, competition to take it away from Boeing would be fierce. Allen desperately wanted to keep the B-52 not only for its profitability but to bring needed jobs to Boeing's Seattle facilities and avoid layoffs. Boeing doggedly tried to make the turboprop work. The project wasn't doing very well, and Colonel Warden, the contract officer under General Wolfe, was losing patience.

This preamble led up to the legend proper, which starts with a meeting on Thursday morning, October 21, 1948, at Wright Field in Dayton, Ohio. Warden had called the meeting to discuss progress on the B-52 prototypes. George Schairer, already the hero of the swept-wing legend, headed the team of three Boeing representatives, which included performance engineer Vaughn Blumenthal and production specialist Art Carlsen. Warden took a look at the report Schairer gave him and stated bluntly that it was no good. He pronounced the turboprop B-52 as good as dead, declaring that it would be officially killed at a meeting in the Pentagon the next week. There would be a new B-52, it would be a jet, and a new development contract would be let. During the discussion that followed, the Boeing engineers won a concession that gave them a small, fighting chance to keep the contract: If, on Monday morning, they could place on Warden's desk a complete, formal proposal for a jet B-52, with drawings and detailed descriptions of its projected physical and performance characteristics, the new contract might go to Boeing without a competition. Warden was talking about a document that normally would take months to prepare, and they had less than four days. What's more, they'd have to work in a hotel in Ohio, with only the records they'd bought with them, far removed from their other records, resources, and vast support network back in Seattle.

As they left Warden's office, the Herculean task looked absolutely impossible, but they had nothing except a weekend to lose by at least trying. They trooped back to their suite on the seventh floor of the Van Cleve hotel. Schairer immediately picked up a phone and got hold of Ed Wells, the vice president of engineering, who was visiting the Wichita plant. Wells said he'd grab some official Boeing proposal forms and graph paper, head for the airport, and join them that night. Schairer then contacted two other top Boeing engineers, performance specialist Bob Withington and structural specialist Maynard Pennell. By what seems an act of Providence, they happened to be visiting Wright Field at the same time to discuss progress on the B-55, a medium-range jet bomber that was essentially an advanced B-47. Both men agreed to stay over and help however they could. The assemblage of experts fortuitously encompassed the major disciplines involved in aircraft design. Schairer went to a hobby shop in Dayton and bought balsa wood, wood-carving knives, doweling, glue, and a can of metallic paint to make a model of the jet B-52 that he planned optimistically to forward with the proposal.

When all six men met at the suite, they decided right away that the only hope they had realistically to come up with an acceptable design was to double the size of the B-55, make necessary modifications, and calculate how the enlarged airplane would perform. Wells bought drafting equipment and went to work designing the landing gear and nacelles (which engineers recognize as two critical design points); Withington laid out the wing (another crucial piece); Pennell and Carlson calculated the weights of aircraft components; Blumenthal worked on the rest of the airplane; and Schairer carved the wooden model. Wells then did the drawings on the glass top of a bureau, and Blumenthal and Withington calculated performance figures.

The men talked among themselves and helped each other. (Although, in retirement, Withington recalled with mock petulance how "Vaughn and I would have liked some help from Schairer, one of the best performance engineers in the world, on performance, but he spent the whole damn time carving his balsa model!") They worked steadily but not frantically, taking nights off. While seemingly bereft of most of the materials to do the job, the men had unique resources in their heads. Extraordinarily intelligent and more experienced than anyone else in the world in designing jet bombers, they had given considerable thought to the basic problems and challenges involved long before arriving in Dayton that week. (Their ability is evidenced by Schairer, Pennell, and Withington all later becoming vice presidents.) Fortunately, they had come with key records and data—and, good engineers that they were, with slide rules—

in their briefcases. Withington had designed a revolutionary variable-thickness wing with a thick root for the B-55 that contributed enormously to the B-52's estimated capabilities. What had seemed at first to be a nearly hopeless endeavor began to look attainable, if just barely. Pennell had done all he could do by Saturday and left. The others finished on Sunday. Withington and Blumenthal wrote the proposal and located a public stenographer to type a good copy. Early Monday morning Schairer walked into Warden's office and laid on his desk a handsome, thirty-three-page, quarter-inch-thick proposal (now the venerated relic) for a B-52 jet bomber, accompanied by a beautiful, fourteen-inch-long wooden model mounted on a stand.

The story has a happy ending. The Air Force gave Boeing the contract without making the company compete for it. That alone would have generated a great legend. What makes the legend pre-eminent, however, is that when the eight-engine B-52 flew for the first time on April 15, 1952, it looked and performed almost exactly like the airplane depicted in words, numbers, and wood on Warden's desk that October 25, 1948. (As the B-52 took off, the normally reserved Bill Allen, standing with other executives on the roof of the administration building across the street from Boeing Field, had waved his arms like a cheerleader, shouting "Pour it to 'em, boy! Pour it to 'em!") Wells reported to the company's board of directors that the test was "the most successful first flight of any airplane the company has ever built."

Ed Wells, who only briefly ran any of Boeing's businesses and never even had overall responsibility for an aircraft development program, was the power behind the throne at Boeing. He exercised incalculable if usually invisible sway over every major decision the company made from the war years through his retirement and even beyond as a consultant. He steered the creation of every airplane from the B-17 through the 757 and 767 jetliners. George Schairer (who had lived across the street from Wells and car-pooled with him during the war) declared that "Wells was the dominating character in the company during the whole period. He had influence over the whole company, even the business side." Two other engineering executives testified to Wells's indispensability. Bill Cook wrote that Wells "was the most valuable employee in the company by far." Maynard Pennell stated that "Wells was the most brilliant engineer we had. He'd go through half a dozen magazines on an airplane trip where I'd go through one." Wells stood constantly at Bill Allen's side, guiding the lawyer through the technical maze of the aircraft business. Wells, given much credit for the stress on integrity in the Boeing culture, is the Saint Peter of all the corporate apostles enshrined by that culture.

Edward Curtis Wells was born on August 26, 1910, in Boise, Idaho, a sparsely populated state that would help to shape Boeing by producing several prominent company leaders. His father worked for the weather bureau. The family had little money, so his mother, who had been a teacher, took in boarders. Shortly after Ed learned to walk, he caught his ring finger in the mechanism of a day bed as it was closing, and the scissoring metal snipped off the tip, leaving him the rest of his life with a short finger ending in a tiny nail. The family moved to Portland, Oregon, when Ed was nine.

Wells aspired to be an automotive engineer and wanted to go to Stanford University. He had to enter nearby Willamette College, however, as his parents couldn't afford four years of Stanford. Wells transferred to the California university for his last two years, majoring in mechanical engineering. His family asserts that he made the highest grades ever achieved in the engineering school with the exception of Herbert Hoover, whom he equaled. He graduated "with great distinction," Stanford's version of summa cum laude, and earned membership in Phi Beta Kappa.

Wells had gotten a summer job with Boeing before his senior year and went to work full-time up in Seattle after graduation. A year later, Chrysler, responding to an application he had mailed in his senior year, offered him a better position in the field that had been his first love. He accepted, resigned from Boeing, and said good-bye to his girl friend—and then had second thoughts. He realized he didn't really want to leave either the girl or the career in aviation. He sent his apologies to Chrysler, arranged to unresign at Boeing, and—two years later—married the young lady, Dorothy

Ostlund. Ed and Dorothy had a honeymoon of only two days because he had to hurry back to the office for a three-week rush assignment: At the age of only twenty-four, he was to lead the initial design effort on the bomber that would become the B-17. His bride hardly saw him in those weeks. On completion of the project's first stage, his superiors, impressed by his performance, gave him responsibility for seeing the design through to the end.

When the prototype proved that his design worked eminently well, and he was tapped to travel to Wright Field, with Egtvedt, to represent the company at the trials, Wells knew that he was headed for a management position. He was eager to pit himself against others in the struggle to climb the corporate ladder. In a letter to his father, who had given him sage advice, he wrote: "It's as you once told me, too, that up the ladder one has to deal more with men than things. . . . Now I'm to have a chance to match my personality and ingenuity with the competition. How I'll measure up remains to be seen." He received his expected promotions. In 1939, when he was named the company's assistant chief engineer, replacing Wellwood Beall, who moved up to chief engineer, he confirmed his high status by buying a home in the Mount Baker District on Lake Washington.

In 1943, when he was just thirty-three years old, Boeing made him chief engineer as Beall rose another rank. The government's domestic wartime propaganda apparatus peddled him hard, christening him "Mr. B-17" and turning him into a celebrity. A newspaper in Oregon carried his story, concluding it with "Thank you, Mr. Wells, America thanks you." *Collier's*, the widely read national magazine, ran a profile extolling him: "[The Axis] has a healthy respect for the 'kid engineer.' . . . [Hermann Goering] well knows the sting of Edward Curtis Wells's engineering skill and daring." He appeared on the national radio program *We, the People*, the first show with a magazine format, to receive an award for accomplishments that "affected the destiny of nations." After the war, popular commentator John D. Vandercook used Wells on a broadcast as an example of talent that must be conserved and encouraged. Northwestern Mutual Life Insurance Company, which Wells served as a director, ran an ad featuring him in *Life*, *Time*, and other large-circulation magazines. Mild-mannered, self-effacing Ed Wells was the biggest showbiz personality Boeing would ever have.

George Schairer was also well on his way toward becoming a towering figure in Boeing sainthood. After Wells, Schairer was probably the second-smartest person at Boeing; and after Wells and the CEOs, he was the most influential person at Boeing during his tenure—like Wells, without ever being totally in charge of businesses or programs. As the top aerodynamicist, he occupied a lofty position; aviation scholars Ronald Miller and David Sawers wrote that aerodynamicists were key figures in aircraft companies "as the first rule of design is to produce an airplane that will not crash." Schairer, of course, did much more than just avoid disaster. He made superlative contributions to Boeing in two ways: He led the company far ahead of the rest of the competitive pack in the design of wings and other aerodynamic features of aircraft, and he recruited men who became outstanding leaders. He hired fifteen engineers into his group, of whom seven rose to vice president.

George S. Schairer was born in Pittsburgh, Pennsylvania, in 1913, the son of an executive with Westinghouse Electric Corporation. He earned his B.S. at Swarthmore College near Philadelphia, and his M.S. in aeronautical engineering at MIT, where he was a student of Jerry Hunsaker, who had sent Tsu Wong to Bill Boeing for the Model C project. He went first to Bendix, which at that time made small aircraft, and then to Consolidated Aircraft for three years. When he couldn't get along with his boss, he looked for another job, and in June 1939 found one with Boeing as chief aerodynamicist; the man who held that post had been killed in the crash of the Stratoliner during the test flight.

Partly because of the efforts of Wells, Schairer, and the others, the B-52 became one of the world's most acclaimed and longest-enduring aircraft. Boeing built 744 of the bombers (initially at six million dollars each), the last in 1962. The Air Force keeps reconditioning and modernizing them and sending them back up in the air. B-52s dropped bombs to help the Desert Storm coalition win the Persian Gulf War. Almost fifty years after the marathon session at the Van Cleve hotel, grandchildren of the first B-52 pilots are

William E. Boeing, a rich man's son, migrated from Detroit to Seattle, made his own fortune in timber, and founded both Boeing and United Airlines. *The Boeing Company Archives*

Workers launch Boeing's first airplane, the model B&W seaplane, into the Duwamish River for trials in 1916. Boeing built only two B&Ws. *The Boeing Company Archives*

Boeing's first building, nicknamed "the red barn," on the banks of the Duwamish River. The picture was taken shortly after the U.S. entered World War I. The soldiers are probably guarding the plant against sabotage. *The Boeing Company Archives*

Three young men who would later become presidents of Boeing pose in this picture around the time of World War I: the first president, Ed Gott (second from left), the second, Phil Johnson (far left), and the third, Claire Egtvedt (far right). The others are unidentified. *The Boeing Company Archives*

Model 40A, a mail plane that was also Boeing's first passenger plane, crosses the Ruby Mountains in Nevada. The window for the small passenger compartment is between the wings. *The Boeing Company Archives*

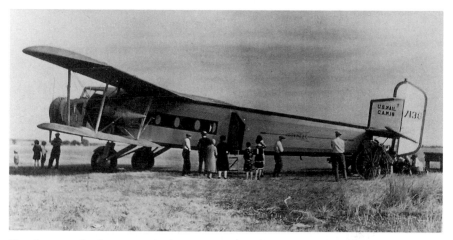

People try to fix the rear end of a Model 80 trimotor airliner that suffered a mishap when landing on a grassy airfield in North Platte, Nebraska. This model first flew in August 1928. *The Boeing Company Archives*

Bill Boeing (center) enjoys a cigarette break, flanked by Phil Johnson (left) and chief engineer Charles Monteith, around 1930, when Boeing was chairman of United Aircraft & Transport. *The Boeing Company Archives*

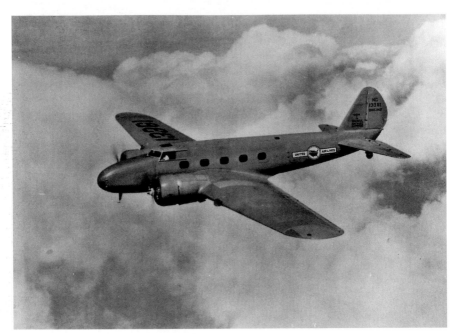

Model 247, the first modern streamlined airliner, entered service with United Airlines in 1933. This was the last time a Boeing passenger airplane led the industry in the propeller era. *The Boeing Company Archives*

Boeing's flying boat, which flew only for Pan American Airways in 1939 as the legendary "Clipper," was huge for its day, as shown by the man standing beneath the tail. *The Boeing Company Archives*

Wellwood Beall, who became one of Boeing's highest-ranking executives, relaxing with two unidentified women in the posh cabin of a Clipper, an aircraft he designed. *The Boeing Company Archives*

Crews work on Stratoliners on the grounds of Boeing's then-new Plant II in Seattle. The Stratoliners were the largest land-based airliners and the first to be pressurized when they went into service in 1940. *The Boeing Company Archives*

Phil Johnson (left) came back from government-imposed "exile" in 1939 to take over the presidency from Claire Egtvedt (right), who was kicked upstairs to the chairmanship. *The Boeing Company Archives*

Oliver West (left) and Phil Johnson survey production of bombers during World War II. West, who ran production during the war, was fired afterward. *The Boeing Company Archives*

Bill Allen was president of Boeing and a widower in 1948 when he married the former Margaret Ellen Field, who became his hostess at their magnificent home in the Highlands. *The Boeing Company Archives*

Boeing's classic old headquarters building was demolished in 1996. The car second from left is a "Boeing," planned after World War II but never built, and apparently inserted into the photo by retouching. *The Boeing Company Archives*

In the 1940s, Wellwood Beall, then vice president of engineering, demonstrates his parlor trick of tearing phone books in half. Bill Allen fired him in 1964 for drinking problems. *The Boeing Company Archives*

Ed Wells (left), the brain behind Boeing's engineering programs for most of the jet era, and aerodynamicist George Schairer (right), the second most influential technical executive under Wells, talk with President Bill Allen. *The Boeing Company Archives*

flying the bombers for the Air Force, and great-grandchildren may be piloting them in the next century.

(We now know that the 1940s was the heyday of Boeing's military business. Nobody in the company or the industry would have believed that, for reasons sometimes clear and sometimes obscure, the B-52 competition would be the last the company would win to be sole producer of a new military airplane.)

The year 1948, when the B-47 had been ordered into production and the B-52 had been turned into a jet in a hotel room, was a time to remember for those happy events in Boeing's corporate life—and for a spectacularly unhappy event, one of the gravest crises ever to strike the company.

=

In 1949, after Dick Henning finished his work on the Stratocruiser, he was appointed lead engineer of electrical design on the B-47. There he got caught up in one of the unbelievable experiences of working with a bureaucracy, another case of military overclassification of secrets. He designed the B-47's radar installation, but the components were so confidential that the Air Force wouldn't give him complete specifications. Dick had to guess at the missing information and, by the laws of chance, often guessed wrong. Not surprisingly, the system didn't work—it couldn't even fit into its allotted space. The installation and the B-47's equipment compartment had to be redesigned and reworked at great expense in money and months of time. (Incredibly, the experience was repeated for the radar on the B-52.)

Dick resumed his work on making relay enclosures safer, this time for the B-47; in 1951, when he finished with the B-47, he moved on to Plant II in Seattle to do the same work on the B-52. He spent twelve years altogether on that project (among others), often working hours at nights and on weekends in his study at home. He was immensely proud of his contributions: "I personally led and directed the development of a whole series of hermetically sealed [air-tight] relays. I was the leader of the movement to provide explosion-proof, hermetically sealed, non-altitude sensitive, dust-proof, large-capacity relays for all sorts of control and power circuits throughout the airplane. . . . Boeing airplanes became the safest from any electrically caused malfunction or explosion at all. We were the first, and in some cases the only ones to provide this complete safety design. . . . There was a great feeling of accomplishment when I left [for a promotion]. . . ."

Dick also devised fireproofing techniques for aircraft electrical systems, and pioneered the development of fire-warning switches on jet engines to alert pilots when they overheated or failed. Again, Dick felt fulfilled professionally: "We made the Boeing products the safest in the world electrically, and I was a great part of that significant improvement. That made me proud."

The good times were marred by a serious accident to Dick's two-year-old baby, much like what had happened to Ed Wells at about the same age. Little Larry and a playmate got to a lawn mower and began exploring it. The friend accidentally pushed it over Larry's hand, slicing off the tip of his right middle finger.

In 1951, the Hennings moved to a better home, a brick house in Brookwood Park in north Seattle ($16,500 price, $3,000 down, 5 percent mortgage). It was near the big Northgate shopping mall, said to be the first truly complete mall in the country. Not part of Seattle proper when he moved in, his neighborhood was soon annexed by the city, raising his taxes almost tenfold, from $12.62 to $124.44. In improving his new property, Dick ran into a problem that bedevils many Seattle residents: large numbers of round, glacially deposited rocks buried in the soil. Using a rake and shovel—and buckets of sweat—he removed thirteen tons of stone from his backyard to make a play area.

Dick loved his job and respected Boeing, but he thought the company could be even better. As usual, he'd act on his conviction and make it a personal responsibility to improve Boeing.

6 || The Workers Unite

Forces that would bring Bill Allen one of his greatest tests had begun to build slowly in the mid-1930s. Personnel practices in the volatile aircraft industry, with its high quitting rate among employees and frequent mass layoffs, were among the least enlightened, probably because most workers were here today and gone tomorrow. At Boeing, as late as 1935, workers hired on by the day, lining up outside the plant and hoping to be selected by the foremen, whose favor employees often had to curry with gifts and means other than good work. Employers didn't feel that employees were a permanent part of the company, so corporations believed they had little responsibility for them and felt no need to cultivate long-term relationships. Boeing paid little attention to its workers, never cultivating them like paternalistic companies such as IBM. Unlike some companies in autos, steel, and other older industries, however, Boeing didn't oppress its workers ruthlessly; it was simply indifferent to them.

In 1935, Congress passed the Wagner Act that encouraged formation of unions. With Seattle a center of labor activity, it was virtually inevitable that Boeing would soon be unionized. President Egtvedt didn't resist unionization, but did try to steer it in the path preferred by the company, toward the American Federation of Labor (AF of L) and away from the more radical Congress of Industrial

Organizations (CIO). Boeing even provided meeting space for visiting AF of L organizers. When the newly formed District Lodge 751 of the International Association of Machinists of the AF of L notified Boeing that it had signed up 70 percent of Boeing's plant workers, the company promptly recognized the lodge as the bargaining agent for its production force without requiring an election. The first contract, for one year, was negotiated in spring 1936.

The next year Boeing was in terrible financial straits, often meeting its payroll with IOUs. When the newspapers reported that the union was after a large wage increase and talking about a possible strike, Boeing's worried bankers told the company that they'd foreclose if the big wage increase was granted. Egtvedt and a couple of his staff members quickly met with District 751's business agent, Sandy Sandvigen, and a couple of his staffers to discuss the crisis. Egtvedt and Sandvigen gave differing accounts of that crucial meeting.

Sandvigen's version, which has become a Machinists' legend, had Egtvedt asking to speak with him in private "Scandinavian to Scandinavian." Sandvigen said the Boeing chief laid out the company's financial position, declared that it was impossible to give a significant wage increase, and concluded that Boeing would have to close down if a strike occurred. Sandvigen remembered that he agreed to take wages off the table if Egtvedt would compromise on the nonwage issues. Egtvedt, with little choice (according to Sandvigen), agreed to virtually all that the union wanted.

Egtvedt, who didn't mention a private meeting with Sandvigen, presented another angle. He said that the union representatives didn't appreciate how bad things were, and at first thought Egtvedt was bluffing. The Boeing president remembered that he had to use harsh language to make them understand the gravity of the situation. Egtvedt recounted the story in a disdainful tone, referring to the "swollen heads" of the union people, telling how he set them straight in no uncertain terms because "they apparently didn't understand just plain language," and admonishing them that they couldn't continue with their "monkey business." Egtvedt stated that Sandvigen agreed to a face-saving arrangement whereby Boeing would raise lower-level labor rates significantly but not other levels, so the total wage package would equal Boeing's proposal. The stories aren't too far apart if it's assumed that each man, in quite human fashion, focused on what he won and overlooked what he had to give up, Sandvigen getting the nonwage concessions and Egtvedt taking the lower wage increase.

The first major problem with the union arose in 1940. As Allen later commented, "there were some union leaders who were anything but constructive—out to get all they could. There were some individuals that were really subversives." There was no denying that Communists had bullied their way into power in the union and gained control. Subversion was occurring at Boeing's plants, and the Communists were suspect. (According to the union but denied by a Boeing official of the time, engineers from Germany who were members of the pro-Nazi German Bund worked for Boeing and were also implicated.) The editor of District 751's newspaper called for the ouster of the Reds, and published names of union leaders he claimed were Communists, including the District's president. The national AF of L intervened, held trials, and expelled the president and forty-nine other members found to be Communists.

Communists weren't the only ones unwelcome in the IAM. The union also excluded women and the people then known as Negroes. When the war started and Boeing needed all the hands it could get, the union dropped its prohibition against women and was persuaded to issue permits to Negroes allowing them to work for the company (but still not to become union members). At the peak of production, Boeing employed sixteen hundred black people. Women constituted about half the workforce by war's end. (Bill Allen shared the union's prewar attitude toward women, believing that their place was in the home, and seems to have paid women on his staff less than men doing the same job.)

During the war, plant employees worked longer hours than in peacetime—often ten hours a day, six days a week. Yet their raises didn't keep up with inflation. As a result, they worked 20 percent longer but for a real income only 5 percent greater. While Boeing was making more money than ever seemed possible, the company was paying its plant employees less than workers doing similar jobs in the East and Midwest, and less than shipyard workers in Seattle. This contributed to Boeing's appalling turnover rate—130 percent a year. Boeing workers blamed the shortfall in real wages not on the company but on the War Labor Board, which controlled wages. (The size of the payroll, virtually all for military work, hardly mattered to Boeing; labor costs were passed directly on to the government under the cost-plus-fixed-fee contracts.) The workers kept expecting the board to redress the problem, but the board always disappointed them. In 1943, the employees heard a rumor that the board was going to allow them only a five-cent-per-hour increase when they felt they needed much, much more to keep up with inflation. Sentiment started to develop around the plants for a strike, but the union had taken a no-strike pledge for the duration of the war. District 751 decided to hold a series of membership meetings to discuss the situation and suggest a plan: They'd hold a general membership meeting and simply not adjourn until they got the requested raise—technically, it wouldn't be a strike.

On February 25, 1943, almost all the workers attended the first of the planned informational meetings, stopping the Boeing production lines. The union leadership, sensing that they had to give their members an outlet for their anger, spontaneously suggested at the end of the meeting that they all march on Seattle's city hall to call attention to their protest. Some eighteen thousand workers shouted in agreement and peacefully marched the one mile to city hall. There the mayor appeared on the balcony and told the protesters he sympathized with them. The marchers dispersed without incident. Instead of returning to work, they went home, so in effect the meeting and march became a one-day strike. The public saw not citizens protesting a legitimate grievance, however, but unionists holding up the government for more money and breaking a pledge by stopping production of airplanes needed in the war, while soldiers not lucky enough to have jobs back home were being killed. Government and military leaders condemned the strike as almost treasonous.

The union persisted in seeking what they felt was an appropriate wage nevertheless. District 751 decided against holding further general membership meetings, but instead held a nonstop meeting of union leaders beginning March 1, 1943. The leaders threatened to turn the conference into a general membership meeting not only at Boeing but at all the aircraft manufacturers if the War Labor Board didn't grant the requested increase. The board relented and granted the raises.

Relations between District 751 and Boeing continued to be good throughout the war. Phil Johnson dealt with the IAM personally, and the union leaders and members liked him. The son of Swedish immigrants who owned a laundry in Seattle, he knew blue-collar people and understood them. He'd been a workingman himself, laboring summers in a machine shop in his high school years, selling tires before going to college, and earning his university tuition by driving a laundry truck. Ed Carrig, then a young union officer, remembered showing up early for a meeting with Boeing officials at Seattle's swank Rainier Club. Participants were slow in arriving, and it was obviously going to be some time before they got down to business. Carroll French, Boeing's manager of industrial relations, was playing a piano in the meeting room. Carrig decided to try to find a drink while he waited. He wandered about the club until he came to a bar where a solitary drinker sat on a stool. Carrig asked the bartender if a nonmember of the club could buy a drink. The man on the stool spoke up, saying "No, but a member can buy you a drink. Have a seat." Carrig looked at him through the mirror over the bottles. It was Phil Johnson. "Is French still playing the piano?" Johnson asked as Carrig sat down and ordered. Carrig nodded. "Let's stay here until he's finished," Johnson said. The two of them drank and chatted awhile, and then went to the meeting together.

Some of Johnson's colleagues felt that a reason the union liked him so much, besides his easy way with all kinds of people, was that he was too nice to them, and that he was giving away the store. In contract negotiations, which were yearly then, Johnson gave the unions almost everything they wanted. Although wage ceilings were set by the War Labor Board, the union asked for and got major concessions from Johnson on workplace policies, most importantly on policies regarding rights of seniority. By war's end, virtually all promotions, transfers between jobs or plants, shift assignments, and layoff and rehiring priority designations were governed by length of union membership.

Among the most nefarious aspects of the seniority system was the process of "bumping" during layoffs. When a position was eliminated during a layoff, the union member in that position had the right to try out for any other blue-collar job held by a person junior to him, at any plant, and had several weeks to prove himself. The person he displaced had the same right. The result was that layoffs triggered massive chain reactions of bumpings. Elimination of just one position could, in principle, cause hundreds of job changes. Large layoffs could and did cause overwhelming dislocations, with vast numbers of people in jobs for which they were inexperienced or, in some cases, jobs that they couldn't handle at all. The bumping process took a long time to play out, moreover; once, Boeing eliminated two hundred positions, but after three and a half months only twenty employees were off the payroll. Production efficiency decreased markedly after even a small layoff.

Johnson didn't resist these severe restrictions on plant management because he faced incentives to accept them and disincentives to fight them. Every airplane Boeing made then was for the war, and Johnson was under tremendous pressure to get the airplanes out as fast as possible, damn the cost and other problems. He wanted to avoid the distractions and problems of battling labor. Since the government paid all costs and a set profit, moreover, Boeing didn't bear the price of the inefficiencies and handicapped management. Johnson had every reason to go along with the union and no reason to buck it—except for the future of Boeing. Archie Logan, Johnson's assistant for labor relations, said he warned Johnson that when peace resumed the union would still have all the onerous clauses in its contracts and Boeing would deeply rue its acquiescence during the war. Logan said that Johnson replied that if caving in was necessary to help win the war, then he'd do it, and that anyway it wasn't his problem—he intended to retire after the war. Then it would be somebody else's headache.

Somebody else, Bill Allen, succeeded to the presidency sooner than Johnson expected. Through no fault of his own, Allen got off to a bad start with labor when the plant workforce was nearly obliterated the very day he assumed the presidency. District 751 felt betrayed. Assurance had been given the union that there would be no sudden, massive layoffs, yet almost overnight the number of Machinist members employed at Boeing went from twenty-six thousand to two hundred. The Army Air Forces had given the assurances to Boeing that orders would taper off. Allen said the AAF did think it was tapering off, and hadn't realized how much work was in the pipeline. (Boeing could fill the remaining orders from its product inventory with finished or partially completed aircraft that didn't require much work.)

Seattle's mayor asked Allen, Egtvedt, and Seattle's union leaders to meet in his office to discuss the layoffs. Allen described the fruitless meeting: "Dick Powell of the union said they were going to see that their paychecks remained the same. That was his contribution. Ward Coley, the business agent for the electrical workers' union—bad actor if ever there was one—made a motion that they recommend that the government take over Boeing, but somebody else pointed out that the government caused the problem. The meeting was just about as destructive as it could be."

Allen could thank Oliver West for another problem related to the massive layoff, which may well have been a factor in West's dismissal several months later. During the war, Boeing's supervisors had been worried about what would happen to them when peace should come and layoffs would be inevitable. (Supervisors, or foremen, are factory workers who have been promoted to the lowest rung of management; they occupy about the same place in the corporate hierarchy as sergeants in the Army or petty officers in the Navy.) Most had accumulated long seniority in the union before being promoted, and wondered if they should drop back down to union jobs and reclaim their union membership and seniority to be protected from being laid off. Logan advised West, then the company's top production executive, that Boeing would have to let go a large number of the supervisors during the expected layoffs; because of the seniority provisions of the union agreement, there would be no way to retain them. According to Logan, West, apparently not willing to lose supervisors but always willing to do whatever it took to maintain production, made a "flat, unequivocal commitment" to them anyway that Boeing would employ them as factory workers if their supervisory positions had to be eliminated.

When the layoffs came, Boeing did try to put surplus supervisors to work in nonsupervisory factory jobs, but the Machinists' union complained. The affronted union declared that Boeing couldn't put the supervisors, who had no seniority, into factory jobs while union members who had any seniority at all were being laid off. The case went to an arbitrator, who upheld the union's objection. On October 26, 1945, Boeing laid off 672 out of some 1,000 supervisors. Three weeks later, the remaining supervisors stayed home in protest, practically shutting the company down. Ironically, the Machinists' union placed ads in Seattle's newspapers condemning the strike for causing work stoppages that resulted in lost wages for its members; the ads referred sardonically to the time off taken by the supervisors, "which they call sick leave and going fishing time." The strikers stayed out five days, but Allen persuaded them there was nothing he could do immediately about the situation.

Archie Logan, although himself one of the hardest of hardball players, bemoaned the betrayal. "[The supervisors] had taken [the company's word] in good faith, and I felt sorry for them because I think if anyone has ever gotten a double cross around here that gang of supervisors got it," he said. Logan snookered the union into an arrangement that let Boeing rehire the supervisors. He got Machinist officials to agree that laid-off employees should fill out forms in January 1946 if they wanted to be recalled. Boeing publicized the requirement in a lengthy announcement written in dense legalese. Not many of those on layoff understood it—which was Logan's purpose—so few applied for recall. He quietly informed the supervisors what to do, and then rehired them. This was a typical Logan maneuver, and a similar ploy would play a crucial role in company history not long afterward. Boeing paid a price for not being true to its word in the first place, however. The supervisors organized their own union, and affiliated as a lodge with the IAM.

Allen felt strongly that the basic problem was the seniority system itself. It fell on his shoulders to confront the legacy of Johnson's union appeasement policy. Allen couldn't promote the best people to job openings, or assign people to jobs, plants, or shifts based on their abilities, or lay off people without causing major disruption and reducing productivity. Boeing had little control over its production personnel—an intolerable situation for any company that wanted to be competitive, especially in the commercial business that Boeing was trying to develop.

Because Boeing had grown so big during the war, and undoubtedly also because of his own inclinations, Allen seldom dealt personally with the union, delegating that responsibility to his labor relations people (although he toured plants and talked with workers almost every week). Needing somebody strong as manager of industrial relations, and feeling that Carroll French wasn't right for the post, Allen replaced him with Archie Logan. Logan, called "Major" after his rank in World War I, reported directly to Allen. Before coming to Boeing, Logan had been general manager at the Seattle *Times*, and vice president for operations at Hearst Consolidated Publications. As he described his duties in those jobs, they included managing responses to walkouts and strikes; unions described him more succinctly as a strikebreaker. He was as rough as anybody he dealt with, and when words couldn't win a dispute he'd sometimes convert adversaries with his fists. Once, when Boeing needed to reach union officials to request workers for a high-priority overtime project, the officials all disappeared because Boeing was displeasing them on another matter. Working his telephone for hours, Logan managed to get hold of the District president, Harold Gibson. After using graphic street language to tell Gibson how contemptible he was, Logan snarled that he'd hired goons to find Gibson and persuade him to provide the workers. Logan declared that he wouldn't call his goons off unless

Gibson got the Machinists to the job in a hurry. It's not clear whether Logan had really sent out goons, but Gibson believed him and rushed the employees to the plant.

Another time during Logan's reign, he asked Ed Carrig and another union officer to meet him in a Boeing building at a certain time. Carrig and his colleague arrived at the guard booth on time, and then cooled their heels a long while waiting for Logan to receive them. Finally, Carrig told the guard they'd have to leave if Logan couldn't see them immediately. The guard pulled his gun, pointed it at Carrig, and told him that if Mr. Logan wanted them for a meeting, they'd stay. Carrig thought the guard was bluffing, but couldn't be sure. Trying to keep his quivering limbs still, he asked his companion if he wanted to leave anyway. The man nodded yes. They both walked away, and, to their immense relief, no shots were fired. Logan was a small-time version of his notorious contemporary, Harry Bennett, the strikebreaking thug and powerful ruler of Ford Motor Company's labor force.

A key moment in Boeing's labor history took place in late 1945, shortly after Allen took office, when he and Logan were seated together on an airplane during a business trip. Logan announced to Allen that one short, simple contract clause could give Boeing the weapon the company needed to solve its labor problems. Logan bragged that even he, not a lawyer like Allen, could write the uncomplicated clause in five minutes. As Logan later described the incident, "He looked at me kind of funny and he reached down [to his] briefcase and pulled out a big yellow piece of paper and handed it to me and said, 'Okay, write it, I'll give you five minutes.'" Logan wrote on the paper and handed it back to Allen. According to Logan, Allen "took it and looked at it and looked at me and said, 'Well, I guess you can.'"

At the next union negotiations, in spring 1946, Logan didn't try to overhaul the agreement. He focused entirely on slipping his magic clause into the contract. Logan said he acted in a low key manner when he presented the proposed contract, giving an explanation for the new clause that was "all sweetness and light," and dismissing its importance. He reported that the IAM negotiator "eyed that thing. He took it down and went over to the office and he asked some attorneys to look at it. He couldn't figure it out. He knew there was a catch in it. . . . But he couldn't find it." Suspicious but unable to discern a trap, the union negotiator bought the clause. "Then we had them," Logan boasted.

Logan would use his tricky clause to spring a trap in future negotiations. During 1946, all was quiet on the labor front. When the 1947 negotiations began, Allen made overhaul of the seniority system his top priority. In a patronizing statement whose message was usually echoed in other confrontations (even decades later), Allen declared, "The company . . . is seeking the first essential to job security—a successful, operating company," as if the union didn't understand that it needed a healthy company. In other words, Boeing knows what's best for all, so the workers should shut up. The IAM said it was willing to negotiate seniority but not give it up entirely. Boeing claimed that, to the contrary, the union would accept little if any change, and didn't want to relinquish the great power that the system gave it. Union and management were in serious conflict on the issue right from the start; observers say progress might have been made if each side had been less confrontational.

The wage issue, although secondary, also found the sides far apart. Boeing offered a fifteen-cent-per-hour increase. The union demanded thirty cents, which would saddle Boeing with labor costs far exceeding those of the company's competitors. The Air Force categorized Boeing as a high-cost supplier, which disadvantaged the company in competition for government business; continuation of the costly seniority policies and implementation of the demanded raise would worsen Boeing's position.

Allen claimed Boeing couldn't live with the seniority and wage demands, and declared that, unless the union moderated its demands, the company would have to move production out of Seattle by sending most of the work to its Wichita plant and farming the rest out to subcontractors. The military was pressing Boeing to take these steps anyway as a security measure. Allen seems to have been dead serious about the threat.

Both sides dug in—and Logan pulled out his ace in the hole, the contract clause he was so proud of. It was an innocent-seeming statement that, if a new agreement were not signed by the stated expiration date of March 16, 1947, the contract would continue in effect past that date until a new compact had been signed. The union, although wary of Boeing's motives, saw no harm in it. In fact, by automatically extending the contract, it would strengthen the IAM against marauding unions that tried to raid the Boeing workforce when District 751's position was weak. If the union went on strike after March 16 when the contract nominally expired (if strikes occurred, they always began after the old contract was up), then it didn't matter if there was an extension—the contract would have no meaning for striking workers, and they wouldn't come back to work until a new contract had been signed. The union hadn't noticed the catch-22 in Logan's clause, however. Another clause in the contract stated that the union could not strike while the contract was in effect. Paired together, this no-strike clause and Logan's contract-extension clause prohibited the union from striking in support of its demands for a new contract. The union couldn't legally strike because the old contract would never expire without a new agreement, so the no-strike clause would remain in effect forever.

If the union struck illegally, Boeing could fire all the strikers and hire new workers on its own terms. The IAM would no longer represent the employees, and would have to vie with competitive unions in an election for a new bargaining agent. If the union did not strike, Boeing could refuse to offer any raise at all until a new agreement was reached with management-acceptable seniority provisions. By ruling out the power to strike for its demands, Logan's clause had removed the teeth and claws of the union.

Given that Boeing was twisting the law, and that no union would knowingly sign away its right to strike, the validity of the clause would obviously be tested in the courts. District 751 decided to ignore the provision. The now-meaningless contract deadline came and went. In April 1947 union leaders gave Boeing notice of intent to strike. On May 24 the general membership voted to authorize a strike. Boeing notified its supervisors of actions to be taken if the workers did walk. Both sides claimed they were willing to arbitrate, but each side wanted arbitration only on its own terms.

The head of the IAM International organization, Harvey Brown, traveled to Seattle from Washington, D.C., in June to see if he could help. The International didn't want a major strike then because the timing was bad politically. Brown met with District 751 leaders and Allen. He argued to District 751 that a strike would be a big mistake because of Logan's clause. The International refused to sanction the planned action.

District 751 held off on its strike. The stalemate continued for months, through the fall and winter—Bill Allen skipped his vacation to deal with the mounting tensions—and into 1948, with union and company negotiators meeting once a week or more. Eventually, both sides agreed they could reach an accommodation on wages (inflation had worked in Boeing's favor, automatically lowering the union demand in constant dollars), but Boeing wouldn't give an inch on seniority, and that became the sticking point. After the one-year anniversary of the nominal contract deadline had passed in March, and two years had gone by since the last pay raise for union members, they grew restive. About the beginning of April, Logan learned that District 751 officials had decided to launch a strike in about three weeks. He got this intelligence through another Logan special weapon: a spy at union headquarters. From the time the strike was planned until it was over, he always knew the union's intentions as they were formed.

Logan alerted Allen to the union leaders' supposedly confidential plans for a strike, and Allen called a special meeting of the board of directors. He told the board that Boeing shouldn't take the strike unless the company was determined to win it, though the travail the company would go through might be great. He didn't think Boeing had a future unless the labor contract was completely rewritten, and so recommended that the company endure the strike. The board backed him up.

On April 20, 1948, the IAM District council met to discuss the strike officially. An International representative came and tried to talk the council members out of it, arguing that Boeing had the upper hand and District 751 was making a strategic mistake. Emotions had come to a boil, however, and the representative was booed from the platform. District 751 voted to strike on April 22 at 12:30 A.M.. The day after the council meeting, the IAM formally notified Boeing that union members would strike the next day, and at the same time raised the demanded hourly wage increase by five cents, to thirty-five cents.

The decision to strike enjoyed strong support among the rank and file. (Long afterward, a man who had been an eighteen-year-old electrician at Boeing and living at home remembered talking with his father, also a Boeing plant worker and union member, about the decision whether to join the picket lines or cross them. His father asked, "What are you going to do?" The son said, "I haven't really made up my mind." The father said, "Let me help you. You go on strike, you got a place to live and eat. You don't, move." The compelling logic won the boy over).

When the appointed time arrived, half an hour after midnight on a Thursday morning, Machinists working the night shift in the plants put away their tools and walked out. Machinists at home refused to report to work for the day shifts. In all, 14,800 members of District 751 went on strike against Boeing. To avoid the appearance of a division between District 751 and the International, the Grand Lodge in Washington, D.C., sanctioned the strike after it started.

In handling, or mishandling, the inception of the strike as it did, District 751 presented Boeing an invaluable gift by making the strike doubly illegal. In June 1947, because of the rash of serious strikes that had broken out since the war, and public sentiment against unions, Congress had passed the Taft-Hartley Act. This law mandated a sixty-day notice of intent to strike. With only a one-day notice having been given, the IAM strike would be the guinea pig for enforcement of Taft-Hartley.

On April 23, Allen sent the head of District 751 a message informing him that because of the violation of both the Taft-Hartley

Act and the no-strike contract clause, the strikers were no longer Boeing employees and the IAM was no longer the bargaining agent for Boeing's plant employees. With that as his legal position, Allen refused throughout the strike ever to meet with IAM officials, or to allow other Boeing officials to participate in such a meeting, even when requested to do so by the U.S. Conciliation Service. As part of his strike management strategy and as a demonstration of his willingness to pull out of Seattle, Allen transferred several million dollars' worth of work to Wichita and subcontractors in Oregon and California.

The foremen's union honored the strike. This was the union that had been formed in the wake of Boeing's not fulfilling its commitment to retain the supervisors during the layoff at war's end. Allen, who wrote in his diary that he considered this a critical problem, ordered them to cross the picket lines or be discharged. The IAM promised that the eventual strike settlement would include reinstating supervisors who stood fast. Some 150 foremen did as Allen ordered. He fired the 225 who stuck with the IAM.

As expected, District 751 filed unfair labor practice charges against Boeing for refusing to bargain. On June 19, the federal district court sided with Boeing, ruling that the strike was illegal. Archie Logan, referring to IAM's "lunkhead counsel," stated, "The strike resulted from poor legal advice the union had . . . [from] very, very inadequate legal counsel" who hadn't recognized the import of Logan's clause or the likelihood of the courts to uphold the clause and the Taft-Hartley Act. Boeing, for its part, fought the strike with every legal weapon at its command. The company got court injunctions to limit picketing and the use of loudspeakers by strikers in picketing areas. Boeing went even further to protect its property rights, mounting machine guns on top of its buildings in case the strike should turn violent.

Bill Allen clearly didn't like or respect District 751. He felt that Communists still had too much influence in the union; several hundred union members were said to be Reds. He criticized its leaders for not taking a "statesmanlike" approach to employee advocacy, presumably meaning that they did not consider the effects of their demands on the company and the long-range good of the workers.

At least by the time the strike was called, Allen clearly wanted to get rid of IAM as the bargaining agent; this was a major motivation for taking the strike. Although Allen had never seen a union he liked, he felt there was a much better alternative, a relatively responsible union with a statesman for a leader, a man whom Allen could socialize with and entertain at his home as he did with the head people among his suppliers, customers, and competitors. The union was the Seattle Teamsters' local, and the statesman was Dave Beck.

Beck would achieve infamy after he seized control of the national Teamsters' organization and became the first Teamsters' leader to be jailed for corruption. (Jimmy Hoffa succeeded him.) In 1948, however, Seattle's business and political Brahmins considered him an enlightened, visionary labor leader. A polished socializer and talker, he worked well within Seattle's power structure. He belonged to exclusive men's clubs, was at home in fancy restaurants, chaired the Community Chest drive, even became a regent of the University of Washington. He contrasted sharply with the dirty-fingernail, rough-hewn leaders of District 751. Less than ten years before he had led goon squads that overturned the trucks of unorganized laundries and truck farmers, and beat up members of the Newsboys' union. Nevertheless, wrote *Time* magazine in its stinging 1948 cover story on Beck, " . . . the great majority of employers think he is wonderful and applaud like happy seals when he speaks at the Chamber of Commerce."

District 751's top people had quite a different view of Beck, reflected in the District's official history. The author couldn't maintain his academic restraint when he described the putative labor statesman: "Dave Beck [was] one of those slimy characters who occasionally manage to worm their way into positions of power in the labor movement. A paunchy, porcine figure, he wallowed in luxurious perks. . . . Always prepared to sign a sweetheart contract, always ready to sell out workers . . . This was the creature with whom Boeing president William Allen preferred to deal."

Allen talked with Beck about the Teamsters taking over as the bargaining unit for Boeing, and the power-hungry Beck leaped at the chance. He set up "Aeronautical Workers and Warehouseman

Helpers Union Local 451" as a Teamsters' adjunct. He opened a hiring hall to recruit scabs for Boeing, signing up workers in his union and sending them through the picket lines. Allen allowed Beck's representatives into the plants to enlist workers who hadn't come through the hiring halls. Beck got national support for his takeover attempt. William Green, president of the AF of L, publicly endorsed Beck's bid to represent Boeing employees. (The Teamsters were members of the AF of L; the IAM had dropped out of the national umbrella group in a policy dispute.)

As the days of the strike turned into weeks, and the weeks into months, individual strikers began to give up and cross the picket lines. Two weeks into the strike, Allen had encouraged the defections by granting the fifteen-cent-per-hour wage increase that District 751 had rejected. With Beck sending in workers, strikers returning, and many jobs being sent to Wichita and subcontractors, Boeing was able to keep limited production going.

District 751 appealed to the National Labor Relations Board to certify its legitimacy as the bargaining unit and force Boeing back into negotiations. On July 20, in a stunning upset to Boeing, the NLRB examiner ruled that the union's strike notice a year before the strike adequately complied with Taft-Hartley, and the long period of negotiations satisfied the intent of the no-strike contract clause, which—the examiner said—was not to be taken literally. The examiner said that the strikers were still Boeing employees, and the company had to recognize District 751 as their bargaining agent and negotiate with the union in good faith. Allen, disgusted, thought the examiner was wrong and the NLRB would overrule him. Allen audaciously refused to comply with what he considered an abominable finding, risking severe penalties for noncompliance.

Hardships overcame many of the Machinists' families, and Allen personally became a target for much of the strikers' anger. He received threats and, fearing for his safety, placed guards around his home.

As the summer wore on, pressures built up on both sides to end the strike. Boeing's workforce was steadily increasing, and District 751 realized that the company might soon be back in full, normal operation, leaving the union and its members out in the cold if the final NLRB ruling went against them. NLRB deliberations leading to that ruling, and then legal appeals by the losing side, would consume more months. If Boeing and the Teamsters succeeded in compelling an election to choose a new bargaining unit, only employees on the job could vote in such an election, and day by day the percentage of Teamsters in the plants grew bigger. Disbursements from the IAM's strike fund were approaching two million dollars, and little money was left. Boeing had filed a multi-million-dollar suit against the union for damages, which grew higher every day. Members who had been unable to find temporary jobs were nearing the end of their rope.

The greatest pressure on Boeing was the NLRB finding. If the board upheld the examiner, Boeing would be liable for back pay to strikers and a fine of $172,000 for every day that it failed to comply with his ruling. Also, the union had countersued Boeing for compensation whose total was swelling. Boeing's major customer, the Air Force, unhappy with delays in its production programs because of the strike, twisted Allen's arm to find a resolution. Allen resisted the pressures and held firm.

When summertime ended and September started to slip away, with Boeing showing no signs of changing its stance, the strikers looked ahead to a bleak Thanksgiving and a December 25 without a Christmas in many of their homes. The union cracked. The strike had exhausted District 751 and its members. The strikers laid down their picket signs and gave up. They returned to work on September 13 totally on Boeing's terms, without a contract, after having been out almost five months. Remaining true to the company's position that those who had walked out had quit their jobs, Boeing coldly made returning strikers fill out employment application forms. The reabsorption of employees took many days as a result. Boeing didn't take all of them back, turning away proven and suspected Communists, and rejecting most of the supervisors whom Allen had fired for not crossing the picket lines. The IAM was in no position to fulfill its commitment to get the supervisors their jobs back; once again their trust had been misplaced.

Bill Allen had won. He had slammed District 751 to the ground, mashed it with his foot, and all but killed it. He hoped the coup de grâce would be delivered to the union by an NLRB ruling favorable to him. The ruling came down at last on November 22, over two months after the strike ended. Allen's hopes were dashed; the board supported its examiner. Boeing immediately filed an appeal, and Allen declared he'd fight the case all the way to the U.S. Supreme Court if he had to. He didn't have to; on May 31, 1949, the appeals court overturned the NLRB ruling, finding that the strike was illegal and District 751 had forfeited its position as bargaining agent.

District 751 was as good as dead. Boeing plant workers would vote in an election to choose a bargaining agent; although the IAM unit could have its name placed on the ballot, Allen couldn't imagine anyone voting for a group that had led its members to such ignominious defeat, especially with the far more attractive Teamsters' union running. The election was held November 1, 1949. The choices were Teamsters' Local 451, IAM District 751, and "no union." The Teamsters campaigned vigorously, and fully expected to walk away with the election. With the limited funds still available, nevertheless, District 751 fought tooth and nail to regain its position. When the votes were counted, Allen could hardly believe the outcome: District 751 won in an incredible landslide, outpolling Beck's group by two to one. Allen had forced the strikers to return to his plants, but their hearts and minds remained on the picket lines. They weren't inclined to vote for the union supported by Allen and his company.

It was a debilitated District 751 that resumed representation of plant workers. When negotiations for a new contract opened in 1950, the union had practically no bargaining strength. Its treasury had been emptied by the strike, and the possibility still existed that Boeing might win its devastating suit for damages; Boeing was then claiming the strike had cost the company over nine million dollars. Another strike—a union's strongest weapon—was out of the question. Allen demanded that District 751 give up the seniority system and the union shop that it had had for thirteen years, and the District had to capitulate.

Allen pressed on with his suit for damages against the IAM International and District 751. In June 1950, the lower court ruled against Boeing, finding that the IAM International couldn't be sued because it didn't call the strike, and District 751 couldn't be sued because Boeing had rescinded the contract. Allen battled all the way to the U.S. Supreme Court, which refused to hear the case. He also lost another ruling by the NLRB. Boeing had legally refused to rehire some two hundred workers who were known Communists—which Allen counted as a key benefit of his win—but the labor board overturned Boeing's refusal to rehire one hundred alleged subversives.

Although Allen had failed to oust District 751 and lost a few other battles, he had won the war. He had succeeded in his top priority of demolishing the rigid seniority system, had held wages to what he considered a competitive level, and had gotten rid of most of the Communists. Allen was well satisfied. He had Archie Logan promoted to vice president.

Trying to cement an important part of his victory, Allen vigorously pushed a Washington state ballot initiative some years later to outlaw the union shop. In remarks to Boeing employees carried on a Seattle TV station, he appealed for help in getting the initiative on the ballot because compulsory unionism "creates an unholy alliance of unscrupulous labor bosses." He wrote a letter to Boeing's managers: "Boeing stands firmly behind Initiative 202. . . . We are directly supporting the effort to gain sufficient signatures to put Initiative 202 on the ballot. . . . I hope that you will sign the petition enclosed, secure the signatures of other persons. . . ." Almost any corporate manager with an instinct for survival would take that as a command. Boeing contributed funds for advertising to persuade citizens to support the measure, and Allen successfully campaigned for the backing of the Republican party. He prevailed in putting the initiative to a vote. At election time, however, the initiative went down to crushing defeat. The Republicans were tarnished, and many of them blamed Allen for setting Washington state Republicanism back by several years.

Despite his onslaught against unions, Allen maintained all along that he was not antiunion, and he resented the antiunion label. He seems to have had a vision in his mind of a kind of union he could support, a responsible, reasonable, and cooperative union that would work hand in hand with the company for the good of all; that such a union didn't exist in reality wasn't his fault.

District 751 has never forgiven Allen for the way he treated the union during the 1948 strike and surrounding events. According to the District's official history: "The changes in labor relations took a definite turn for the worse after death of [Johnson] and election of William M. Allen. . . . He brought a lawyer's mind to the job. He also brought a certain legalistic meanness, an attention to the contract and to legality, and a disregard for the worker except as an instrument in the process of production." Union retirees still tell a joke from the Allen era: It seems that various companies and organizations in the Seattle area sponsored an annual rodeo. The head of each sponsoring group rode a horse in the opening parade. Boeing was a sponsor, and one year Bill Allen was given a white mare to ride. He asked if instead he could have the white stallion he'd had the year before. A rodeo official said, "But Mr. Allen, this mare is the same horse you rode last year." Allen insisted he'd ridden a stallion. The official asked why he was so sure it was a stallion. "Well," Allen explained, "as we paraded in front of the crowd, I kept hearing people shout, 'Look at that big prick on the white horse!'"

Like Southerners who will never forget the Civil War, old-timers at the union keep alive the memory of the strike and the bad feelings toward the executives who fought them and the scabs who crossed the picket lines. There have even been instances of children of scabs who grew up, got jobs at Boeing, and were ostracized by other workers because of their parents.

Some union veterans, however, are willing to "give the devil his due," as Ed Carrig put it. They grudgingly credit Allen with leading Boeing to greatness, creating more jobs, and ultimately improving the lot of the workers. Boeing believes the company could not have survived, let alone prospered, without the leadership Allen provided in 1948. Looking back years later, Lowell Mickelwait, Boeing's attorney during the strike, concluded, "The successful end to the 1948 strike enabled Boeing to become a major factor in the industry."

★ ★ ★

In few companies are professional employees unionized. Most professionals identify with management, and many if not most of them want to become managers. Engineers especially tend to feel that management will reward merit and take care of them without being pushed. They don't sympathize with the "us against them" attitude of many unions.

Although Seattle was a hotbed of unionism in the mid-1940s, and aircraft manufacturers then paid little attention to their employees, engineers at Boeing generally had no interest in unionizing. They felt well treated and secure, although they didn't like what they felt was tyrannical rule by middle managers. A crisis erupted in September 1945, however. District 751 announced that, using legal stratagems allowed by the Wagner Act, the IAM intended to take over the engineers and bargain for contracts to cover them. Since production workers would constitute the vast majority of District 751 members, and their needs and desires were often opposed to those of professionals, the engineers panicked.

A small organization that served as a bargaining unit for engineers in several Seattle-area companies had been formed the year before. Called the Seattle Professional Engineering Employees Association (SPEEA), it was crusading for Boeing employees to join. When Boeing's engineers realized to their horror that they had to find a "white knight" to rescue them from the IAM, they turned to SPEEA.

Allen was of two minds about SPEEA. On the one hand he, too, was appalled at the thought of an IAM takeover. On the other hand, he was unalterably opposed to any existing union. Allen seems not to have feared a successful IAM takeover as much as the engineers. He held a huge dinner for engineers and their wives at the Masonic Hall. Allen gave the after-dinner talk, urging the engineers to hold off on unionizing and describing the harmful effects of unions and strikes on companies, employees, and especially on families (inviting the wives had been more than a gracious gesture).

As much as the engineers respected Boeing's top management, they were still more influenced by the IAM menace; their feelings against middle management intimidation also came into play. The month after the IAM's takeover announcement, 60 percent of Boeing's engineers petitioned to have SPEEA represent them in bargaining. On May 8, 1946, the NLRB held a certification election among the engineers, with SPEEA and IAM on the ballot. SPEEA won with an impressive four out of five engineers voting for the group. SPEEA didn't call itself a union, and the group served no union functions then except contract bargaining. It saved the engineers from the IAM, however, and gave them a voice to upper management. Although Allen hadn't welcomed SPEEA, it aspired to be close to the ideal union that he might embrace.

SPEEA began negotiating a contract with Boeing only two weeks after it won certification. Archie Logan treated SPEEA with the same coarse, bullying manner he used toward the IAM, which infuriated the engineers. Feeling that it was getting nowhere with the company, SPEEA decided it had to display some muscle itself to gain respect. The unit threatened to set up an office to comb the United States for engineering jobs and hire away from Boeing every engineer it could find a job for. Boeing took notice, and negotiations moved quickly to a conclusion acceptable to both sides. Relations between Logan and SPEEA remained tense, however, and got no better as time went by. Logan, whose macho mind-set couldn't comprehend the intellectual approach and sensitivities of engineers, complained to Ed Wells that he just couldn't understand them. Wells arranged for a rising engineering manager who had been one of the first officers in SPEEA to spend part of his time advising Logan. The young adviser, who had a monogram for a nickname and was destined to play a major role in Boeing's history, was a man called "T" Wilson.

As a consequence of the 1950 certification battle between the IAM and the Teamsters, the engineers also had to vote again, choosing among SPEEA, IAM, and the Teamsters. This time Allen seems to have accepted SPEEA as the least of union evils and encouraged the engineers to recertify their bargaining unit. SPEEA again won with a comfortable 81 percent of the vote.

In SPEEA's early days at Boeing, one of its main goals was to end a stifling practice called the Gentlemen's Agreement. This was an informal pact by members of the Aircraft Industry Association stipulating that a company would not offer a job to an engineer at another company without the permission of the other company. This inhibited engineers from changing jobs and had the effect of holding down engineering salaries. SPEEA's efforts against the agreement helped to end it. Although SPEEA tried to avoid confrontations, its leaders got tough when they felt they were losing respect. Once, the group got Hughes Aircraft Corporation to offer irresistible jobs to seven key engineers in one Boeing department. The men all left, virtually shutting down the department and increasing SPEEA's bargaining power. This feistiness would surface every so often, erupting into a major show of force in a later era.

After Bill Allen had started at Boeing, and perhaps partly because of getting absorbed in a new job, his personal life gradually returned to normal, and the pain of Dorothy's death receded. At the same time, he drew closer to a woman named Mef, who had been a friend of Dorothy's. He had first mentioned her in his diary entry for Sunday, October 14, 1944: "To Mef's for dinner." He recorded that four couples were also guests. Mef was an attractive young blonde, born Margaret Ellen Field, initials MEF, who was always called by her acronymic nickname. At thirty-one years of age, she was thirteen years younger than Allen. Mef had divorced a philandering husband and had rejoined the social crowd at the Highlands, where she had grown up. Like Allen, she had two small daughters.

Allen felt he was too old for Mef, but they began seeing more and more of each other, sometimes just the two of them together, sometimes in the doings of their Highlands set. By the end of 1944, they were getting together almost every day. Allen grew uneasy, perhaps because of the age difference, perhaps because he wasn't ready yet for another emotional commitment. In March 1945, about the time he committed to Boeing, he and Mef uneasily agreed to limit their contacts to twice a week for the next half year, presumably then either to get serious or break off from each other entirely. The agreement didn't last long; they were soon seeing each other frequently. On September 17, 1945, not long after Allen occupied his Boeing office, and two weeks after his agreement with Mef would have ended, he jotted in his diary that he had taken her to have cocktails with some admirals. From then on, he escorted her to social events connected with his business where other men took their wives.

Allen's relationship with Mef had reached a plateau, and it continued on that level for three years. Mef became unhappy with her status, especially when friends began to ask exactly what that status was. The great 1948 strike was under way and it was no time to press the issue, but when the crisis was over she made her move. A petite but strong woman, she gave Allen an ultimatum: Either we get married, or we split. Allen protested again that he was too old, but he didn't want to lose her. He asked her to marry him and, faster than a speeding jet, she said "yes." In his strange fashion, Allen wrote nothing about his decision to remarry in his diary; with few exceptions, he filled the diary with the trivia of everyday life but ignored major personal and business moments. His first diary entry concerning his impending marriage was on December 6: "Big excitement. The kids find out Mef and I are to be married."

Because Tuesday, December 28, was his wedding day was no good reason for Allen to skip work. He and Mef got their wedding license that morning, then, dependably, he went to the office until mid-afternoon. He returned home, put on his tux, and went to the Highlands chapel for his wedding, with no time wasted. A bishop officiated, and the church was filled with friends. Afterward, he and Mef went down to Los Angeles for a combination honeymoon and business trip. On their return, she moved into his big house and they merged their families.

A woman who knew Allen well observed that his second marriage was an excellent arrangement and that Mef was a great asset for him. As a child of the Highlands, Mef understood and accepted the demands that Boeing made on Allen's time. (Almost literally born to be a Highlands hostess, she'd prove invaluable to his business. She sometimes accompanied him on his weekly plant tours. They'd often entertain at their estate, holding events ranging from small dinners to parties for three hundred Boeing managers; "bashes of the first order" that would go on past dawn, one participant recollected. Allen loved to dance in the game room in those glamorous days. Guests included airline and aircraft industry executives, politicians, rulers such as Jordan's King Hussein, military leaders such as Eisenhower, and occasionally other celebrities. Bob Six, head of Continental Airlines, once came to a party with his wife, Broadway star Ethel Merman, who sang all her songs from her latest musical.) It's difficult to fathom Allen's feelings about Mef from his diary, which is essentially passionless throughout, but two comments in a long passage of reminiscence are consistent with a typical marriage. At the end of 1959, reviewing the past decade, he wrote, "Mef and I were married in 1948. Life became better." In the same entry, he listed six things to be thankful for, of which the first is "A fine wife, she makes a number one effort to help me."

The 1948 strike drastically slowed early production of the Stratocruiser, Boeing's luxury airliner whose development had already been much delayed. The slowdown not only forced postponement of deliveries, but raised inventory financing costs and lost Boeing possible orders. Government certification of airplanes added to the stretch-out, taking months and millions of dollars more than Boeing had expected, partly because of bad luck; a rash of airline accidents just before the certification process began had pressured the regulators to conduct an exceedingly prolonged, detailed, and rigorous evaluation. The Stratocruiser wasn't certified until the end of 1948. Pan Am didn't get its first delivery until January 1949, two years late. (Wellwood Beall had to send a case of Scotch to Pan Am's engineering manager to pay off a bet they'd made on delivery time.) At a ceremony at National Airport in Washington, D.C., President Truman's daughter, Margaret, christened the airplane *Clipper America*. Northwest Airlines, in no mood to forgive and forget, sued Boeing over the delays in its deliveries. The holdups made the hard sales job even tougher.

The Stratocruiser's problems in development and production were but a prelude to horrendous problems in service. The airplane's propulsion system—engine and propellers—was a source of never-ending troubles; it would make Boeing engineers hate pistons and propellers. The engine, the Pratt & Whitney Wasp Major, was the largest and most complex engine ever installed on an airliner. The last word in piston-driven aircraft engines, it proved conclusively that the technology had reached its limits. The power plant had twenty-eight cylinders arranged in four rows; because the cylinders looked something like corncobs, the machine was dubbed the "corn-cob" engine. The power plant, as it turned out, was too big. It could never take in enough air to cool itself and so frequently suffered from overheating. Production models of the C 97 using the corncob engine entered military service about the same time as the Strato-cruiser went commercial. Engine failures caused so many forced landings and ocean ditchings that crews, playing on the name of the best-known military transport of the time, the Globemaster, began calling Boeing's transport "the Ditchmaster." Stratocruisers suffered similar mishaps on airline flights. The engines performed poorly and uneconomically besides. They never achieved their rated horse-power in flight. Maintaining the engines was complicated and ex-pensive; maintenance cost per mile was twice as high as Douglas's competitive DC-6.

The propellers were no great shakes, either—literally. The Hamilton Standard propellers were a new kind made of hollow metal filled and tipped with plastic. The tips kept flying off and causing severe vibrations, shaking the airliners so severely that twice they went out of control and crashed, killing their passengers.

The disastrous propulsion system caused the end of the Strato-cruiser. The last airplane rolled out of the plant in 1950. Despite all the problems, airlines bought fifty-six Stratocruisers, six more than the projected breakeven number. Because of all the problems, however, development and production had cost much more than projected, and Boeing lost over fifteen million dollars on the model. The significance of the Stratocruiser lies in its being Boeing's last propeller-driven airliner, and in making Boeing eager to abandon pro-pellers and piston engines for something better as soon as possible.

★ ★ ★

Because Dick Henning's father had been a union official, Dick had a personal interest in the labor movement and had acquired some familiarity with labor law. The founders of Boeing's SPEEA unit invited him to help write the group's constitution. Still simmering over Boeing's refusal to pay his business expenses during the war, he accepted eagerly and joined the delegation that drafted the document in a craft room at downtown Seattle's YMCA building. He volunteered to participate in SPEEA's working groups and served on the committee that negotiated SPEEA's first contract. During the bargaining, and after SPEEA displayed its power, "Our relationships [with the company representatives] were very cordial and meaningful," he remembered. He ran for an office, was voted in, and took aim at the top post.

Dick rose within SPEEA's hierarchy, being elected chairman of SPEEA's executive committee in 1949. Two years later, he achieved his highest noncareer ambition when he won the association's presidency. This position gave him the prestige of a second office, which SPEEA rented in an office building in downtown Seattle. Dick repeated his victory in 1952. While president, Dick led the formation of a national umbrella organization, Scientists and Engineers of America, to coordinate the activities of groups similar to SPEEA. He turned down the full-time presidency of the organization (which lasted only four years) to stay at Boeing.

Although a manager on the B-47 program had tried unsuccessfully to block Dick's assignment to the project because of his SPEEA activities, Dick was gratified to experience little friction otherwise between himself and his superiors over his labor involvement. That was important to him because he was striving assiduously to work himself up from his SPEEA-represented job to a management position.

7 || Allen's Historic Gamble

The jetliner revolution lifted off like big rockets—incredibly slowly at first. After the war, Allen had thought about developing a jet-propelled passenger airplane, and he knew that his competitors were thinking the same thing. Each aircraft manufacturer was eager to be the first to offer a jetliner, and afraid to be left behind if another beat that company to it. The manufacturers had been impressed by the jet fighters that Germany had introduced during the war, and knew that with jet bombers under development, it was only a matter of time before passenger jets would fill the skies. The industrialists thought that time would be years, however. In America, no one moved to implement the radical technology.

The British, as the jet engine pioneers, wanted desperately to spearhead commercial application. They saw themselves capturing the jetliner market before the others got started, and vaulting to world leadership in the commercial aircraft industry. Encouraged and supported by the British government, the de Havilland Company in October 1946 launched a project to develop a jetliner.

Allen had to decide whether to respond. If de Havilland captured the world jetliner market, it would be difficult if not impossible for Boeing to force its way in. Allen might miss a fabulous business opportunity if he didn't meet the British challenge, so he took a hard look at the latest studies his engineers and marketing people had done of the jetliner forecast. The biggest drawback was their heavy thirst for fuel. This would limit their range because they couldn't go as far per load of fuel as propeller-driven planes. Fuel costs would be more expensive per mile of travel. To operate economically, jetliners would have to be bigger and carry more paying passengers than propeller-driven airplanes, but jet engines weren't powerful enough to propel big aircraft. Jets had such low thrust at low speeds in particular that extralong runways would probably be needed, and jetliners might need auxiliary rocket thrusters for takeoff. The engines operated at high temperatures that were hard on metals, so they had to be made with new heat-resistant alloys that hadn't been tested long in service; they might break down frequently (although Boeing's early experience with the B-47 tended to dispel that fear). Jet bombers were hard to fly, moreover, and would require extensive modification for passenger service; no one was certain that this could be done.

Jet speeds, at almost twice the miles per hour of conventional airliners, would certainly attract passengers. It seemed, however, that when jet flights came about they'd require such steep fares that only the rich could afford them (like today's Concorde supersonic transport). Because of all the technical and economic objections to jetliners, and the innate conservatism of airlines due to their momentous safety responsibilities, most carriers had no immediate interest in the new technology. For many of the same reasons, the Army Air Forces didn't want jet transports just then.

With so many problems not yet solved, and virtually no customers interested at the moment in jet passenger planes or military transports, Allen concluded that jet engines weren't ready to power airliners quite yet, despite what the British believed. He'd hold off on committing the large sums that would be necessary to develop them, while keeping an eye on de Havilland and his other competitors, and periodically reviewing his decision. Allen's confrères at other companies made similar judgments. Allen accelerated his Stratocruiser project and the other manufacturers went back to work on their own conventional airliners.

The aircraft makers all realized that piston-engined aircraft were approaching their ultimate in speed, range, and efficiency, however. They'd undoubtedly be succeeded soon by a new generation of flying machines. Most of the manufacturers and airlines thought that the new-technology airliners, rather than being purely jet-powered, would be propelled by the hybrid turboprop, with its turbine-powered propellers. Turboprops would be more efficient and hence cheaper than pistons, while avoiding many of the shortcomings of pure jets. Over the years that turboprops were flying, jet propulsion technology would be ripening for use in the following generation of airliners. (After its initial enthusiasm for jets, the military, too, was then pushing turboprops for its bombers and transports.) Expectations for the turboprop generation became the conventional wisdom in the aviation community, and most of the major manufacturers began planning to make the hybrids.

Except Boeing. The engineers in Seattle flirted with the idea of equipping the Stratocruiser with turboprops, but never got serious about it. Alone among aircraft manufacturers outside Britain, they saw how fast the jet was coming along. From the time they first heard of jet engines during the war, Boeing executives almost continuously had one study or another going on about the possibilities for commercial use. Early on, with the B-47 experience, Boeing had learned jet airframe and engine technology better than anybody else. This was a great advantage because jet design was more complicated than design of propeller-driven planes. There were few options in where to locate piston engines, for example, but many options for jets (on the wing, in the tail, against the body). Wings were straight out and fairly standard in size and shape for propeller-driven airplanes, but designers had to choose sweepback angles and configurations for jets. Control systems for jets, too, presented unique challenges. Boeing added to this keen knowledge an ardent enthusiasm for jets born of happiness with the B-47 and unhappiness with the Stratocruiser.

The tempo of Boeing's interest in jets picked up considerably in 1948. After jet engines proved superior to turboprops in the dramatic episode of the B-52 redesign that year, Ed Wells was convinced that successful jetliners could be built much sooner than engineers at other companies thought. The latest Boeing study of jetliner possibilities concluded, moreover, that a jet passenger airplane could be economical in five years.

In 1949, while the Yanks waited for jetliner technology to mature, the British flew the world's first jet passenger airplane, which de Havilland called the Comet, and began several years of flight testing. The company had achieved the honor despite being short of capital to do a first-class job of designing, making, and marketing the airplane. Like many first-of-a-kind products, the airplane had many limitations. A small, four-engine jetliner able to hold only thirty-six passengers, having a range of only fifteen hundred miles, it was frightfully expensive to buy and operate. It could hit five hundred miles per hour, but its wings were only barely swept back, making it aerodynamically inefficient, so it couldn't take full advantage of its engines for greater speed. Rudimentary flaps gave the craft poor takeoff and landing characteristics. As the airplane was largely handmade, its manufacturing costs were high. Neither the engines nor the airframe had the benefit of the wealth of experience developing military jets that American companies were accumulating.

Jetliner fever infected Boeing's engineers when they heard about the Comet's flights. Developing a jet would be dauntingly expensive, however. Boeing didn't have the money to attempt it, and Bill Allen didn't think any of his competitors did, either. With the British government subsidizing development of the Comet, he grudgingly decided that the U.S. government would have to subsidize jetliner development in this country. An article that appeared in Boeing's employee magazine and was signed by Wellwood Beall articulated the company's stand. The article concluded, "Government financial aid will be required if we are to overtake and pass the subsidized British aircraft industry in its bid for domination of the future jet transport field." Beall said flatly, "No company can risk its capital in the building of a wholly new type of airplane, such as the jet transport." Doubtlessly figuring that Boeing, with its experience in designing big jet airplanes, would have an excellent chance to win a competition for a government jetliner contract, Allen pressed the industry's trade group, the Aircraft Industry Association, to lobby for a federal program. Boeing itself fought hard for federal help. As Allen described the efforts, "We didn't have very much money, and if we could have gotten the government support, why, that would have been what we really needed, and we tried and we tried and we tried." He managed to get a bill considered by Congress, whose members were indignant that the first flight of a jetliner had been made in England, but the aircraft industry failed to unite behind it, and the measure died. If the United States was to produce jetliners, the initiative would somehow have to come from private enterprise.

Early in 1950, Allen learned of a Lockheed move that threw a scare into him. A top engineer from that company was calling on airlines to show them Lockheed's idea for a jetliner and ask them to help finance its development. To head off a coup by his southern California competitor, Allen swiftly ordered his engineers to prepare a similar sales pitch based on their jetliner concepts. Boeing's designers had several notions all based on the idea of making development affordable by borrowing heavily from designs and tooling for the company's current products, and avoiding where they could the risk of trying anything new. Allen then boldly sent his executives to airlines throughout the world, even including Russia, to sell the ideas and shake loose development funds. His emissaries tried hard but returned empty-handed. No one wanted to pay a bundle of money to serve as a guinea pig for what seemed to them a dubious technology. Allen then tried resourcefully to interest the Air Force in a tanker based on Boeing's concepts but, despite their good experience with the B-47, the generals were still leery of jet transports and tankers. Although denied the exuberance of a victory, Allen could enjoy the feeling of relief when Lockheed met with the same turndowns. A manufacturer wanting to produce a jetliner would be on its own—no government money, no airline money.

This experience reinforced the substantial opposition to jetliners within Boeing. Outside the engineering area, most executives resisted an attempt to get into the commercial jet business. They argued persuasively that Boeing was a proven loser in the commercial field—every one of the company's airliners had lost money—and a proven winner in the military field, where several products were making good money and highly promising developments were under way. The opponents contended that Boeing should play to its strength and avoid its weakness. No customer anywhere in the world wanted a Boeing jetliner, moreover. Why bother? Allen found these arguments convincing, especially since jetliner development would take so much money. A pro-jet executive annoyed Allen by pushing to produce a jetliner on speculation, developing it first and selling it later as they had done with the Stratocruiser. "Christ, whose money are you spending?" Allen snapped. Reminiscing years later, Allen remembered, "From time to time different people in the organization talked to me about jet transport development. When we got down to the economics of it, it always appeared to me that the risk involved of launching into a jet transport project, at least the way we did the Stratocruiser, was more than we could undertake."

On the other hand, most engineering executives favored jetliners, Wellwood Beall among them. They argued that the commercial market promised to be too large to ignore, and that it was bad business to rely solely on military contracts, which went up and down with changes in the world situation and American defense policy. In the summer of 1950, hoping to ignite enthusiasm in Allen for jetliners, Beall worked on him to go to the Farnborough Air Show in England, where representatives of the aviation industries gathered every year. Beall told Allen that the Comet was scheduled to put on a demonstration and that Boeing's president should see it. Allen reluctantly agreed to go.

Allen had never flown in the B-47, so his knowledge of jet performance came from reports and not personal experience. Allen well knew how convincing hands-on involvement can be; he himself had arranged General Wolfe's ride on the B-47 that persuaded Wolfe to order the bomber into production. On August 28, the pro-jetliner crowd therefore got a bonus when Allen stopped in Wichita on his way to Europe and was offered and accepted a chance to fly in a B-47. The effect the ride had on him is well captured by an exuberant interview he gave later: "It gave me a terrific lift, and a great amount of enthusiasm because of the smoothness of flight, feeling of power, and lack of vibration, and the way the airplane performed. I mean you went so far and so high and so fast as contrasted with anything else. I mean I remember I got off that airplane and got right into the DC-6 flying to Chicago and I thought I never would get there. . . . I couldn't talk about anything but the B-47."

In England, he beheld the Comet in flight. Ed Wells also saw the demonstration and felt more than ever that the jetliner's time had come. Allen and several Boeing executives discussed the possibilities of commercial jets at dinner after watching the Comet's performance. Allen expressed deep reservations, cited losses on the Stratocruiser, and wondered if Boeing shouldn't stick to what it knew best and was doing best—military work. He seems to have been playing devil's advocate. When he got home, Beall sensed that he was "really hot" on jetliners for several months. Allen himself later recalled, "The B-47 ride in Wichita is what really stimulated me toward" a jetliner and "There wasn't much doubt in my mind of the direction we were moving" after seeing the Comet.

Another B-47 exhibition early in 1951 further charged Allen up. He was in Wichita with John McCone, then undersecretary for air (and later head of the CIA). Both men were flying to Washington, D.C., from Wichita. McCone was a native of Seattle and a member of the Highlands clique. He and Allen had been friends before McCone rose to high government rank. Allen asked if he could accompany McCone in his Air Force Constellation, and McCone invited him aboard. A B-47 took off at the same time as the Connie. McCone asked his pilot to radio the B-47 pilot to fly by. Allen later told an interviewer that the B-47 "just flew right by us, and it made you feel, riding in the Constellation, like you were backing up, like you were going to California." The B-47 flew back and forth and around the Connie for several hundred miles "to make us feel we certainly are out-dated."

Allen was tugged one way by the promise of the exciting new technology. Then he was pulled the other way by his own innate conservatism. The pro-jetliner faction would mesmerize him one day, and the anti-jetliner camp would discourage him the next day. Events were friendly to the "antis." The Korean War had started the summer of Allen's trip to England, and most of his attention and Boeing's resources were directed toward speeded-up military development and production. Beall was sorry to see that the naysayers had cooled Allen's ardor for a commercial jet program by mid-1951.

Beall needn't have worried. In an astounding conversion not many months later, and with surprising conviction, Allen let Boeing staffers know during the first days of 1952 not only that he now favored Boeing's production of jetliners if possible, but that he wanted to launch development as quickly as the corporation could move.

Allen's epiphany came about as the result of an uncommon conjunction of events and trends in the late fall of 1951 as portentous as the rare, brief conjunctions of planets that moved astrologers ages ago to forecast great happenings. The exact instant had arrived for Boeing to make its move, and Allen was alert enough to snatch the opportunity. In conversation years after, he mentioned four factors that influenced him: high present and future profits, and the excess profits tax; an impressive concept for a jetliner; the need for jet tankers; and the probability of a commercial market. In other words, Allen saw at that point that Boeing had a good, attractive idea for a jetliner, the company could finance its development, and the customers seemed ready to buy. At least two other factors were likely also at work: De Havilland and some other competitors were threatening, and Boeing had lost one of the period's last big military contracts. This was a defining moment, the decision that made the company what it is today.

The biggest obstacle to jetliners in Allen's mind had been the economics, and the first factor he mentioned related to the money angle. Boeing earned all its money in the defense industry then, and the cold war and the Korean War, which was still being fought in the fall of 1951, made the times highly profitable. The aircraft industry had regained its World War II position as the nation's largest industry. Boeing participated fully in the growth with its B-47 bomber, C-97 transport, and KC-97 tanker. Boeing was doing so well that it had become the number one contractor in dollar value of sales to the Pentagon. With the B-52 almost ready to fly, the future promised to be even more profitable. The idea of self-financing jetliner development could no longer be dismissed out of hand now that Boeing was in the money.

As 1951 drew to a close, Allen could see that Boeing's year-end financial figures would be outstanding. He was of course delighted about the company's prospects. He worried, however, about the disposition of its profits. Because an excess profits tax was in effect during the Korean War, Boeing's tax bracket was a near-confiscatory 82 percent. ("Excess" profits were defined essentially as those exceeding profits in the 1946–1949 period immediately preceding the Korean War, when Boeing had made little money.) Boeing's stockholders could keep only eighteen cents out of every dollar of profit their investments earned, and they'd have to turn even more over to the government through personal income taxes if Boeing distributed the profits as dividends. Prudent money management called for Allen to spend most profits on improving the business and claiming those expenditures as business deductions, which would not be taxed. The company would be in a stronger position to make even more money, which would be reflected in the higher price of its stock, so he'd keep the investors—his bosses—happy. Allen had to find a big tax deduction. The best way for Boeing to plow its profits back into the business and claim a huge deduction was to develop a new aircraft with the company's own money. In a perverse way, Boeing's backbreaking tax burden gave the company a competitive edge in development programs. Douglas was only in the 68 percent bracket, and Lockheed's rate was way down at 48 percent. Boeing "saved" eighty-two cents of every dollar that the company sheltered from taxes; Douglas saved only sixty-eight cents and Lockheed banked a mere forty-eight cents. The economics of jetliner development had been transformed from an obstacle for Boeing to an advantage.

Allen had to have a promising jetliner concept to develop. In 1950, nobody had liked the economical jet transport concepts based on existing aircraft that Boeing had tried to peddle. Just recently, in August 1951, Boeing had tried unsuccessfully to sell the Air Force on the idea of modifying a KC-97 tanker to take jet engines. Neither the airline industry nor the Air Force wanted tired retreads. Allen had told his engineers to start anew and come up with the best concept they could for a jet to serve as either tanker or jetliner, borrowing from previous airplanes when there was no better approach, but with no attempt to economize by adopting used designs or tooling. When the engineers presented their fresh concept to him, Allen loved it. He described his feelings to a colleague in typical corporatese: "I had a terrific amount of enthusiasm for the airplane." The power plant would be a civilian version of the J-57 engine that Pratt & Whitney was developing for the B-52. The powerful J-57 had just been tested for the first time, and engineers at Boeing and Pratt & Whitney were almost dancing at the exciting results. Boeing calculated that the engine would do three times as much work as the props on the leading airliner, the DC-6, at only double the operating cost. The long-sought economical engine for jetliners had arrived. To Boeing's great advantage, it was the only company in the industry that knew the details of the engine's performance, which were a military secret.

Customers weren't yet asking for jet transports, but now Allen could clearly see the benefits of jet tankers for the Air Force and foresaw the money airlines could make with jetliners, so he was sure he could persuade the buyers. The most compelling need was for jet tankers. Flying together in a refueling operation was difficult for the jet B-47 and a propeller-driven tanker; there was a serious mismatch in speeds. The highest speed that the tanker could fly was not much more than the slowest speed that a B-47 could fly without losing lift. The situation would be even worse when the Air Force started flying bigger, faster B-52s in a few years. Allen had little doubt that the Air Force would soon see the necessity for hundreds of jet tankers.

The commercial outlook had also brightened. Contributing to this upturn were the introduction of coach fares in 1948, which proved a tremendous marketing success, and the outstanding safety record being compiled by the airlines compared with prewar statistics. By late 1951, the number of passengers and the need for new airliners were growing.

At the same time, the military aircraft business was being threatened. In the government's fiscal year of 1951, missile production had risen sharply, reaching five times what it had been the year before. Guided missiles had suddenly become an important part of military arsenals. Allen must have seen that missiles might someday drastically reduce if not eliminate Boeing's main business in bombers and the tankers to refuel them. One countermeasure against such an eventuality was to get Boeing into the missile business, which Allen prudently had done. The amount of money to be made in the new field, however, and Boeing's ability to succeed in it were both uncertain. Getting back into airliners would be a wise precaution.

Allen, guided by Ed Wells, firmly believed that the next generation of passenger airplanes would be propelled by pure jets. If Boeing waited until Douglas and the others came out with jetliners, however, there would be no hope of wresting the market away from them. Being first in a market was especially important in the airliner business. Customers tended to standardize on one manufacturer for their fleets because of the economies, such as needing only one stock of expensive spare parts instead of stocks for the airplanes of several manufacturers. If Boeing were ever going to get back in the commercial field, it had to get there first and head everybody else off. And if it were to get there first, the time to strike was at hand.

Allen had to watch de Havilland and his other competitors for the jetliner market. He must have known that over in England the Comet was doing well in flight testing and would likely enter commercial service before long. The first Comet model was too ineffectual to be a threat in itself. Once de Havilland got its toehold in the market and gained experience with jetliners, however, the British company could be expected to come out with effective, economical Comets. Across the channel in France, Sud Aviation, a large aircraft manufacturer, was getting serious about a jetliner, and word of this may well have spread through the gossipy industry to Allen.

In the United States, Lockheed remained poised to leap into the arena.

The giant of the industry was sleeping as far as jetliners were concerned. Without Boeing's sophisticated knowledge of jet airplanes and experience with them, Douglas didn't think the time for jet transports had yet arrived, and was pouring all its energies into development of its next propeller-driven airplane, the DC-7. Only two other American companies had the technical and financial resources to launch a jetliner: North American, which was concentrating on fighters and had no interest in transports, and Convair. Convair, like Boeing best known for its long-range heavy bombers and transports, was waiting with Douglas for jet technology to advance to a point where the company could trust it to power a commercial airliner.

Boeing had lost a competition earlier in 1951 that might have played a role in making up Allen's mind. Lockheed had won a big contract that Allen had hoped to get for producing a turboprop transport. (Although Boeing didn't think much of turboprops, the Air Force did, and for the right price Boeing would produce one.) With the development phase of the B-52 winding down and no new project scheduled to absorb all his engineers, Allen was faced with having to lay off valuable talent. Only one more major Air Force contract, that for an advanced bomber, was scheduled to be let in the current cycle. After it was awarded at the end of 1952, there would be no more development plums for several years (excepting the jet tanker that Allen was sure the Air Force would have to add). Allen couldn't count on winning it, and indeed may have found the political realities unfavorable to Boeing. (Convair later got the contract.) He wanted a substantial new program to occupy his prized engineers. Mounting a project himself would solve the problem. Unless Boeing had a civilian airplane to offer after the Korean War, moreover, the company would be right back in the hole it had fallen into after World War II.

Allen figured that the best way to persuade the airlines and Air Force of the value of jetliners and jet tankers, within a time that suited him, was to provide a demonstration jet transport that they could see and fly, and whose performance they could analyze. On the basis of his own experience with the B-47, he could appreciate the convincing force of thrilling flights as opposed to the cold words and numbers of the usual sales presentation. Allen gave top priority to the tanker because the need for it was most urgent, but he hoped that one prototype could serve to win over both military and civilian decision makers. As he recounted in a rambling but revealing interview in later years, "We had all the know-how we needed to build a jet tanker. And our experience with jet airplanes had clearly demonstrated that the time was ripe for such a plane. I became convinced that it was just a matter of time until the Air Force should have one—it would have to have one. The need was there; as a matter of fact we were late on the need. So it seemed to me that there was inescapably a definite military market, regardless of what came up on the commercial. I was just as sure there'd be a commercial market, but I realized that might be longer delayed. Therefore, it didn't take too much gray matter to wonder if we couldn't stimulate it by a prototype and in turn see if that prototype couldn't accomplish two purposes." Allen worried, however, that customers might view one prototype serving two purposes as an unimpressive compromise that wouldn't sway anyone. He asked Ed Wells if he thought just one prototype would do for both tanker and jetliner. Wells did some digging that indicated no one would be turned off by a single, all-purpose demonstration airplane.

Allen worked out a development strategy to minimize risk and cost. Professor Charles Bright judged that "Allen's series of financial maneuvers must be one of the shrewdest coups in business history." After designing and building the tanker/jetliner prototype, he'd try to produce the tanker first. If, and he fervently hoped when, the Air Force placed an order, Boeing could recover much of its heavy investment in the prototype from Independent Research and Development funds. IR&D funding was money that the military added to payments to contractors who successfully developed defense equipment on their own; the military paid for both development and production, whether equipment was made to order or built on speculation. Boeing's designers would make the jetliner have as much in common with the tanker as possible, and Allen would try to get the Air Force to approve use of tanker tooling (which the Air Force would own and lease to Boeing) for the jetliner, just as Beall had done by using C-97 tooling for the Stratocruiser; airplane tooling is specially designed and expensive, so the move would save Boeing much money, even allowing for the fees the Air Force would charge. Any bugs in the basic design found in shaking out the tanker during its early days in service would be worked out at government expense. The tanker would in effect serve as a second prototype for the jetliner, which engineers like to have for revolutionary airplanes. If the Air Force for some reason didn't buy the tanker, Boeing could go right to the commercial market. If the Air Force bought but the hoped-for commercial market never developed, nothing much was lost and the anti-jetliner faction in Boeing would be all smiles. If the Air Force did buy the tanker and Boeing also succeeded in the commercial field, Allen would have seized the whole jet market from Douglas, Lockheed, and the others. The vision captivated him.

Allen was a realist and not a helmet-and-goggles romantic, however. The tremendous risks he saw tempered his enthusiasm:

- The projected cost of the prototype was $13.5 to $15 million, which would be a great strain on the company. The figure was about a quarter of Boeing's net worth—a huge gamble. Development of the jetliner and tanker from the prototype would take additional staggering investments. If the airplanes went into production, Boeing would be spending more than it was making in the early years, and could get in the hole by hundreds of millions of dollars.
- Boeing had to maintain a high profit level to make use of the jumbo tax deductions.
- The project's enormous drain on Boeing's cash meant that the company couldn't undertake any other significant projects while the jet transport effort was under way; if it flopped, the company might have nothing else to fall back on.
- Boeing might have misjudged the readiness of jet technology and could be overconfident of its own abilities to make jet transports.

- There was no guarantee that the Air Force would allow Boeing to use its tanker production facilities for the jetliner.
- Once the Air Force was convinced of the need for a jet tanker, the generals might hold a competition for a design instead of buying Boeing's airplane "off the shelf."
- Even if Douglas or Lockheed or other competitors came in late, they might get all the commercial business because Boeing was a loser in passenger airplanes, and airlines preferred to buy from winners.
- Airlines were meeting the growth in ticket sales by buying new propeller driven airplanes with twenty-year lifetimes. Boeing's jetliner would have to be so good that the airlines would be willing to scrap their pricey new conventional airplanes and replace them with the even costlier jet model.
- Despite Wells's assurances to Allen, the Air Force and the airlines might be put off by the compromises that Boeing would have to make in building a single prototype.
- There was no guarantee that the civil aviation authority would certify a jetliner: they had no standards for jetliners, since commercial jets didn't exist yet, and there was no telling what objections bureaucrats might come up with.
- If one of the first new jets crashed with a full passenger load and everybody aboard was killed, it would be the worst accident in airline history because a jetliner would carry twice as many people as propeller-driven airplanes; the resulting headlines would scare off passengers and airlines.
- Boeing always faced the ordinary risks of its business, such as the chance that the economy might turn down and airlines wouldn't or couldn't order new airplanes; the potential deleterious consequences of these risks loomed larger than usual because Boeing would spread itself so thin financially.

There were conceivable scenarios (that happened to other companies) by which Boeing could lose all the money it invested in the transport and even go bankrupt. Whether to set out in pursuit of the jet transport markets was a choice to be made with great care. When he decided to go, Allen believed he had to be bold. Explaining the principles that guided him at times such as these, Allen once showed an interviewer a plaque on his office wall with a quotation from Theodore Roosevelt that, he said, expressed his own philosophy of life better than he could ever hope to say it:

> It is not the critic who counts, not the man who points out how the strong man stumbles or where the doer of deeds could have done them better. The credit belongs to the man who is actually in the arena, whose face is marked by dust and sweat and blood, who strives valiantly, who errs and comes up short again and again, who knows the great enthusiasms, the great devotions and spends himself in a worthy cause. Who at the best knows in the end the triumphs of high achievements and who at the worst, if he fails, at least fails while daring greatly, so that his place will never be with those cold and timid souls who know neither defeat nor victory.

The first indication that most of Allen's staff people had that he had made up his mind for a jet transport was a memo he wrote to them in the first week of 1952. He asked them to research the answers to several questions he had about taking on the tremendous project: Do we have the engineering manpower to do the job? Do we have the manufacturing manpower? Do we have space? How much would it cost? Could we write it off currently as we go along? The memo led to a series of meetings with the staff on each question. As far as Allen was concerned, the answers they gave just about sewed up the case for the new airplane.

Wellwood Beall, to whom the sales department reported, wanted to name the airplane the "Jet Stratoliner," but the public relations department wanted it known by a short, distinctive model number that would fit easily into headlines. By Boeing's numbering system, the jetliner should have been given the designation "Model 700." Public relations won the struggle, proposing that a sexier model number become the aircraft's sole name: the 707.

Launching development of a new airplane required approval by the board of directors. Allen set the vote for the April 22 meeting. He asked his top executives in all business areas—design, production, marketing, finance—to report their most up-to-date views on the project to him the day before the meeting, presumably so he could back off from a commitment or postpone it if any late information put the success of the program in doubt. On April 21, Allen convened a meeting with all the executives. He went around the room and got all their opinions. No one raised any objections that would halt the project. Allen was satisfied. It was time to put the chips on the table.

The board of directors' vote was really a formality; the majority of members were inside directors—Allen, Egtvedt, Wells, and four other Boeing executives who worked for Allen—and he knew they'd all vote with him. The measure would definitely be approved, no matter how the six outside or nonemployee directors, the minority, voted. Surprisingly, however, given the fearsome risks, the controversial nature of the decision, and Allen's having taken a long time himself to come around to favor jet transports, his colleagues reported that he hadn't tried hard in advance to win the support of the outside members. Although he had the necessary votes in his pocket, no chairman likes to make a major move with the board split, and yet Allen chanced that by not fully preparing the outsiders to accept his recommendation. The full support of the board for the ambitious project was up in the air as Allen confirmed his intentions with Boeing's vice presidents.

The board meeting took place the next day at 1 P.M., after the company's annual shareholders' meeting. The directors' meeting opened routinely and dealt with general business matters until the last item on the agenda. The landmark 707 discussion would climax the day. At that point, a puzzling scene took place. Three of the outside directors got up and left the boardroom, not to return until the next meeting. The minutes of the meeting don't explain why the men declined to participate in one of the most momentous board decisions in corporate history. Given Allen's failure to win them over ahead of time, however, a likely assumption is that they were opposed to gambling the company's fortunes on the uncertain project, or felt they were unprepared to make an informed, considered decision. Knowing the program would go ahead anyway, it may be that they didn't want to let it get off to a bad start by spoiling a unanimous vote of approval.

Allen started off the discussion of the 707 by saying that the transport was needed for the military "as well as the commercial transport field," stressing the primacy of the tanker version. Several Boeing executives gave the results of their technical and marketing studies of the 707 project. The treasurer reported that he had asked the U.S. Treasury for a ruling on the expenditures to be sure that they could be deducted as current expenses rather than amortized over a number of deliveries, a crucial element of Allen's strategy. Wellwood Beall reported that Pratt & Whitney had indicated informally that it would donate the expensive engines for the prototype. The secretary noted for his minutes that "it was understood that one or more competitors were engaged in the design and/or construction of a jet transport." People made presentations showing that tooling would probably cost fifty to sixty million dollars, and other expenses could push total investment to at least one hundred million dollars—these figures always grew—before the first delivery.

The secretary also noted that "a spirited discussion then ensued," presumably between the three remaining outside directors and the seven inside directors who had already held their discussions. Beall remembered later that there wasn't really much argument, however, and in the end the directors who were there all agreed to support the project. They passed a historic resolution, contingent on the expected favorable tax ruling: "RESOLVED that management proceed with the program for the design and construction of a Model 707 jet transport. . . ."

Design and eventually production took place at the government-owned plant in Renton, the former B-29 factory. Allen began driving down to Renton at least once a week to check on progress and to show the engineers on the project how important he considered it. He kept the 707 launch secret until August so as not to spur on competitors; initial work was done in a walled-off section at Renton. He had to announce the project when he sent out sales teams, but even then he downplayed its significance. The company's annual report for 1952 would bury notice of the project in a routine discussion of company events.

Allen tried an interesting bit of gamesmanship to avoid waking his competitors. For the development phase of the project, the company dropped the 707 designation and renamed the prototype "Model 367-80." The 367 number designated the airplanes that the military called the C-97 transport and KC-97 tanker; "-80" indicated a variation of the basic design. Allen hoped that when competitors learned about the project, they'd think Boeing was merely adapting the KC-97 to jets, an approach the company had in fact tried earlier to sell. Some Boeing veterans think that Allen had a double motive in assigning the designation. His engineers were much more excited about the commercial possibilities than the military, so the new designation would serve them as a constant reminder that the prototypes's tanker role had the higher priority. Informally at Boeing, the prototype redesignated the 367-80 began to be called simply the "Dash 80," the name by which history still knows it. (Interestingly, however, Allen himself always called it "the 707.")

On May 2, less that two weeks after the 707 launch, the Comet made its first commercial flight, from London to Johannesburg, beginning regular service to Africa, India, and the Far East. (It had to refuel every fifteen hundred miles, and so couldn't cross the Atlantic.) Jet speed attracted passengers right from the start, and the Comets were filled on almost every flight. The jetliner was profitable despite having operating costs nearly three times those of the best-selling DC-6. The economics were fragile, however. As soon as the 707 or any other competitor started flying commercially and attracting a share of the passengers, Comets would no longer fly full and wouldn't cover their appalling operating costs, so they'd lose money. As expected, de Havilland announced that it would soon introduce more economical versions: the Comet II in 1954 and Comet III—about twice as big as the Comet I—in 1956. Late in 1952, Juan Trippe of Pan American stunned American aircraft manufacturers by placing firm orders for three Comet IIIs.

Two other aircraft manufacturers, both European, launched jet transport projects in 1952. Vickers in England started the V-1000 program which, like the 707 effort, aimed to develop a large jet military transport that could readily be modified to a jetliner. Sud in France began to develop a jetliner smaller than the 707 or V-1000.

Except for Boeing, American aircraft manufacturers were amazingly blind to what was happening. The Gross brothers who ran Lockheed down in Los Angeles decided that the jetliner development they'd been considering would be too expensive without government aid, and still thought that the turboprop would come first. They believed that by 1965 only 1 percent of airliners would be jets. In 1952, when Boeing became pregnant with the 707, as company executives sometimes put it, Lockheed turned the other way and abandoned its jetliner plans, concentrating on developing turboprop airliners. The top engineers at Lockheed's cross-city rival, Douglas, realized what was going on, however. Douglas's vice president of engineering, who had a design study under way on a jetliner, predicted in 1952 that a successful commercial jetliner would be flying for an airline in five years. Douglas's chief engineer repeatedly urged his chairman to conclude the study and start on a jetliner prototype. Donald Douglas ignored his technical advisers because he didn't think there was any hurry. He was sure that if the 707 project ever began to look like a winner, his company could immediately launch its own jetliner project and make up much of the lost time by skipping a prototype and going right to a production aircraft. Remembering his good fortune in improving on Boeing's short-lived Model 247 to make the dazzlingly successful DC-3 in the early 1930s, Douglas dismissed Boeing's lead and said airily, "There may be some distinction in being first to build a jet transport. It is our ambition at Douglas to build the best and the most successful."

The airlines encouraged Douglas to ignore Boeing, primarily because of their bad experiences with the Stratocruiser (and perhaps taken in by the "Model 367-80" fiction; the Stratocruiser was a commercial derivative of the Model 367 series). They felt they could buy the radically new technologies embedded in a jetliner only from a company in which they had the greatest confidence, and that was Douglas. C. R. Smith, head of American

Airlines, and Pat Patterson, head of United Airlines, both bad-mouthed Boeing. Smith, urging Donald Douglas to pay no attention to Boeing and to concentrate on developing the propeller-driven DC-7, told him straight-out that no one would ever buy a Boeing jetliner. In a speech, Smith proclaimed, "We are all of us still intrigued by the glamor of the jet airplane, but neither we nor you, the consumer, can now afford it. . . ." He cited fuel consumption, noise, and the estimated four-million-dollar price. "We can't go backward to the jet. I'm interested in cheap transportation and a more efficient machine, not in more expensive machines." Patterson said he believed that 50 or 60 commercial jets would take care of the needs of all domestic airlines. Douglas's marketing people were hardly more optimistic, forecasting that the worldwide market would buy 250 jetliners at most.

The military had a better grasp of technological realities, however. As Allen had hoped, the Air Force began to show an interest in a jet tanker. In January 1954, Allen took another risk and ordered preliminary work to begin for tanker production, although the prototype was four months from being finished. Boeing wasn't to have the order automatically, however. Hope for a sale without a contest vanished when the Air Force announced a competition for the best tanker concept; the service would fund development of the winner and probably place an order with the winning company. Allen would just have to hope that Boeing's superior jet skills and its long head start would knock the competition dead.

About noon on Sunday, January 10, 1954, off the west coast of Italy, an incident occurred that affected Boeing's business environment. In a boat between the islands of Elba and Montecristo, a fisherman heard an unusual roar overhead, looked up, and saw an airplane. "Then there were a series of blasts. The next thing I saw was a streak of smoke plunging perpendicularly into the sea," he related. Investigators found that the aircraft he had seen disintegrate was a Comet. All thirty-five persons on board were killed. Not long after, in a nightmare for the British, a second Comet exploded in midair and killed everyone on it. These were not the first Comet accidents. Previously, two of the planes had crashed shortly after takeoff, with passengers killed in the second crash. All Comets were grounded pending an investigation of the crashes and explosions. The public was made to wonder about readiness of jetliner technology. Juan Trippe canceled Pan American's order for three Comets.

By contrast, times were bright at Boeing. In spring 1954, defense business was going so well that the board of directors voted a two-for-one stock split. Saturday, May 15, 1954, was a special day for Boeing's commercial business. The Dash 80 was ready to be unveiled. In an emotional ceremony, the plane was rolled out of the Renton factory, precisely at the 4 P.M. shift change, to the cheers of assembled employees. To mark the memorable occasion, Bill Boeing himself attended as guest of honor, and his wife, Bertha, christened the company's offspring. Wellwood Beall wrote the words she used for the dedication, and he tried (unsuccessfully, as it turned out) to get his way on the jetliner's name: "I christen thee the airplane of tomorrow, the Boeing Jet Stratoliner and Stratotanker." An onlooker noted that Bill Boeing had tears in his eyes during the ceremony. (He died aboard his yacht on September 28, 1956, never having backtracked on his resolution to clear out of the aircraft business: His twenty-two-million-dollar estate included not a single share of Boeing stock.)

The Dash 80 was configured as a tanker and had only four windows. Multicolored, it had a silver belly, a broad copper-colored stripe running along the window line that flared up like the wings on Mercury's helmet above the windows of the flight deck and a top that was light yellow. The wings, swept back thirty-five degrees, were also light yellow, with copper-colored flaps and engine pods. Four jet engines hung in pods from the wings and jutted forward of the wings. Cabin width of 132 inches was the same as that of the Stratocruiser.

Taxi testing—trying out as many characteristics of the plane as possible on the ground before the dangerous first flight—began almost immediately. The tests went on without a hitch for several days, but on May 21 test pilot Tex Johnston was testing the brakes when the left landing gear collapsed, dropping the left wing and allowing an engine pod to hit the runway. If the problem hadn't surfaced until the prototype had flown and was landing, the accident might have killed the test-flight crew and destroyed the prototype. The defect turned out to be a combination of a design flaw that overstressed a landing gear part, and the part being made from improperly treated metal that the manufacturing people had thought adequate for the prototype. Fixing the faults would take six precious weeks. When Ed Wells reported the findings to Allen, Wells feared there was a real possibility he'd be reprimanded and perhaps demoted, but the boss accepted the bad news stoically.

In July, the Dash 80 was ready to graduate from waddling on the ground to flying in its native element, the most eagerly anticipated technical milestone of the jet transport program. The first flight was scheduled for 7 A.M., Thursday, July 15. Dawn arrived that day with Seattle's infamous overcast, but clearing was predicted by noon. The flight was postponed until 2 P.M. The sun broke through at lunchtime as forecast, and crowds of spectators headed out to the areas surrounding the airfield at Renton. The atmosphere was tense as usual for the first flight of a new model, but not nearly as thick with foreboding as when Boeing's first jet airplane, the B-47, had taken its inaugural flight almost seven years previously. Years of test flying each B-47 as it came out of the factory, and over two years of B-52 test flying, had given Boeing confidence in its jet airplanes. Even so, when Tex Johnston shook hands with Bill Allen before boarding the airplane, Tex noticed that Allen, who had so much riding on the success of the Dash 80, looked stooped with care.

Allen watched the bearer of his hopes take off into the partly cloudy sky, and wrote a terse description for his diary, with a little more feeling than usual: "July 15th was the big day. In about 2000 feet she lifted from Renton Field and climbed into the blue. The timing was perfect, for on that day *Time* magazine was on the stands featuring Boeing and the 707. After an hour and a half she landed at Boeing Field. What a day." Modest and restrained even in his diary, Allen failed to note that *Time*'s cover for that issue was a portrait of himself. Tex observed that Allen stood taller after the successful flight. A car drove up behind Boeing's president and someone yanked him out of the way. "If it had hit me, I wouldn't have felt it," he said.

Time's cover subject was undoubtedly overjoyed that the test hadn't given him anything dramatic to record in his diary. The flight hadn't been without its moments, however. The official photograph of the cruising Dash 80 that Boeing released afterward, taken from a chase plane, was an unusual view looking down on the airplane instead of the traditional side or front view. A knowledgeable person looking at the photo sees that the Dash 80's flaps were down, an odd position during cruise. The company photographer didn't snap a conventional picture because the landing gear was down, too, and that would have seemed strange even to a nonexpert. Johnston hadn't been able to raise the gear and flaps after takeoff because their hydraulic controls wouldn't work. He stayed aloft after determining that there was no danger and he could complete part of the first flight-test program.

For the first couple of weeks the test flights went well, delighting Allen by revealing that the engines actually did five times as much work as those on the DC-6 instead of the calculated three times. The 707 would be even more attractive to customers than anticipated. Boeing's luck changed on August 5. When Johnston landed and applied the brakes, the aircraft's equivalent of a car's master cylinder failed and the brakes lost all pressure, making them useless. The prototype had no thrust reversers on the engines to slow it down. Shooting along the ground at over one hundred miles per hour, Johnston veered off the runway onto grass and tried turning sharply to stop the hurtling craft. The airplane slowed but was still rolling when the nose landing gear hit concrete construction debris and broke. Johnston and most of the Dash 80 were OK, but the near disaster shocked Allen. In one of the more emotional entries in his diary, he wrote: "Will I ever forget Thursday, August 5th. We were entertaining the AIA [Aircraft Industry Association] that weekend. Had planned 707 to fly for them. . . . Then came a shattering call, the 707 had no brakes. Tex attempted a ground loop. Knocked off nose gear. Boy what a day. We flew B-52 for AIA instead."

The Air Force, recognizing late its need for jet tankers, as Allen had foreseen, told him it would place an interim order with Boeing to serve its requirements, which had become critical, until the tanker competition had been decided and the service could get the bulk of its tankers from the winner, be it Boeing or a rival. Allen immediately ordered the acceleration of engineering and tooling for a production tanker. In August 1954 the Air Force officially ordered twenty-nine Boeing tankers to be delivered in October 1956; since January, Allen had sunk over one and a half million dollars into preparations for tanker production, so he was much pleased by the order.

Then the Air Force announced the winner of the jet tanker competition—and, as signified by many long faces in Seattle, it wasn't Boeing. Because Boeing had generated its concept before the Air Force announced its requirements, the company's tanker would not exactly match those requirements; certain aspects, such as deck height and fuselage width, were a compromise with the jetliner that Boeing also hoped to make out of the Dash 80. Lockheed issued a proposal keyed to the requirements and won the contract award with a tanker concept having the jets mounted on the fuselage. Jack Steiner, who headed the team that made Boeing's proposal in the competition, is sure that politics played its pervasive role, too. He points out that Lockheed's home state of California, a political heavyweight, was angered by its aircraft companies losing the B-47 and B-52 contracts to Boeing. Allen felt the same way. Shortly before the tanker competition had ended, he wrote in his diary, "We may lose because of (a) a desire to spread wealth and (b) [a desire to] establish a competitive type." So Boeing's best chance to capture the jet transport business had been crushed. Allen had to pin all his hopes on the less certain success of the commercial version.

In October 1954, after the first phase of flight testing had proved the Dash 80 safe and flushed out most of the initial glitches, Allen started giving demonstration flights to airline pilots and others influential in airline buying decisions. The guests were impressed by their first flights at high altitude well above the weather, where piston engines don't work efficiently—the quietude, the freedom from vibration, and, for pilots, the ease of control. The resistance of the airlines to jets began to melt away. Allen sensed they'd soon be ready to buy.

Allen's first guests aboard the Dash 80 had been Pan Am executives who worked for Juan Trippe, and his consultant, Charles Lindbergh. Excited about their first jet flight, they infected Trippe with their enthusiasm. Always eager to be first with new airplanes, Trippe sprang into action. He wanted competition among manufacturers to reduce the jet price. In his usual aggressive, cagey style, he created the rivalry. He gave Donald Douglas his wake-up call, notifying Douglas that jet technology was ready for the airlines and Pan Am was looking to buy. Douglas ordered his designers to work up a detailed concept for a jetliner, which would be called the DC-8. Trippe tried to get Robert Gross at Lockheed to reconsider jetliners, but Gross wouldn't hear of it. Trippe nevertheless had engineered a situation he liked: two manufacturers who would compete with each other to give him what he wanted.

Douglas had not absolutely committed to building a jetliner, however—and neither had Boeing. Bill Allen was even showing signs of cold feet as he considered the impact on Boeing. In his diary entry for November 25, 1954, Allen wrote: "We are suffering from growing pains. Our organization has its hands full. Could we handle a commercial jet transport without (a) jeopardizing existing projects and (b) jeopardizing future bomber effort?" Boeing's 1954 annual report, written a couple of months later, was the company's first annual report to highlight the Dash 80. The report gave the project a big splash, including a color centerfold of an artist's rendition of the airplane. The text was tentative about a commercial version: "Our entry into the commercial field is as yet undetermined. We desire such a commercial development if it can be accomplished on a sound financial basis without interfering with our military commitments. . . . The company is hopeful of entering the commercial field, but the decision is dependent on military requirements and the financial feasibility of such an undertaking." Besides stating the realities of the situation for stockholders, Allen clearly wanted to assure the Air Force—then the company's only customer—that its needs were paramount.

In March 1955, an unusual announcement from the Pentagon about jet tankers turned frowns to big smiles in Seattle and reinvigorated the jet transport program. The need for the tankers had gone from crucial to desperate. The Air Force was so impressed by the performance of the Dash 80 and the plans for the jet tanker—now known as the KC-135—that the service was canceling the Lockheed production contract (before the airplane had been built) and would buy all its tankers from Boeing, starting with an order for three hundred worth seven hundred million dollars. The KC-135 may not have been everything the Air Force wanted down to the last specified millimeter, and it may not have been stamped MADE IN CALIFORNIA, but it would be a superb airplane based on an essentially proven design—and would be available in quantity long before any product from Lockheed. Allen's prophecies had been vindicated.

Allen had one more strategic objective to reach before he'd consider ordering the jetliner into production: that the Air Force allow Boeing to use the KC-135 production line for the commercial airplane, too. It would save Boeing millions of dollars in duplicating tooling and would be another step in improving the economics and lowering the risk of the jetliner endeavor. As Boeing argued to the Air Force, payment for use of the facilities would also make the KC-135 more economical. In July 1955, after negotiations and a meeting between Allen and Air Force Secretary Harold Talbott, the service agreed to the proposal in return for Boeing paying for a share of the Air Force's tooling and plant space. While waiting for the Air Force deal to come through, however, Allen had lost precious months of his lead over Donald Douglas, who was sure to enter the jetliner development race eventually. Nevertheless, almost everything had now fallen into place for undertaking the jetliner project.

There's no public record of what quieted Allen's concern that a jetliner program might interfere with military projects. Once financing was assured for the commercial airplane, Allen ordered engineering on it to begin. The passenger airplane assumed the original designation for the jet transport, the 707. The Dash 80 design, which incorporated B-47 and B-52 bomber technology, would have to be substantially revised to make a passenger airplane that airlines would buy. Noise was still a problem, for instance. Boeing had decided that the 707 had to be bigger than the Dash 80 to carry more passengers, so the engineers had to widen and lengthen the fuselage, and increase the number of seats from eighty to one hundred. (The changes had already been incorporated in the KC-135 fuselage, for production compatibility.) Engineers estimated that the airplane would sell for $5.5 million, but the airlines argued that $4 million was the limit of their financing ability. Allen ordered his engineers to squeeze costs out until the plane could be sold for $4.5 million. He also made organizational changes to give the jet business the attention it needed to grow, which would culminate the next year in formation of a separate airliner division. Boeing's salesmen were euphoric about their prospects. One of them later described his feelings: "Everybody was going to sign up with Boeing! We just thought there was going to be a real bonanza."

Events in Europe that spring increased the tempo of the arriving jet age. In France, Sud's short-range jet, the Caravelle—not a direct competitor to the longer-ranged 707—flew for the first time on May 12. In Russia, a large jetliner known as the TU-104 made its first flight on June 17, a milestone in aviation technology even though the Soviet Union presented no commercial threat to manufacturers in the West.

It was true, however, as the naysayers pointed out, that the world wasn't ready for jetliners. Lack of a jetliner infrastructure was among the concerns that gave airlines pause about adopting jet technology. Airports, for example, would need new fueling equipment and processes to handle jet fuel, which was kerosene and not the gasoline that conventional airliners burned. Airports would also need longer and stronger runways for the big jets, larger hangars, redesigned loading and servicing equipment, jet-engine starting carts, and who knew what else. The problem was the catch-22 that faces many innovators, adding yet another layer of risk to Boeing's big gamble. The world wouldn't change to accommodate a new technology until there was a new technology to accommodate. All Allen could do was plow ahead and trust that jetliners would prove so attractive that the world would have to catch up.

As the general public became aware that the jet age was dawning, fear mongers exploited the opportunity to seize the stage. They warned that jetliner noise would be intolerable; New York refused permission for the Dash 80 to land there on its first transcontinental flight and considered permanently banning jetliners from its airports. Stewardesses, as female flight attendants were called then, were warned that if they flew on jetliners they'd become sterile, have menstrual problems, and get varicose veins. An expert warned that if airlines converted all their airplanes to jetliners, by the end of the century ten thousand people would be killed annually in crashes. The warnings were clear: A technology forced on the public by greedy businessmen and allowed by an uncaring government was going to be awful, simply awful.

Despite the obstacles, jetliners every day moved closer to actuality. In Los Angeles, Douglas's engineers produced their concept for the DC-8. The company's board of directors approved it, and in June 1955 Donald Douglas ordered full-scale development to begin. As he commented resignedly to an interviewer, "Our hand has been forced. We had to go into the building of the DC-8 as a jet transport or else give up building airplanes." By starting so late, however, Douglas had accumulated severe handicaps. With no prototype, he'd have to go straight into production, whereas Boeing in effect would have two prototypes with the Dash 80 and the KC-135. The DC-8 had to make or break itself in the commercial market, while Boeing had the military market as a cushion with its tanker version. The Douglas company would have to pay all development and production costs itself, while the military would be sharing many costs with Boeing.

With many of the Dash 80 design details and performance figures known within the aviation community, Douglas used that experimental craft to some degree as its own prototype from a distance. Not having time to correct mistakes, Douglas played it safe with wholesale copying of the successful Dash 80. A joke current at

Boeing then had a visitor on a tour of Douglas's Santa Monica facilities asking, "Where's the DC-8 prototype?" The guide answers, "Oh, that's in the Seattle facilities."

On the other hand, Douglas had vastly superior savvy in the commercial marketplace and had the confidence of the world's airlines. Having stolen the 247 market away from Boeing with the later DC-3—basically a much improved 247—and the Stratoliner market with the later and better DC-4, Douglas was confident that it could once again cook Boeing's goose. Douglas was a formidable opponent, and Boeing clearly had a fight on its hands.

Neither the 707 nor the DC-8 was ideal for Trippe because westbound transatlantic flights would have to stop in Newfoundland (like most propeller-driven airplanes). Trippe wanted larger jets with bigger engines and wings that could carry more passengers and fuel, and fly directly from Europe to the United States; even though the 707 would be larger than the Dash 80, it wouldn't be as roomy as Trippe liked. Pratt & Whitney was developing its biggest engine ever, the J75 for the Air Force. It was supposed to be a military secret, but Trippe found out about it through his wide-ranging contacts. If adapted to commercial aircraft, the power plant would be powerful enough to grant Trippe his desire. He asked Allen and Douglas to switch from the current, smaller Pratt & Whitney engine to the planned bigger one, and enlarge their jetliners and give them longer range. Both men refused, citing the risk that would be piled atop risk if they based their plans on engines that hadn't been developed yet and might not succeed, and that might not be modified for commercial use even if they were successfully produced. Allen added that Boeing's development was too far along even to think about such a major design overhaul. Boeing's costs would explode beyond reason, especially because the overhaul would make it impossible to build the jetliner with KC-135 tooling.

Not discouraged, Trippe made a deal with Pratt & Whitney: If Pratt would produce a civilian version of the J75, he'd buy forty million dollars' worth of the engines even though he had no aircraft to mount them on at the moment. He encouraged Pratt to shake hands on the arrangement by hinting he'd buy the engine with transatlantic capability that Rolls-Royce was trying to develop if Pratt refused. Then he went back to Allen and Douglas, announced that he'd lessened the engine risk, and asked them again to build the airplane he needed. Allen shook his head and said he just couldn't do it because his already high risk would still be increased, and the costs would kill him.

Donald Douglas considered the proposition, however. The engine change would add to his risks, and so would departing from the jetliner size and range that had been proved practical by Boeing's Dash 80. On the other hand, the changes wouldn't add much to his costs since design of the aircraft and tooling weren't far along, and of course he had no savings to protect like those Allen was counting on from using KC-135 tooling. Douglas knew that Allen had refused to go along with Trippe. If Douglas should successfully produce Trippe's airplane, he'd lock up the orders from Pan Am and all the other international carriers. Since the 707 probably couldn't fly coast-to-coast nonstop in the face of strong head winds frequently met in the westward direction, but Trippe's jetliner could, most of the domestic orders would be sure to follow. Producing a reconfigured DC-8 was more daring than he would have liked, but Douglas saw his chance to make up lost ground and kill the 707 and maybe even Boeing with it. The DC-8 would be able to fly with the older J57 engine until the new J75 was ready, although performance during the interim would be short of the airplane's capabilities. He told Trippe that yes, indeed, he'd be glad to accommodate such a valued customer as Pan Am.

Trippe and Douglas had substantially altered the jetliner contest. On one side now was Boeing, a company little respected by airlines. Experienced in building large jet bombers, Boeing offered early delivery of an adequate jetliner based on a proven prototype. On the other side was Douglas, a company with no comparable experience and no prototype, and perhaps a year behind Boeing in delivery capability. Douglas was well respected by the airlines, however, and offered a larger, longer-ranged, more powerful jetliner that could cross the Atlantic or the country nonstop. The odds seemed to have tipped abruptly in favor of the Californians.

Douglas's engineers made a few other departures from the Dash 80 to increase the sales appeal of the DC-8. They swept the wings back slightly less than the angle of the Dash 80 wings, for instance, sacrificing about twenty miles per hour in speed but, Douglas claimed, making its jetliner easier and safer to fly than the 707.

Douglas clearly could compete with Boeing in fundamental technical capability. It was highly questionable whether Boeing could compete with Douglas in marketing capability. Boeing started off handicapped by its lack of respect: Airlines regarded Boeing as a company with its heart in military airplanes, a company that treated its airline customers too casually and didn't pay enough attention to their concerns. Boeing's executives thought their greatest obstacle to selling the 707 was the airlines' bad attitude toward the company. Boeing would have to sell itself as well as its airplane with a sales force much less experienced than Douglas's force. Allen put his top people to work selling: he sent Wellwood Beall with a team to Europe. They would simply have to outhustle and outdeal Douglas. In an article about the enthusiastic, conservative Seattle airplane salesmen, *Fortune* magazine described them as "rosy cheeked engineers wearing wing-tipped shoes."

Whenever possible, Allen used his strongest weapon, the Dash 80, to impress potential customers. Trotting it out, he emphasized that Boeing had an honest-to-goodness, high-flying passenger airplane, while Douglas had nothing but drawings and high hopes. This led to one of the most often repeated of the many yarns that Boeing employees like to tell about their company. On a summer Sunday in 1955, the leaders of the aircraft and airline industries were in Seattle for trade association conventions at the same time that the Gold Cup hydroplane races were being held on Lake Washington. Boeing rented three yachts and invited the aviation leaders and other VIPs aboard to watch the races. During the meet, the Dash 80 was to fly overhead and make a low pass over the yachts. Allen, the host, was beaming on one of the yachts as the Dash 80 came into view only about three hundred feet up, jets roaring, and all heads turned to watch. Suddenly a wing dipped and kept on dipping. The airplane was on its side and then on its back, rotating on its axis, as it flew over the yachts. Tex Johnston was barrel rolling one of the biggest airplanes in the world! Stunt flying the craft in which Allen had sunk much of Boeing's fortune and all its hopes! Allen watched, stunned, as the craft completed the roll, straightened, and flew off to the cheers of his guests. Allen breathed easier. Then, in the distance, the airplane turned and headed back toward the yachts. When a wing started dipping again, Allen could feel the blood draining from his face. He could hardly believe it. But, yes, around the airplane went again, slowly rolling right above the yachts. Trying to calm himself, Allen asked Larry Bell, the head of Bell Aircraft, who was standing beside him, if he could have one of Bell's heart pills.

The next morning Allen called George Schairer, Johnston's boss, and told him to bring Tex to the president's office. When they entered the office, they found Ed Wells with Allen. Neither man was smiling, neither gave more than a perfunctory greeting. Schairer and Johnston sat down in silence. Allen asked Schairer if he had told Johnston to do the rolls. Tex interjected a "no" and took full responsibility. Allen asked him why he had endangered the Dash 80 and the survival of the corporation with a silly stunt. Johnston defended his barrel roll by stating there was no danger at all. He explained that, as long as the pilot keeps a force of one g acting on the airplane as gravity normally does, it doesn't matter to the aircraft what its angle is in relation to the ground. (Johnston didn't mention it, but a flight test engineer on the airplane hadn't known Tex was going to roll and wasn't even belted up, yet he was hardly aware that the airplane had turned over. Nor, sensibly, did Johnston mention that he'd rolled the Dash 80 twice before on test flights.) "Any airplane that you can't roll just ain't safe to fly," he concluded. Allen nevertheless told him never to do it again, if only because Boeing was trying to win the respect of the airlines. Allen declared that hot-rodding gave Boeing an image of irresponsibility and upset the insurance company.

(Unbowed, Johnston later gave famed entertainer and aviation enthusiast Arthur Godfrey a ride on a KC-135 test flight. Johnston knocked Godfrey's socks off by barrel rolling the tanker. The antic remained a secret between the two men until Johnston left Boeing. Many knowledgeable persons thought the Dash 80 barrel roll had impressed people with the ruggedness of the airplane and Boeing's confidence in its abilities. Years later Johnston and Allen were talking at a party at Allen's house. Allen was well lubricated and mellow, and Johnston figured it was a good time to rehash the incident of the Dash 80 barrel rolls. He jabbed Allen's chest with a forefinger and asked, "Bill, are you willing to admit finally that slow rolling the 707 over the Gold Cup course was probably the greatest thing that ever happened to that program?" Allen's face suddenly hardened. He snapped a sharp "no!" and walked away. Only near the end of his career did Allen finally mention the barrel roll lightheartedly, introducing the topic in a speech by saying, "It has been many, many years since I could discuss this incident with even a modicum of humor." Colleagues say he never forgave Johnston for what Allen always considered a childish prank.)

Technology isn't everything for a passenger airplane—aesthetics count highly, and that wasn't Boeing's forte. For the design of the passenger spaces in the 707, Boeing contracted with the industrial design firm of Walter Dorwin Teague, which had done the Stratoliner and Stratocruiser cabins. Frank Del Giudice, the lead designer, felt that his main challenge was to overcome the feeling of being in a long, narrow, crowded tunnel. To break up visually the monotony of the 130-foot-long interior, he divided the seats into blocks of bright colors, and emphasized the overhead passenger service units and interruptions in the ceiling that carried life rafts. Most important, he recommended that the planned number of windows be increased so there would be one beside every row of seats no matter how the seats were sized or arranged. This would let in more sunlight, counter the closed-in feeling, and give passengers something interesting to look at. (This turned out to be one of the 707's major attractions. Douglas at first put windows in the DC-8 only for every other row.) Del Giudice also made the interior in modular sections so that airlines could more easily customize their airplanes, and made the cabin quickly washable because jetliners, needing less engine maintenance than props, would spend less time on the ground. One of Del Giudice's most influential innovations was his use of vinyl-clad aluminum for the cabin sidewalls; this find turned out to be the most practical, most economical, and most easily decorated sidewall material. Just as the 707's engineers set the technical pattern for jetliners, Del Giudice introduced the jet style.

Staid, conservative Boeing had to learn modern marketing ways for its war with Douglas, as when it put on demonstrations of its product. "Hoopla" was alien to the Boeing culture, dominated as it was by engineers who thought plain facts and figures should be enough to convince anyone. Allen, no engineer but matter-of-fact in his own right, also found showmanship distasteful. Douglas, influenced perhaps by its proximity to the movie colony, was a master at theatricality, however, and Allen felt he had to answer in kind. If Douglas was Hollywood, Boeing would be Broadway. Allen paid Walter Dorwin Teague, his New York consultant, half a million dollars to build a mock-up of the 707 cabin in Manhattan and arrange a stagey exhibit for groups of potential customers. Teague replicated an attractive airport boarding area. Boeing's customers would gather there for a brief introduction to the 707, and then "board" the jetliner, entering the cabin mock-up. Although not part of a real airplane, the mock-up was realistic in every detail. The customers would take their seats and go through a simulated flight, starting with leaving from the gate, and would hear all the appropriate noises and announcements by cabin attendants and captain.

Douglas wasn't the only competitor Allen had to worry about in mid-1955. He also had to keep his eye on Vickers over in England—until the British government helped him out. As the prototype of the Vickers jet tanker neared completion, a real threat to Boeing and Douglas, Her Majesty's government decided to economize by canceling the project. Without the funds to carry on itself, Vickers dropped the transport and ended any chance of a commercial version. Thus ended the intriguing possibility of a three-way race for jetliner supremacy. About this time Lord Hives, head of Rolls-Royce, is said to have seen the Dash 80 and remarked, "This is the end of British aviation."

The first 707 order offered to Allen was a large one, for a fleet of two dozen jetliners selling for around one hundred million dollars—and Allen spurned it. He was considering the source. Howard

Hughes, noted even then for his eccentricities and unpredictable ways, wanted to beat Juan Trippe for recognition as the first to fly jetliners. Hughes tried to place the order with a provision that TWA, the airline he controlled, could fly 707s exclusively for a year. Allen, sensing nothing but trouble from dealing with the wacky Hughes and confident of his ability to make major sales elsewhere, wisely turned him down.

Allen itched to sell the first 707s to Trippe because Pan Am was the world's foremost airline; if Pan Am bought, other airlines would tend to follow its lead. Even though Douglas was building the jetliner Trippe lusted for, Allen hoped that Pan Am, like the Air Force, would find his earlier delivery dates and surer, proto-type-based technology irresistible. Since Boeing would certainly deliver 707s to someone before Douglas could get any DC-8s out of its factory, Trippe would have to buy from Boeing to be first in the world with practical jet passenger airplanes, a distinction he craved.

Early in October 1955, Trippe was ready to make the first serious tender for jetliners. The Pan Am chief planned a mammoth purchase, forty-five jetliners that Boeing priced at over $190 million, the largest single purchase of commercial airplanes ever. Trippe invited Allen and his staff, and Donald Douglas and his staff, to Pan Am's New York headquarters to make sales pitches. Allen and a small army of engineers and financial and marketing experts flew east and ascended to Trippe's offices, then in the Chrysler Building. During Boeing's presentation, Trippe asked the price and how Boeing arrived at it. Clyde Skeen, Boeing's controller, said the price was $4.28 million per airplane, including engines, and went through his pricing methodology. Trippe replied that the Douglas people in the next room were asking only $3.9 million. Allen broke in, saying, "Juan, I believe Mr. Skeen was wrong. Our price is $3.9 million." Boeing would lose money at that figure, but Allen felt this was a must-win order; he could raise the price for future purchases once the Pan Am buy triggered the expected avalanche of orders. Allen completed his sales talk, and he and his colleagues flew back to Seattle. They felt good about the arguments they had presented and were pretty sure they had landed the contract, but fretted while they waited for word from Pan Am.

Within days, Frank Gledhill, Pan Am's purchasing agent, flew west to give the word personally. He first met with Wellwood Beall. Sitting down in Beall's office, Gledhill delivered unexpected and demoralizing news: Pan Am was splitting its order, taking twenty-five DC-8s and only twenty 707s. His explanation of Pan Am's reasons and plans shocked Beall. Trippe didn't want any 707s at all. He was ordering twenty only to salvage the claim to be first in the industry with jets. He'd replace them with DC-8s as soon as the Douglas products were available, and would never even consider the Boeing airplanes again. Size and range were the overpowering considerations. DC-8s would be much more profitable for Pan Am, and that's really all that counted. Allen spoke later with Trippe. The Pan Am head thought few airlines would find the 707 worthwhile and predicted that Boeing wouldn't sell any more than 100 of them, far short of Boeing's initial breakeven projection of 150 sales. If the other airlines took their cues from Trippe as expected, Boeing was headed for a bath in the tens of millions of dollars at least, and the collapse of any realistic chance for a commercial business.

Stunned, Allen pulled himself together and moved rapidly to rescue his jetliner program. His actions show that he was willing to increase the cost and risk of the program if that could save it, and if the expected returns would justify it. His technical people told him that they could probably change the design at an acceptable cost, so the 707 could take the big J75 engine and cross the Atlantic and the United States nonstop. Allen ordered his engineers to decide broadly on the needed changes immediately. He wanted to promise the redesign to Pan Am at least to stop them from repudiating the 707s they'd already bought, and to give his jetliner a fighting chance in negotiations with other airlines sure to come up soon. A team of engineers set to work on the changes. George Schairer and another engineer went to New York to find out what would make Pan Am happy, and discuss possible changes as they were conceived and phoned in from Seattle. In about a week, Boeing had a new concept for a 707. The company would widen and redesign the

wing, and make the adaptations for the J75 engine. Boeing nicknamed the new model the "Intercontinental," and changed its
numerical designation from 707-120 to 707-320. Pan Am agreed
to take the Intercontinental for the last half of its deliveries, when
the J75 was planned to be ready. On October 13, Pan Am made the
public announcement of its split order. Other airlines began to call
to schedule presentations. Few were enthusiastic about jetliners, but
none wanted to be left behind. The stampede into the jet age was
under way.

Allen wondered if Boeing should make the 707 larger, too, to
compete with the DC-8 on size as well. His advisors were overwhelmingly against this because they thought it would require an unbearably expensive overhaul of the design, so different from the KC-135
that Boeing could no longer use the tanker's production line.

Soon Maynard Pennell, the 707's chief engineer, led a group
to Chicago to pitch the 707 to Pat Patterson of United Airlines.
Another large order, for thirty jetliners and some $120 million, was
at stake. Pennell knew that he had a tough sell, since Patterson,
although (perhaps because) he had been with United when it was
part of Boeing, plainly didn't like doing business with Boeing, for
reasons never made public. Patterson gleefully took the group to a
special room at United's headquarters. In the room were life-size
mock-ups of sections of the 707 and DC-8 cabins, placed end to
end. Patterson led the Boeing men through the mock-ups, entering
the DC-8 end. The men stood comfortably in the aisle between
two rows of three seats each, noting the spacious overhead bins.
Ahead they could see the 707 section. While only three inches narrower in diameter, it seemed much smaller. They stepped into the
707 aisle, flanked by one row of three seats and one of only two seats.
They felt cramped. The overhead bins were puny. Embarrassed and
dejected, the men hardly needed any comment from Patterson. He
gave them his opinions anyway, forcefully pointing out the shortcomings of the Boeing cabin. On October 25, United made its dis-
couraging announcement: all DC-8s, no 707s.

American Airlines took the next place in the line for orders,
wanting thirty-two jetliners. Allen heard that American wanted the

early deliveries that he could promise, and would like to order from him because of Boeing's experience in building large jets, but the 707 was smaller than the carrier wanted. American's president, C. R. Smith, told Bill Allen, moreover, that he hated the idea of getting another Boeing airliner that was really a tanker hybrid: American had had bad experiences with the Stratocruiser, based largely on the KC-97 tanker. He didn't like the compromises involved. Smith wanted Boeing to wise up and design a jetliner with nobody but the airlines in mind. Also at this time, messages were arriving from Boeing salesmen across the Atlantic that the European airlines strongly favored the larger DC-8. A picture comes to the imagination of a grinning Donald Douglas in Los Angeles savoring the aroma of goose being cooked.

The realization that the 707 was as good as dead hit Allen on a Thursday. He had an appointment with Smith to make his formal 707 presentation on Monday. Allen had to make the most critical quick decision of his life. The only way to revive the 707 was to enlarge it to match the DC-8. But that would mean expensive redesign and greater departure from the tested Dash 80 configuration. Above all, it would entail abandoning use of 85 percent of the KC-135 tooling, a cornerstone of his 707 financial strategy. On the other hand, the 707 project wasn't quite as risky as it was when he had set out. The prototype had been completed and had demonstrated the basic soundness of Boeing's technical approach, and the tanker had been sold. Boeing's other business had continued to boom, generating large profits and high promise. (Boeing would declare another two-for-one stock split the next year, and would set company records for sales and profits a year later.) Allen hadn't been completely sure at the start that airlines would buy jets so soon; now they were jostling each other in their rush to place orders—big orders. The market he had only guessed at was there for certain. The right airplane would make a lot of money.

Allen made up his mind: He decided to go for it if he could, if the redesign wouldn't require essentially abandoning the present 707 design. He asked his engineers to see what they could do about widening the fuselage and, while they were at it, if they could also lengthen it to respond to airline criticisms that both the 707 and the DC-8 were too short. If it could be done, he had to have all the information for a new presentation by the time he walked into Smith's office in four days. Once again, Boeing's engineers tackled a seemingly impossible deadline.

Allen had their answer before he shook hands with Smith. Smith was surprised when Allen launched into a presentation on a new jetliner that would be an inch wider in diameter than the DC-8 and almost eight feet longer, and could carry more cargo than the Douglas airplane; it would be about twice as big as the biggest propeller-driven airliner. Allen's engineers had come through again. With their help, he hadn't just matched Douglas's bet, he'd raised the ante.

Smith, delighted at being offered exactly what he wanted, announced on November 8 that he was ordering all 707 Intercontinentals—no DC-8s. The reaction in Seattle went unrecorded, but it must have been party time. Good news piled on top of good news when Boeing's engineers finished designing the new wing, churned out in a phenomenally short six weeks. Five percent more efficient than the DC-8's wing, it allowed Allen to advertise that the Intercontinental could fly farther nonstop than the DC-8. (Boeing ranks the Intercontinental wing as one of the company's greatest engineering achievements.) Before long, Pan Am canceled its DC-8s and changed its entire order to Intercontinentals, except for an early six 707–120s that would make it the first airline with jets. With Allen sweetening his deals by undercutting Douglas three hundred thousand dollars on the price (and both companies selling below cost in the early going), the world's jetliner orders started to go Boeing's way more often than not. As a result of Allen's daring and his engineers' skills, Boeing had risen in a flash from defeated, dying combatant to victorious giant killer. Boeing's salesmen also contributed to the wins with their enthusiasm and energy if not polish. A foreign airline executive who bought 707s mused about the sale: "I don't know how Boeing sold anything. They gave us the impression of being hicks." Others smiled at salesmen they called "the country boys from behind the Cascades."

The battle between Boeing and Douglas was fierce. Allen told a security analysts' meeting at the time: "[Competition] is not limited to a basic selling price; it involves extending credit to the purchaser or taking trade-ins of used airplanes or both. . . ." Airlines tried to unload their used props on the manufacturers because the used airplane market had collapsed as airlines the world over bought the new jetliners and got rid of their fleets of props. One Allen tactic was outspending Douglas to make sales. Boeing and the 707 program were in much stronger financial shape than Douglas and the DC-8 program. Besides taking the sales losses that Allen mentioned, he also accommodated almost every wish of his customers to individualize their airplanes. Braniff, for example, asked for and got a model tailored to the special high-altitude requirements of La Paz, Bolivia. These modifications cost Boeing dearly, but Douglas couldn't match them, so Allen wrote up the orders. He always counted on more than making up the deficits once the good reputation of the 707 and Boeing itself were well established with the airlines. In business-school lingo, he was buying market share.

Boeing took away Douglas's most impressive customer when Secretary of State John Foster Dulles pointed out to President Eisenhower that Russian Premier Nikita Khrushchev was upstaging the American president by flying to international meetings in a TU-104 jet. With symbols and impressions so important in politics, Eisenhower asked Air Force General Curtis LeMay to recommend a jetliner for him. LeMay endorsed the 707 because of exceptional Air Force experience with its sister aircraft, the KC-135 tanker. Eisenhower immediately ordered three 707s for use by the executive branch; when the president was aboard one of the airplanes, it became Air Force One. The Boeing jetliners replaced Douglas and Lockheed airplanes that had served presidents for many years.

While Boeing and Douglas were duking it out, a third competitor entered the jet arena through a back entrance. Convair, a company much like Boeing, had been waiting until it could be absolutely sure that jet technology was ready for passenger airplanes.

Convair launched development of a medium-range jetliner smaller than the 707 and DC-8 to serve routes that didn't require such large craft. Although the market for a smaller jet was limited, Allen saw that Boeing could make money building an airplane for it. He also reasoned that Convair, once established in the jetliner market, would be a serious competitor in all size ranges; he could help to safeguard Boeing's position in the market by beating back Convair with a better small jetliner.

In 1956, taking the measure of Convair's jetliner, the 880, Allen decided he could best it with a smaller, lighter, and less expensive version of the 707. He got his designers started on a 707 variation to be called the Model 717. (It was still basically a 707; Boeing didn't explain why it wasn't designated 707-dash-something.) In 1957, Convair was nearing the end of negotiations on a sale to United Airlines, having agreed to eighteen of nineteen articles in a sales contract. Allen stepped in and offered United a better deal, killing the Convair sale and snatching an order for twenty-eight airplanes. One of the personal peculiarities that sometimes intrude on the sterile world of business changed the designation of the plane. Pat Patterson of United didn't like the two sevens in 717 and 707; this was said to be one of his reasons for not buying the 707. To accommodate his idiosyncrasy and help to make the sale, Allen withdrew the 717 model number and renamed the jetliner the 720.

Stung but not beaten, Convair counterpunched by introducing a technology that was to revolutionize jet engines. The company modified the 880 to take a new power plant developed by GE called the fan jet; the turbine not only provided jet propulsion but also turned a fan within the nacelle. The fan acted much like a propeller for additional propulsion. The engine promised to be more powerful and economical, and quieter than conventional jets of the same weight, providing greatly increased speed, range, and fuel efficiency. Convair bestowed a new model number on the airplane, calling it the 990, and in early 1958 got American Airlines interested in buying it. Allen, searching for a way to respond, learned that Pratt & Whitney was developing a fan jet, although unenthusiastically, not confident that its promises would be fulfilled. (Pratt & Whitney executives enjoyed quipping that the fan jet, which passed voluminous air in its exhaust, was "just a lot of hot air.") Allen leaned on the engine manufacturer to speed up the project and quickly modified the 720 to take the new engine. One day a short while later, American Airlines was to sign its contract with Convair at noon. Ed Wells and a party from Boeing showed up at American's offices first thing that morning, pitched the 720 equipped with the Pratt & Whitney fan jet, and stole a large part of the order from Convair.

The 720 was so much better than the 990 that Boeing went on to garner most of the sales in the market niche for small jets. Boeing's success played a large role in knocking Convair (now known as General Dynamics) out of the jetliner business completely.

The competition between Boeing and Convair had two long-lasting effects. One was the industry-wide adoption of fan jets. C. R. Smith of American Airlines, as a result of his carrier's experience flying airplanes with the engines, called them "the greatest advance in air transportation since the jet itself." They increased range by as much as 50 percent and reduced fuel consumption by as much as 25 percent. Fan jets quickly became the standard engines on all jetliners and ended any remaining controversy about props versus jets; for all but the smallest airplanes, props were undeniably dead. The other significant consequence of the competition was that Boeing learned it was good business to offer different models to pinpoint airline markets; Ed Wells is credited with recognizing and promoting this as a key strategy. This market differentiation began the "family of models" idea that's been as important to Boeing's success as it's been to the automotive companies. Just as a car buyer could purchase any of several models from GM, ranging from a small Chevy to a big Caddy, to suit his needs and bank account, so an airline would be able to buy any of several models from Boeing to fit its routes and treasury. The multimodel approach hadn't been practical with propeller-driven airliners, whose size range is much narrower than that of jetliners.

A milestone in Boeing's history occurred during the 720 days. Douglas was still king of the commercial skies, having built over half the airliners flying in the world. In fall 1957, the tally of jetliner sales reached 145 for the 707 and 124 for the DC-8. Boeing had taken the lead in passenger jet sales, which it steadily lengthened and holds to this day. Allen said nothing for the record, but he must have been pleased professionally and personally. He never expressed his feelings about Donald Douglas explicitly in his diary, but he seemed to think his fellow Scottish-American pompous. Allen inserted two brief mentions of Douglas in his diary, both in connection with meetings of the Aircraft Industry Association. The references contain a hint of disdain: in 1948, "Mr. Douglas puts on a performance"; and in 1950, "Mr. Douglas and I had our usual argument." The personal rivalry ended in 1957, when Douglas retired.

The Comet, the world's first jetliner and once a competitive threat to Boeing, surfaced again in 1958 after having been out of service over four and a half years. De Havilland had located and corrected the design flaw responsible for the crashes on takeoff, and found the cause of the mysterious midair explosions. The disintegrations resulted from fatigue in the fuselage metal caused by the repeated stresses of pressurizing and depressurizing. As the metal in a window frame had been pushed back and forth this way, a small crack had formed. Then, as the window frame flexed in turbulent air, the crack had shot several feet along the fuselage, which blew apart from the force of the pressurized air within, like a balloon bursting when blown up too much. (Boeing had designed ways to prevent cracks from growing into a problem on the 707.) None of the Comet accidents resulted from problems peculiar to jet technology, so they had no effect on the willingness of airlines to buy 707s.

The incident that triggered the Comet's metal fatigue problem illustrates the meticulous care that must be taken in designing airplanes or changing designs. The Comet had been conceived with dimpled rivet heads. The stresses that led to the blowups occurred because de Havilland switched to countersunk rivets for production convenience without realizing the consequences. Reaming the holes for the new kind of rivets created sharp edges that initiated the cracks.

The grounding of the Comets had almost bankrupted de Havilland, which survived only through government intervention. De Havilland, realizing the hopelessness of trying to put its original model or even a close derivative back in service, had accelerated its jetliner development program. The company reentered the market with its Comet IV, which went into service three weeks before the inaugural flight of Pan Am's first 707. Beating the 707 into airline schedules did little for the Comet IV, however. The 707 (and later the DC-8) proved so superior to the Comet that the de Havilland airplane sank into oblivion.

On a gorgeous Sunday in late April 1958, when Boeing had been putting the finishing touches on the first 707 it would deliver to Pan Am, Bill Allen felt good about life. He experienced a feeling of tranquility at home unusual enough to record in his diary: "As I sit by the window, I look out on blooming rhododendrons, azaleas, dogwoods, magnolias, etc. A beautiful time of the year in Seattle. I am playing Beethoven's sixth (pastoral)—a peaceful and thrilling feeling comes over me."

Soon Juan Trippe took possession of his first 707. In a ceremony to commemorate the occasion, the country's First Lady, Mamie Eisenhower, christened the jetliner *America*. After a shakedown period, Pan Am made a special "first commercial flight" of the 707, for VIPs only, on October 19. Fitted out like a club car, the 707-120 flew from New York to Brussels. Pan Am flew the first regularly scheduled 707 commercial flight, from New York to Paris, on October 26. The 707-320, the Intercontinental, entered service in spring of 1959. The DC-8 made its first commercial flight in September 1959. Overall, it was not quite as good as the Intercontinental; according to design experts, even Boeing's cabin features had it all over Douglas's.

In 1959, the Martin Company, a major producer of propeller-driven airliners and potential rival for Boeing and Douglas in jetliners, realized the futility of trying to catch up with the jet leaders. Acknowledging the demise of props, Martin gave up the passenger airplane business completely. As the world entered the decade of the 1960s, the only remaining strong competitors in the airliner business were Boeing and Douglas. Less than eight years before, the thought of this happening would have been considered absolutely absurd.

In one of aviation history's greatest anticlimaxes, Lockheed's Electra turboprop made its debut in early 1959, joining the American Airlines fleet. Before American's C. R. Smith had been converted from jet skeptic to believer, he was a staunch advocate of props and professed faith in the coming of the turboprop era. Smith had held a competition to develop a turboprop airliner, which American would help to launch, and Lockheed had won. Now that it was ready, it wasn't of much use. Although economical for short ranges, the Electra couldn't compete with pure jets for most flights. To make matters worse, 3 of the ill-starred Electras crashed in the next year. With the Electra's poorly timed debut and soiled reputation, only 176 were sold, and Lockheed lost millions. Within just a few years, passengers hardly ever saw propellers on big airplanes at airports anymore.

Aviation leaders in those days all seemed to have their Howard Hughes stories, and Allen had his. He told of Mef answering the phone at nine one night and calling out that it was Howard Hughes. Knowing the quirks of the pioneer aviator and aviation tycoon, Allen went into his library, lay down on the davenport, and got comfortable before picking up the receiver and greeting Hughes. Hughes chattered nonstop until 1:30 A.M. before Allen could hang up. Such personal relationship as the two men had—the reclusive Hughes was the only major airline figure Allen had never met in person—was shattered after Hughes finally bought 707s with no strings attached. Hughes was impressed by the Dash 80; as a friendly gesture, Allen offered to send it to him for a day, so he could fly it. Hughes kept asking for one more day until a week had gone by. Allen ordered his crew to bring the plane back. When Hughes learned of the order, he immediately called Allen and pleaded for one more day. Allen told him no, and explained that the prototype was needed for testing. Hughes said nobody had ever talked to him that way. Allen replied that there was a first time for everything. Hughes said he'd never buy another Boeing plane. Allen said that was too damn bad. "So that was the end of Allen and Hughes," the Boeing chief concluded. (Subsequently, TWA made only one small Boeing purchase until after Hughes lost control of the airline in the mid-1960s;

because of TWA's limited needs and finances in that period, however, the carrier might not have given Boeing a substantial order anyway.)

Boeing had to make two major changes in the design of the 707 after production and deliveries started, both for reasons of safety. The need for the first change became apparent when the cause of the Comet's two crashes on takeoff (not the midair explosions) was found to be insufficient lift at takeoff speeds. Analyzing the finding, Boeing engineers realized the 707 could encounter the same problem. Boeing incorporated a device known as a leading edge flap into its design and fitted them on all 707s, including those already produced.

The need for the second change was revealed on August 15, 1959. As an American Airlines 707 on a training flight, with no passengers, approached Grumman Field on Long Island, New York, the power to two engines was cut way back to simulate an emergency condition. Flying at about five hundred feet, the pilot made a left turn to line up for a landing. As he came out of the turn, his airplane began to Dutch roll. The pilot couldn't handle it. After only fifteen seconds, the jet suddenly flipped upside down and two engines tore off. The airplane crashed on its back and exploded, killing the crew. Two months later, a Boeing training flight for Braniff personnel Dutch rolled near Seattle, lost three engines, and crashed, killing four people. Then Pan Am and Air France training flights flipped over, tearing off engines, but managed to land safely. The accidents occurred when extraordinary flight emergencies were simulated while pilots were training, but they should not have happened under any circumstances. Boeing had to contend with the fact that, under rare conditions, the 707 would Dutch roll. (It wasn't publicly explained why the "Little Herbie" yaw damper didn't prevent the accidents.) The British refused to grant the 707 a certificate of airworthiness until the flaw was fixed. Safety is priority number one for aircraft engineers, but they can't always think of everything that could go wrong; disasters befalling their creations weigh heavily on their minds. Bill Cook, an engineering manager who played a key role in the 707 project, acknowledged that, in designing the 707, ". . . the XB-47 Dutch roll unfortunately had been forgotten. . . ." Maynard Pennell, chief engineer for 707 development, confessed there was a deficiency in the design of the 707. "We should have paid more attention to the 707's Dutch roll properties. . . . The only thing I'd have done differently on the planes I worked on was to avoid the Dutch roll problem," he admitted. It was solved primarily by enlarging the tail. Boeing again retrofitted the changes on 707s already in service. Altogether, the changes cost Boeing $150 million.

The 707 program almost collapsed one night in February 1959. An incident came perilously close to making travelers afraid to fly on the 707, although it had nothing to do with Boeing or the jetliner's design. Only a few months after commercial 707 service began, one of Pan Am's first jetliners was thirty-five thousand feet over the Atlantic on a scheduled flight from Paris to New York, with 119 passengers and a crew of 10. The captain had left the flight deck to use the lavatory, with the controls on autopilot and the copilot in charge. The captain stayed awhile in the cabin to have a cup of coffee with his wife and a Pan Am executive. (It was then legal for the pilot to leave the flight deck.) Suddenly the airplane pitched nose downward and began diving, then rolling. The captain struggled to get back to his post. Reaching the flight deck, he clambered into his seat and righted the airplane, pulling it out of its dive barely seconds before it would have plunged into the ocean, never to be seen again. A passenger broke an ankle, and several blacked out from g-forces as the power-diving airplane had leveled off, permanently twisting its wings from the strain. The incident was never satisfactorily explained, but the 707 itself wasn't implicated. If the airplane had gone into the water with all its passengers, nevertheless, nobody would have known what happened, and the resulting black headlines and doubts about the 707's airworthiness might have spelled the end of the jetliner.

The technical success of the 707 was never in as much question as its financial success. The initially projected breakeven point of 150 deliveries (when all the money Boeing spent on developing, producing, and selling the airplanes would equal the money the company received for them) became meaningless after Allen started spending money lavishly on design changes and sales incentives. In October 1957, as development was winding down, *Fortune* magazine had published its estimate of expenses that would be incurred by delivery time. The publication figured that the total would run to about $185 million: $16 million on the prototype; $100 million in engineering and tooling; $35 million in plant and equipment; $7 million to develop a thrust reverser and sound suppressor; $4–$5 million on advertising and sales; and about $23 million for flight testing, research, and other costs. Development costs ended up twice as high as predicted, and production costs, too, soared way over estimates. These steep expenditures moved the break-even point far out to around 400 deliveries.

Incredibly, it wasn't until 1964, nine years after Boeing sold its first 707, and twelve years after the company started heavy spending specifically for the prototype, that Boeing recouped its entire investment in the jetliner. Making up for losses to inflation would take another dozen or so additional sales. That was just to get its money back—to get out of the red. Only then would Boeing have begun to turn a true profit; it would take several more years to accumulate an adequate return on investment.

The expenditure on all aircraft delivered to the break-even point was over two billion dollars. Most of this was money spent to build individual airplanes, so-called recurring costs that were recovered relatively quickly on delivery. Never before, however, had an aircraft manufacturer laid out so much money before making anything on it. Partly, this was due to the greatly increased complexity and gargantuan size of jetliners compared to their predecessor airliners, and the accompanying evolution of aircraft plants from what were essentially sheet-metal bending shops to highly capital-intensive machine shops. Manufacturing inefficiencies contributed; many were wartime attitudes and practices that were hard to uproot. The outpouring of money to survive and eventually to beat Douglas later in the program also played a large part. Boeing's run of high profits ended in 1959, halved by losses from the first full year of money-draining 707 production. Allen blamed management for some of the costliness; in 1960, he replaced the head of the 707 program.

The profit Boeing made out of the entire KC-135/707 program is a business secret. Fragmentary data about costs have become available, but all figures about any aircraft development program have to be looked at cautiously. Even the break-even information may not be all it seems because so much depends on unknown accounting choices. We're in the dark, for example, on how joint costs, such as expenditures for the Dash 80, were apportioned. Sometimes, moreover, numbers are presented without being tagged as before tax or after tax. And the lucrative follow-on business in spare parts can turn losses into gains; the Stratocruiser program was reported to be ultimately profitable, for instance, when long-continuing sales of spare parts were figured in. So complex are the accounting equations that even Boeing may not be precisely sure of its profit. One senior executive admitted, "Locating the break-even point is like finding a will-o'-the-wisp." Whether the 707 by itself made much money is anybody's guess.

Sales of the KC-135 and 707 do seem to leave room for a healthy profit, however. Boeing made 820 KC-135s, closing down production in 1966. The Air Force keeps renovating the ageless airplanes, and in the mid-1990s they remain the primary U.S. tankers. *Fortune* magazine called the 707 "the biggest triumph in the history of the [aviation] industry." On average, 707s reportedly sold for 25 percent more than the cost of making them, development expenditures and taxes aside. Boeing produced 725 of the jetliners, the last one in 1978. Boeing didn't close the production line until May of 1991, nevertheless, because the 707 went on to another life in a slightly different form. The company made 68 special 707s for the Pentagon's Airborne Warning and Control System—the airplanes with the huge, funny-looking antenna sprouting mushroom-like from the top that became well known during the Gulf War. The popular 707 had one of the longest continuous production runs in aviation history, and hundreds are still in service.

Boeing probably made a decent return on its investment in the tanker/jetliner program. But even if it hadn't, even if the company had lost a little money, Bill Allen probably would have been ecstatic because of the nonmonetary value that the company gained from the venture. Boeing went from almost a zero in the passenger airplane business to the dominant company globally in current sales. After a shaky start, Boeing earned the respect and confidence of the world's air carriers with its attractive product and responsiveness to the airlines' needs and wants. Allen's jet program strengthened Boeing's leading military position and put the company firmly in the desirable commercial business while killing off, weakening, or overshadowing all its competitors. His strategy paid off in success that few other chief executive officers have ever enjoyed.

Boeing had Douglas bleeding and on the ropes. Although Allen had spent more than Douglas on sales incentives, it's generally agreed that Douglas poured much more money in total into the DC-8 than Allen put into his 707. Boeing's competence in producing big jets and Allen's financial strategy made the difference. For one thing, Douglas sorely missed having the prototype that formed the basis of the Allen grand plan. It wasn't enough trying to play copycat; Douglas had to pay dearly for late design changes and major tooling alterations of a kind that Allen obviated with his Dash 80. Two economists conducted different studies of the finances of the two companies in 1959 and 1960. The first study estimated that Douglas by then had spent $65 million more than Boeing on its jetliner, and the year-later report found a difference of $133 million. The DC-8 program was a financial bog of quicksand that nearly dragged Douglas down. The company never sold enough DC-8s to recover its huge investment, and would likely have gone bankrupt but for its military and government business. Arthur E. Raymond, Douglas's vice president of engineering, said of the program: "Probably it would be about the biggest project ever taken on by any company in the United States. It almost broke the company, but not quite." Douglas yet lived, and even before delivering its first DC-8 had already begun planning another jetliner to knock Boeing out the next time the two companies would fight.

Airlines had been expecting a break-in period of little or no profit or even losses from their jetliners. They charged premium fares for flights on jets to recoup their expected greater expenses. Some airlines put lounge areas ahead of the first-class seats, thinking that jet passengers would require premium service. To their astonishment, airlines made large amounts of money right from the first booking. They quickly dropped the jet surcharges and lowered fares to attract even more passengers. They replaced the fancy lounges with money-making seats. The carriers made so much money because jets turned out, astoundingly, to be much cheaper to own and operate than the airliners they obsoleted, and attracted many more passengers with their phenomenal speed, fewer refueling stops, surprisingly greater comfort, and—eventually—lower fares.

Despite the high prices of jetliners, they saved their owners piles of money because they carried many more passengers (or cargo tons) per year than the props had, and had significantly lower operating costs: They needed far less maintenance and demanded much less payout for fuel. The big jets carried around twice as many passengers per trip, they were so fast that trip times were greatly reduced and therefore the airplanes could make more trips per year, and they spent more time in the air instead of on the ground for maintenance. The passenger load was doubled while maintaining the size of the flight-deck crews, thereby halving the cost per passenger for crew salaries, which are among an airline's biggest outlays. A Boeing executive expressed jetliner economics simply: "The 707 cost twice as much as a piston airplane, but had four times the productivity, so it had two times the earning capacity."

Airlines were happy with the unexpectedly low operating expenses. Jet engines proved so rugged and reliable that they flew four times longer between overhauls than the pistons, and needed to be replaced much less often. The military had only recently discovered this. The Air Force had a warehouse full of old, unneeded B-47 engines because the Pentagon had ordered a large number of spares based on experience with rapidly aging piston engines. The biggest surprise to most airlines was fuel cost. Carriers had feared that fuel expenses would be the Achilles' heel of jetliners. Far from greatly exceeding the fuel costs of props, however, jet fuel payments turned out to be significantly lower. Not only did jets burn less fuel than anticipated, but the cost of jet fuel—kerosene—was much cheaper than that of the pricey high-octane gasoline that piston engines drank.

One quality was uppermost in travelers' minds when they thought of jetliners—blazing speed. In the 1960s, the word "jet" became synonymous with speedy. On a 707, a passenger could fly a mind-boggling 600 miles per hour instead of the 350 miles per hour of props. Boeing's big passenger airplanes flew even faster than the fighters of World War II, which now seemed slow at 450 miles per hour! The New York–Los Angeles flight dropped from eight hours to a little over five hours. On many routes, the range as well as the swiftness of jets decreased total travel time because airlines eliminated intermediate stops on many routes and made them direct flights. Jet speeds inspired the early 1960s French farce *Boeing! Boeing!*, which also appeared in translation on Broadway. Set at the time propeller-driven flights were ending, it concerned three stewardesses who shared an apartment in Paris and arranged their flight schedules so that only one girl occupied the rooms at a time. They didn't know they also shared the same boyfriend until, with much hilarity, rapid 707s got them back so soon that their stays overlapped.

Passengers were delighted to find that jets made flying much more comfortable than they were used to. Jet engines operated efficiently at much higher altitudes than reciprocating engines, so jetliners could fly above most of the turbulence that often made prop flights so rough. Their swept-wing design and great speed, moreover, tended to smooth out the ride even in rough air. Amazingly, considering the earsplitting noise people were subjected to when they watched jet takeoffs and landings, passengers found jetliners to be considerably quieter than props. Jetliners freed travelers from the vibration they had to put up with on props; one airline ad, which impressed many potential fliers, pictured a boy in a 707 almost unbelievably balancing a coin on edge on his tray table. With less to go wrong than on props, jets established greater safety records. Jetliners also recorded more on-time performances because, with their great speeds, they were less affected by winds. Jet propulsion was a rare technology that exhibited virtually all pluses and—except for airport noise—no minuses for its manufacturers, operators, or customers.

Attracted by the speed and high quality of jet flying, and soon the lower fares, passengers flocked to the jetliners, causing a boom in air travel: In the first two years of scheduled jetliner flights, air travel almost doubled. For the first time, it was not just the well-to-do who could afford air travel. Soon, the number of passengers traveling by passenger airplane across the North Atlantic exceeded the number traveling by ship. This was ominous for ocean liners: By making several trips for each one made by an ocean liner, a jetliner could carry more passengers at much less cost. As a primary means of travel, ocean liners were doomed. And, only months into the jet age, few passengers were willing to travel long distances by prop anymore. United Airlines, which had given the DC-8 its first big exclusive order, had to discontinue its transcontinental prop flights until it could get its late deliveries from Douglas; the carrier's former coast-to-coast passengers were flying in 707s delivered early to rival airlines.

Although jet technology was overwhelmingly beneficial, the introduction of jetliners was not without problems, minor and major. A new medical disorder, jet lag, arose because jet flights across time zones shifted eating and sleeping schedules so fast that the body had too little time to adjust. More significantly, the problem of jet noise in communities surrounding airports surfaced right at the beginning. A few days after American Airlines started 707 service to Dallas, a sign appeared on an apartment house in nearby Fort Worth: JETS GO HOME. (Forty years later, communities, airlines, and aircraft manufacturers are still arguing about airport noise.)

Maynard Pennell stated proudly that his airplane "changed the world." The jetliner revolution started by the 707 clearly has had a profound effect upon society. A mass commercial air-travel market didn't exist before the pioneering Boeing jetliner. The tourist industry has exploded because jetliners have made long-distance travel possible for many people for the first time. The airline industry itself has grown into a giant business. The rise of multinational megacorporations owes much to the airplanes that make it easy for executives to travel from one part of the company to another, perhaps halfway around the world. Shuttle diplomacy enabled by jetliners has transformed the conduct of international politics. Scholars can now go anywhere in the world to do research or teach. Performers can do shows in New York today and London tomorrow. Professional and major college sports have expanded tremendously because teams—no matter where their home city—can play anyone, anywhere, at almost any time. Anyone with enough money can join the newly created jet set and roam the globe attending parties. The 707 and its successors and imitators have shrunk the world and made all of us neighbors to each other.

The 707 ignited a true technological revolution. The duel with Douglas replayed the clash between the Boeing 247 and the Douglas DC-3 two decades before that had started the era of sleek, modern-looking airplanes, when many travelers first soared into the skies. This time, the clash between the two rivals produced the jetliner era that took hordes of travelers skyward—and, in this rematch, Boeing came out on top because it dared greater risks.

Boeing won the first time it bet the company. But it would have to lay the company on the line again and again.

=

Besides working strenuously at his desk and drafting table in his Boeing office, and often on a table covered with Boeing work in his den at home, Dick Henning tried to make himself more attractive for promotion to management in other ways. He joined the Toastmasters Club to improve his public speaking skills, and took night courses in electronics at the University of Washington.

On March 1, 1952, at the age of thirty-seven, Dick achieved his career goal: He was promoted to engineering electrical group leader for the B-52A—a management position. The new title carried a big bump in salary, a 15 percent increase to nearly eight thousand dollars a year. There was a bittersweet aspect to his promotion: Dick had to give up his cherished SPEEA membership and activities, since he had moved to the other side of the divide between labor and management. To fulfill his personal commitment to service, he became active in his neighborhood club and eventually was elected its president.

Dick continued his design work even as he assumed new administrative duties, and this led to an unusual opportunity for him. He personally developed a wire clamp for jet engines that incorporated fiberglass impregnated with silicone to resist extreme heat or cold and corrosion. Engineers normally sign over to their companies the rights to inventions they make on the job. Boeing's patent attorneys thought the design would be challenged, however, and they considered the cost of defending a patent to be more than the invention was worth. Dick asked if he could patent his brainchild himself, and the company gave up its prerogative. In 1955, he applied for the patent and spent twenty-five hundred dollars in fees and lawyer's costs to pursue it. The patent was granted in 1960—and never challenged. Every jet engine uses around 125 of the clamps, and the devices are installed on missiles and spacecraft, too. In 1988, the last time Dick counted, some 25 million clamps had been sold. This technical achievement earned him not only professional satisfaction but also money—several thousand dollars in royalties annually for fourteen years.

Dick directed development of the electrical, radio, and radar systems for the long-lived B-52, finishing in 1958. He was profoundly satisfied by the fruits of his own labor and that of his team, which then numbered 135 engineers: "The best, most reliable electrical system for airplanes ever produced. On time and within budget. Lowest failure rate in Boeing engineering history. . . . We were exceedingly proud to say, 'This is ours. . . . We did good!'" Boeing rewarded Dick financially for his successful military jet program, giving him a bonus of thirty-one shares of the corporation's stock worth $1,247.25 and a raise in salary to $17,520 a year.

One of the highlights of Dick's managerial career had nothing to do with engineering per se. In 1954, when desegregation in the United States began in earnest with the Supreme Court decision known as *Brown v. Board of Education of Topeka*, Dick began to hire Negro engineers. He thought he signed on more of them than anybody else in Boeing then. He had faith that his hiring criteria would select good employees no matter what their color. In reviewing résumés, he always looked first at the last lines, those that describe miscellaneous activities and memberships. He checked for signs of what he described as good family values: participation in church groups, the YMCA, Boy Scouts, and similar religious and civic organizations. His approach was practical as well as philosophic: Most of his employees had to have secret clearances from the government, and people with all-American backgrounds were likely to pass scrutiny. The next résumé entry Dick scanned was the one listing schools attended: graduates from what he considered good schools rated high priority. Without consciously trying to do so, Dick was searching for people who were clones of himself culturally, one of the most common personnel selection techniques among managers everywhere—except that he excluded race from consideration.

Feeling comfortable financially in the last years of the B-52 program, Dick bought an upscale Chrysler New Yorker and, as a second car, a five-year-old blue Plymouth coupe. He took his family on vacation to New York City, where they enjoyed going to Broadway, seeing *Damn Yankees* and *My Fair Lady*. His grandest sign of affluence was the purchase of an estate on Mercer Island in Lake Washington. The island, five and one-half miles long, three miles at its widest, and little-developed although only two miles from downtown Seattle, was a fashionable location that attracted many Boeing executives. The biggest draw for the Hennings was the opportunity to enroll eleven-year-old Larry in a school system reputed to be the best in the state. The fourteen-room brick house, surrounded by over three acres of pines, firs, and alders well over a hundred feet tall in a woods heavily populated by raccoons, and including a trout pond, cost $33,500 (with mortgage payments of $168 per month). A driveway 450 feet long led to the huge house. Dick and June christened the property "Rainbow Springs." June's mother, separated from her husband, moved into an apartment in the basement. With plenty of room for a big dog, the Hennings bought a German shepherd, which they named Madchen, German for "little girl."

Dick had started smoking Camels in his sophomore year in college, and by the time of the move to Mercer Island was up to two and a half packs a day. He achieved a personal triumph when he kicked the habit in 1957.

In 1958, Boeing presented Dick his next major assignment, transferring him to the exciting new world of aerospace: electrical unit chief for instrumentation and wiring for the Minuteman, an intercontinental ballistic missile with a nuclear warhead. Boeing had just gotten the contract to assemble the missiles and manage their installation in underground silos throughout the country. Dick's first task would be to direct design of instrumentation and wiring for the prototype, to be tested at Cape Canaveral. He looked forward to an interesting job working for an interesting man—the young comer he had associated with at SPEEA, T Wilson.

8 ‖ Beating the Competitors

In 1956, when Allen started planning to modify the 707 into the 720 and joust with Convair's 880 for the favor of customers who wanted a jetliner smaller than the 707, he also ordered a study to begin on the possibilities for a jetliner specially designed for the cheaper, medium-sized jetliner market. Although the 707 hadn't yet flown, and its success was still far from certain, the aircraft business demands such long-term thinking that Allen had to make moves then based on potential business conditions ten years hence. He set in motion a train of events that would lead to a choice harder for him to make than his 1951 decision for the 707.

The new model would be called the 727 (following the 707 and the 720, which was then designated the 717). It would mark a departure for Boeing—the first time the company would offer a major new airliner that had shrunk in size and range from its predecessors. For years, the developers would argue over the proper size and range for the new jetliner. Unlike the scenario in which a similar decision had been made for the 707, the arena for medium-sized jetliners was then crowded with contenders whose presence complicated the judgment. France's Caravelle was a medium-sized jetliner. Britain's de Havilland was planning an entry. Convair's 880 was still in the running. Lockheed's Electra was also still around; although it was a turboprop and not a jetliner, it offered economics for the short-range market that were tough to beat. Boeing's own 720 would take some of the market. Douglas was sure to put up a contender.

The studies showed that it was worthwhile to start design of the 727. In 1958, with design work on the 707 completed and an internal report showing the need for a project to sustain sales and employment in the early 1960s, Allen asked the directors to approve the project tentatively. They did, provided that before production he get preliminary orders from at least two of the big four airlines: United, American, TWA, and Eastern. A young engineering manager named Jack Steiner was named to head the 727 program.

Boeing's chief financial officer, Hal Haynes, whose conservative approach to the business kept Boeing sounder financially than its competitors, asked Steiner to come to his office. The engineer was shocked at what Haynes had to say. The vice president told Steiner that the 727 program would ruin Boeing financially and urged him, for the good of the corporation, to use his position to stop the project before neither of them had a company to work for anymore. He pointed out that the market was overcrowded, the 727 would cannibalize the 720's share of the market, and Boeing couldn't afford another big gamble because the 707 was in a financial deep hole and digging itself deeper every day. Steiner learned that the opponents to Boeing's entry into the commercial field hadn't been mollified by the early successes of the 707; most people outside the engineering groups still thought the company should stay with its military business and give up pipe dreams of commercial success. Steiner didn't buy their arguments at all. He remained a staunch believer in Boeing's jetliner business, and resigned himself to fighting off anti-727 sniping from within the company even as he grappled with the program's thorny technical and marketing problems. (The intracompany guerrilla warfare eventually became a case study in the Harvard Business School.)

Meeting the board's launch criteria wasn't going to be easy. The effect of the condition was to mandate prelaunch sales to both United and Eastern; TWA was in no financial shape to buy airplanes from anybody, and American had tied itself firmly to the Electra.

Allen courted both airlines but found himself in a dilemma: United wanted four-engine airplanes, to be sure its flights had enough power for reliable service into and out of its high-altitude hub at Denver; Eastern wanted a more economical two-engine airplane for its East Coast routes. During the evolution of the 727, the number and placement of engines was the hottest topic in the engineering building. Economy dictates having the fewest engines that can provide the needed power; for the same total thrust, two engines are cheaper both to buy and to operate than four. At the time, passengers and pilots alike felt safer with four engines, however, and it wasn't certain that two engines would be powerful enough. Federal regulators were skeptical about two-engine passenger airplanes, moreover.

Douglas compounded Allen's problem by announcing that it was planning to come out with a small, four-engine version of the DC-8, to be called the DC-9. Douglas tentatively agreed to sell it to United, provided that Douglas could get a second launch customer. At the same time, other competition was disappearing. The Electra, with its accidents, and the 880, with its mortal wounds inflicted by the 720, were sinking from their problems. Caravelles were proving uneconomical, and poor service by Rolls-Royce, which made the Caravelle's engines, was infuriating customers. In negotiations with airlines, moreover, the French offered the jetliner on a "take it or leave it" basis: they wouldn't modify the aircraft at all to suit individual customers. Most airlines chose the "leave it" option. Only the British Trident, which was over a year ahead of the 727 in development, and the promised DC-9 remained as strong competitors. The Trident, named for its three engines, was made by de Havilland, of Comet infamy.

Allen immediately ordered a full-scale reevaluation of the 727 program. The study concluded that Boeing could still develop a profitable 727 if the airplane were made larger than had been planned, directly countering the DC-9 and only slightly smaller than the 720. Boeing calculated that an airline operating a fleet of fifty 727s would save thirty million dollars a year over a fleet of 720s, so Allen would have to accept the end to sales of that model. The 727 would be larger than all the other airplanes in its class save the DC-9.

The newly conceived 727 would also share the most prominent features of its cross-Atlantic rival, the Trident: three engines located in the tail area, difficult to design but a compromise acceptable to both United and Eastern, and an unusual T tail, with the horizontal member at the top of the vertical member instead of at the bottom.

Allen also more sharply defined his target market and presented his engineers with the difficult assignment of designing an airplane to fit the market. The 727 would serve customers who wanted a jetliner that was economical for medium-length flights. An aircraft is most efficient at cruising speeds, and least efficient when taking off and landing. Shorter cruises mean less efficient flights and worse economics; at the same time, shorter flights compete with ground transportation for passengers, so economics become more important. The 727 would fly routes where the economics of turboprops were hard to beat, and use airports where turboprops ruled the scene. It would take off and land in a short distance, so it could use smaller airports that couldn't handle the big 707s and DC-8s. Boeing couldn't compete on price in the market: the company would compete on performance, lifetime economics, versatility, and quality. Allen hoped to garner four hundred orders.

Boeing and Douglas hadn't been face-to-face in this new arena long when the Californians blinked. The airlines had gone into a financial slump; after the initial surge of traffic induced by the 707 and DC-8, ticket sales had declined, worsening the financial burden the airlines had taken on when they bought the big jets. Few customers were in a buying mood, and Douglas couldn't meet its goal to get a second customer for the DC-9 before the company proceeded with the airplane. Douglas exercised the clause in its agreement with United that enabled Douglas to escape if it couldn't reach its target, and the company abandoned the market that would have been served by a small DC-8. Bill Allen moved quickly to agree with United to sell them forty 727s and, despite the airline recession, captured another forty sales to Eastern. He put in his own escape clauses: If he hadn't sold a total of one hundred 727s by December 1, 1960, he could pull out of the deals.

Boeing adopted the 707 fusclage for the new jetliner, thus saving on design, tooling, and learning curve ("break-in") manufacturing costs. The company incorporated special design features in hopes of attracting military purchases as a secondary market (a vain attempt, as it turned out).

Boeing wanted the 727 to be the first airliner with fully powered controls (like power steering and power brakes in a car). The industry recognized that the best job of designing controls had been done by the Lockheed engineer responsible for the Electra's controls. The people in charge of the 727 program were euphoric to learn that, of all the luck, this man had retired, sailed his yacht up the coast, and moored it on Lake Union to enjoy his declining years. The Boeing people approached him excitedly about coming out of retirement to design the 727 controls. "We convinced him he needed us to buy another yacht," Steiner explained, and the Lockheed veteran agreed to commute down to the Renton plant every day until the job was done. Boeing described his accomplishment on the 727 as a major advancement in airliner control systems.

The price that Allen was quoting the airlines for the 727 was $4.2 million. He tried hard to woo airline executives, treating them to cruises of Puget Sound on a yacht and entertaining them at dinners when they were in Seattle to discuss the 727. Wellwood Beall and his wife, Jeanne, usually hosted the airline people at the Bealls' home on Friday, and Bill and Mef Allen would have the VIPs over on Saturday. Because the airlines were in such a bad way financially, however, and skittish about a jetliner with fewer than four engines, Allen had to give up hope of landing the remaining twenty orders before his deadline.

Allen confronted his biggest decision since he had resolved to produce the 707 nine years before. By December 1, he had to choose whether to be cautious by following Douglas and bailing out of the 727 project, or be daring and commit the 727 to production despite not getting the orders he had deemed necessary. Once again, he had enormous risks to reckon with. This time, however, there would be no military orders and tooling to lessen the commercial investment and risk, and the cancellation of the excess profits tax at the end of the Korean War had ended the accompanying tax incentives. Boeing was already hundreds of millions of dollars in the red because of the 707, and estimated that cash requirements for the 727 would build up to at least $130 million before first delivery. Allen thought the airlines would order the 727 when their recession began to wane, but he couldn't be sure of that, nor could he know how long the slump would last.

Boeing couldn't afford a prototype and would go straight to production, so the technical risks would be greater than they had been in the Dash 80 days. Allen made the technical risks even bigger by promising Eastern that the airline could operate a Boston–LaGuardia–Washington–Atlanta–Miami 727 flight without refueling, and by giving Eastern an incredible guarantee: that Miami-bound 727 flights would be able to take off from a certain short, tricky runway at New York's La Guardia Airport, meet the airport's tough noise restrictions, and on the return leg land on the same runway, which had a difficult approach. The technology that would allow a jetliner to do all that didn't exist yet, and no jetliner had yet been approved for operation at La Guardia. Jack Steiner declared later, "From a technical standpoint, the 727 program must be classed as a very risky program, because the goals were known to be barely attainable—if attainable at all."

On top of the special 727 risks, Boeing of course faced the everyday risks of its volatile business, which inflated the gamble of the jetliner program. The total risk, while not as huge as the uncertainty surrounding the 707 program, was still considerable, especially given Boeing's slim financial resources. "The 727 program was probably among the largest risk ventures by private enterprise of any kind compared to the capitalization of the firm. . . . I went to Wall Street again and again for Allen," Steiner said. While he didn't think that the threat of Boeing's corporate death loomed as large as it had in the last decade, Boeing would still be crippled if the jetliner didn't work out. On the other hand, Boeing's competitive position would be severely weakened if the company's rivals seized the market for the airplane.

Allen was in somewhat the same position as Donald Douglas had been when Allen had refused initially to gamble on the availability of a big new engine for the 707 to suit Juan Trippe, and Douglas had seized the opening for his DC-8. Now the Douglas company had backed down and presented an opening for Allen. If he took it, he could win round two from Douglas, further diminishing his great rival's competitive strength and helping to secure Boeing's position at the top of the jetliner business.

At the board meeting of October 31, the directors expressed confidence in whatever decision Allen might make. Allen knew that he was in the wrong line of work if he couldn't step up to a good bet. He decided to go for it. On November 30, 1960, Allen signed contracts with United and Eastern for a total (counting an option United took on another twenty 727s) of $420 million—then the largest single transaction in commercial aviation history.

Tall—six feet three inches—and slender Jack Steiner, with a rich, bass voice as distinctive as his height, would continue to lead the 727 design program in its last phase. It's unusual for one person to head aircraft design in all its stages—conceptual, early design, final design—as Steiner did. A Seattle native of Scottish and Swiss-German extraction, he had grown up in the fine Queen Anne Hill neighborhood. Steiner came to Boeing in 1941 after graduating from the University of Washington at the top of his aeronautical engineering class and earning a master's degree at MIT. Assigned to the B-29 program, he alternated with his boss as an engineer on test flights. (So it was the boss who was killed and not Steiner in the fatal crash at the edge of Boeing Field). He rose to a major aerodynamics design position in the 707 program. Steiner became "Mr. 727," a champion of the program against all enemies and adversaries, and a super salesman to banks whose financing was needed, other investors, and customers.

A workaholic's workaholic, he spent almost every waking minute on the program. The company allowed him two full-time secretaries, one on a night shift. On many days he didn't get home until after midnight. Steiner's boss at one time, Mal Stamper, thought Steiner needed a break. Stamper and his wife invited Steiner and his wife, Dorothy, on a ski trip. A man who worked for Steiner got a phone call from him while he was in the mountains, but his voice was muffled. "Stamper doesn't want me to discuss business this weekend. I'm calling from a closet," he explained.

(Rare among executives, Steiner volunteers to point out the contributions of his wife to his career. "Dorothy took care of our three children and everything else at home while I was on the 727," he relates. Dorothy often brought dinner to his office so they could enjoy a meal together. Steiner proudly discusses how she gave him the support that helped him in his many confrontations at work. He met Dorothy, a tall blonde from Alaska, at college. He explains that one reason he didn't go for his Ph.D. was that he had to marry her so he wouldn't lose her.)

Jack Steiner was blessed by having a young head of technology, Joe Sutter, who was on his way to becoming one of the industry's top designers. As Steiner's team drove full blast toward production, the single greatest challenge it faced was the wings: Wide, high-lift wings were best for slow takeoffs and landings at small fields but narrow wings were most desirable for cruising at jet speed. Clever engineering solved the problem and got Allen out of the hole he'd dug for himself in promising to meet Eastern's seemingly unfillable requirements. Boeing's engineers devised an innovative, complex, but highly effective flap system, involving "triple slotted" flaps, that was the making of the 727. When deployed (to much whirring and unfolding that would be obvious to sometimes uneasy passengers) the flaps would increase wing area by 25 percent and radically change wing shape. (Later, a joke in the aviation community had the pilot of a 727, after taking off, telling the copilot to put the wings back together again.)

The original 727, headed for eventual service with Eastern Airlines but painted copper and yellow like the Dash 80 prototype, rolled out on November 27, 1962. In the long genesis of the 727, this represented the ninth complete design and the expenditure so far of $150 million. The airplane first flew on February 9, 1963. As it took off, spectators heard two bangs: The middle engine had surged or, in lay terms, backfired. The pilot, controlling his fear, eased off on the throttle and had no more engine problems through-out the flight. When the airplane landed safely, Bill Allen was so excited that he jumped up and came down with one foot in a mud puddle.

The surge was the first symptom of serious problems with the engine caused partly by the air intake design, which had to be slightly modified, but mostly by the haste in which Pratt & Whitney had to put the power plant together. Engines self-destructed several times on flight tests. "It was a terrible engine," as Steiner remembered. The problems took a long time to fix and triggered "a big row with Pratt," according to Steiner, although eventually the engine worked fine. Joe Sutter thought Pratt uncooperative in finding solutions, foreshadowing a major rupture in relations between the two com-panies in a later project.

Sales continued to be slow even as jetliner passenger traffic began a new period of rapid growth and the airline industry's finances improved. Allen moved aggressively to get sales going. Even before flight tests were finished, he sent the fourth 727 produced on a tour of the United States and the world to impress customers with its virtues, sometimes flying aboard the airplane himself. The jetliner showed that it was more nimble than its competitors, able to climb and descend faster, which are abilities critical to the use of small airports. Surprising even its creators, the 727 got 10 percent better mileage than expected. Hangar tests had revealed that the airplane could carry a load 10 percent greater than anticipated. In combination, these two bonuses would allow each 727 a saving of more than two million dollars over anticipated costs in ten years of operation. Not for the first time in the history of jet aircraft, cus-tomers were so impressed by seeing an actual airplane and flying in it, and studying performance figures from real (not simulated) flights, that they opened their treasuries and began to buy. The Trident never had a chance; it couldn't go as far on a load of fuel or carry as many passengers, and its operating costs were slightly higher.

The first 727 was delivered to Eastern Airlines in October 1963, and made its first scheduled commercial flight in February 1964.

Since Allen didn't have to buy market share for the 727, or use price cuts and expensive customization as weapons in cutthroat competition as he did with the 707, the 727 entered service on a sound financial footing. Hard figures on total development and production costs aren't available, but the project seems to have come in close to budget and to have broken even quickly at a low number of sales.

Boeing's jetliner program as a whole reached notable milestones as the 727 began to infiltrate airline fleets. In 1964, commercial sales for the first time exceeded military and government sales. The next year, Boeing passenger airplanes became the most widely used: 36.2 percent of all passenger airliners flying had been made by Boeing, compared with 26.8 percent for Douglas aircraft. (In 1946, the figures had been 95.4 percent for Douglas and 0.8 percent for Boeing.)

Although elated by the successful conclusion of 727 development and high promise for the jetliner's future, Boeing executives were sobered by four 727 crashes that took 264 lives in a half-year period in late 1965 and early 1966. Federal investigators exonerated the jetliner and blamed pilots for not flying the airplane properly. The pilots had failed to follow the special techniques required to handle a combination of the 727's high rate of descent and engines that took seven or eight seconds to go from idle to full power.

The tragedies had no effect on orders. The 727 sold and sold and sold, making all sales forecasts look silly. For its second jetliner, Boeing had picked just the right size, range, and qualities. By the time Boeing ended production in 1984, airlines had ordered 1,831 of the jetliners. It was then the best-selling and most profitable airliner in aviation history. Boeing emerged from the second commercial battle of the jetliner age as the undefeated, undisputed champion, stronger than ever and dreaming of even greater feats. The relatively smooth 727 program, however, had not prepared Boeing for the bruises and bloodshed it would have to suffer in future campaigns.

Wellwood Beall and Bill Allen often ate together and bantered with each other, but beneath the lightheartedness was an undercurrent that swept both men to the most traumatic moment of their careers in February 1964, the same month that the 727 made its first commercial flight. Beall was then senior vice president in charge of engineering and sales, and a member of the board of directors. He and Allen had gotten along well. Wellwood and Jeanne Beall vacationed with Bill and Mef Allen at least once, in Bermuda. They'd been neighbors at the Highlands for many years. They kidded one another, like the time Allen joshed Beall about his car. Allen drove a plain Mercury to work every morning down Route 5. One day at lunch, he needled Beall and his public relations chief, Carl Cleveland, about the fancy Ford Thunderbirds they drove. "I guess you're getting too old for other things, so you go in for these sporty cars," he smirked. Cleveland said Allen would change his mind if he ever drove a T-bird, and offered to exchange cars for a day. Allen accepted the offer. A few days later his brand-new Thunderbird joined the others parked in the garage below the headquarters building.

A legend at Boeing for his "dining room table" design of the Pan Am Clipper, Beall had become a superb salesman, especially for military products. He was well liked and respected by Boeing's customers. General Curtis LeMay, Air Force chief of staff, stayed with the Bealls whenever he was in Seattle.

Beall liked drinking. During World War II, he had quipped to a *Fortune* magazine reporter, "I used to think that the wartime diet [on business flights] consisted exclusively of airline chicken legs and double martinis," and "I have a philosophy about trouble. When I see that I'm not getting any place, I telephone my beautiful wife and invite her out for dinner somewhere. I have a couple of stiff drinks, a fine dinner, and by the time she's told me what she's had to take from the laundry, I've completely forgotten I ever had any real problems."

Beall spent much of his time entertaining customers, and that meant drinking with them—often, getting drunk with them. The challenge for executives in that position is to not drink so much that they lose their judgment. Beall had lost his sense of when to slow down or stop drinking. He got too drunk at parties for customers, behaving boorishly and embarrassing himself and Boeing. He made business deals while intoxicated that no sober executive would dream of. Allen warned him several times that he had to regain control. There had always been a tension in the relationship between Beall, the party animal, and Allen, the dour Methodist. (The only mention of Beall in Allen's diary is in 1945: "Wellwood tears telephone book in two.") In business, Beall always pushed for concessions to customers, arguing that the volume of sales produced by generosity would in the long run be more profitable than stingy deals that won fewer customers. Allen carped that Beall was giving away the store.

The tensions increased as Beall's drinking problem grew worse. Beall groused to friends that Allen always blamed him when anything went wrong. Allen told colleagues that Beall wasn't producing anymore. (Boeing hadn't won a military aircraft-development competition in seventeen years and had recently failed to win several contracts that Allen dearly wanted. It's not known if Allen faulted Beall in any way for the losses, but clearly the situation wasn't favorable to the company's military glad-hander-in-chief. With the commercial business passing the military side in volume, moreover, Beall's importance may have diminished.)

That February, Beall and George Schairer went to New York to see a customer. Beall got drunk again and made commitments that he shouldn't have. When he realized what he'd done, he told Schairer that Allen would fire him when they got back to Seattle. On the day he returned to Boeing headquarters, Allen summoned him. In a confrontation that a mutual friend described as emotionally shattering for both men, Allen, as Beall had predicted, asked for his aide's resignation. Beall, then fifty-seven years old, left immediately. After a few months, he accepted a position at Douglas as executive vice president–operations, and was elected to Douglas's board of directors. His former colleagues at Boeing saw his hand in several Douglas successes over the next several years and felt that Douglas's competitive position had been strengthened at Boeing's expense. Some wondered if Allen couldn't have worked out some arrangement to keep Beall at Boeing and away from Douglas, but the details of their parting and any realistic possibilities for alternative resolutions never became generally known.

★ ★ ★

Although Boeing had not suffered a strike since 1948, the major issue in that labor war had lain dormant, and in the mid-1960s it came back to life again. Allen had replaced the detested seniority system with a system based on performance evaluations by managers. District 751 complained that the new system was being administered unfairly, and wanted to reinstate a degree of seniority. The other major issue in the 1962 negotiations was the IAM's desire to get back the union shop. Allen, of course, vehemently opposed any slipping back to the old ways.

District 751 termed Boeing's contract offer an "insult" and described it as an "attempt to smash the union." On August 25, the membership voted to authorize a strike when the contract expired on September 15. The events leading to the Cuban missile crisis were under way, and President Kennedy didn't want a strike at a key defense supplier. Two days before the strike deadline, he appointed a special panel, the President's Aerospace Board, to investigate the labor situation at Boeing and make recommendations. The union agreed to contract extensions while the board conducted its hearings and wrote its report. Allen believed the board was politically inspired, and cooperated only because he had to.

The board's report came out in mid-January 1963. It certainly sounded politically inspired. The board agreed with the union on virtually all points and couched its findings in union-style rhetoric that could have been written at IAM headquarters. The board assumed, for example, that opposition to union shops is unquestionably evil. The report preached, "It is axiomatic that taxation without representation is tyranny. The reverse is equally true. The enjoyment of the fruits of representation without payment of one's proportionate share of the cost is similarly repugnant. . . . The Boeing management has no monopoly on either patriotism or wisdom, and some tangible recognition of that fact would be very much in order at this point." Not surprisingly, the IAM offered to abide by the recommendations, and Allen ignored them.

In late January, IAM members voted not to accept Boeing's contract offer. President Kennedy maneuvered to delay a strike further by invoking the Taft-Hartley Act and appointing a board of inquiry, which mandated an eighty-day cooling-off period. "Any interruption of the production of aircraft, missiles or spacecraft at the Boeing Company would be a serious threat to this nation's defense effort," he declared. The union suggested arbitration, but Allen refused. On March 14, Washington state politicians jumped on Boeing. The state senate called on the company "to demonstrate a sense of responsibility and moral obligation to the citizens of the community, state, and nation by agreeing to a contract settlement based on the President's Aerospace Panel's report." Washington's Governor Albert Rosellini issued a similar statement. Soon after, Allen calmly submitted another contract proposal that was little changed from the original offer. Union members again voted it down, and IAM's leaders announced that the workers would strike in early May. The day before the walkout was to begin, Boeing and the IAM agreed on terms. Allen hadn't compromised meaningfully on either seniority or the union shop, but both sides declared victory.

The seniority issue refused to die, and two years later it was back on the table again. Each side determined to win a clear victory this time. The union announced a strike for September 15, 1965. Neither Boeing nor the IAM would give in, and on the appointed day the workers walked off the job, the first time they had done so in over seventeen years.

Somewhat surprisingly, Allen made the first move toward a negotiated settlement. He offered to study Boeing's merit system and consider changes. Nineteen days into the strike, the union agreed to call off the action for six months, but set March 31, 1966, for a new strike unless Boeing submitted an acceptable proposal. In a very Boeinglike way, the company undertook an engineering approach to the study. Analysts pored over records of decisions made under the merit system and compared them with actions that would have been taken under a seniority system. They were astonished to find that around 95 percent of promotions and layoffs would have been the same under either system, although it made sense when they thought about it: The people who could do the jobs best were usually the ones who had been doing them longest. Allen therefore offered to convert to a seniority system for promotions and layoffs, except that a certain small percentage of decisions each year would be based on the company's assessment of merit. With the Federal Mediation Service catalyzing the discussions, the union bought the arrangement. Nothing really changed, but everyone was happy.

When Douglas pulled its four-engine DC-9 out of the competition with the 727 for the medium-size jetliner market, the company hadn't given up on the airplane entirely. The Californians saw a market for a small jetliner, and shrewdly decided to take that business over while Bill Allen was too busy developing the 727 to give them any trouble. Douglas changed the DC-9 concept to that of a small, two-engine airplane and put its designers back to work.

Allen, too, had recognized the market for a small jetliner but, as Douglas knew, couldn't spare any resources for it at least until the first 727 had been delivered. Meanwhile, Douglas got the small DC-9 well under way and began taking orders. At the same time, the British Aircraft Corporation had identified the small-jetliner opportunity and was developing and selling its entry in this field, the BAC-111. There proved to be a large demand for that kind of airplane, and by spring of 1964 every major U.S. airline except United and Eastern had ordered a twin-jet.

In May, with his 727 burden largely unloaded, Allen ordered a study made of the possibilities for a smaller Boeing jetliner. The review concluded that the DC-9 was an adequate although not invincible competitor worldwide, but the BAC-111 wouldn't have many takers, at least in this country. The study determined that, despite the competitors, who were two years ahead of Boeing in the marketplace, the company could make money if it hurried up and made a better airplane. Allen wasn't convinced Boeing could catch up but decided to start development of an economy-sized jetliner to be called the 737, soon nicknamed "the baby Boeing." In November, the board of directors approved the first stage of 737 development.

Allen tried to arouse interest in the new jetliner at United, Eastern, and Germany's Lufthansa, which was shopping for a small jetliner and whose routes were ideally suited to such an airplane. The Germans showed the greatest enthusiasm, so Allen tentatively considered them a possible launch customer. But when Lufthansa scheduled February 19, 1965, to make its decision on which airplane to buy and get a commitment from its manufacturer, Allen balked. He wasn't ready to move that soon and wasn't sure he wanted to move at all. As the end of January 1965 approached, some two hundred DC-9s and almost one hundred BAC-111s had been ordered—an impressive head start that gave Allen pause.

Allen also worried that Boeing would be taking on too much. He hoped to get the contracts soon for both the huge new military transport, the C-5, a Boeing idea that the Air Force was planning to implement, and the commercial Supersonic Transport (SST) that the Kennedy administration was preparing to finance. Too, it looked as if Boeing would soon have to develop a jetliner bigger than the 707 to stay competitive. The company was deeply involved in missile and spacecraft programs, and of course was busily producing 707s and 727s.

Boeing's forte was big aircraft, where the greatest profit was likely to be made, moreover, and Allen wasn't sure the company should go after the low end of the market. Boeing was in good financial shape, and the risk wouldn't be as great as it had been for the first two jetliners, but the estimated loss of $150 million if the 737 were developed but didn't sell would still be staggering. He seriously doubted that the 737 showed enough promise to justify that gamble. He deferred his decision until he'd consulted with the board of directors at the February 1 meeting in New Orleans.

Jack Steiner was now head of the 737 program, and he brought all the energy to his new assignment that he had devoted to the 727. He saw Allen wavering and felt that it was his job to make sure his program moved forward despite the boss's misgivings. One of Steiner's neighbors was Ned Skinner, a Seattle real estate developer who was on Boeing's board of directors. The Steiner and Skinner children played tennis together. Steiner got together with his neighbor and made a forceful pitch for the 737. He persuaded Skinner that the 737 was important to Boeing's future and that the company should commit to Lufthansa. Skinner was so sold on the project that he arranged for Steiner to make his case to three other outside directors—all without Bill Allen knowing a thing about it. When Steiner's support among the outside directors was added to the 737 believers among the inside directors (some of whom regarded the 737 as at least a loss leader to corral new customers for all Boeing's jetliners), Steiner had a majority.

At the New Orleans meeting, the directors successfully pressed Allen to make the Lufthansa deal and commit the 737 to production against his better judgment. He found out that Steiner had engineered his predicament, and he was not amused. He called Steiner to his office as soon as he got back to Seattle. When Steiner entered, Allen shook a finger at him and asked, "Are you aware of what happened in New Orleans?" Steiner responded that he'd heard some stories about it, but not very much. Allen demanded to know if he'd lobbied the directors, and Steiner had to tell him the whole story. Allen stuck his finger right in front of Steiner's nose and commanded angrily, "Jack, don't ever, ever do that again." He let his naughty engineer go with that and, as far as Steiner knew, never held the incident against him. Allen was now stuck with the project, and resolved to do his best with it. A few days later, he inscribed in his diary, "Get 737 going—start long pull to make it a successful program."

Lufthansa got offers from Boeing and Douglas to provide jetliners. The airline slightly preferred the 737 and liked the idea of having the special influence on design accorded to an airliner's launch customer. Lufthansa feared that Boeing might back out of a deal if no other customers could be found, however, thus leaving the airline short of the jetliners it needed. The Germans asked Allen to agree to a contract provision for a penalty of ten million dollars should Boeing renege, but he talked them out of it. During the airline's February 19 board meeting to make the choice, the chairman got the head of Boeing's airliner division out of bed at 3 A.M. Seattle time with a phone call to his home. He asked for and got the executive's personal assurance that Boeing would fill Lufthansa's order no matter what. Satisfied, the Germans bought twenty-one 737s for four million dollars each and became Boeing's first foreign launch customer.

Allen figured he also had to snag Eastern or United to make the 737 successful financially. Eastern was leaning toward a 737 purchase. Douglas felt that Eastern was the key to the success of its own program, however, and vowed not to let the order get away. Like Allen fighting for 707 customers a few years before by making major late design changes, Douglas promised Eastern that it would enlarge the DC-9 and make major revisions to suit the airline. Eastern took the company up on its offer.

That left United as a must-win for Allen. United knew it had strong leverage and used it. That airline, too, pushed for a bigger airplane, and Allen bowed to its wishes. United also wanted a long-term, financially attractive package involving a balance between their 737s and 727s, with 737 orders replacing some 727 orders. Allen agreed. On the day United was to decide, Steiner invited a couple of dozen coworkers to his house to celebrate if the decision were favorable, and to commiserate if it were not. Greased by Allen's concessions, the deal went through. United bought forty 737s and took options on thirty more. Some 150 people had actually gathered at the Steiners' by the time word came through, and they went wild, smashing down a bedroom door.

All three manufacturers of small jetliners had to choose a compromise between speed and economy: the narrower the cabin, the faster the airplane but the higher the cost per seat-mile (number of seats on an airplane multiplied by the miles covered on a flight). Douglas and British Aircraft tilted in favor of speed and so made narrow fuselages. Boeing opted for economy and gave the 737 the same wide fuselage as the 707 and 727. The airplane would be slower than its competitors by fifteen miles per hour—only a couple of minutes over the short routes it would fly—but the fuselage commonality with Boeing's other jetliners would save money for Boeing as well as the airlines because of the learning-curve in manufacturing. The roomier cabin also made the 737 more attractive to passengers than its rivals. Boeing took advantage of this for the 737 sales campaign. The company put together what the salesmen called a dirty mock-up—dirty as in "dirty pool." It was like the end-to-end mock-ups of the 707 and DC-8 cabins that United Airlines had built when it was deciding which big jetliner to buy. Customers would be led into a mock-up of a section of the 737 cabin. Walking through, they stepped into the narrower, cramped DC-9 cabin mock-up. Continuing on, they entered the still more constricted BAC-111 mock-up. It was a powerful sales tool.

The British airplane was no competition and soon faded away. The remaining contestants, the 737 and DC-9, were closely matched, but the larger battle between the two companies that made them was distinctly uneven. Since the 707 had forged ahead of the DC-8, Douglas had been Boeing's patsy, and the current clash threatened to put Douglas on the canvas for good.

Douglas was weak because of its own mistakes as well as the beatings by the Seattle terror. After World War II, Donald Douglas had gone softheaded. In one of the most incredible stories in corporate history, he had taken up with a party girl, made her his mistress, and then installed her in a powerful position in his company between himself and his vice presidents. Many executives left, and Douglas's commercial and military businesses both suffered. When the founder retired in 1957, he named his son, Donald junior, to succeed him. Junior alienated more executives, many of whom also deserted, further eroding the company's management capabilities. One big mistake the son made was to change the accounting system to write off development expenses over the long term instead of the short term. This allowed the company to look more profitable than it really was during aircraft development programs, and obscured dangerous overspending.

Douglas spent so much on the DC-8 that it came close to going out of business, and was still deeply in debt when it undertook DC-9 development. When Allen launched the 737 program, he again forced Douglas to the brink. Douglas spent too much in revamping the DC-9 to snatch the Eastern Airlines order away from Boeing. Then Douglas cut prices below cost to beat its northern rival to further orders, which came pouring in—not for a profit but a huge loss that the company couldn't withstand. By year-end 1966, Douglas realized that it couldn't survive. The company had to merge with a stronger firm or go bankrupt. McDonnell, a military aircraft manufacturer headquartered in Saint Louis and eager to get into the commercial business, bid the winning offer. On January 13, 1967, McDonnell took over Douglas and formed the new McDonnell Douglas Corporation.

The 737 made its first flight on April 9, 1967, and was delivered to Lufthansa and United in December. Although the 737 program didn't destroy Boeing because the company was in good financial shape, nevertheless it was a near disaster from the standpoints of finances, technology, and labor politics. Allen had been right in his doubts about the program: It was so compressed to catch up to Douglas that many mistakes were made in design and early production, and so many other programs at Boeing had higher priority that the 737 wasn't given the wherewithal it needed to get off to a good start. The production programs for the 707 and 727, and a project to stretch the 727, had first call on resources. Boeing was deeply involved in work on the SST, the number one development project. The company worked long and hard to get the Air Force's C-5 contract. Boeing lost the contract but immediately started on its own project to develop a huge jetliner, the 747, which had second priority for designers and other development resources. Boeing executives never revealed the development budget overrun for the 737, but admitted it was dreadful, the worst by far of the company's three jetliners. Allen had made a manufacturing decision that was partly to blame—to build a new factory near Plant II and make the 737 there, instead of Wichita, which had badly wanted the program. With hindsight, his advisers realized it would have been cheaper to make the airplane in Kansas. New employees were assigned to 737 production, learned by their mistakes in that job, and when they got good were transferred to the 707 or 727, pushing 737 manufacturing costs deep into the red. Although Steiner survived, several vice presidents were forced out because of the mess, and talented executives avoided assignment to the program because it became known as a career killer.

The first 737 had serious design problems with its wing, the flaps and slats on the wing, the nacelles (which contain the engines), and the landing gear. When flying, the airplane had more drag from air resistance than desirable. The worst mistake had been in the thrust reversers, which turn the jet exhaust backward to slow the airplane on landing. They had hardly any effect at all on the airplane's speed. Boeing couldn't fix the reversers before the 737 went into service, and had to caution pilots about using the practically worthless devices, especially on runways slick with rain or ice. Boeing spent twenty-four million dollars to redesign and retrofit the reversers. The delivery of the first 737s had been two months late, and Lufthansa management was furious about the lemons that Boeing handed them.

The most grievous blow to the 737, however, came not from any slipups by Boeing or even from the company's own unions, but from the pilots' union, the Air Line Pilots Association (ALPA). One of an airline's biggest operating expenses was crew costs. A major goal as aircraft technology advanced was to eliminate the need for the flight engineer and get the flight-deck crew down to just two, pilot and copilot. That technology had arrived by the 1960s, and all three of the small jetliners had been designed for only two crew members. FAA regulations allowed airplanes under a certain weight to be certified routinely for two-person operation. The DC-9 and BAC-111 met the requirement and were certified. The ALPA campaigned for a lighter maximum weight, and the standard was lowered before the 737 was ready for certification. It was too heavy under the new rule. The Boeing airplane would have to demonstrate its two-person capability in rigorous special tests by the Federal Aviation Administration, which would consider the results of those tests in ruling on the application for two-person certification.

The 737 passed the tests, and the FAA announced that it could be certified for two-person operation. The ALPA challenged the finding, claiming that a third crew member was necessary for safety. Ian McIntyre, author of a study of the aircraft industry, wrote of the union members, "The root cause of their hostility was classically Luddite—they were opposed to the idea because it would mean fewer jobs." The third person in the 737 did nothing and was no more useful than the fireman that unions imposed on railroads long after there were any fires to tend. The FAA bent to the ALPA pressure, however, and denied certification. The featherbedding resulted in the absurd situation where only one aircraft among three of the same general type and size was required to carry three crew members. This impediment so handicapped the 737 economically that it made few sales in the United States even after all its initial problems had been rectified for many years. For the second time since pilots muscled the 247 into an uneconomical design, Boeing airliners had been victimized by the shortsighted self-interest of the people who flew the airplanes.

Orders plummeted because of the three-person requirement and the airplane's hard-to-shake reputation as a dog. Deeply discouraged, Tex Boullioun and Hal Haynes discussed abandoning the program, but resolved to stick with it as long as there was a glimmer of hope; scrapping an airplane in production would be a drastic step, a first for Boeing, and neither man relished making the move. With sales in the United States and Europe at a level barely enough to keep the 737 program going, Boeing turned to an overlooked market—the many tiny airlines in the Third World, especially African countries. The company developed an option for the 737 that could shield engines from stones thrown up by the wheels during takeoff and landing, allowing the airplane to operate on the gravel runways often found in underdeveloped countries. Individual sales were usually only for one, two, or three aircraft, unlike the dozens of airplanes often sold at a time to major airlines, but Boeing had found a niche that kept the 737 program alive if not robust.

In 1980, Boeing embarked on a complete overhaul of the 737, producing a new version called the 737–300. The next year, a presidential panel ruled that two-man crews were safe on all airplanes in the 737's class. With an attractive new look, improved performance and economics, and the three-man albatross removed, the 737 began to sell as briskly as Boeing's first two jetliners. It successfully fought off its McDonnell Douglas counterpart, the DC-9-80, later redesignated the MD-80; Britain's BAC-111 was out of the picture, a failure. The 737 did so well that by October 1985 sales had reached 1,418, passing McDonnell Douglas's 1,400. So much money had been poured into the 737, however, and so little earned out of it until development of the 737-300, that the Baby Boeing program didn't break even until the mid-1980s, almost two decades after the jetliner's first scheduled flight with an airline. The popular, rejuvenated 737 passed another milestone in February 1990, when the 1,832d airplane rolled out of the plant, surpassing the 727 as commercial aviation's production champ. Boeing introduced further 737 models over the years and was planning new derivatives even in the mid-1990s. Thirty years after its development, the 737 was the best-selling jetliner in the world.

The small-to-medium-sized jetliners continued the transportation revolution started by their big brothers, as they became the major intercity carriers. Yet, despite the 737's importance, a person intimately familiar with Boeing's business has wondered if the 737's success in its later years outweighs the troubles it caused in its wretched youth. He suggests that an analysis of the 737's investments, profits, and losses based on the time value of money might prove sobering. Although the 737 was last in priority during development, it nevertheless did consume limited financial, engineering, and other resources when the company had too many projects competing for those resources, and Boeing's other programs suffered. If all the company's losses and missed opportunities caused by the 737 program were accounted for, it might be deemed a failure; Boeing arguably might have been better off in the long run not participating in the small jetliner market, or developing an entry later and perhaps differently than it did. A rigorous analysis is impossible, so no one today knows for sure if Bill Allen's reluctant decision in 1965 to develop the 737 then was right or wrong. It's clear, however, that costly 737 development and other events of the late 1960s combined to drag the company to the edge of financial ruin in the 1970s.

In the mid-1990s, Boeing is hard at work on a research project on the 737 that the company wishes it never had to undertake. The reason for the project goes back to March 3, 1991, when a United Airlines 737 with 20 passengers and 5 crew members was about to land at the Colorado Springs airport. Suddenly it nosed over and dived into the ground, killing all aboard. Two and a half years later, on September 8, 1994, a USAir 737 was approaching the Pittsburgh airport, a little over a mile high, with 127 passengers and a crew of 5. The jetliner rolled belly-up, banked, and plunged nose first into a woods. No one survived. Both crashes are among the few whose causes have never been found, and where nobody—at Boeing, the airlines, the investigating agencies—even has a good guess. The incidents are a total mystery. Given the thousands upon thousands of landings that 737s made before and since with no trouble, the chance of something similar happening again is obviously tiny, but Boeing engineers and manufacturing people won't feel comfortable until they've determined if they were in any way responsible.

=

In 1959, T Wilson, head of Boeing's Minuteman program, assigned Dick Henning to develop a proposal to win the thirteen-million-dollar contract for a reliability program to assure that Minuteman missiles never failed. Wilson was putting Dick on the spot; previous reliability proposals had been turned down as too costly. Dick's big moment in his new job was to take place on Tuesday morning, January 19, 1960, when he'd make an oral presentation of his proposal to government representatives. The night before, a slight infection that had been simmering in a toe flared up into a major illness. The pain became excruciating, and Dick developed a fever. At midnight, he went to a doctor and had outpatient surgery. He couldn't sleep most of the night but dozed off toward dawn. June let him sleep as long as he could and didn't wake him up for work. When Dick awoke and saw that the time was nine-thirty, he was furious at June. He rushed to get ready, sped to his office, and hobbled out in front of his audience on crutches. Boeing won the reliability contract. For this instance of devotion to duty and because of the nature of his assignment, his coworkers nicknamed him "Old Reliable."

Typically, Dick wasn't named head of the reliability program he had conceived; Boeing hired a veteran reliability expert for the job. Wilson named Dick to an important management post in the program, however, and raised his salary to $18,576 a year. Dick established the world's largest data bank of aerospace failures, including information on both military and commercial aircraft, spacecraft, and missiles; almost every Boeing civilian and military customer feeds data into the bank. In 1962, Dick was promoted to the new position of aerospace reliability assurance chief. Dick admitted that he felt "very proud to have been the first to be selected for such a venture."

After Dick had been in his new job a little over a year, he was tapped for a special assignment: staff assistant to Wilson in charge of preparing Boeing's Minuteman branch for an Industrial Management Assistance Survey by the Air Force. Again he took over a project that had been botched by others. The survey was a review of how a company controlled costs, schedules, and technical performance on Air Force contracts. Boeing had done poorly on the last survey, with ninety findings against the company—mostly, Dick believed, because the employees who responded for Boeing had submitted erroneous information and not because of real flaws. Dick understood that Secretary of Defense Robert McNamara disliked Boeing because of a disagreement on a subcontract Ford had from Boeing when McNamara had been a Ford executive, and that McNamara used the first IMA survey to justify his refusal to award Boeing contracts (although there was no hard evidence for this, and McNamara refuses to discuss his attitude toward Boeing). Working ten-to-twelve-hour days for over a year, Dick got the branch ready and prepared the responses. The Air Force turned up only nine findings against the company, a top mark, and ranked Boeing as the best in the country in systems management. Increased Air Force funding followed for Boeing, and promotions and raises followed for Dick. In 1963, he and June bought a white Chrysler Imperial.

In 1966, Dick's son, Larry, graduated from high school, got married, and was preparing to enter a junior college when he was drafted. His son, Scott, Dick's first grandchild, was born in the spring of 1967. The next year, Larry was shipped to Vietnam. A call from Larry's wife shocked Dick when she passed word that his son had been wounded in the Mekong delta. Larry won a Purple Heart but was sent back into action.

Dick began working on an informal basis with the team that was preparing a proposal for the contract to develop an Airborne Warning and Control System (AWACS); Boeing wanted to adapt 707s to the task. In 1967, his salary was boosted to $26,350, and he was formally transferred to the AWACS proposal group.

Arriving at work every day in the '69 Plymouth that he and June had bought as a second car, Dick Henning labored with the AWACS engineering team on the proposal to adapt 707s to an Airborne Warning and Control System (which next year won the contract). He disagreed so strongly with a superior's disposition of certain government funds already allotted for the project that he asked for and got a letter from the boss clearing him of any responsibility for violating terms of the contract in his area. The superior's actions eventually resulted in a fine by the Pentagon's contract audit agency for contract nonperformance, but the letter in Dick's file kept him out of trouble. "Without the letter, I'd have been hung out to dry," Dick declared.

In May 1969, Dick celebrated his thirtieth anniversary with Boeing, and the company gave him a couple of presents. First, he was promoted to engineering manager—executive grade. Second, he and June drove down to the Boeing Space Center in Kent, south of Seattle, where he received an Accutron watch at a ceremony honoring the veterans of three decades. He pronounced the evening "a night to be proud of."

His next assignment transferred him to a program that produced one of Boeing's proudest achievements—and some of its sorriest times.

9 || The Incredibles

In 1965, Bill Allen commanded wars against Douglas on two fronts. The first was the confrontation over small jetliners, where the DC-9 jumped out to an early lead and Allen unenthusiastically answered by launching the 737. The second was in the battle over large jetliners, where Douglas threatened to seize the market from the 707 with a new DC-8. The market had changed, largely due to the success of the 707 and DC-8. People had learned jets were safe, comfortable, and fast; the idea of air travel vacations for the masses was catching on; and travelers were switching from ships and trains to jets. People had more disposable income than they'd had when the jetliners first flew. As a result, every year people flew in ever greater numbers. Air traffic was growing at 15 percent a year and was expected to grow at that rate indefinitely—the number of people flying would double every five years.

The airlines wanted to handle the throngs with bigger airplanes rather than more airplanes. Larger jetliners gave economies of scale: The cost per seat-mile was lower; lower costs allowed lower fares that would attract still more passengers. Larger jetliners also would solve the problem of congested airports and airways that grew steadily worse as the plants of Boeing, Douglas, and other manufacturers disgorged more and more airplanes—the number of airliners produced was doubling every two years. Busy airports were approaching the maximum number of takeoffs and landings they could accommodate, and the air traffic control system along busy routes was getting clogged. The only way to get many more passengers into the air was to fly bigger airplanes.

Developing a big new jetliner would be horrendously expensive. Douglas, however, pulled a rabbit out of its hat, showing that it could produce a larger airplane with hardly any effort. Anticipating the need for more airplane, the DC-8 designers had made the fuselage capable of being significantly lengthened, or—as the surgery came to be called—"stretched." In 1965, they made cuts in the airplane, inserted plugs of new fuselage totaling seventy more seats, and sewed it back up again. New orders started to swing toward Douglas. Allen's engineers looked into stretching the 707, but the airplane wasn't made for that; for one thing, the tail of a stretched 707 would drag on the runway every time it took off. The designers considered making the fuselage taller and adding an upper deck, but that idea literally wouldn't fly. There was absolutely no way that Allen could forsake the market for big jets—that's where the most money was and where Boeing's abilities were unparalleled. He had no choice but to begin planning a mammoth development program on top of the 737 effort and the SST project.

Allen wanted to piggyback again on a contract for a new military transport. GE had conceived a huge new engine that would be two and a half to three times more powerful than the one on the 707. Boeing envisioned these engines powering a gigantic transport that would cut down drastically on the number of aircraft needed for airlift operations, providing spectacular new capabilities and economies. Just 12 airplanes of the size Boeing had in mind could have handled the entire Berlin airlift of 1948, which required 224 aircraft. Boeing submitted an unsolicited preliminary proposal for the company's brainchild that persuaded Pentagon officials to sponsor development of such an airplane, which the Air Force designated the C-5. Boeing then helped the officials to write the budget paper submitted to Congress to get the project started. Required to hold competitive bidding, the Air Force in May 1964 requested preliminary conceptual studies from Boeing and all other interested aircraft manufacturers. This resulted in Boeing, Douglas, and Lockheed all getting contracts to prepare final bids.

To lead Boeing's project, Allen chose aeronautical engineer Thornton A. "T" Wilson, formerly head of Boeing's highly success-ful Minuteman intercontinental ballistic missile program and newly elected vice president for operations and planning. By the April 1965 deadline, Boeing put together a proposal so big that the documen-tation filled the cargo airplane that flew it to Washington, D.C. Douglas and Lockheed produced similar outpourings: the total weight of all the contractors' documentation was 35 tons. *Business Week* magazine called the competition "the most strenuous in aero-space history." Wilson was proud of Boeing's entry; much later, he said Boeing had never been as well prepared to win a government contract as it was then (nor, according to Wilson, has it been as well prepared since the C-5). Boeing bid $2.3 billion for the fixed-price contract to design and build 115 C-5s.

A source selection board would recommend a winner to Secre-tary of Defense McNamara. Shortly after Labor Day 1965, the Air Force called the bidders together to go over the results of the source selection board review. The board had no criticisms of Boeing's de-sign; the spokesman simply said to the engineers, "You guys have a hell of a good proposal. Let's have a cup of coffee." The board did criticize Boeing for its cost projections, however, stating that the bid would have to be lowered $100 million to be acceptable. Allen could do that only by forgoing a profit for this initial order and persuading his suppliers to cut prices. He decided that would be worthwhile for him and his suppliers, considering that he might make money on future orders, and the project would save Boeing hundreds of mil-lions of dollars in development costs and result in a transport that the company would use as the basis for a highly profitable jetliner. Allen sliced his bid, and the board recommended that the contract go to Boeing. Boeing officials who had gone to the meeting, including Bill Allen and T Wilson, celebrated their great victory on the flight home; one of them remembers that they all "got stewed."

McNamara's official decision was announced publicly on Sep-tember 30, 1965: Lockheed. Allen and Wilson were incredulous.

Lockheed had bid an absurdly low $1.9 billion. McNamara had made his decision on price alone and a promise by Lockheed to improve its much inferior design. Boeing and other observers had another explanation, however—Lockheed's political clout and savvy. Lockheed would build the C-5 at its plant in Marietta, Georgia, a half hour away from Atlanta. Senator Richard Russell of Georgia was chairman of the Senate Armed Services Committee. Anything Russell may have done was behind the scenes, but Boeing strongly suspected that his intervention—on top of McNamara's reputed dislike of Boeing—was the real reason the secretary again overruled the source selection board, as he had done when the board had recommended Boeing for the TFX fighter contract. Berkeley Rice, author of a book on the C-5 affair, wrote that Lockheed executives deliberately bid much less than they knew the plane would cost: "Much of the trouble with the C-5 program was due to a deliberate buy-in by Lockheed. . . . Lockheed was probably counting on later design changes and repricing to raise the price well beyond that of the contract."

Wilson, heartily seconded by other executives who worked on the C-5 proposal, puts Boeing's view of the competition succinctly: "We were screwed." A member of the source selection board agreed. "There's no doubt that Boeing got screwed," he admitted. The incident further increased the contempt for Robert McNamara felt by many (and quite possibly all) Boeing executives who worked on defense programs and proposals while he was in charge. "Probably the worst secretary of defense the country ever had," was one executive's unkind assessment. "About as useful as George McGovern," said another in the business world's ultimate put-down.

(As the source selection board had predicted, Lockheed's C-5 project ran way beyond its time schedule and budget. Lockheed incurred an unprecedented overrun of two billion dollars for fewer planes—81 instead of 115—and thus tripled the price per plane. It was the first defense program to have an overrun exceeding a billion dollars, and was one of the costliest military projects in history.)

★ ★ ★

Boeing had begun laying preliminary plans for a large new four-engine commercial jetliner based on the new generation of powerful new engines even before the C-5 competition took place. Engineers drew rough designs for double-decker airplanes carrying 250, 300, and 350 passengers. The company printed brochures about each airplane and made presentations to the major airlines, soliciting reaction. To Boeing's surprise, nearly all the airlines went for the largest airplane, the 350-seat model.

Juan Trippe of Pan Am was especially enthusiastic about the big airplane, and suggested that it be made even bigger, to hold 400 or more passengers. He envisioned an airplane that would be the cheapest ever to fly, with seat-mile costs some 30 percent lower than that of the 707. Trippe was eager for Pan Am to be the first airline to fly the new giant jetliner for two reasons. One, he wanted to maintain Pan Am's reputation for always being first with the latest and best aircraft. Two, so-called launch customers could influence the characteristics designed into the aircraft, so Trippe would be in a good position to get exactly the jetliner he wanted for Pan Am. For its part, Boeing wanted Pan Am as the launch customer. Pan Am was the world's dominant international carrier, and Boeing, using the same reasoning as on the 707 program, felt that a large initial order for the new airplane from Pan Am would force the other airlines to order the jetliner for themselves.

Every summer, Boeing rented John Wayne's yacht, the *Wild Goose*, and Bill and Mef Allen took Trippe and other business associates to fish for salmon and trout in Alaskan waters. On the voyage in late summer of 1965, the Trippes and two other couples went along. During the cruise, Trippe solidified his intention to be the launch customer for the new plane.

On Allen's return to Seattle, he ordered the design effort on the "new technology plane," as it was then called, to begin immediately. As overall head of the program, Allen chose the man who had headed the immensely successful engineering effort on the 727, Jack Steiner. He promoted Steiner to vice president–product development.

Joe Sutter, who had played important roles in developing the 707, 727, and 737 was chosen to be head engineer and designer. He was on vacation at his summer cabin on Hood Canal, a fjordlike part of Puget Sound southwest of Seattle that—uncommon in those waters—has temperatures warm enough to permit swimming. The cabin didn't have a phone, but Sutter had left the number of a neighbor for emergencies. His boss reached him through the neighbor, informed him of his promotion, and told him to forget his vacation and return right away—Allen was in a hellacious hurry to get the new airplane under way. (Ruefully, Sutter says this was typical: "I don't think that I had more than one week off at a stretch in forty years.") Although Sutter was delighted at his elevation and rushed back, he viewed it as kind of a consolation prize. He thought Boeing was putting its top talent into the more glamorous, more technologically challenging, and potentially more profitable SST project; engineers on the way up were being assigned to the SST.

The big new jetliner became the second of the two Boeing airplanes identified primarily with one man, as the 727 had been linked with Jack Steiner, and that person was Joe Sutter. Like Steiner, Sutter had been born in Seattle and went to the University of Washington to study aeronautical engineering. In his senior year, he happened to be on a hill overlooking Boeing Field, watching the airplanes, when test pilot Eddie Allen tried to land his flaming, smoking B-29 and crashed into the factory on the edge of the field. No university lecture could have impressed Sutter more with the dangers of aviation and the responsibilities of aircraft designers. Having been in the Naval ROTC, Sutter entered the wartime Navy as soon as he graduated in 1943. When he got out in 1945, he worked briefly for Douglas and then came back home to work for Boeing, where he was assigned to Stratocruiser development. He remained on the commercial airplane side and rose fast, his promotion to his new post and a raise to $29,565 a year being the latest recognition of his abilities.

Although Trippe was serious about ordering the new airplane, he didn't want to commit Pan Am irrevocably until the winner of the C-5 competition was chosen. When he learned before the official announcement that Lockheed had won, he immediately phoned

Lockheed chairman Robert Gross and asked if he wanted to build a commercial version. Gross, knowing (as the government did not yet know) that Lockheed would have its hands full with the C-5, told Trippe he'd get back to him when Lockheed was ready. (He never did get back.) Douglas for the moment was happy with its stretched DC-8; although the company was thinking about building a bigger airplane, there was no sense of urgency. Trippe couldn't wait for either Lockheed or Douglas, so he decided to cement the deal with Boeing.

On October 28, Boeing sent a long official letter of intent to Pan Am. When signed by Pan Am, the document would commit both companies to exercise their best efforts to launch the new airplane. By then, Boeing's new jetliner had been given a model number: 747. The letter described the 747 as an airplane that would carry 350 to 400 passengers—three times the size of the 707—fly at nine-tenths the speed of sound, cover a range of nearly fifty-nine hundred miles, and cost fifteen million to eighteen million dollars. The letter declared Pan Am's intent to buy 25 747s, and stated that Boeing would be under no obligation to continue development of the airplane if the company could not get preliminary firm orders for fifty aircraft. According to the terms, Pan Am would agree to graduated payments beginning immediately after signing the contract and ending with payment of half the total price for all airplanes six months before delivery of the first aircraft. (Normal purchase terms called for only a 25 percent down payment.) In recognition of Pan Am's role in sharing the risk and financing, the airline would also share in the profits of the first 150 airplanes. (Pan Am didn't expect to make any money from this provision, figuring that Boeing wouldn't break even until at least 200 airplanes had been sold.)

The letter also contained specifications on delivery date and weight that would later cause one of business history's titanic corporate clashes. The agreement called for the first aircraft to be delivered in the last quarter of 1969, in time for the big Christmas travel season, and a "substantial number" to be delivered before the summer (the tourist season) of 1970—an incredibly short development and production schedule. And a seemingly innocuous clause specified the plane's weight—no more than 550,000 pounds—which was important to the carrier because each excess pound cuts into profits.

Allen and Trippe scheduled a meeting about the airplane at Pan Am headquarters in New York on the Monday after Thanksgiving weekend. Allen recorded the plans for the meeting in his diary that weekend, noting his concern with the risk involved in using private funds to develop a commercial airplane on the same scale as the multi-billion-dollar C-5: "On Monday I go to New York for meeting with Pan Am on 747. The big problems confronting the Boeing company are: 1. Should we go forward on 747, a large subsonic transport capable of carrying up to 400 passengers—or for use as a cargo plane. The risk would be enormous. . . . It is becoming clear to me that if we move forward on 747 we should raise some equity capital. . . . The risks are becoming so great that we need more of a capital margin than we have."

Allen's mention of the 747's use as a cargo plane was an important point. He and Trippe expected that virtually all overseas passenger flights in ten years or so would be made by SSTs, and so wanted 747's designed to be easily modified to carry cargo. It was to be the first commercial airplane ever designed from the beginning with special provisions for carrying cargo.

On December 22, Bruce Connelly, head of Boeing's airliner division, sent a follow-up letter of intent to Trippe restating and refining the provisions of the earlier letter. It pinned down delivery of the first two airplanes to November 1969 and guaranteed that Pan Am would get most of the first 747s made. (Trippe had refused to sign an earlier draft of the letter because those guarantees weren't strong enough.)

Allen and Trippe both wanted to develop and produce the 747 as fast as possible. Allen had to stanch the flow of orders going to Douglas for its stretched DC-8—which first flew in 1965—and head off Boeing's competitors, who also knew the needs of the airlines and were likely to launch very large airplanes any day. Lockheed in particular might design a big jetliner one step behind the C-5. Allen knew the advantages of being first in the market, as he had been with the 707, and the agonies of playing catch-up, as he was doing with the 737.

If any other company should build a competitive large jetliner before the 747, Trippe's rivals would buy it and get ahead of him in the transoceanic market. Pan Am badly needed more airplanes quickly, but Trippe, who always seemed in a hurry anyway, had decided to wait for the next generation. Trippe couldn't wait too long, however, and had a much greater sense of urgency than Allen. Allen and Trippe both wanted to get the 747 out and serving as many years as possible before the SST made it obsolete as a passenger airplane.

To save design and production time, Sutter decided to make the 747 essentially a greatly enlarged version of the 707, the airplane it was to replace. He'd hardly advance the technology at all. He expected that carryover from Boeing's preliminary work on the C-5 would also save some time.

All three of the world's major jet engine manufacturers wanted to be selected for the 747. Rolls-Royce planned a radical departure in technology: using a composite material (fibers embedded in a plastic matrix) instead of metal for the fan blades. Sutter met with Rolls's chief engineer at the Englishman's suite in New York's Ritz Towers hotel. The engineer had prepared a dramatic demonstration of the ruggedness of Hyfil, as Rolls called the composite. He strode into his bedroom and came back carrying a Hyfil blade. "Watch this," he bid, and swung the blade down on a coffee table. The blade sliced right through the thick wood, and the engineer stepped back, looking smug. Unfortunately for Rolls, coffee tables didn't often enter engines during flight, so the FAA didn't consider them a significant threat to airline safety. Big birds were a threat, however, and only a chicken test would satisfy the FAA and Boeing.

Chicken tests are assuredly the most ludicrous scientific procedures in the world, especially since they're conducted solemnly in the advanced engineering facilities of the high-tech aerospace industry. Their purpose is to ascertain how the vulnerable parts of a jetliner will react when the airplane collides with heavy birds while it's zooming along at close to the speed of sound. These occurrences happen often enough to be a major concern to governments, airlines, and aircraft manufacturers. The experimenters load live chickens (properly anesthetized, the public relations people are quick to make clear) into large, compressed-air cannons. The big guns are then aimed at the engines, windshields, or other targets on stationary airplanes. When engines are involved, tests are run at various throttle settings. At the command to fire, the chickens, martyrs to progress, are shot with jet speed at the bull's-eyes. It's easy to identify the senior people in the laboratory groups—they're the ones who don't have to mop up afterward.

The Hyfil blades flunked the chicken test. They disintegrated when the birds were shot into the mouths of Rolls engines. Boeing engineers traveled to England several times, furthermore, and concluded that the technology was premature; they were sure the blades would not hold up long in use, birds or no birds. Boeing executives also thought Rolls's manufacturing capabilities and financial resources were inadequate. Boeing scratched Rolls from the competition.

The engine GE was producing for the C-5 wasn't directly suitable for the 747; in particular, it was too slow and noisy for a jetliner. GE found the differences so great that the company would have to mount a separate development program to produce the engine Boeing required. Jack Parker, head of GE's engine business, thought the ambitious three-year timetable for the 747 was absurd, especially since engines normally took a year longer to develop than airframes. C-5 engine development would have top claim on GE's engine resources, moreover. Parker called Bill Allen and told him GE couldn't possibly make the engine unless the development schedule were extended at least another year. Allen responded that Trippe wouldn't stand for that, so GE pulled out of the race.

That left Pratt & Whitney, which then made 90 percent of the world's jet engines. Allen felt that Pratt had become complacent, and he had hoped to energize the engine maker by giving the 747 business to someone else. Somewhat reluctantly, he turned back to his familiar old supplier. Pratt executives had no doubts that they could meet the demanding schedule, so Allen put them on his team. Pratt's eagle logo would fly under the wings of the 747.

Before Boeing would sink too much more money into the 747 project, the Boeing and Pan Am boards of directors had to approve the program. The boards would have to make their decisions without the detailed analysis of projected costs and revenues that today's boards expect, and that many other companies were making even back then. Boeing didn't do a sophisticated market analysis of potential 747 sales, nor did Pan Am do such an analysis of potential income from the 747. Allen and Trippe both relied on simple data and the informal judgments of themselves and their staffs.

Lacking good numbers, Allen had only a general idea of how much money the 747 project would take. Boeing estimated "at least" five hundred million dollars. This would be more than the initial investments for the 707, 727, and 737 combined. It would be the largest private investment in aviation history and perhaps the largest private business investment ever. Boeing had cash to spend from earnings; the 1965 annual report said that profits had "far exceeded those of any previous year in the company's history." Bill Allen estimated he could raise another hundred million dollars from a new stock issue. The rest would come from Pan Am and lenders.

The stockholders and lenders would be taking incomparable risks, even greater than those of the 707 gamble. The 747 would not use a proven military design, and Boeing could not rely on military orders if the jetliner should fail. The power plant would not be adapted from a successful military design, and the outcome of engine development, which was as risky as the airframe project, wouldn't be known until the airplanes were ready to have the jets bolted on. Boeing would rush to construct the monstrous plant needed to make the 747 as the airplane was being designed, and would rely on the builders working on their own tight schedule to finish the facility in time to make the first airplanes. The huge bulk of the airplane might present unthought-of problems. Competitors might produce big jetliners more attractive to the airlines. The 747 might not meet payload, range, speed, or economy targets—and so not sell. And, of course, projections of the need for the big airplane might be wrong, especially if the airline industry should be in another of its downturns when the airplane came out. Boeing admitted in its annual report that "the costs and overall financial risks of the program and the demands on facilities, engineering, and management are substantially greater than for any of the company's previous commercial programs. . . ." Bankruptcy was a very real possibility.

Jack Steiner believes that Allen and Trippe shared a personal motive, besides their business reasons, for taking on the 747 gamble and hurrying to complete the monumental project. Steiner points out that Bill Allen was sixty-five years old, and Juan Trippe was sixty-six. Steiner thinks both men urgently wanted to create the 747 as a monument to themselves and a farewell to the industry. "It was a situation where two men wanted to make a stake in the ground that everybody would look at and remember them," Steiner contends.

Boeing's board met on February 28, 1966, to consider the 747. Allen and his staff made presentations on the project, and board members toured the mock-up of the 747's interior at Renton. John Yeasting, president of the airliner division, presided over the presentations and gave his division's recommendations. The secretary noted in the minutes of the meeting, "During the entire presentation a large number of questions were asked by the directors, and following Mr. Yeasting's presentation of the recommendations there was extensive discussion." Board members questioned Allen's staff closely about the market for the airplane and its economics. They feared that the 747 might be so gargantuan that it would miss the market for an airplane intermediate in size between the new airplane and the 707; competitors might design airplanes of this in-between size to take away sales of 747s for the shorter routes. The staff members had to admit it was a "tremendous worry" and that there was a need for a smaller, twin-engine airplane; Boeing was conceding this market to anyone who cared to serve it. If an entry did appear in the twin-engine market, however, Allen thought Boeing could quickly produce a small 747 derivative to capture a slice of the market.

Board member Crawford Greenwalt, chairman of Du Pont, asked about the 747's expected return on investment, a quantitative measurement of the kind to which Boeing paid little attention.

Yeasting, an accountant who had been Boeing's chief financial officer before taking over the airliner division, replied diffidently that he thought someone had looked into that but he couldn't recall what figure they came up with. Greenwalt laid his head on the table, put his hands over his head, and moaned, "My God, these guys don't even know what the return on investment on this thing is!"

It must have been clear to Greenwalt and other board members that Boeing would stretch itself thin—maybe too thin—by committing itself to the project. Boeing was undergoing the greatest growth spurt in its history, in both aircraft programs and buildings. The 737 was in deep trouble and draining funds, development of a 727 derivative was taking more money, and the SST required still more spending. All the projects taxed Boeing's resources in labor and facilities. (Wellwood Beall, talking to a reporter at his new offices at Douglas, commented on Boeing's plans: "If they do the 747, they'll have to get out of the SST—you can't do everything." Boeing continued its SST project, however, and at the end of 1966 won the intense competition for partial government funding.) Greenwalt observed that if 747 development got in trouble, they could always back out. Allen, shocked, replied, "Back out! If the Boeing Company says we'll build it, we will build it, even if it takes the entire company."

Of the thirteen board members, Egtvedt and three others were missing. (Chairman Egtvedt, who for most of the past quarter-century had had little more to do than officially preside over board meetings, retired a few days later. He died on October 20, 1975.) Despite reservations, Boeing's board, by a unanimous vote of those present, approved launching the 747 project and issuing new shares to finance it, tripling the company's authorized capital stock.

The board affirmed the tentative arrangement with Pan Am that Boeing could pull out of the project if it didn't have fifty orders for the 747, and added the deadline of August 1. A pullout by Boeing would be a serious setback to Pan Am, which needed new airplanes of some kind, and preferably the 747, by 1970. Trippe encouraged Boeing to see the project through by getting Allen to agree that Boeing would pay Pan Am ten million dollars if Boeing did quit, and that Pan Am would pay Boeing ten million dollars if the company did not quit—a side bet, as it were, on the main crapshoot.

Pan Am also faced bankruptcy if the airline's 747s didn't work out. Boeing and Pan Am negotiated a final price of $18,767,000 per jetliner, and slightly higher for two airplanes that would be rigged as freighters. The sum for all twenty-five planes, with spare parts and other extras, would be $550 million, about the same as Pan Am's total passenger revenue for 1965 (Pan Am's highest revenue on record). It was the most expensive airline order in history. And that was just the starting price when the contract was signed; Boeing prudently negotiated an inflation clause, the first in the aircraft industry, which stipulated that the price would rise with increases in labor and wholesale costs. Fifty percent of the amount due had to be delivered half a year before Pan Am got its hands on the first 747, and before the FAA decided whether to certify the aircraft. Ground support equipment at all the airports used by the leviathan of the air would be a separate major investment in itself: larger baggage carts, stronger airplane tugs, new lifts for cargo containers, et cetera.

On April 12, 1966, on the fifty-second floor of Pan Am's new curved tablet of a building atop Grand Central Station, Trippe's board of directors approved the contract with Boeing, which incorporated most of the provisions of the letters of intent; the specified weight, however, had risen to 655,000 pounds. The contract was signed the next day.

On the same day that Pan Am's board met, the third company in the daring partnership, Pratt & Whitney, officially committed to developing and building the engines. Boeing's contract with Pan Am called for Boeing to take complete responsibility for engine selection and performance. (Today, airlines negotiate separately with engine manufacturers.) By developing a commercial engine without a military predecessor—the first time this had been attempted—and having at least a year less than usual to do it, Pratt was also taking a gamble that could bankrupt the company; the corporation would

George Schairer sent this historic letter from Germany to Boeing only days after the shooting stopped, explaining the swept-wing concept that he had found in captured German files. *The Boeing Company Archives*

A B-47 flies over farmland near Wichita, where it was made. Boeing's original jet airplane, the bomber first flew on December 17, 1947, and gave Boeing the lead in jet technology. *The Boeing Company Archives*

Union members walk a picket line during the bitter 1948 strike of almost five months, Boeing's longest work stoppage. *The Boeing Company Archives*

Archie Logan (center), the industrial relations manager who helped to crush the Machinists' union in 1948, signs an agreement. Looking on are the union's District 751 president, Harold Gibson (left), and Boeing labor executive James Esary. *The Boeing Company Archives*

A Stratocruiser, Boeing's luxurious airliner version of the C-97 military cargo aircraft (in turn based on the B-29 bomber), emerges from the factory in the late 1940s. *The Boeing Company Archives*

Five of the six men who designed the B-52 over a weekend in a hotel room in Dayton, Ohio, discuss the legendary incident. Left to right: George Schairer, holding the wooden model he carved that weekend, Vaughn Blumenthal, Maynard Pennell, Ed Wells, and Art Carlsen. (Bob Withington is missing.) *The Boeing Company Archives*

The B-52, the second and last jet bomber Boeing ever designed, takes off from Boeing Field on its maiden flight on April 15, 1952, which Ed Wells then called "the most successful first flight of any aircraft the company has ever built." *The Boeing Company Archives*

Bill Boeing (left), in his mid-seventies and long retired from his company, and president Bill Allen look over the Dash 80, the 707 prototype, under construction. *The Boeing Company Archives*

The Dash 80, the prototype to both the 707 and the first jet military tanker, the KC-135, takes off from Renton Field on July 15, 1954, for its first flight. *The Boeing Company Archives*

The big 707, the world's first successful jetliner, flies over the Cascade Mountains. The 707 made its first scheduled commercial flight on October 26, 1958. *The Boeing Company Archives*

VIPs tour the cabin of the medium-sized 727 on rollout day, November 27, 1962, while stewardesses of the first airlines to fly it pose for the cameras. *The Boeing Company Archives*

Jack Steiner, "Mr. 727" and one of the foremost design engineers in jetliner history, poses with models of the 727 (lower left) and three of the other airplanes he worked on: 747 (upper left), 707 (upper right), and 737. *The Boeing Company Archives*

The misty vision of Mt. Rainier, the massive dormant volcano in the Cascades that symbolizes Seattle, looms behind 727s and 707s parked at Renton Field. *The Boeing Company Archives*

Workers at Renton put the finishing touches on a 737, Boeing's smallest jetliner, nicknamed "Baby Boeing." The 737 entered service on February 10, 1968. *The Boeing Company Archives*

Bill Allen (left) and his long-time friend and business sparring partner, Juan Trippe, head of Pan Am, get together at an industry affair. *The Boeing Company Archives*

Joe Sutter, designer of the 747, stands near the first of his creations to roll out. Retired, Sutter has urged that his 747 be stretched, which seems likely for the latter 1990s. *The Boeing Company Archives*

place about a billion dollars at risk. In some respects, Pratt's bet was even riskier because there are more uncertainties in developing an engine. With only slight exaggeration, a Pratt executive averred, "Designing an engine is an art, not engineering." The total to be spent by the three companies together on their joint program was probably exceeded in history only by major military projects. Except for some limited escape provisions, there was no backing out now; the perilous journey for all the partners had begun.

Allen lined up his financing for the 747 program: raising $122 million by selling stock, $130 million from convertible debentures, commitments from institutional lenders for $175 million, and revolving credit from a group of banks.

Even though engineers had been at work on the design for half a year, critical final decisions had not yet been made on the airplane's shape and precise size. The designers couldn't simply lengthen the 707 fuselage to accommodate the trebled passenger load; a giant pencil-shaped plane wouldn't work. The designers decided to keep the 707 fuselage width but to lengthen it to the limit, double the height, and give it two decks. Trippe loved the idea, and looked forward to promoting double-deck flights in Pan Am's ads. Optimism over the double-decker proved premature, however. The engineers ran into insoluble problems in trying to provide for ground operations—servicing, cargo handling, and especially emergency evacuation.

The designers hadn't seriously considered widening the fuselage because it would add significantly to the airplane's weight. Stymied on the double-decker, they looked again at the wide cabin, and this time saw several attractions. A circular fuselage with two aisles in the cabin and holding nine passengers abreast, which Boeing's advisers at Pan Am considered an attractive arrangement, would also exactly accommodate two standard-sized cargo containers placed side by side. Compared to the double-decker, the wide-body would also allow more efficient routing of the wires, cables, and pipes that run out of sight through a fuselage in the hollows between the inner and outer surfaces. The plane also looked well proportioned— better than the double-decker—an informal criterion among aeronautical engineers that has proven sound. Chief engineer Joe Sutter figured that the substantial gains were worth the weight penalty.

Allen and Sutter had to persuade Trippe that the wide-body was better than the two decks he liked so much. Sutter thought the wide-body was so much more attractive that it would sell itself, so he had rough mock-ups made of both versions. They showed Trippe and his staff the double-deck mock-up, then walked them over to the wide-body simulation. Pan Am's chief engineer converted to the wide-body as soon as he saw how much more cargo space it offered. Trippe, keeping a poker face, said nothing. Sutter showed him the flight deck. The flight deck on the wide-body had been raised to an upper level for the freighter role that was thought to be the 747's main function in the future; the nose would tilt up to load cargo. The top of the airplane had to slope down to the main deck for aerodynamic reasons, leaving an empty space behind the flight deck. Trippe asked what the space was for. Sutter said he thought it could be used as a crew rest area on long flights with two crews. Trippe said, "No, this space will be used for passengers." That's how Allen and Sutter learned that Trippe had bought the wide-body idea. Since Trippe liked the space, Sutter enlarged it a bit. (The hump enclosing the flight deck and upper passenger section would become the world's most recognizable aircraft feature, readily identifying the airplane even to laymen for whom all jetliners otherwise look alike.)

The finished mock-up, which cost a million dollars, impressed everyone who saw it. Visitors were dazzled by their first sight of an airplane cabin that looked more like a cavernous room than a narrow tube. When Pat Patterson, the head of United Airlines, stepped through the doorway into the mock-up, he stood there, took it all in for a moment, and then exclaimed, "Jesus Christ!" For a while afterward, the 747 was known among United executives as "the Savior airplane."

Trippe had a change of his own that he wanted Boeing to adopt. Engine manufacturers normally kept improving their designs while their engines were in service; three years after it started flying, Pratt's engine could be expected to be more powerful than it was at first and capable of propelling a larger airplane. Reminiscent of the time he bought underpowered DC-8s in expectation of bigger engines, Trippe decided he could sacrifice 747 performance in the first years in exchange for a larger airplane that would perform outstandingly when the new engines came out. Boeing complied with his wish to make the wide-body airplane longer to carry more passengers or freight.

Simultaneously with designing the 747, Boeing had to select a site for a new plant and finish constructing the factory in time for the first phases of airplane production, which would begin before the design was completed. The size of the 747 dictated that the plant be of grand dimensions, too. Boeing expected to produce seven airplanes a month at peak production. The vast volume of the main structure would put it in the *Guinness Book of World Records* as the largest commercial building on earth and one of the largest buildings of any kind.

Having learned a lesson from Lockheed about the importance of political factors in plant location, Boeing hired a consulting firm to help find a site in California, whose size gave it much more powerful congressional representation than Washington state enjoyed. California was home to most of Boeing's subcontractors, moreover, which would shorten transportation time for subassemblies. Boeing had flirted with California before, but not this seriously. The company picked a location near Oakland, across the bay from San Francisco, took options on the land, and began laying plans to build, equip, and man the new facility there. It quickly became apparent, however, that placing the plant near Oakland instead of in the Puget Sound area with the rest of Boeing would severely disrupt the 747 project. The impact would be especially hard on personnel: People involved in development would have to move, many would refuse, and replacements would have to be hired. This would slow down development and take much more time than the tight schedule allowed. Allen, perhaps with a sigh of resignation, decided that Boeing again had to abandon its California dream and keep the 747 at home.

Boeing's first choice in the Puget Sound area was near McChord Air Force Base south of Tacoma, but two homeowners at the site wouldn't sell. Boeing was considering alternatives when the fifth location on its list offered the company a package of incentives that proved irresistible. The chosen land was seven hundred wooded acres next to an airfield near Everett, an old lumber-mill town close by Seattle to the north. It offered political advantages of a sort, too: Washington's U.S. senators Scoop Jackson and Warren Magnuson ("Maggie") were both from Everett. Boeing speedily acquired the property and began digging. Together with other construction that would get under way in 1966, the Everett endeavor would constitute the biggest expansion of facilities in Boeing's history.

As an international carrier, Pan Am depended heavily on backing from the U.S. government when the airline dealt with other countries, so Trippe was exquisitely sensitive to his standing with Washington, D.C. President Johnson had asked business voluntarily to put plant expansions and capital spending on hold to curb inflation during the Vietnam War. Trippe knew that, unless he impressed Johnson with the importance of the 747 project, the president wouldn't be happy about Pan Am, Boeing, Pratt & Whitney, and a vast network of subcontractors launching a multibillion-dollar program then. Besides tending to worsen inflation, the efforts would draw heavily on aircraft industry facilities, labor, and strategic materials vital to the war. Bill Allen had to be concerned about the possibility, however remote, that Johnson would call on the companies to postpone the program to avoid sapping the country's military strength while our boys were dying overseas. Allen and Trippe met in the nation's capital, and Trippe called on defense secretary McNamara. Allen sat the meeting out because it would have been awkward: McNamara and Allen were angry with each other over three projects where McNamara had opposed Boeing—the TFX fighter, C-5, and SST. Bolstering Boeing's suspicions about the secretary's feelings toward the company, McNamara told Trippe he wished that Pan Am could wait for Lockheed to make a commercial version of the C-5. (In asking Congress to fund the C-5, McNamara had mentioned a commercial spin-off as one of his justifications.) Allen and Trippe both met with Johnson and persuaded him that their program should go forward.

With the Pan Am order secure and the 747 program well on its way, Boeing approached other airlines to sell the airplane. The first stop was TWA, Boeing's second priority after Pan Am. TWA's response was disheartening. Charles Tillinghast, head of the carrier, tried to persuade Allen to build something smaller. Although TWA needed bigger airplanes than were then on the market, Tillinghast didn't want an airplane as gigantic as the 747, or as underpowered as the model was to be at first. The airline bought the 747 only because it was the sole big airplane available and TWA competed with Pan Am on some overseas routes. Tillinghast wasn't happy, however. Eastern Airlines also gave Boeing's salesmen a frosty reception. That airline, too, tried to persuade Boeing to make a smaller airplane, needed for its domestic routes, but Boeing wouldn't—couldn't—budge. American Airlines desired a jetliner quite a bit smaller, with only two engines, and had even sent a letter to all the world's airliner manufacturers asking them to make the airline's ideal model. Boeing got the same cheerless response almost everywhere: The company had gone too far in sizing the plane; airlines wanted something big, but not *that* big.

Fortunately, however, Boeing had played its cards right in allying itself first with Pan Am. Pan Am always set the standard for the latest in air travel, and other airlines had to order the new airplane to keep up. Trippe's influence pervaded the whole industry; airlines that didn't compete with Pan Am were afraid that an airline they did contend with would buy the 747 and get ahead of them. Many airlines needed bigger airplanes, moreover, and Boeing had the only one in the large-sized market. In fact, the 747 garnered more orders before its first flight than any airplane in history (orders that could be canceled, however, if the airplane couldn't fly as fast, as far, as cheaply, or with as many passengers as promised).

After Pan Am had signed the contract, the 747 project was taken out of Jack Steiner's product development group and made a separate group befitting its importance and need for autonomy. Steiner expected to be named head of the new group and be given the chance to repeat his success with the 727. Instead, Allen made a surprising choice for leader of the project as overall manager of design, plant construction, initial production, and marketing. Completely outside the Boeing mainstream, he was not an aeronautical engineer, had never worked on an aircraft project in his life, and had made his mark with General Motors before joining Boeing in midcareer. Allen's pick was Malcolm Stamper, an electrical engineer who had worked on GM's missile programs and whom Allen had recruited four years before to build up Boeing's aerospace electronics capabilities. In June 1965, he had been named a corporate vice president, and Allen assigned him to try to make something of the company's stunted, floundering turbine division, a survivor of the postwar diversification efforts. When the 747 program started a few months later, Allen decided to save the money needed to invigorate the turbine division and instead sell the division for much-needed cash to finance development of the new airplane. He told Stamper to arrange the sale. After the engineer had sold the division, putting himself out of a job, Allen asked him what he'd like to do next. "How about working on your toughest problem," Stamper answered. Allen said that was the 747 program and asked Stamper if he'd like to run it. Stamper, who laces his conversation with self-deprecating humor, replied, "The only airplane I ever built had rubber bands on it!" Allen, Stamper's biggest booster but no barrel of laughs, didn't crack a smile. "Do you want to build it or don't you?" he responded humorlessly. Stamper snapped his quick response, "You bet!" and Allen pronounced it his.

Steiner feels that the 747 program was taken from him because he warned his boss, Tex Boullioun, that 747 manufacturing would suffer a "massive overrun" of its budget unless the project were delayed a year. Boullioun, says Steiner, told him, "Maybe you're not the right guy to manage it," and maybe they needed someone who wasn't "tied in with the old manufacturing element," someone who could find a way to make the planes in the allotted time without spending all the money Steiner thought the compressed program would take. Others have suggested that Allen had soured on Steiner because of the engineer's lobbying of the board on the 737, but Steiner doesn't believe this. Allen was grooming Stamper for higher office, and it could simply be that the 747 challenge was the best means available to prove Stamper in a highly visible mission and let him learn the aircraft business.

One of Stamper's first decisions, in early 1966, was to set December 17, 1968, the anniversary of the Wright brothers' first flight, as the target for the first 747 flight. Considerably less than three years away, the deadline would be almost impossible to meet. Because of the terribly short timetable, construction was as rushed as the rest of the project. Finding the work site to be an area of hills covered by alders and firs, the builders bulldozed the tops of the hills into a flat, clear space so construction could begin. (Before the job was over, the Caterpillar and John Deere equipment would move as much earth as their predecessor machinery had moved in building the Panama Canal and the Grand Coulee Dam combined.) It began to rain while the work was in progress, and kept raining so long that even Seattleites, used to frequent drizzle, began talking about the deluge. It rained for a memorable sixty-seven days straight and turned Boeing's property into a mud puddle of—fittingly— gargantuan extent. The skeletons of buildings arose despite the obstacles, and before long the first enclosed structures appeared. As soon as part of a building was enclosed but before there was heat, office equipment was moved in, and engineers, staff people, and managers reported to work, often in hard hats. Stamper boosted morale by declaring to these employees that they were doing an incredible job and distributing hats, T-shirts, and coffee mugs with the logo THE INCREDIBLES printed on them.

No jetliner Boeing had ever produced (or ever would produce, through at least the 777) had been developed on such a short schedule. Jetliners generally went through years of preliminary design, when the concept was probed thoroughly and abundant data were gathered for the more detailed design phase; the 747 had only about half a year of preliminary design, with almost no opportunities for data-gathering studies. That was all the time Sutter had to define the airplane, and compute its weights, performance, and cost-related data. The 747 had little more than three and a half more years of detailed design before being handed over to the customer; designers usually spent much more time than that on the details. Because of the telescoped schedule for 747 development, many design tasks that would ordinarily take place one after the other would instead have to be done at the same time. Sutter called the 747 working environment "a real pressure cooker."

Sutter had to contend with office politics as well as technical problems. The engineering vice president appointed an assistant to Sutter who acted as if he were in charge. Sutter went to the vice president and laid it on the line: "It's either me or him." The assistant was transferred to another project.

The rushed schedule caused problems, complicated by more design work having to be done than the company had counted on; almost nothing from the C-5 studies proved worthwhile in the 747 program, so Sutter couldn't skip any work. One problem was especially insidious. Month by month, the difficulty steadily worsened until by mid-1967 it was recognized as a crisis that could undo the whole program. The predicament was caused by the airplane designer's worst enemy: weight. The 747 was getting too fat. The jetliner was ballooning in the rush to throw the design together and make it suitable for cargo as well as passengers. The excess poundage meant that the airplane could carry fewer ticket-buying passengers or less revenue-generating cargo. A special team was assembled and told to find every unnecessary ounce in the design and cut it out. The fat-finding squad got rid of ten whole tons, but it still wasn't enough. Boeing's grapevine hummed with the word that Sutter was having trouble hanging on to his job because of the crisis.

On June 9, 1967, Bruce Connelly, then Boeing's vice president–sales, sent a letter to General Larry Kuter, Pan Am's vice president–technical staff, saying that the 747 would exceed the 2 percent weight variance allowed in the contract. The amount by which the 747 was overweight at that point was unclear, but seemed to have been close to another ten tons; Kuter calculated that the fat represented a loss to Pan Am of perhaps twenty thousand dollars per flight. Pan Am replied that Boeing would be held to the contractual commitments. Boeing retorted that most of the extra weight was due to changes and additions that Pan Am itself had insisted on. Pan Am disagreed. Sutter gave a presentation to Pan Am trying to prove that two-thirds of the weight gain could be attributed to the airline's gluttony and not Boeing's carelessness. Pan Am charged that the problem was really Boeing's miscalculation of weights at the outset.

The abbreviated development schedule resulted in other aircraft features deviating from the contract as well. Pan Am found fault with almost every aspect of the design: range, payload, speed, cruising altitude, and engine noise. The airline told Boeing that the 747 now proposed was completely unacceptable. In July, at a series of meetings in Seattle about the crisis, the Pan Am staff squeezed Boeing hard to fulfill the contract to the letter. Fighting deviously for some "give" from Pan Am while Trippe's team was in Seattle, Boeing announced an order for thirteen 747s that it had received in May from United Airlines. The story made front-page headlines in Seattle's newspapers; the Pan Am staff felt that Boeing was trying to get the message across that Boeing didn't depend on their business entirely. In October, continuing the war of nerves, Pan Am let Boeing know that Kuter was meeting with Douglas to discuss plans for the new large airplane that Douglas was thinking of building.

Pan Am notified Boeing that grounds existed for a breach of contract suit and pressed harder for Boeing to live up to the letter of the contract. In Seattle, Allen met with his legal advisers to discuss how to respond to a possible suit. As Kuter admitted later, however, Pan Am never seriously considered suing. The airline knew it was demanding too much from Boeing; Pan Am privately thought of the contract specifications as ideals. Winning a suit, moreover, would either force cancellation of the 747 and thus bankrupt Boeing, or force Boeing to change partners in designing the 747 and modify the design to satisfy Pan Am's competitors. Either way, Pan Am would lose out on getting a jetliner it desperately needed, a good airplane if not the best possible. The airline might also lose one of only three companies able to provide airplanes. Under Trippe's direction, Pan Am's strategy all along had been to negotiate the hardest contract it could, and then use it to hold Boeing's feet to the fire to be sure of getting the best airplane under the best terms. Trippe wouldn't ruin Boeing—but he fully intended to exact severe financial penalties from his 747 supplier for missing the targets.

Commenting later on how hot he had made things for Boeing, Trippe said, "Bill Allen took his coat off a few times." In the way that many politicians fight furiously against one another one minute and socialize amicably the next, however, the Trippes and Allens played golf at the Homestead in West Virginia, the Trippes had the Allens to their vacation house at the swank Cotton Bay Club on Eleuthera in the Bahamas, and the couples took their annual August cruise together to fish in Alaskan waters.

Boeing didn't feel it could squeeze out any more weight from the 747. The only way remaining to meet the performance specifications Pan Am insisted on was to increase the thrust of the engines. Allen asked Pratt to build an even bigger engine than planned. Already held to a nearly impossible schedule, Pratt agreed to the increase but asked for a delay in the program. Allen's own designers would have liked an extension. Allen felt many pressures to continue on the present timetable, however. First was Pan Am's adamancy about sticking to the contract provisions, including the schedule. Boeing wouldn't get the agreed payments from Pan Am needed to finance the project and might have to pay steep penalties if the company didn't fulfill the provisions; Boeing figured that a delay of six to nine months would cost the company $250 million to $400 million. Second, orders for the 747 were pouring in, and Allen felt that a delay would turn off the spigot. Allen also felt that a delay in filling the orders would be bad for Boeing's reputation. Allen didn't want to lose any of the lead he had over his competitors, moreover: Douglas and Lockheed both had preliminary design work under way on large jetliners. Allen told Pratt that he'd rather cancel the 747 program than accept a delay. At that point Pratt had more invested in the new engine than Boeing had in the airframe. Pratt bowed to Boeing's pressure and promised to build a larger engine than planned and do it in the original time.

The bigger engine would of course cost more than the original engine—$350 million more. Pan Am expected Boeing to pay the difference; Boeing said Pan Am should pay it. This disagreement widened the conflict between the two companies, which became so heated that the 747 deal came close to coming apart. Pratt brought the program back from the brink by offering to absorb the cost increase itself.

Because so much had to be done simultaneously, 747 development demanded more engineers than usual on a design project. According to one estimate, well over six thousand engineers—more than half Boeing's total engineering force—were working on the 747 at one point. The number vastly exceeded the figure that Allen and his advisors had expected, and represented huge unplanned expenditures. To make matters worse, the problem caught Allen and Stamper by surprise; they didn't find out about the unexpected labor requirement until it was well advanced and they were suddenly faced with the need for legions of engineers. This predicament further worsened relations between Sutter and Stamper, already strained by the weight crisis (although Sutter didn't report directly to Stamper—he worked two organizational levels below him—and seems not to have been directly responsible for keeping him in the dark).

In the fall of 1967, actions by Boeing's rivals strengthened Allen's resolve to get the 747 flying as soon as possible. Lockheed started taking orders for its first jetliner. Two months later, Douglas began soliciting customers for its new large jetliner. Both designs had been influenced by the letter that Frank Kolk, chief engineer of American Airlines, had sent to all the world's airliner manufacturers. Kolk had described the kind of jetliner American would like to buy, which would be a wide-body with only two engines, larger than the 707 but much smaller than Boeing's planned 747, and aimed primarily at the domestic market. Kolk's letter had stimulated much discussion in the airline industry about the ideal jetliner for the next generation; as the result of wordplay on Kolk's name, a homonym of a popular soft drink, his concept became known in the industry as the "Kolk machine."

Most of the other airlines agreed that the best jetliner should be smaller than the 747 but larger than the Kolk machine, with three engines. TWA pushed Lockheed to develop that airline's particular three-engine vision, while United got behind Douglas; although both airlines influenced the designs, neither exerted the powerful force that Pan Am focused on Boeing. Lockheed (which never did make a jetliner out of its giant C-5 military transport) called its airplane the L-1011, or the Tristar; Douglas named its three-engine offering the DC-10. Lockheed selected Rolls-Royce to make engines for the L-1011. Rolls, like Pratt, agreed to build the engine in three years; Rolls seemed confident that it could be done, unlike Pratt, which by late 1967, at least, was having its doubts. Douglas bought its DC-10 engine from General Electric.

Fortune magazine, referring to the Lockheed and Douglas airplanes as "airbuses," ran an article titled WHY BOEING IS MISSING THE BUS, which criticized Boeing for developing the 747 monstrosity and not pursuing what the editors deemed the smarter course of building something closer to a Kolk machine. The article clucked that the 747 "conceivably might become the first Boeing airliner since the Stratocruiser not to show a substantial profit."

Boeing had a glaring problem in its management structure in the fall of 1967, and the difficulty centered on a failure by Bill Allen. He had expected to be retired already. Almost ten years before, he had noted in his diary, "Our normal retirement age is 65. I should certainly retire by that time." Allen turned sixty-seven that September, however. He was still holding on to power, and no one had yet been designated to take over. The board of directors may have been restive; when Egtvedt had retired the year before, the directors had not named Allen to replace him as chairman, perhaps a pointed omission to pressure him into designating a new president and heir apparent before they'd promote him.

Allen was trying. Over two years before, he had chosen a successor and had been grooming him to take over—tall, good-looking John Yeasting. On July 6, 1965, Allen had written a resolution in his diary: "Implement my succession program as rapidly as practicable. I shall be 65 in less than two months. My objectives: a. Make way for my successor as soon as this can be arranged. The problem is to get the best possible successor for J. O. Yeasting as head of Commercial Airplane Division. b. Continue to serve the Boeing company. . . ." Then, on Thanksgiving weekend of 1965, he penned a follow-on resolution: "Continue to press for John to get into a position to take over." The plan seems to have been to promote Yeasting from the airliner division to the Boeing presidency. After a short time proving and seasoning himself, Yeasting would have been made CEO. There's no indication why this didn't happen in late 1965 or early 1966; there had surely been time to have found a successor for Yeasting in his divisional job by then. Yeasting was sure that the outside directors thought him too old—only five years younger than Allen. Thwarted in his first choice, Allen reportedly picked as his second choice large, mustachioed George Stoner, who had shone as head of Boeing's aerospace business. If the report is true, Allen was frustrated again, because the board also passed over Stoner. At some point, Allen is said to have wanted to pass the mantle to accountant Clyde Skeen, but Skeen left to go to another company. Allen, desperate to find someone, may have signaled another choice at the board meeting of February 28, 1966. As management's candidate for the board opening created by Egtvedt's retirement, he proposed a talented young executive: T Wilson. Wilson had been elected vice president in 1963 when he was in charge of the Minuteman missile program (Boeing's most successful nonairplane venture), and a year later Allen put him in charge of operations (Boeing's word for manufacturing) and planning. Wilson was elected to the board and named executive vice president in 1966. Wilson, a basic man, is blunt about the frantic selection process: "Allen got his tit caught in a wringer and I was in the right place at the right time."

Wilson's performance impressed Jim Prince, Allen's closest adviser after Ed Wells, who had moved from their old law firm to Boeing as Allen's assistant. He pushed for Wilson's confirmation as the next CEO. Swayed by Prince's arguments, Allen firmly settled on Wilson and recommended that the board of directors officially tap him to be Boeing's next leader. On April 29, 1968, the board elevated Allen to the chairmanship and named Wilson president (at a salary of $130,830 a year). Allen retained his responsibilities as CEO and thus still ran the company.

In contrast to the usual tendency of managers to hire and promote people like themselves, Allen had chosen a man about as unlike him as anyone he could find at Boeing. Thornton A. Wilson, forty-seven years old, was a rangy six-footer with a craggy, impassive face and dark brown eyes under slightly drooping lids. He had an aquiline nose like Charles de Gaulle's, framed by big ears. He was a Democrat in a world of Republicans. Born February 8, 1921, in Sikeston, Missouri, he spoke in midwestern nasal tones. He was raised on a farm; because of his earthy language, artless, down-home manner, and rustic visage, he would have looked natural all his life in a straw hat and bib overalls. Like his father after whom he was named, Wilson was always called simply "T." (At Boeing, he signed memos by just scrawling a big *T* at the bottom.) Sikeston, in the southeastern corner of the state, isn't far from Arkansas, Mississippi, Tennessee, and Kentucky; Wilson says it's really part of the South. The family farm had black sharecroppers, who so admired Wilson's father that many named sons after him. To this day, the name "T" is common in the black community in that area. The names of his mother and brother perfectly fill out the rural setting of Wilson's early life: Daffodil and Jasper. Mrs. Wilson worked as a seamstress.

In 1933, the rock bottom of the Depression, when Wilson was twelve, his family joined the legions of those who lost their farms. They moved to Jefferson City, the state capital, where his father got a job in the Missouri highway department. (He eventually became head of the department.) In high school, Wilson became a championship swimmer and coached the team in a year when it had no regular coach. (Remarkably, a teammate, John Opel, became head of IBM.) After graduation, he enrolled in a junior college in Jefferson City because it was cheap. While there, he learned to fly in the government's Civilian Pilot Training Program (but never piloted an airplane afterward). After two years, he transferred to a four-year college, choosing Iowa State University because the University of Missouri didn't have a swim team. He studied aeronautical engineering and was named captain of the swim team.

As his college years neared their end in 1943, Wilson applied to every aircraft company on the West Coast for a job. All the salary offers he got were about the same, but his fiancée, Grace Miller, was from Seattle, so he picked Boeing. He was assigned as a draftsman to the C-97 transport project, then in its conceptual stage. After he had proved his worth, the company shifted him to B-29 development, which the government had designated essential to the war effort, to shield him from the draft. He was placed in the aerodynamics section of the project. Realizing that he'd progress faster in his career if he had a degree from a school with a more prestigious aeronautical department than Iowa State, he left Boeing after the war to improve his education. First he returned to his alma mater for a year to expand his mathematical skills while teaching there part-time, and then transferred to the highly regarded California Institute of Technology. He got his master's degree in aeronautical engineering from Cal Tech in 1948.

Again Wilson applied to several companies. Boeing asked him back but North American offered the most. Boeing raised its offer higher than North American's, but Wilson drove a hard bargain, refusing that salary before finally accepting. He was placed on the aerodynamics team for the long final development stage of the B-47 before it went into production. He became an active member of SPEEA, serving as an officer, because he didn't like the way its leaders were running the bargaining unit. (No stranger to union tactics, he had led a strike by students in high school to get a new recreation area.) When the overall project engineer on the B-52 program had a heart attack, T was named to replace him for the latter stage of the program. Wilson was devoted to his work, usually reporting to the office at 6:30 A.M.

In 1952, Boeing selected Wilson for the Sloan Fellowship Program. Boeing had begun sending its most promising young executives for a year of study at the Sloan School of Management at MIT. Wilson was impressed by the caliber of the faculty. He took courses from luminaries such as economist Paul Samuelson and George Shultz (later named U.S. secretary of state), who filled him with ideas for improving Boeing. Wilson, who had married Grace, enjoyed himself immensely socially as well as academically, and described his time at MIT as "probably the greatest year my wife and I ever had." At about that time, T and Grace had their first child, a boy who became T III. Later in his childhood, little T contracted spinal meningitis and, tragically, lost his hearing. The Wilsons eventually produced another boy and adopted a girl.

Wilson led the successful Minuteman missile proposal team and became general manager of the Minuteman program. He turned down Allen's first offer of a headquarters position because he wanted to finish his Minuteman work. In 1964, when he was a vice president at the corporate offices, an executive search firm—a "headhunter"—asked him to interview for the top job at Thiokol, the rocket manufacturer. With Allen facing retirement, Wilson knew he had a shot at the presidency, but felt this might be an opportunity too good to pass up. He told Allen about the contact, saying he felt as if he were having his first affair because he wanted to have the interview. Allen told him to go ahead but not to make a commitment until they had talked again. Wilson flew to the search firm's New York office. During the interview, the headhunter admitted he hadn't realized how close Wilson was to "grabbing the brass ring" at Boeing, and told him he'd be foolish to take the slot at the much smaller Thiokol.

When Wilson's election to the presidency was announced, the grapevine at Boeing was overloaded by people trying to find out what he was like. He was described as brilliant and decisive, with superb managerial skills. Supremely self-confident, at times arrogant, he was known occasionally to ignore expert advisers and even defy his superiors to pursue what he considered the correct course. He got away with it because he was almost always right and had the political savvy to make sure his supporters always had more power than his enemies. People said he was brutally frank, nothing subtle about him, never leaving any doubt what he expected of you or what he thought of you. He was often abrupt, sometimes to the point of being rude. He tended to be autocratic, keeping his reasons for decisions to himself, unlike Allen, who relied heavily on discussion and consensus. Wilson was infamous among those who had worked with him for his impatience and short temper—and for being quick to fire or transfer people who didn't measure up to his standards or whom he no longer needed. He himself described what he called his philosophy of management: "Get rid of the bums and the cream will rise to the top." As one of his closest associates later described him, in words that marked the friend as one of Wilson's men, "There wasn't any of this industrial welfare shit with T." In the same vein, another good friend commented, "T didn't worry about people issues. His attitude was 'Screw 'em.'" You didn't cross Wilson; Steiner said he'd never have lobbied for the 737 behind Wilson's back as he'd done with Allen. Yet he had a keen memory for people he worked with and their families. (Long into retirement, Wilson was asked if he remembered an engineer who had once worked for him named Dick Henning. Without hesitation he replied, "Absolutely. His dad was a business agent for the IAM in the Midwest.")

An interesting incident occurred soon after Wilson became president. He redecorated the office he'd inherited, and installed a private bathroom with a shower—the first private shower in any Boeing office. One day, Allen called and asked him to come over to discuss an important matter. Wilson came immediately. When the discussion was over, Allen asked if Wilson could show him the redone office. Wilson protested that he'd just held a meeting in the office and it was a mess, but Allen said he'd like to see it anyway. Wilson took him to the new quarters. As Allen peeked in the bathroom, the shower door opened and a cute young blond woman, wrapped only in a towel, stepped out and exclaimed, pouting, "T, you promised we'd be alone!" Wilson looked about to come unglued and must have envisioned his career disappearing down the shower drain. Suddenly a bunch of other executives appeared, looking in on the scene and laughing. Allen, too, was convulsed. Wilson's tormentors had hired the girl, a beauty contest winner, in an elaborate practical joke. Such jokes seem to be part of Boeing's culture, and executives like to recount them. Wilson enjoyed telling the "blond" story on himself afterward, but usually wouldn't stand for being made to look foolish; ordinary mortals at Boeing would never have dared to pull such a stunt.

Like most leaders when they come to power, Wilson turned to associates he knew best when making appointments, but some people thought he took the crony system to new lengths at Boeing. Minuteman veterans started to assume important posts throughout the company, sometimes meeting resentment from those who believed success on an aircraft program should be the principal criterion for the top jobs.

Not long after Wilson's ascension, Allen promoted Yeasting out of the airliner division and made him an executive vice president at corporate headquarters. Wilson, in his capacity as president, chose Yeasting's replacement at the division. He picked Tex Boullioun, who had served with Wilson on the Minuteman missile program and had gone on to work for Yeasting. Pan Am and Pratt welcomed the move. They felt that Yeasting, the accountant who had long been in charge of corporate finance before becoming a division head, paid more attention to contract legalities than to producing a satisfactory 747. When Boullioun, whose background was in engineering and production, took over, Boeing's partners felt he took their technical objections seriously. (Sadly, both Yeasting and Stoner contracted cancer, and neither man could have served long at the top. Yeasting died in 1970, Stoner in 1971.)

In a surprise move a month after Wilson was clearly designated as Allen's successor, Juan Trippe retired from Pan Am. The two giants of the 747 program were both abandoning it before completion. Harold Gray succeeded Trippe as Pan Am's chairman and CEO, and Najeeb Halaby became president. Larry Kuter was named executive vice president.

The personnel changes at the tops of the two companies did nothing to improve the working relationship between them. Boullioun described an acerbic bargaining session: "Allen and I were negotiating with Halaby and Kuter. . . . And they were being so mean, so tough, that finally Bill said, 'I'm about to throw up. I'm going to leave, catch an airplane immediately, and I'm going back to Seattle. It's all yours. I can't stand it anymore.' And damned if he didn't!"

Boeing executives thought Kuter particularly unreasonable and not very smart, although he had graduated near the top of his West

Point class. Wilson flatly told Halaby, whom he considered intelligent and reasonable, that he wouldn't deal with Kuter.

Up at Everett, Joe Sutter plowed ahead designing the 747. He was guided by a thick manual officially titled "Model 747 Design Objectives and Criteria" but unofficially called "the bible." Every Boeing airplane design effort was guided by its own bible, which incorporated lessons learned from all previous Boeing design experience. Boeing considered the information top secret and limited the number of copies in distribution. Sutter was astonished when a group of visiting Russians, ostensibly considering buying 747s, asked him about the bible; they had learned about the guide when a salesman unthinkingly mentioned it. The real purpose of the Russian mission surfaced when the leader of the group offered Sutter one million dollars for the bible. Sutter refused, and the Soviets raised their offer. Sutter demurred again and ended the meeting, spurning a final offer of ten million dollars as he showed the spies to the door.

There was no letup in the hectic, almost (but not quite) slapdash pace of the design work. Because they had no time to do studies when questions came up, the engineers often made decisions by guessing or compromising, accepting solutions they knew to be workable and safe but probably not the best. Manufacturing of parts began when their design was supposedly fixed, even before overall development was completed, but twice as many expensive changes involving remanufacturing had to be made in the "final" parts designs than in any other Boeing project. The early 747s looked almost as if they'd been just thrown together in too much of a hurry. An executive on the project sighed that the airplanes "probably had one thousand pounds of shims" (used to smooth out poorly fitting joints when fuselage sections are joined).

The chaos of the emergency evacuation tests was typical of many other aspects of the project. Like every airplane, the 747 had to be designed so passengers could evacuate it completely in ninety seconds in an emergency. Tests had to be run under simulated emergency conditions with full passenger loads, including representative samples of men, women, children, and people over sixty years old. The tests were dangerous, and every manufacturer that performed them expected injuries. Nevertheless, hundreds of people volunteered for each 747 test; for one trial, a Lions Club provided subjects who were paid twenty-five dollars each. Volunteers had to slide down chutes from a height of sixteen feet and, in the case of the 747 upper deck, sit in a sling and ride it down thirty feet. The tests turned out to be nightmares. Two or three people broke bones in each trial, and many sustained friction burns from the slides. A volunteer was pushed off the upper deck before his sling was fully secured and landed hard on the concrete, snapping several bones but glad to be alive.

After the 747's nose had been designed, a veteran engineer who reviewed the plans pointed out a basic flaw in the structure. The nose had to be completely redesigned at great expense. (Airflow around today's snoot is so smooth that the nose portion of the cabin is the quietest seating location. When Sutter flies on his creation, he always tries to get an aisle seat in row three.)

Despite the frenzy and multitude of glitches at Everett, however, Boeing executives considered their project to be roughly on target to produce an airframe that was at least acceptable to Pan Am and other airlines. A continent away, in Hartford, Connecticut, Pratt was working double time to develop the 747 engine called the JT9D, but was getting results that Boeing did not consider acceptable. Wilson didn't believe the truncated development schedule was any excuse, and thought seriously about going back to GE or Rolls-Royce to see if one of them could build an alternative to the JT9D. He assigned an engineer named Bert Welliver to study the situation and make a recommendation. After three months of study, Welliver gave a presentation to Wilson detailing serious problems with the JT9D but concluding that Boeing should stick with it and get Pratt to redesign the engine. Wilson told Welliver to give the same presentation to Pratt's top engineering executives.

When Welliver finished his presentation at the engine maker's offices, Pratt's engineers argued that none of his criticisms were valid. Frustrated, he blurted out, "You're going to redesign the fan, and you're going to redesign the compressor [the fan and compressor are the main parts of a jet engine], and you're going to do it now, or you're going to do it later, so you might as well get on with it." Driven beyond his limits by Welliver's criticisms and bluntness, Pratt's senior engineer lunged across the table, grabbed Welliver by the tie, yanked him off his feet, and pulled him over the table. While Welliver was choking, the Pratt executive yelled that the work he was demanding would cost one hundred million dollars. Shaken, Welliver escaped from Hartford, returned to Seattle, and reported his misadventure to Wilson. The Boeing president phoned Bill Gwynne, the head of Pratt & Whitney, and told him he'd better make Welliver happy about the engines or Boeing wouldn't buy any of them. (Pratt denies the story, but if one assumes it's true, the engine maker had picked on the wrong man—Welliver eventually became a senior vice president at Boeing.)

The finished 747 was born on Monday, September 30, 1968, a chilly and typically overcast Seattle fall day, when it rolled out of the gigantic manufacturing hangar that had nurtured it. The Everett facility had been completed at a total cost of two hundred million dollars. Visitors to the rollout saw a gargantuan main building that covered forty-three acres; someone calculated that there was enough room inside to play forty football games simultaneously. Boeing said clouds could form in the building's two hundred million cubic feet.

Wilson served as MC for the rollout ceremonies, which began with a half hour of speeches before the airplane's emergence. Then Mal Stamper stepped up to the podium and intoned the command for the hangar door to be opened and the 747 to be brought forth. When the door—which was the size of a football field—had been ponderously lifted, an aircraft tug slowly and reverently pulled out the first 747, which was white with a red stripe down the window line. (Gone were the copper and mustard yellow rollout colors that had always been decreed by the now-departed Wellwood Beall.) The

Everett High School band played "Pomp and Circumstance" as the 747 majestically entered the outside world. The size of the behemoth awed the spectators. The monstrous tail reached as high as a six-story building. It was pointed out that the fuselage extended twice as long as the Wright brothers' first flight, and that the vast hollows in the wings would carry enough fuel to drive the average automobile ten thousand miles a year for seventy years. Boeing proclaimed that the newborn airplane weighed two and half times as much as the company's next biggest jetliner, the 707. Those who had had the tour of the interior mock-up had seen that the cabin was a cavern twenty feet wide and nine feet high, with seats that Pan Am had insisted be larger than usual to accommodate posteriors that the airline was sure were growing bigger.

Boeing had deliberately made the 747 larger than airlines could fully use at that moment. Aircraft manufacturers always introduced models that were bigger than required at first so that, as air traffic grew, in a few years they would be sized right and then, eventually, would be too small and be ready for replacement—and then the design would be stretched. The wings were truly huge, looking to the day when the body would be stretched. Lengthening the body is a simple redesign compared to enlarging a wing, so the wing was made big enough at the start to support the weight of a fully loaded and stretched 747 with bigger engines. What's more, tests had shown the wing to be 16 percent stronger than the target—so the plane could carry more passengers and cargo, or more fuel (and thus go farther), than planned.

Decals of the twenty-six airlines that had ordered the 747 adorned the nose of Boeing's latest creation. When the tug pulling the 747 came to a stop, the airplane was surrounded by stewardesses from the purchasing airlines, each woman carrying a champagne bottle. At a signal from Stamper, they assaulted the aircraft, breaking their bottles on designated tough portions and dedicating it to some now-forgotten piety. Representatives of each of Boeing's other jetliners—a 707, 727, and 737—made low passes over the Everett facility, welcoming their new sister into the Boeing family.

Some reporters called the 747 "the jumbo jet," and the term started to catch on. Boeing didn't like it. "We didn't think it sounded clean and sporty and fast. It sounded like a lumbering elephant," Stamper recollected. The company at first refused to use the term, but it became established as the 747's nickname.

Boeing had orders for almost two hundred jumbos, which apparently made the airplane a business success, barring technical problems. (Allen had won his ten-million-dollar bet with Trippe about getting fifty orders by August 1966.) The company optimistically increased the planned production rate to eight and a half airplanes a month, to be turned out by twenty-five thousand employees.

Although the 747 had looked ready for flight at the rollout, much work remained to be done before it was set even for taxiing tests. It wasn't until January 1969 that it took to the runway for the ground run-throughs. One of the first findings was that the designers had made a big mistake about controlling the jumbo on the ground. They had thought the pilot could steer it with the jets, so the wheels wouldn't need steering capability. The engineers were dead wrong. It cost five million dollars more to make the wheels steerable.

Four months after rollout the airplane was ready for flight test, which was set for February 9, 1969. Bill Allen came rushing back from a visit to the Trippes' house in the Bahamas. (Trippe, retired, stayed in the islands.) Test pilot Jack Waddell would take the jumbo up. (His predecessor, Tex Johnston, had quit test piloting and eventually left Boeing after losing out in a power struggle between his flight-test group and the design engineering organization.) A copilot and flight engineer would fill out the crew. Allen, long-faced and tense, spoke with Waddell just before the pilot boarded the airplane. Unthinkingly, Allen told Waddell, "Jack, I hope you understand that the future of the Boeing Company rides with you guys this morning." That's not what Waddell needed to hear. He was trying to focus sharply on his dangerous task at hand and wanted to avoid the distractions that would come with dwelling on possible disasters. "Bill, up to now I haven't been feeling any pressure. I'm sure glad you let me know," Waddell replied in a mild reproof to his boss.

Shortly before noon, the 747 roared down the runway, pouring all its power into acceleration. Halfway along, when it reached 150 miles per hour, the huge building with wings soared into the sky, one of the largest heavier-than-air structures ever to become airborne. Up, up, up it went, thrilling spectators who thronged the surrounding area. Sutter's wife, Nancy, broke into tears. For all its bulk, the jumbo flew beautifully, delighting all those whose lives, fortunes, and reputations it carried. Waddell, continuously reporting by radio to the crowd of engineers and executives back at the field, successfully ran a series of tests before attempting to answer one of the most critical questions: Was the 747 susceptible to the infamous Dutch roll instability that had wrecked 707s and killed crew members? With everyone at full alert, none more so than the crew, Waddell announced he was ready to try going into Dutch roll. He kicked the rudder pedal. The airplane wiggled—and then settled back into steady flight instead of going wild. There was no Dutch roll. The engineers who had paid special attention to designing a tail that would prevent the malady were deeply gratified.

The 747 passed several more tests until Waddell experimented with the rear flaps, wing sections that extend back and downward for takeoff and landing. Suddenly the crew and those listening on the radio heard a loud clunk, and the airplane began to quiver. The flight engineer went to a window and saw that a section of flap had come loose and wedged in a gap, where it was vibrating. The condition wasn't serious, but Waddell prudently decided to end the test session and come down. Now he faced another unknown: From a flight deck thirty feet above the runway—three stories—could he land the jumbo safely and smoothly? Some pilots expected 747 landings to be awkward and accident-prone because the person at the controls would be so high off the runway. Waddell found out after flying about an hour and a quarter. The fledgling 747 made an unusually fast—because of the bad flaps—but otherwise near-perfect landing. Waddell had no trouble at all. Despite the airplane's elephantine size, designers had given the airplane such superb handling characteristics that on this flight (and later ones) the 747 proved, amazingly, to be the easiest jetliner to land.

On the first flight, Waddell didn't conduct the most perilous test: investigation of any flutter problems. When parts of an airplane start to flutter in the airstream, which blows over jetliners at wind speeds like a super tornado, clawing for the tiniest weaknesses, the craft can shake itself apart in just seconds. Test pilots induce flutter conditions slowly and carefully, so they can pull back at the slightest hint of impending catastrophe. On subsequent flights, Waddell conducted the delicate maneuvers—and the news wasn't good. Strong hints abounded. The 747 would flutter badly under certain conditions. The problem so threatened the jumbo's airworthiness that Ed Wells assigned Jack Steiner to head a special team to solve it, anticipating weeks of work. The flutter gremlin exhibited such stubbornness, however, that the team had to fight for half a year before knocking it out. (Flutter can often be defeated by strategic placement of weight, much like the process of balancing an automobile wheel by positioning lead weights at just the right spots on its rim. For the earliest 747s, Boeing engineers hit on an ingenious solution involving the embedding of pellets of the heaviest available metal, uranium—depleted of its fissionable isotope—in the nacelles.)

Flight tests continued while the work of the flutter group dragged on; the trials also took longer than expected because an unusually severe winter delayed many tests. Those who worked on and around the flights found that the sheer size and power of the jumbo took getting used to. Ordinary wheel chocks were useless to keep the jumbo in place while the engines were revved up if there was the least bit of ice or snow on the ground. The engine exhaust knocked over a light plane and a car parked too close to the runway. Tragically, a small jet photographing the giant flew too close behind it, got caught in the turbulence of the wake and exhaust, and was knocked out of the air.

A problem that seems almost silly nevertheless threatened the delivery schedule. A jetliner's food carts are made to the same exacting standards as the rest of the airplane. Boeing couldn't find a supplier who could make satisfactory carts. Despairing of locating a reliable company on time, Boeing itself finally set up a firm in California to produce good carts.

The most disturbing problems that showed up in the flight tests were not with the airframe or its contents but the engine. As Boeing's engine study had shown, the JT9D simply couldn't do the job. It couldn't even get close to thrust or fuel consumption specifications. To be sure, it could get the jumbo into the air and fly it for a relatively short distance. But 747s powered by the JT9D couldn't carry as many passengers or fly them as fast or as far as the airplane that Pan Am had ordered, and they had an insatiable thirst for fuel. (The 747 could fly faster than any airliner in history—0.84 Mach, or 623 miles per hour. Pan Am had specified 0.9 Mach, or 667 miles per hour, however. Boeing was partly responsible for the shortfall of 44 miles per hour. The more the wings are swept back, the faster an airplane can fly. The ideal sweep for Pan Am's goal was forty degrees. Sweepback introduces control difficulties, however, and Boeing was reluctant to go much beyond the thirty-five-degree sweep of its previous jetliners. Boeing compromised by splitting the difference with 37.5 degrees.)

The bad news about the engines got much worse as flight testing continued. Not only did they not work well, they often didn't work at all. They tended to flame out when pilots called for more power. On the ground, strong winds could blow them out. The engines broke down at an alarming rate. During flight testing, Boeing went through eighty-seven engines, including fifty-five that self-destructed. Maddeningly, engines that didn't break down gradually lost a significant amount of their already low power levels and burned even more fuel.

The top people at Pan Am were furious. As they saw it, even when the engines worked, the 747 might be good for short, heavily traveled routes but not the long routes that Pan Am typically flew. The carrier would not get the airplane in which it had invested so much money and which it needed so badly.

Boeing blamed Pratt's top management. Boeing's executives felt that their counterparts at Pratt worried more about Pratt's bottom line than about the engines, and didn't do nearly enough to solve the problems. As Sutter analyzed the situation, "Rather than complete their job prior to delivering engines, they let the bugs and problems emerge after the airplanes are in service; at that point, the carriers and manufacturers share the problem and are expected to pick up part of the bill." Whenever Everett's engineers referred among themselves.to the Pratt engineer who traveled west regularly to brief them on the engine's progress, they used the nickname they had bestowed on him: "the lying cocksucker." (The aerospace industry isn't known for delicacy of language.) Engine manufacturers retort that airframe people try to blame others for problems they've created themselves, and, anyway, no part of a new airplane lives up to advance billing. "Planes are always heavier and draggier than you predict, and engines never measure up to expectations on weight and performance," an engine company executive philosophized. At any rate, Boeing felt that Pratt's attitude was even worse than it had been on the 727 program. The anger that Boeing executives and engineers on the 747 project felt toward Pratt bordered on hatred, and their feelings hardly diminished over the years. (Much later, when nearing retirement, Wilson told an interviewer that he had never forgiven Pratt.)

To achieve some kind of working relationship between the two companies, Stamper held a meeting in Bermuda between the top Boeing and Pratt people on the project, inviting three men from each company and their wives. "I had to include the wives—if the men were alone they'd have killed each other," he explained. The participants dubbed it "the love-in," and one of the Pratt men reported back to his troops that it was "extremely productive."

Boeing followed up the love-in with another, larger meeting in Seattle—a big mistake. The attendees from Hartford felt that it became a "beat on Pratt" session. Bernie Schmickrath, the engine maker's engineering vice president (and later company president), declared that Pratt was fixing the technical problem under discussion. A Boeing executive shot back a threat: "We'll go to the FAA [Federal Aviation Administration] for an airworthiness directive if you don't fix it." Such a directive would condemn the engine and jeopardize both its future and Pratt & Whitney's. Schmickrath, redfaced, rose and shouted, "Why don't you go fuck yourself!" and stalked out. (Schmickrath would never again visit Boeing.)

While the engine problems were being resolved, life went on at Boeing. A landmark event in the company's history took place quietly, with no fanfare and little immediate impact on programs or policies. In April 1969, after having gradually transferred his duties to T Wilson, Bill Allen stepped aside and the board of directors elected Wilson the new CEO. Although late—Allen was sixty-eight—the transition had been well prepared and was virtually seamless. Allen continued as chairman and studiously avoided giving unsolicited advice or comments to his successor. He looked forward to spending more time with Mef at the Highlands and their summer home on Orcas Island in the San Juan Islands of Washington state.

As the new head of Boeing, Wilson underwent an initiation ritual into a unique secret society that, on the face of it (but with little substantiating evidence), seems to vindicate those who see vast conspiracies at work in major industries. Called the Conquistadores del Cielo, Spanish for "Conquerors of the Sky," the group was founded in 1937 by Jack Frye, head of TWA. The group inducts top executives from aviation-related businesses all over the world. Members gather at a remote location every year for five days to rough it and play cowboy—whether competitors or allies, friends or enemies the rest of the year. (In the 1990s, the society met at Wyoming's A Bar A Ranch, owned by the chairman of Lear Gates.) An initiate had to dress in a velvet and brocade costume, redden his lips with lipstick, and paint on a black goatee and mustache. In a torch-lit nighttime ceremony, surrounded by others in costume, he was sworn into the elite band.

Boeing flew a 747 to the Paris air show that spring. Boeing and the Soviet Union had made an unusual deal that they carried out privately during the show. Russia was the world leader in the technology of processing titanium. Boeing used titanium in the 747 landing gear, and planned to make most of the SST (then still a hot project) out of the strong, light metal. Boeing was the world leader in designing engine placement for jetliners (a task involving highly complex physics and mathematics), and the Soviets were far behind. Boeing offered to trade its engine placement secrets for Russia's titanium processing secrets. The Soviets' keen interest in such matters already having been well demonstrated to Joe Sutter, the two parties struck a deal. Engineers from the two countries met in a secluded room at a French restaurant. The Russians agreed to go first and spent an hour candidly telling Boeing's engineers everything they wanted to know. Then Joe Sutter spent ninety minutes revealing all to the Russians, drawing on the tablecloth to illustrate his points. At the end of the meeting, the Soviets packed up the tablecloth, and both delegations left feeling they'd gotten a good bargain.

Nothing any of the partners in the 747 program did seemed to make the others happy. Pan Am was peeved at Boeing for not painting the plane it flew to Paris in Pan Am's colors; Boeing explained that this would discourage sales to other airlines. Pan Am then asked for and got Boeing's permission to have Pan Am's large Paris staff give tours of the plane to VIPs at the show.

In April, the same month that Allen passed the CEO title to Wilson, Allen's protégé Mal Stamper was promoted to vice president and general manager of the whole Commercial Airplane Group. Stamper, the outsider whose appointment as head of the 747 program was controversial within Boeing, was (and remains) proud of his role in the project. Working days that were often eighteen hours long, seven days a week (he remembers taking a complete day off only once, a Christmas) for over three years, he built Everett, started it up, and literally got the 747 off the ground. No one worked harder and probably no one worked as many hours a day on the program as he did. (His workday followed an odd pattern. Stamper would arrive late in the morning and work until early the next morning.) Some people say his lack of both aeronautical and manufacturing expertise contributed to huge overruns in the labor and financial budgets, and technical problems with the airframe and engine (since oversight of Pratt was a Boeing management responsibility). Stamper could be glib; he didn't impress one major supplier, who described him as "all throttle and no airspeed." Perhaps no one could have done better, however, given Pan Am's demands, the nearly impossible timetable, and the system Stamper inherited and had little time to change. An executive who worked closely with him declared, "The guy who made the 747 program happen was Stamper. He cajoled, bullied, bribed—all kinds of things to keep that program going." Jack Steiner, citing Stamper's success in maintaining the support of the board of directors for the project, admitted, "The 747 might have died but for Stamper." When Stamper returned home one night to the Highlands, where he had moved when he got the 747 assignment, he found that someone had left a plaque at his front door. It was inscribed with the inspirational quotation from Theodore Roosevelt about courage that Stamper had seen on a similar plaque on Bill Allen's office wall. Stamper knew that the anonymous gift-giver had to be his neighbor, the Rough Riders fan.

An unusual aspect of the 747 program compared to other Boeing programs was the high management turnover. Some people burnt out because of the onerous pace. Stamper transferred many executives involuntarily out of the program, however, and some retired early rather than work with him. There's no question that the resulting turmoil caused difficulties. But Stamper's admirers say he made the moves and applied the pressures because the problems would have been worse otherwise. He doesn't seem to have been entirely ruthless about it. One manager is still puzzled that Stamper praised him, gave him a raise, and forced him off the 747 and into a job elsewhere in the company.

Stamper apparently wasn't able to touch the engineers, however, probably because of the power of Ed Wells. A manager in the 747 program explained, "In this company you don't touch the engineers. Nobody's ever been fired out of engineering that I'm aware of, unless for something illegal." (Tex Boullioun, whose actions then as head of the airliner division were sometimes thwarted by Wells's power, is one of the few veterans of those days who doesn't speak reverently of Wells.) Had it not been for these politics, one wonders what might have been the fate of Joe Sutter, who didn't get along well with Stamper. During one of their tense meetings, Stamper brought up a sore point. At the start of the program, he had set the anniversary of the Wright brothers' historic accomplishment, December 17, as the deadline for the first 747 flight. The engineers missed the date by seven and a half weeks. People experienced with other development programs considered the 5 percent overrun of the time budget over the almost three-year period to be insignificant. Stamper nevertheless felt that the person most responsible for the development schedule, Joe Sutter, had failed him on this project where time was of the essence. Stamper went to a cabinet and took out a model about a foot long of the Wright brothers' first airplane. He told Sutter that he'd had fifty such models made and had planned to present them proudly to key people on the program at a ceremony after the December 17 flight. Noting that the models were nothing but junk now, he swung the one he held and smashed it on the desk in front of Sutter, breaking it into several pieces. Sutter picked up the scraps and left. (Glued back together, the model sits in Sutter's retirement den.)

With Stamper's promotion, the 747 program had to march to its conclusion without his immediate participation. Shortly after flight tests had started, the jetliner had begun tests for FAA certification. Boeing and Pan Am knew that the FAA would be particularly stringent because of the nature of the aircraft: the first jumbo jet, carrying an unprecedented number of passengers, having no military predecessor, and (the FAA being a political body) attracting worldwide attention. Fortunately, no problems surfaced to disqualify the aircraft. The FAA determined that the engine difficulties wouldn't compromise safety and so passed the power plants, although just barely. The only glitch in the certification process was emergency passenger evacuation from the upper deck. The FAA wouldn't certify the upper deck for assigned seats until the doors off the deck were redesigned. (Airlines used the space as a lounge until then.) The airplane was certified in December 1969—one of the fastest certifications ever, and especially remarkable for such a complex, novel airplane.

Pan Am had learned in October that Boeing would miss its promised November delivery date, and wasn't happy that the first 747s wouldn't be delivered in time for Christmas travelers to buy tickets for jumbo jet flights. The deal between Boeing and Pan Am had a kind of automatic penalty, since Boeing wouldn't get the final half of Pan Am's payment until the airplanes were delivered.

These payments had become vitally important to Boeing because of a crisis precipitated by an incredible turn of events in the economy, the airline and aircraft industries, and Boeing itself. The year 1968 had been a high point for the economy and Boeing's business. The airlines were booming. Boeing sold a record 376 airplanes that year. Then Boeing's world fell apart. A recession began even before 1968 was out, and downturns are almost always especially bad for capital goods producers such as Boeing. At the same time, airline costs rose and financing became harder to obtain. Air traffic, instead of rising 15 percent a year as predicted, rose at a much lower rate, especially in the United States. The lower than expected rate was due partly to the recession and partly to mistaken forecasts, which underestimated the large portion of traffic growth that had come about because travelers were switching from trains and ocean liners to airplanes; that part of the growth stopped after train and airplane passengers completed the switch. Saddled by debt from their enthusiastic purchases of the first jetliners, moreover, the airlines couldn't afford to buy many new aircraft, and certainly not the most expensive offering, the 747. Most domestic airlines wanted to put off buying any new airplanes; orders for all models fell way off, and airlines began to cancel orders. If carriers absolutely had to acquire aircraft or lose business, they tended to buy Lockheed's L-1011 or Douglas's DC-10, whose smaller size was now better fitted to the less than expected passenger traffic in the United States, and which cost a third less. Boeing came to realize an even more sickening truth: The company had erred from the very beginning in its reading of market needs. The 747 had always been much too big. Even allowing for new models being on the large side to provide for market growth, airlines would never have needed an airplane that size for years, as many carriers had been telling Boeing.

The element that turned these setbacks into an emergency for Boeing was one for which the company's management had to accept responsibility: the feared results of Boeing's taking on too much had come to pass. In trying to do more than they could handle, Boeing's managers had let development and manufacturing costs spin out of control. "Let's face it," Steiner said. "On the 747, we bit off more than we could chew." Overspending on the 747 program and other projects had drained Boeing's treasury. Stamper told an interviewer, "We never let money stand in the way of performance on the 747 project." Management seemed to expect demand for the 747 to be so great that it would pay for any overrun. At one point Boeing was spending $15 million a day on the new airplane. (Many of the costs, to be sure, were unavoidable consequences of increased size and greater complexity. Aviation historian Peter W. Brooks, citing the 747 among other models, concluded, "Every time there's a major step forward in transport aircraft technology, the cost in constant dollars of launching a new type of airliner increases by a factor of about four.") Boeing has admitted spending $750 million on 747 development, almost equal to Boeing's net worth of $762 million recorded in the annual report for 1965, the year the project started. Several people connected with the project say more realistic accounting would put the bill in the billions of dollars, maybe several billion. Whichever estimate was correct, Boeing couldn't afford it. Bankruptcy wasn't out of the question. The banks were putting pressure on Boeing to get its deliveries back on schedule and collect the payments to stave off insolvency. In November 1969, a rumor swept the nation's financial markets that T Wilson would be replaced or Boeing would be taken over by one of its banking creditors. Bill Allen had to put out an official statement denying the gossip.

There was a major drawback to relying on Pan Am's payments to avoid financial ruin: The airline wanted delivery soon of 747s with the characteristics spelled out in the contract; it did not want delivery of what it considered an inferior product. Pan Am threatened not to take delivery even when Boeing would tender the airplane. Boeing then hinted that, despite contract clauses giving Pan Am the first 747s, there were legal grounds to deliver airplanes to TWA first. Boeing was sending a 747 to Hawaii for high-temperature tests. In a bit of gamesmanship, the company painted the airplane in TWA colors. Pan Am learned of this on November 20, when the airplane was on its way. Kuter called Boullioun in a rage at what he called "this patent attempt to associate TWA with the first 747 flight to the Pacific, particularly in view of Boeing's refusal to paint the Paris air show 747 in Pan Am colors." Boeing's point made, Boullioun radioed the pilot to turn around and come back.

Boeing announced the company would be ready to deliver a soon-to-be-certified 747 on Monday, December 1 (but not in time for Pan Am to train flight crews and carry out other preliminaries that would be necessary for the airplane to carry part of the Christmas crowd.) Pan Am sent a flight crew to Seattle to accept delivery, but told Boeing it would withhold four million dollars from the final payment on each airplane until Boeing fixed twenty problems Pan Am had enumerated—most but not all of them engine-related—and the aircraft could perform according to specifications. Pan Am, with its long routes, was most disturbed by the 747's being 7 percent short on range.

On Tuesday, Wilson and Boullioun flew to New York and met with Halaby. Wilson told Halaby he couldn't deliver the airplanes unless Pan Am paid Boeing in full, pleading that withholding payments would bankrupt Boeing. Halaby, unaware of the awful extent of Boeing's crisis, didn't believe it, and threatened to sue Boeing for damages caused by nonperformance. Gamesmanship reached higher levels the next day when Halaby ordered his flight crew in Seattle to forget the 747 delivery and return home. Boullioun let Halaby know that TWA was planning 747 demonstration flights in the New York area on December 12 if Pan Am didn't take the airplane.

Gamesmanship became hardball on Friday. Boullioun told Halaby that Boeing planned to officially tender the 747 to Pan Am on Monday for delivery three days later. If Pan Am did not accept delivery then, Boeing would consider the deal with Pan Am off and the companies would next meet in court.

On Monday, after several calls back and forth between New York and Seattle, Boullioun agreed to defer the delivery until Thursday.

Late Thursday, Wilson called Halaby. They negotiated some more for over an hour and finally reached a compromise. Pan Am would take the airplane but would withhold two million dollars. Wilson agreed, knowing he'd save half by withholding one million dollars from his payments to Pratt & Whitney. TWA would have to wait a few months for its 747s.

Pan Am set the christening of its new 747 for January 15, 1970, and the first commercial flight for January 21. The nation's First Lady, Pat Nixon, christened the airplane at Dulles Airport, naming it *Clipper Young America*. Six days later, 332 guests and 20 crew members assembled at Kennedy Airport in New York for the first commercial flight, to London. Departure was delayed by bugs in doors and the cargo hold. Then the airplane taxied out to the runway, but had to return when an engine temperature ran too high. Pan Am had to switch airplanes, bringing in the second airplane Boeing had recently delivered, which was being used for training. A slowdown by air traffic controllers compounded the débâcle by delaying takeoff again. Finally, nearly seven hours late but with the holiday mood of the passengers hardly dampened, the 747 took off and headed toward England. The flight itself was uneventful.

The mishaps on that occasion were a harbinger of what would happen on many succeeding flights of 747s with the early, unreliable engines. Flights were often delayed or canceled outright. Others took off, got partway to their destinations, and then were forced to turn back by engine malfunctions. Some engines lost parts, and one caught fire. The engines didn't cause all the horrors, however. The lever that attendants pushed to steady the doors when they had been opened looked like the nearby lever used to inflate the emergency evacuation chutes; two flights were delayed by the hours it took to restore the chutes. The FAA seriously considered grounding the 747s, but determined that passengers, although inconvenienced, were never in danger. The agency let the jumbos fly.

A frequent source of trouble was a device that incorporated one of the 747's few advanced technologies, a device that seemed to most passengers one of the lowest forms of technology: the passenger service and entertainment console, which includes the call button, bell, and light; music; and movie audio. Sutter tried to save weight in the long wiring usually needed for the sets. He installed the airline industry's first multiplexed consoles, where electronic devices send signals for different functions over the same wires, thus reducing the number of wires needed. Not yet broken in, the advanced passenger consoles frequently had fits and got their signals crossed; on several flights, the cabin attendant call bells went off every time the volume of the movie audio increased.

Airport conditions often compounded the passengers' distress. Many airports weren't ready to deal with four hundred or so passengers—and their luggage—arriving all at once, so arriving travelers frequently found themselves awash in mass confusion.

Unlike invited passengers on the ceremonial first flight, whose trip was a lark, regular travelers didn't take these later flights from hell in the party spirit. The 747 acquired a new nickname: "the Dumbo jet."

There seemed no end to problems with the engines. Airlines found that they wore out quicker than expected because pilots had to fly them at hotter than recommended temperatures to get the necessary power. Nearly overwhelmed by all the problems, Halaby thought of grounding his 747 fleet and bringing a major damage suit against Boeing. He rejected the thought when he realized the action would probably bankrupt both companies.

Pratt's problems compounded when the company couldn't make engines fast enough to keep up with Boeing's record production pace on the airframes. Boeing began to leave newly made planes without engines—"gliders," Boeing employees called them—parked on the delivery ramp at Everett, with concrete blocks hanging from the empty engine mounts to keep the airplanes from tipping over. The number of "gliders" reached thirty early in 1970 and inspired a nickname among the harassed Pratt people: "the aluminum avalanche." Boeing had more than its net worth locked up in this parked inventory. Analysts figured that, with interest rates at then-record highs, Boeing paid $150 million in interest on cash it had to borrow until the company could deliver completed planes and collect final payments. On top of this loss, Boeing had to pay penalties to airlines because of late deliveries and unsatisfactory performance.

Wilson was more than fed up with Pratt. He yearned to have GE develop engines for the 747 so customers could order some engine other than one made in Hartford, even though Boeing would have to spend $150 million for additional design work and certification for a new engine. He thought that was the only way for the 747 program to get healthy. His analysts told him, however, that offering GE engines would gain him at most only five more customers for the 747 and thus lose money. But after GE offered to split the cost of the redesign, he determined to go ahead and do it. (More than a third of 747s sold later were ordered with GE engines, and Boeing thinks a significant portion represented sales that would not have been made otherwise.) Rolls-Royce also developed a 747 engine without Hyfil fan blades, and Wilson heartily welcomed the British to the table.

Pratt was nevertheless far from the only source of problems. In manufacturing the 747, Boeing produced its share. Poor management of parts inventories resulted in as many as a thousand part shortages a day. These shortages, plus the many new parts that had to be made or ordered when the design changed during production, resulted in airplanes having to be finished after they left the assembly line, delaying the production schedule and increasing the cost of manufacture.

Most Boeing people and other commentators who have written or spoken about the 747 program attribute its initial shortcomings and problems mostly to pressures from Pan Am and failures by Pratt. A refreshing exception is the pithy analysis by Dean Thornton, one of Boeing's earthy executives, in the T Wilson style, who later became president of the airliner division and a strong candidate to head the corporation. His straightforward response to an interviewer would probably be shared by any MBA classes that used it as a case history: "We screwed up the 747 badly. . . . We did not do an adequate early development program, so we had huge cost overruns, our schedule was in trouble, the engine guys screwed up as well. But we shouldn't have let them screw up. We sued Pratt, but I think Boeing has to take a fair share of credit for that screwup. In my opinion, most of our screwups are two-thirds to three-quarters something we do. Typically a businessman is the greatest rationalizer in the world. He'll figure out a way why whatever this bad thing was is events beyond his control. But I maintain, 'Bullshit!'"

Boeing had sought compensation for financial damages in its suit against Pratt but settled out of court in return for business concessions.

Pan Am, despite its unhappiness with the performances of Boeing and Pratt, actually liked the 747 itself. After taking delivery of their twenty-fifth and last airplane under their contract in the summer of 1970, the airline exercised an option to buy eight more. Following a year of flying the 747, Halaby prophesied, "It will . . . serve as a new base for resuming the growth of airline earnings." (Unfortunately for Pan Am, the number of passengers flying Pan Am plummeted in the recession that began in late 1968, and a long time passed before passenger traffic fully utilized its 747s; Pan Am had been unduly optimistic in its forecasts. Burdened by its overinvestment in the 747, America's premier international carrier never fully recovered its financial health and, its condition worsened by poor management, went bankrupt in 1991.)

Douglas's DC-10 flew for the first time in August 1970, about the same time that Boeing delivered its twenty-fifth 747 to Pan Am. Lockheed's L-1011 first went into the air three months later. They both entered commercial service the next year. The airplanes were similar in almost every aspect, including price, since their makers were working from basically the same airline-generated concept. They carried two-thirds the passenger load of 747s, had one-half the range, and cost two-thirds as much. Except for transoceanic routes, on which the 747 was still the favored airplane, the DC-10 was outselling the 747 domestically and in total worldwide sales. Douglas talked about designing a family of jetliners and regaining the top position in the aircraft industry.

But it was already apparent that Douglas and Lockheed had made a big mistake by coming out simultaneously with nearly identical models of that particular size and range. The market for that type of airplane was only big enough for one entry to succeed. The capacity of the type was close enough to the 747 that the Boeing airplane competed with them for some routes. One of them should have been a smaller, twin-engine airplane, of the kind Boeing had forgone when it chose to pursue the 747. As it was, Douglas and Lockheed split the market. Neither was selling as many airplanes as anticipated. The competition between the two was the most savage the industry had ever seen. The airplanes were so much alike that prices and delivery dates rather than capabilities became the focus of the cutthroat competition. Both companies slashed prices to the bone and made no profit. (Later, when the DC-10 had a series of well-publicized accidents, some observers claimed that fierce cost cutting had compromised safety.) Lockheed had special problems. With no background in designing and manufacturing jetliners, Lockheed spent more to produce its airplane than the company had expected. Then Rolls-Royce went bankrupt trying to produce the L-1011 engine on an accelerated schedule, and the engine was delayed while Rolls arranged a bailout by the British government. Like a country watching its two enemies wage devastating war on each other, Boeing could watch the commercial contest and take satisfaction that, at a time when the Seattle company was vulnerable, its competitors in Los Angeles were fighting and weakening each other.

Lockheed killed the L-1011 at the end of 1981 after selling only 244 airplanes, fewer than half the number needed to break even. Lockheed lost an estimated $2.5 billion on the program. The reputation of the DC-10 had been ruined by three fatal crashes, the last and worst occurring in May 1979 at Chicago and killing 273 people. The last passenger version of the DC-10 rolled out of the Santa Monica plant at the end of 1980. Douglas had sold only 446, not enough to break even.

Tex Boullioun was renowned as a gambler, in both the gaming and the business sense, and as "the World's Greatest Airplane Salesman" for the many deals he swung for Boeing. (An Arkansas native who always retained a trace of his Little Rock drawl, he earned the nickname "Tex" for betting a month's salary on the University of Texas football team, and winning. He attended but didn't graduate from

Texas because "I majored in motorcycles and tennis." Motorcycling to Seattle to start his job with Boeing in 1940, he lost his bike in a poker game in Portland and had to hitchhike the rest of the way.) Both aspects of his personality helped him win a 747 order from Singapore's airline when the carrier had tentatively selected a DC-10. Executives of the airline thought the 747 was too big. Tex offered them one of the bets that Boeing likes to make with customers from time to time. He offered to sell them a 747 with a contract providing that Boeing would make up any loss the airline might suffer from attracting too few passengers to the jumbo, while the airline would pass on to Boeing all profits from carrying more passengers on the 747 than the DC-10 could have accommodated. Impressed, the Singaporeans decided Boeing must be sure it could win that bet, so they bought the 747 on standard terms. "They were real happy in just a few years, because they'd have paid us a bundle," Boullioun chortled.

The airlines themselves chose the cabin décor of the airplanes they bought, and the wives of the top executives often advised their husbands in this matter. At the time of the 747, Audrey Meadows, who costarred as Alice with Jackie Gleason in *The Honeymooners* TV series, was wed to Bob Six, the star-marrying head of Continental Airlines. She played a major role in designing Continental's 747 passenger space, which aviation writer Robert Serling called "one of the most beautiful interiors ever put into any airplane."

Despite the hastily created 747 design, initial engine problems, manufacturing mistakes, and some annoying new-plane glitches, the airlines flying the jumbo discovered over the years that it was a fine, safe airplane. Most of the engine difficulties were overcome after the 747 had been flying for two or three years, although Sutter wasn't fully satisfied with the power plant for ten years. Pan Am reported that—engines notably excepted—the airline experienced no bugs at all in the airplane's flying qualities or control systems, never had to ground the jetliner, and overall found fewer flaws than in other new aircraft. Insurance actuaries had predicted that 747s would suffer three fatal crashes in the first year and a half. In the first ten years of service, the actual experience of the 747 was five fatal crashes, including three laid to pilot error. The 747's safety record is unmatched, partly because Sutter took advantage of the airplane's immense size to install fail-safe "quadruple redundancy" in many structures and systems. If a structure or system and two of its back-ups fail, a fourth comes into play.

Because orders slowed to a trickle after the initial rush to buy the 747, it wasn't until 1978 that sales reached the official break-even point of four hundred established early in the program—meaningless when achieved because of the stupendous budget overrun.

Sales of the 747 took off in the late 1970s with the improved general and airline-industry economies, and a growing demand for airplane seats that finally caught up to the size of the premature jumbo jet. Another factor driving sales upward was increased use of the 747's capabilities for carrying freight, which are unparalleled in the industry. "The SST did the 747 a real favor" by forcing designers to build in special cargo-carrying characteristics, Joe Sutter commented. The orders included those for the 747s that serve as Air Force One, the president's airplane, and the commander in chief's flying command post. At some airports, such as New York's Kennedy Airport, most of the occupied gates have 747s in front of them.

The 747 has undergone numerous design changes, but it remains today the largest jetliner, and the cheapest per seat-mile to operate; with improvements over the years, it's now 45 percent less expensive per seat-mile than the 707. Airlines make a great deal of money from it, which is why Boeing also makes a great deal of money. It has become a cash cow, a product Boeing milks steadily for high profits. In 1992, an analyst concluded that seventy cents of every dollar that Boeing makes comes from 747 sales. Joe Sutter, still a Boeing consultant, campaigned after retiring for Boeing to stretch the 747 to hold over five hundred passengers. (He admits that its never having been stretched all these years may indicate that it was too big when introduced.) Boeing has stated that it believes it will be producing 747s well into the next century.

The 747 is still the only true jumbo jet—a Boeing monopoly that, given today's enormous development costs, will probably never be matched by any other single company. A member of Boeing's board of directors summed up its importance to the company: "The 747 has been the greatest program that ever happened. The 747 has put us in a strong position for three decades. Just unbelievable!"

The greatest importance of the 747 to the world at large comes from its cheap operating costs per passenger, its economies of scale. The jumbo extended the revolution begun by the 707. The sharp drop in the cost to airlines of long-distance flying allowed the carriers to pass on much of the savings to travelers, making transcontinental and intercontinental trips affordable to many for the first time. Few people of modest means could fly overseas on vacation before the 747, for example; now such holidays are fairly common.

Although the 747 in its mature years helped Boeing to the pinnacle of financial success, the trauma of its birth nearly destroyed the company.

In 1969, Dick Henning was transferred to the 747 project, promoted to quality assurance chief on the program, and assigned to make the 747 the world's most reliable airplane. He described his new job as being "vigorously to design the airplane so well that there are few major failures and a minimum of maintenance." A long commute and stretched hours made the workweek a killer. The Everett plant was thirty-seven miles from his home on Mercer Island, and he averaged ten hours a day on the job. On the drives, he dreamed of really making it big at Boeing, parlaying his accomplishments in reliability engineering to become the top corporate man in charge of reliability for the entire company.

Before long, however, Dick realized that his current job wouldn't be a stepping-stone. He'd been put in a terrible position. He reported to the service department, where jobs would depend on the number and kind of bugs on the 747: The less reliable the airplane was, the more money, employees, and power the department would get. Dick's incentives and those of his superiors were totally at odds. As Dick explained, "It should be obvious that I was attempting to put the maintainability people out of work. So to be forced to report to them was a travesty of management planning. I could never forgive the Commercial Division management for that blunder."

Dick's unhappiness at Everett increased in the spring of 1970 when he tried to get 747 program management to institute a procedure he had successfully introduced on the Minuteman program. He wanted a special display to be set up in the engineering control room. All the major engineering problems affecting delivery and customer acceptance would be posted to focus everybody's attention on what had to be fixed. He cataloged the eleven significant 747 problems, ranging from fluorescent-light ballast failures and toilet fixture and water fittings problems to snags with engine power indicators, doors, and thrust reversers; failures of the passenger entertainment system were also on his list. "Management refused and as a result dragged their feet, costing the company lots of money on the startup of the 747. The crunch [Boeing's idiom for the big financial crisis] was partially brought on by engineering not reacting fast enough to high-impact cost failures we had identified which were chewing up the budget. There was overspending by everybody on the project," Dick lamented. He was convinced that the managers of the commercial project didn't like someone coming over from the military side and trying to tell them what to do.

Dick's anger at management probably stems as much from what happened later in 1970 as from his frustrations in trying to do a good job on the 747. The director of commercial engineering called and asked Dick to come down to his office at Renton to discuss an important matter. Because Dick was so dedicated to his career and company, what happened when he arrived mocked his principles and shattered his life.

10 ‖ Boeing's City and State

Management mistakes on the 747 project were the biggest single cause within the company of Boeing's financial crisis that began in 1969, but basic organizational and management flaws originating many years before had set the company up for the near catastrophe.

The problems went back to the beginning of World War II. Boeing and other aircraft manufacturers were ordered to produce as many airplanes as they could in the shortest time. The government would pay whatever it took, as when Phil Johnson essentially bought labor peace for Boeing's wartime contracts. The aircraft companies grew into huge organizations geared to churning out product without regard to cost or efficiency. Engineers gave little thought to the cost of producing their creations and looked down their noses at the people, few of them engineers, in charge of bending the metal and working the riveting guns; engineers ignored suggestions for economy that came from the shop people. Promotions came thick and fast in the ballooning companies, often to people who found themselves beyond their depth, thus lowering the overall competency of management. The companies continued in this way after the war, since government was still the largest customer by far and often insisted on speed in design and production to the detriment of economy. Little was done to regain the efficiencies of the early 1930s. Boeing's tradition of high productivity, which had helped the company survive after the First World War, went out the window. In Seattle, Boeing's ponderous ways earned it the nickname "the Lazy B." Always, more and more people were hired to do by brute force what was not being done by efficiency. Boeing (and the other aircraft manufacturers weaned on military work) would rather have hired a legion of mediocre engineers than a few good ones; throwing people at problems was one of Boeing's particular weaknesses. Communication between individuals and subunits within these large groups was poor, compounding the inefficiency.

Overmanning and inefficient work raised the costs of development and manufacturing, thus increasing the risk of producing a new airplane, making profits less than they might have been, and worsening the chances for survival in a financial crisis. Other factors also raised the costs and risks. As Boeing and other manufacturers pursued greater performance and reliability from their airplanes, aircraft technology grew increasingly complex year by year. Designs became more sophisticated. Regulators demanded increased provisions for safety. Aircraft became stuffed with more and more equipment that was more and more complicated, and that often required extensive handcrafting. As production methods matured, such as machining metal for the skins of wings and fuselages, tooling became more extensive, more complicated, and more expensive—greater than other costs. Boeing estimated that the cost of producing a new airliner increased 7 percent a year in constant dollars due to the application of new technology alone. The rapidly changing technology was one reason that Boeing had difficulty forecasting its ultimate investment in the 747.

Boeing managers ignored or simply accepted the rising costs and inefficiencies. Business boomed and Boeing expanded in the mid-1960s, making a nice total profit on its great volume of sales despite the deeply embedded uneconomical practices. In 1966, as often happens, the corrosive effects of the practices began to reveal themselves when they made other problems worse. The short 1965 strike threw the company out of equilibrium, and Boeing had a much harder time than it should have had regaining its balance and stabilizing. As a result, 707s weren't being finished on the assembly lines and had to be parked at Renton to await completion, tying up millions of dollars (foreshadowing the 747 "gliders" four years later at Everett). Boeing started missing delivery-date commitments—almost a capital offense in the aircraft industry—as the unfinished 707s sat there. (Aircraft deliveries didn't get back on schedule until January 1968.) Boeing's supply of cash dwindled to an uncomfortable low. T Wilson, then head of operations at corporate headquarters, asked all Seattle-area plant managers to cut unnecessary expenses to improve cash flow; not much happened because the managers weren't convinced they had serious problems.

If Allen, alerted by the problems that surfaced in 1966, had taken a good look at his company, figured how adverse circumstances might affect it, and initiated fundamental changes, Boeing might have been spared much of the agony that followed. Neither Allen nor the other managers could believe how bad off the company was, however, even when what should have been unmistakable signs of collapse began to appear in late 1968. Managers continued their record pace of recruiting and hiring that had more than doubled the Seattle area payroll between mid-1965 and 1968, for example. In January 1969, a Boeing vice president described their rosy view in a speech to the Renton Chamber of Commerce: "The commercial airplane market is still expanding. . . . Our forecasters are estimating that the air transport market will continue to grow at about 10% to 12% per year." Shortly after that talk, however, when the managers saw the official 1968 accounting numbers, they had to accept what was happening. Then it hit them hard. They were suddenly faced with almost out-of-control costs and the near certainty of much less income than planned. They were in deep trouble—"in deep yogurt," as the saying goes at Boeing.

Because of the cost overruns, compounded by the loss of down payments that would have accompanied airplane orders that were anticipated but never gotten in the severe recession, Boeing began to greatly increase its borrowing. Money had gotten tight, and the company had to borrow at the rate of 10 percent. Boeing's debt quickly surpassed its net worth of $796 million and eventually reached $1.2 billion; interest payments amounted to over $100 million a year.

Almost without realizing what happened, in an incredible turn of events, Boeing found itself on the verge of extinction. The debt burden reached the point where Boeing's banks and other creditors had the legal right to force the company into bankruptcy. Tex Boullioun and Mal Stamper, who by then ran the airliner division together, undertook a tour in which they visited forty-two banks to calm the lenders' fears. The banks would no longer lend money, however. Boeing turned to the company's main suppliers—principally Northrop, Rockwell, Pratt & Whitney, and Rohr—and got them to agree to defer billings until the crisis was over; it was in the suppliers' interest to keep Boeing out of bankruptcy and, they hoped, able eventually to pay them off fully.

A chain of weekly newspapers heard of all the problems and planned to report that Boeing would go bankrupt. Learning this, and realizing that such a story would trigger a forced bankruptcy, Boeing successfully threatened to sue the newspapers if they ran the report.

By October 1969, Boeing's situation was desperate. Within two months, the company would run out of cash to meet its huge payroll and cover its other bills: the company would have to declare bankruptcy. Strangely, neither the senior executives nor the board of directors could admit to themselves how bad things were; it was as if they were in a psychological state of denial. Then Wilson, who had been CEO less than half a year, woke up one night and saw the picture clearly as if in a revelation: Boeing was going to go broke—no doubt about it—unless something drastic were done. He sat on the edge of his bed thinking about what might happen. He knew that the government wouldn't let a vital military contractor go bankrupt. Nor would the banks stand by while Boeing went under; they'd step in and try to straighten Boeing out in their own way to safeguard their investments. But Wilson didn't want to ruin Boeing's reputation for reliability, or let outsiders exert control over Boeing, by seeking a bailout from anyone (as Lockheed did in similar circumstances almost three years later).

Sitting there in the dark, Wilson realized that, before long, the board of directors wouldn't be able to overlook the obvious. He reasoned that the board would have no choice politically but to fire him and appoint some man from outside the company to run Boeing, someone "who had ink and ice water running in his veins." An outsider hired only to keep Boeing solvent probably wouldn't really understand the company, would think only of avoiding extinction, and wouldn't give a thought to Boeing's long-term future. This hired gun would undoubtedly cancel the money-losing 747 program, since no one could prove it would ever make a profit. Boeing would survive but, with nothing invested in tomorrow, would become a second-rate player in the industry. Wilson decided that, as long as something drastic was bound to happen, he might as well do it himself, but in a knowledgeable way that would salvage the long-term programs providing Boeing's only hope for continued greatness.

A salient factor in deciding what to do came from an observation Wilson had made shortly after becoming CEO. Sensing wasteful overmanning, he had placed a hiring freeze on the company. The labor force in the aircraft industry is so transient that this action alone would soon drop the payroll by something like twenty thousand as people left and weren't replaced. After several months and the loss of thousands of employees, the company's output hadn't gone down. Productivity, output per employee, had therefore gone up. The same thing had happened several years previously when Wilson had decimated the Minuteman workforce. His suspicions that the company was overpopulated had been confirmed.

Wilson was also certain by then that the problems went beyond simple overmanning. Boeing, he thought, had grown not only fat but also lethargic: he essentially agreed with the "Lazy B" taunt. In engineering, managers were missing deadlines and overrunning budgets. In manufacturing, he felt that managers were keeping deadwood—people who weren't on top of their jobs or working hard enough. He was convinced Allen had been too lenient and allowed incompetent people to stay on at all levels, especially in the airliner division.

The next morning Wilson called his old friend Tex Boullioun up to his office for a discussion. He told Tex about his sleepless night and ruminations, and his decision to be the "ink and ice water guy" himself. He said he'd concluded that the best way to save Boeing was to emphasize cutting the payroll instead of programs, and that Tex had to reduce his commercial division operating budget by one hundred million dollars. Before Tex left, Wilson told him pointedly, "If they do fire me, there's one guy going before me."

Wilson let it be known that Boeing could no longer pay employees who weren't pulling their weight. He announced to his top managers, "We can afford no more tolerance toward employees who do not produce or whose capabilities are marginal." Even some of those who produced, including Wilson himself, had to make sacrifices. He cut the salaries of almost all Boeing senior executives, slashing his own salary from $140,000 to $75,000, and suspended all bonuses. He told *Forbes* magazine that his job, as he saw it, was to "keep one step ahead of the bankers, but also to maintain the ability to bounce back when the curves [on the business charts] head up again."

Because of the generally poor conditions in the aircraft industry, all the manufacturers were laying off then. A company's payroll is a huge drain on cash, an outflow readily if not happily turned off. Dutch Kindelberger, head of North American Aviation, put it well when he explained the importance of cutting the payroll as soon as times turn bad in aerospace: "If I stub my toe and fall while running to lay off people, we're liable to lose our shirts."

Wilson's hatchet man for the layoffs was his assistant and right-hand man, Wes Maulden, who had degrees in economics and industrial management. Maulden was one of the strangest and nastiest high corporate executives anywhere. He kept his office dark, with the blinds drawn and only a single, low-wattage lamp for light. He rarely sat behind his desk, favoring an overstuffed chair next to a low coffee table, on which he spread his work. Secretaries could hardly see to take dictation. When his secretary brought coffee, he'd yell if the cup handle wasn't placed exactly so he could reach out and take the cup without twisting his hand. He'd read the papers in his in-basket and throw them over his shoulder onto the floor for his secretary to pick up. He fired one secretary after another for not catering to his whims. Maulden once bragged to another man's secretary about how he had kept her boss from being promoted. "Maulden was heartless. He terrified people," one associate remembered with a shudder.

Maulden was one of the best administrators Boeing ever had, however, and Wilson often used him to troubleshoot major problems. Because he did such a good job and didn't cause trouble for other executives, Boeing, like other corporations then (and many now), didn't care how he treated the people under him. With that strange bureaucratic insensitivity, some Boeing executives even today, almost all nice people in their personal lives, tell stories about Maulden's callousness—not to mention a deceased vice president's sexual exploitation of secretaries—with a smile and a shake of the head. Maulden was eventually promoted to senior vice president, Boeing's highest vice presidential rank.

Wilson stopped subcontracting as much work as possible and brought it in-house, but that couldn't stop the layoffs. They began shortly after Wilson ordered the drastic budget cuts, and accelerated toward the end of the year, ruining the holidays for many in Seattle. Wilson turned the Boeing employment office into an outplacement office that tried to find jobs for people in other companies.

At the end of the November meeting of the board of directors, all of whom were now fully aware of Boeing's precarious position, Wilson suggested canceling the December meeting because of the holidays. George Weyerhaeuser declared that Boeing was in such trouble—among the company's many problems, it was headed for its first annual operating loss in twenty-two years—that the meeting should be held as scheduled, and it was.

What started as a severe layoff turned into a tragedy for which the word "bloodbath" seems too mild. Wilson thought the layoff would enable Boeing to turn the corner, but it didn't. There had to be a second layoff. And then another. Wave after wave of layoffs swept over the company in the next couple of years. Wilson maintains that Boeing kept up its output and improved its productivity with the first workforce reduction of thirty thousand. The greater part of the total reductions cut not only fat, however, but especially in the final rounds, muscle and sinew, too, resulting in losses of production and capabilities. Wilson told *Forbes* magazine that this wasn't all bad: "Quite frankly, I'd have to say that as the layoffs went on, some of our people also began working a little harder." (Retirements, resignations, and deaths also removed a significant number from the payroll. Retirements were heavy. During World War II, many men too old for service had gone to work at aircraft plants, and a large number had stayed on after the war. Many of those who stayed started reaching retirement age in the late 1960s. Few people resigned. Most of the great number of transient workers, who ordinarily would have quit, decided to stay on and hope they'd get laid off so they could collect layoff benefits.) Boeing's headquarters wasn't spared. The corporate staff dropped from seventeen hundred employees to only two hundred as employees were laid off or transferred to other sites. Eleven vice presidents left.

The layoffs had a domino effect on other Seattle businesses. As the flow of cash from Boeing into the Seattle economy through workers' pay envelopes diminished and Seattle's economy stalled, other businesses also had to lay off. Some of the laid-off people left the Seattle area, more than a few of them slinking away in the middle of the night, leaving mortgages and other debts behind. Surprisingly, nevertheless, 85 percent of them stayed. The governor of Washington expressed surprise that unemployment and welfare claims didn't rise nearly as much as such a large number of laid-off residents would indicate, however. Boeing theorized that the explanation lay in the numbers of housewives, students, and other transient workers at its plants who simply left the workforce.

Many if not most of those who stayed, to be sure, remained because they couldn't find jobs elsewhere, especially those who were looking for work in the poor aerospace economy nationwide. So many more men than usual were home all day that the number of household burglaries declined significantly.

The often unendurable stresses of being laid off, or being threatened with layoff, caused an increase in medical problems in Seattle among workers and family members, even little children sensitive to their parents' tensions. Psychiatric and other stress-related problems increased, and the suicide rate went up. Some laid-off people couldn't handle the blow to their self-esteem. There were men who couldn't tell their wives they'd been laid off. One man would get up in the morning, dress as if for work, drive off, walk around the waterfront all day, and then go home. He kept up this charade for weeks, until the lack of paychecks betrayed him. The psychological problems were probably worst for engineers and other white-collar workers. The multitude who couldn't find jobs in their professions often had to apply for food stamps and take menial jobs to survive and wait out the downturn. In Seattle, the waiter who ground pepper for your salad, the befuddled taxi driver who wasn't quite sure of the address you gave him, the unsmiling gas station attendant who wiped your windshield—all might have until recently been high-salaried Boeing employees. People's lives were so shattered that some of them never were able to pick up the pieces.

Many laid-off employees were bitter. Jack Steiner, who was put in charge of all aircraft production except for 747s in June 1970, recalls getting phone calls at all hours at work and at home from friends and others he knew well who had been let go, all saying basically the same thing: "I've been a loyal employee for so many years. What are you doing to me?" Steiner got a letter from an employee who quoted the Twenty-third Psalm and said the only reason Steiner wouldn't be afraid in the valley of death is that he must be the biggest son of a bitch in the valley.

As on battlefields, the distressed workers sought some relief from their misery in humor. When the pace of laying off reached its peak, a joke went around Boeing about the difference between an optimist and a pessimist at the company: An optimist brings his lunch to work, and a pessimist parks his car with the engine running. A small amount of hiring, for key jobs, went on even as the layoffs mounted. So chaotic was the turmoil, however, that the left hand sometimes didn't know what the right hand was doing. One man was hired from another part of the country, moved to Seattle, reported to his new job one morning, and was laid off in the afternoon. (He was reinstated on appeal.)

Boeing's troubles could hardly get worse, but on Tuesday, January 13, 1970, they did. Wilson boarded a Northwest flight to Washington, D.C., to attend the christening of Pan Am's first 747 by Pat Nixon two days later. As SeaTac airport dropped away, Wilson felt pains in his chest. They soon got worse, and he felt as though his chest were being crushed. He had had a minor heart attack two years before, and knew what was happening. He pushed the call button and told the flight attendant. She looked at his ashen face and rushed to tell the captain, who immediately headed his airplane to the nearest field, the Spokane airport. He had to dump much of his full load of fuel to make a safe landing. An ambulance met Wilson and sped him to Deaconess Hospital. His heart gave out and stopped. Not many years before, the doctors would have pulled the sheet over his head. Instead, they slapped cardiac electric jump-start paddles on his chest and hit the switch. His body jumped and his heart fired up again. Wilson was in intensive care for days, but gradually improved and started what promised to be a long recuperation.

On Saturday, January 31, Bill Allen, in one of his most anguished diary entries, summarized what was happening at Boeing and to himself as the result of Wilson's near death and the company's financial emergency:

> This is written early in the morning. I awoke early worrying about the financial situation at Boeing. On Jan. 13, T Wilson suffered a heart attack. At an emergency meeting held the next morning, the directors concluded I should resume chief executive responsibilities until T was able to resume. He was brought back from Spokane yesterday, but it will be at least a month before he can be back, if then. This has been one of the most strenuous and worrisome

periods I have ever experienced. Went to Europe—Rome, London, Paris and Hamburg—in effort to solidify position of 747. On return found that our credit situation had become critical. That we would probably need greater borrowings, if they could be obtained. Haynes [Boeing's controller] and others will meet with National City and investment bankers on Tuesday. It would serve no good purpose for me to speculate on outcome. Clearly everyone, creditors, customers, stockholders, employees will be better off if sufficient credit can be obtained to get through this critical period. During the time when our problems are being solved I must:

1. Resolutely stay with the ship. Hopefully, T will be back soon, but I must not push him back into the harness to the detriment of his health.

2. Face the problems without flinching. Do what is best for the creditors, customers, stockholders, and employees.

3. I must not let these monumental problems destroy me. I must learn to be able to put them aside so as to get the required sleep and relaxation. At this writing I am not doing this. It is very difficult to free your mind of the worries in order to get the sleep needed to be fresh to meet the problems the following day. I must learn to live with this critical situation until it is solved.

He told Mef he felt obligated to run the company as T would, but didn't like having to think like T. Nor did he like being beholden to bankers, whom he regarded as overpaid and underworked.

T wasn't back a month later as Allen had hoped. Nor two months later. The harrowing experience had wrecked his health, and he was considering retiring. On March 28, *Business Week* magazine reported: "Most Boeing watchers do not think that Wilson will take up the chief executive's reins again on a full- time basis, and believe that Allen will be largely a caretaker until a new chief executive is found." The magazine related that, because the Boeing staff expected a new man to take over shortly but didn't know who, there was a growing factionalism among executives who were frightened and wanted to bet on the right horse.

Another month went by. Wilson turned the corner and, feeling much better, thought no more of giving up his job. He planned to stay home a little longer, however, to avoid any chance of a relapse. He changed his mind abruptly when he got wind of a situation at Boeing headquarters. Throwing on his business suit, jumping in his car, and racing north to the Boeing complex, he forgot recuperating at home. He'd heard that the board of directors was about to replace him in the presidency with someone else, Allen's protégé and a favorite of many other board members, too: Mal Stamper. Wilson found the choice of Stamper especially alarming because he had little regard for the controversial aircraft industry alien. T's return to work and resumption of power forestalled any move to nudge him aside.

The crisis in the airline industry deepened as President Nixon's anti-inflation efforts took hold in late 1970 and intensified the recession. This was one reason Boeing couldn't get out of its hole. During one period, Boeing didn't sell a single airplane to any U.S. trunk airline, the core of its business, for seventeen months. Because airlines often found themselves unable to take delivery of completed airplanes of any kind, Boeing found itself in the same position as in 1966, with finished airplanes parked and awaiting buyers. By the end of 1970, the total of airplanes parked at Renton—not counting 747s parked at Everett—reached twenty-four, costing about two million dollars a month in interest, insurance, taxes, and other costs. Jack Steiner confessed that, because he was under great pressure to unload the airplanes, he had some moved in back of a hangar where they couldn't easily be seen, hoping that "out of sight, out of mind" would work on his superiors.

In 1970, Boeing's lead bank turned down Allen and Haynes for an increase in the company's credit limit. By early 1971, Boeing was more than one billion dollars in debt.

Boeing's workforce received yet another crushing blow on March 24, 1971, when Congress canceled the SST on good economic and questionable environmental grounds. Some 8,000 people, mostly engineers, were laid off in one day alone as that project folded. Boeing had hit what would prove to be the bottom of its employment trough.

The slaughter reduced the number of employees by an astounding two-thirds; Boeing's employment went from roughly 150,000 to 50,000. Economic depression smothered Seattle. Mordant humor surfaced again when it looked as if the emigration of laid-off Seattleites to other cities would turn into an exodus. Two residents used their own money to put a message on a billboard on the Pacific Highway, which runs by SeaTac airport, so it could be seen by people catching flights or headed south out of the city. A newspaper photographer took a picture of the billboard, and wire services sent the photo to publications all over the country. It became a symbol of what was happening to Seattle and Boeing. The sign read: WILL THE LAST PERSON LEAVING SEATTLE TURN OUT THE LIGHTS?

Wilson told people that he had no choice but to order the layoffs, and that they would have happened anyway had Boeing replaced him with an "ink and ice water" guy or gone bankrupt. Wanting always to be seen as tough, he went so far as to claim that the action was so clearly necessary, almost out of his hands, that it didn't affect him emotionally. He told a story about himself that belied this, however: "I went into a plant and I was deep in thought. I was walking with my head down and I ran into this old aerodynamicist I used to work for. He brought me up short and said, 'Hey, get your chin off your chest; you look like an old man.' It dawned on me that the men don't want the president of their company walking around looking depressed." (In retirement, reflecting on those times, he admitted that the emotional strain of firing so many people had contributed to his heart attack.)

Although the SST cancellation marked the end of a great Boeing dream and was devastating to those who lost their jobs, it contributed greatly to the survival of Boeing. The company stopped paying its share of the program, which amounted to several million dollars a year. The government, moreover, paid Boeing back for the money the company had already spent: $31.6 million. Wilson characterized the refund as "manna from heaven." Since no other company could undertake an SST program, moreover, Boeing got rid of the expensive millstone without losing ground to a competitor.

In fighting for Boeing's survival and return to prosperity, Wilson got rid of buildings and other facilities as well as employees. These asset sales saved on maintenance, taxes, and insurance; improved efficiency by consolidating functions, many of which were then being performed by skeleton crews; and brought in much-needed cash. As with employees, sentimentality played no part; old Plant I, at Bill Boeing's original factory site on the Duwamish River near the junction with Puget Sound, was sold to the Seattle Port Authority (except for the very first building, the "red barn," which was eventually moved to Seattle's Museum of Flight). One of the newest buildings, constructed to produce the 737, was put up for sale, and 737 production was moved to Renton. Steiner bemoaned having to move "out of new and very beautiful facilities into old and more dismal ones." This effort disposed of about ten million square feet of space. Sales of tools, machinery, equipment, and furniture raised over thirty million dollars.

Not even aircraft programs were sacrosanct. The 737, mired in all the problems it had at the beginning, hadn't sold well and its future was then doubtful. Wilson was prepared to sell the whole program to another manufacturer. MITI, Japan's trade agency, wanted Japanese companies to buy the business. Negotiations became serious, but the Japanese backed out when they decided the plan wasn't feasible.

While shedding many facilities, Boeing cut back on maintenance of its remaining properties to save money. At Everett, managers turned off the lights and heat in some offices and rest rooms, and marked the areas DEACTIVATED. The company stopped painting its buildings and let its grass and indoor decorative plants die, accepting the impoverished appearance as only a reflection of reality. The lavatories at the Renton facility symbolized Boeing's degraded condition. Management ordered that several toilets in each lavatory be boarded up so they wouldn't have to be cleaned, and stopped regular swabbing of the floors. The cleaning frequency was raised only when a fungus started to grow on the floors, and management became concerned that health authorities might close the plant.

★ ★ ★

Unfortunately, Boeing's problems were so immense that they couldn't stop at the plant gates. They engulfed not just a corporation, but a whole community. In 1969, checks from Boeing sustained a fifth of the Seattle area's economy. When those checks stopped coming, the city started hurting—badly. Among the earliest casualties were automobile dealerships that sold mid- and high-priced models, as people decided to hang on to their old cars and put off buying new ones if they could, or buy cheaper models if they had to; at least five dealers in the area went out of business in the first half of 1970. In the same period, hotel and motel occupancy in the region dropped 25 percent as business slowed down. By the end of 1971, unemployment in Seattle was the highest in the country at 12 percent, twice the national average and the worst in any major city since the Great Depression. The area unemployment figure rose to 17 percent at the peak of the layoffs. Real estate sales dropped 40 percent, and automobile sales 35 percent. Repercussions were felt all over the country, especially in Boeing's other plant communities and southern California, where 942 of Boeing's subcontractors lost much of their business.

The Boeing recession, as it was known in Seattle, had at least one major positive consequence. Some laid-off engineers started their own businesses or joined others who did, with ventures in burgeoning computer-related fields being most common. These firms played a key role in the eventual expansion and diversification of Seattle's economy.

Several questions about the 747 program provoke debate, among them whether the program should have been launched when it was or whether it should have been deferred until Boeing was in a better position to undertake it. Had Boeing known that the dreadful recession of 1968–1971 was coming, and that sales would drop to almost nothing for so long, presumably the company would have waited until a better time for the 747. Critics say that, even without this prescience, Boeing should have passed on the 747 until the company was better prepared. Boeing had a full plate of other programs already. The company had grown too fast and too much, was poorly managed in many respects, and was grossly inefficient; complex programs such as the 747 need sharp, well-functioning organizations if they're not to spin out of control. Boeing made a mistake in judging how badly the airlines wanted or needed a plane as big as the 747 then. And Boeing probably gambled too much knowing that, in its cyclical business, severe downturns are always around the corner, downturns that could prove disastrous if they follow the tongue-in-cheek (but so often valid) Murphy's law: Things always happen in the worst possible way or at the worst possible time—in this case, just as the pricey new airplane went to market.

Joe Sutter is glad the project wasn't postponed, however. He feels that it had to get started when Boeing was flying high, as it was in the mid-1960s. The project would certainly never have started later, during the recession, and might never have happened at all if Allen hadn't moved when he did; Boeing would then be without its biggest moneymaker today. Sutter believes that Allen had a gut feeling the airplane was needed and would be successful, but knew that a close examination by conventional analysis would doom the project; according to Sutter, Allen rushed the project through so no one would have time to raise logical but—in Allen's view—unhelpful objections. Allen, says Sutter, felt he had to seize the opportunity.

Given what Boeing knew when the engine problems surfaced, the company might have been smart then to have accepted the penalties for delay, stiff as they were, and taken half a year longer or so; the money to be saved in nonrush development costs could well have exceeded the amount to be lost in penalties. As Sutter pointed out, however, a delay would have moved the program into the recession and would probably have resulted in cancellation; with millions sunk into the project and no 747s to sell to recoup its investment, Boeing might have gone bankrupt.

Commenting on the inaction by Boeing's board of directors before the crisis, Wilson said, "It was kind of amazing that the board didn't recognize that we were going broke" and "The board was too dumb to know it." At no point along Boeing's road to near ruination, from the beginning of the 747 project until the depths of despair in 1971, did the board ever act independently of management. The directors never applied the brakes, urged caution, or called a halt to rash action. Wilson said there were too many inside directors. The majority of directors were employees. Their boss was the chairman of the board, Bill Allen. Allen clearly wanted the 747 project to go forward, and apparently would brook no doubts or doubters. Employees smart enough to get on the board of directors aren't so dumb as to go against their boss on a matter of the greatest importance to him. (In the mid-1990s, Boeing had only two inside directors.)

Boeing today remains the greatest individual economic and political force in Seattle and Washington state. A 1989 study detailed the economic relationships between Boeing and the Puget Sound region and the state. One of every seventeen workers overall in the Puget Sound area, and half of all manufacturing workers, had jobs at Boeing. One person in five depended either directly or indirectly on Boeing jobs. The study identified Boeing as the state's largest private employer and "the single most important factor affecting the Washington economy." The report showed that each Boeing job indirectly supported 2.8 other jobs in the state economy, for a total of 230,000 other jobs, and supported the equivalent of 17,628 small Washington businesses. The researchers concluded that, although Washington had diversified and grown economically in recent years, Boeing had grown, too, so the state depended on the company as much as ever.

The author of a 1972 book about Seattle quoted an anonymous Boeing executive about the downside of being so influential: "Boeing management will be happy when we don't stand so much alone in supporting the local economy. It's gotten so that, when the aircraft business sags, and so do we, Seattle and all the towns around start pointing their fingers at us and asking for a magic answer." The executive may get his wish in the 1990s, as Seattle's explosive economic growth brings a flood of dollars in from other sources.

Most of Boeing's economic impact in its home state is from its weighty payroll, which is even more influential than suggested just by the numbers of employees in the workforce because they're paid so well: In 1996, Boeing's factory workers earned an average of over fifty thousand dollars a year in base wages, overtime pay, and bonuses. A 1993 study showed they make half again as much as other Seattle workers. Apparently largely by the company's design, much less of the impact is due to Boeing's mighty purchasing power. Trying to lessen the local impact of the periodic severe business turndowns that are the curse of the aircraft industry, Boeing has never encouraged a concentration of its suppliers in Washington state. Indeed, the company spreads its purchases all over the country and even the world; a rundown once showed Boeing buying only 12 percent of its needs from Washington vendors.

To avoid being a target for accusations and complaints about its influence, or assertions that Seattle is a company town, Boeing historically kept its profile as low as it could in the city. The company firmly believed in the business maxim "The bigger the profile, the bigger the target." That's one reason Boeing has steadfastly refused to move downtown, besides being better able to keep its nose to the grindstone by staying where the grindstone is. Every so often colleagues in the city's business community mount an effort to persuade their Boeing neighbors to join the rest of the gang, but Boeing's chairmen have been wary of moving into a conspicuous "Boeing Building." Likewise, Boeing donated consistently if not bounteously to regional charitable and cultural causes, but invariably behind the scenes and often anonymously. There's no "Boeing Amphitheater" or "Boeing Arts Center" anywhere around. Even the nonprofit Museum of Flight, while established with Boeing funds and in the middle of Boeing properties, doesn't bear the company's name. Boeing welcomed neither the glare of the spotlight nor the sounds of rattling cups from the army of supplicants that would arise if word spread that the company was shoveling out cash.

Leaders of Boeing today believe the company didn't give as much as it could, and hunkered down too far when it did give. People didn't know anything about the Boeing rulers who were making decisions that affected everyone in the area. Even the downtown skyscraper crowd didn't know much about them. Fear, distrust, and suspicion of the company's motives began to cause problems. Not knowing much about Boeing's gifts, furthermore, critics accused the company of not caring about its community and being a poor corporate citizen. As a remedy, Chairman Frank Shrontz has taken judicious steps to make Boeing more visible and better known and appreciated at home. He allows somewhat more publicity for the company, Boeing executives consort more frequently with Seattle's movers and shakers (although, as Boeing is an international business, local business dealings will never become the top priority), and the corporation has become more generous as well as more visible in contributing to local causes. Shrontz went further, establishing a multi-million-dollar trust fund to provide contributions during business slumps and rating managers partly on how well they discharged community responsibilities.

Boeing has historically been more forceful in local and state politics than it's been in public relations. During the 1960s, the company offered courses in public affairs for employees to take on their own time, apparently in an effort—which was successful—to get more Boeing people active in civic groups and elected to local offices. Presumably, these people sympathized with the company's view on regional issues.

Boeing clearly doesn't always get its way in local matters, however, at least not easily, as evidenced by two battles over corporate headquarters. Although the corporation eschews moving its front office to downtown Seattle, it isn't irrevocably committed to the present site. In the late 1970s, Wilson wanted to move to a location just west of SeaTac airport. People close to the proposed new facility didn't want it, citing the noise of executive helicopters taking off and landing. The protesters managed to tie the matter up in legal proceedings for four years. The state supreme court finally found for Boeing, but by that time the company had given up and refurbished its old headquarters.

Another controversy involving headquarters erupted in 1990 when the owners of Longacres racetrack sold their property to Boeing. The company would have put up several nonmanufacturing buildings, including a new head office, on the land, which is near the Renton plant and a bit closer to SeaTac than the old head-quarters. The track was a Seattle institution, however, and the keystone of a four-hundred-million-dollar-a-year thoroughbred race horse industry that directly and indirectly supported fifteen thousand jobs. Again citizens blocked construction, hoping another buyer could be found who would keep the track open or at least, environmentalists hoped, convert it into park land. Again, legal ma-neuvering stalled the project for almost four years. Boeing ultimately prevailed, but again the top executives stayed put (at least for the time being), with only a customer training facility erected on the site.

People in Seattle generally have the impression, nevertheless, that whatever Boeing wants from the state government, it gets. The *Economist* magazine reported in 1991, "Few bills pass the Wash-ington state legislature without Boeing's approval." A crude joke (entirely fabricated to make a point) went around Olympia, the state capital, getting laughs with a punch line that had the governor per-forming fellatio on a Boeing lobbyist.

Bud Coffey, Boeing's longtime chief lobbyist, retired in 1995 but still reports to work every day as a consultant. Hanging on his office wall is the original art for a political cartoon from a Washing-ton state newspaper. It shows what would happen (supposedly) if Boeing were a school instead of a business. A caricature of Coffey as a school official shows politicians falling all over themselves to offer him more money, buildings, equipment, teachers. Coffey, whom a legislative reporter called "the ultimate lobbyist," is astute enough not to have hung the cartoon unless it were not true. Not true, at least, in the sense that Boeing does not rule tyrannically over Olympia, and does not exercise sweeping power or insatiable greed. Coffey headed what still is the most powerful and effective lobby in the capital by far. The company itself is smart and sophisticated enough, however, not to overreach and, in the end, destroy its un-paralleled effectiveness.

It is true that Boeing seeks to identify and influence every bill that might affect its business significantly; as a member of the Olympia press corps put it, "No law that Boeing is interested in passes without their fingerprints." Boeing's major legislative interests lie in taxes, labor, and the environment. The company seldom attempts to get favorable legislation passed; most of its efforts are directed to killing unfavorable legislation. For example, the state has exempted Boeing from its steep sales tax: the company argues that, as it operates in an international market, it would go out of business were it the only competitor having to pay millions of dollars per sale in Washington taxes. Every so often a legislator tries to slip the tax through, nevertheless, and Boeing goes all out to defeat the measure—always successfully. (Boeing already pays hundreds of millions of dollars annually in state and local taxes.) Boeing has rarely tasted defeat when it set out to kill any major bill.

Boeing exerts enormous legitimate power as Washington state's five-hundred-pound gorilla, whose huge number of jobs and river of greenbacks flowing into Washington's economy command the respect of virtually all the state's elected politicians. The company has no need, even if it were so inclined, to use illegitimate or unethical means to achieve its ends. Because the company doesn't want to dilute its influence by involving itself in scandals, Bill Allen instructed his lobbyists, "Don't do anything you wouldn't want to read on the front page of a paper or have to lie about under oath." As a result, Boeing's reputation in Olympia is spotless.

Boeing also strives hard to keep itself free of partisanship, working with and contributing to Democrats and Republicans, liberals and conservatives, especially incumbents; for one thing, the company never wants to be affected by the often fickle shifts of power. Once a Boeing lobbyist attended a postelection victory meeting of Republicans, where certain Democrats were targeted for political destruction. When his superiors found out he'd been there, they yanked him out of Olympia and transferred him to a nonlobbying job. Even some Democrats pleaded unsuccessfully for Boeing to reinstate him.

Boeing is a loner in Olympia: the company is so strong that it hardly ever needs to form coalitions with other businesses, and pays little attention to their efforts. A natural alliance with the IAM District 751 lobby occurs, however, on the many occasions that the company's interests and those of its workers coincide. The Boeing-IAM team is virtually unbeatable; the IAM has the most powerful union lobby in Olympia.

The most striking characteristic of Boeing's state lobbying operation, remarked on by virtually everyone familiar with the activity, is its obsession with keeping out of sight. Boeing is clearly deeply afraid that stories and photographs in newspapers, and segments on TV, of Boeing at work in Olympia would confirm peoples' suspicions that Boeing controls the state, and provoke public hostility. Legislators, for their part, fear that publicized contacts with Boeing's lobbyists might make them seem the company's puppets. Consequently, the company stations only two or three employees in Olympia, and maintains most of its lobbying staff at its headquarters, a little over an hour away up I-5 or just a short hop by helicopter. Boeing representatives almost never testify at hearings in the capitol, preferring to talk discreetly with legislators in their offices. Nor do they talk to the media on the record about bills, or distribute press releases about legislative issues, or allow their pictures to be taken on lobbying missions—they've been known literally to run away when cameras appeared. Although Boeing contributes amply to political campaigns, it takes care never to be the largest and therefore most conspicuous donor. Boeing does much of its lobbying when the legislature isn't in session, visiting legislative districts unobtrusively and hosting lawmakers on plant visits. Boeing's lobbyists try to spend time with each legislator important to the company if they feel the person will listen.

The union of Boeing and Seattle is like some marriages. One partner is pretty, the other a stalwart breadwinner. They're proud of their spouses, usually tolerate each other's faults, and fight and make up every so often. For the most part, they feel comfortable together, and would rather have the other as a mate than not. In the early 1970s, Boeing was flat on its back, Seattle was suffering, and both wondered if they would ever get well again.

=

Dick Henning described what happened to him in late 1970 when he was called into the office of the director of commercial engineering: The director "opened a conversation that lasted less than two minutes, got an urgent telephone call—so he said—of a reported late afternoon management meeting, and he handed me a release form and walked out of his office leaving me standing with my mouth wide open. I was in utter shock." Dick realized he'd been told "to make my own way—after thirty-two years of dedicated service. . . . I was devastated." He'd lost the job he'd had within Boeing, but had such high seniority that the corporation kept him on the payroll at full salary for the time being, and would assign him to small, odd jobs as they came up. But his boss's manner of dismissing him had been more like telling him to get lost. Dazed, yet a professional conditioned always to think of the company, Dick was hurt that no one had asked for his opinions on "the future of reliability on the 747, or what the overall plan was shaping up to become, the plan for the future."

"I was frightened, and so was June," Dick remembered. He was in extreme danger of being laid off for good. With his prospects slim for landing another good job at the age of fifty-five, they had to husband their resources. That meant selling their biggest extravagance, Rainbow Springs, their idyllic estate on Mercer Island. With the housing market glutted by homes of departing ex–Boeing employees and others wounded by the depression in the area, Dick could get only what he lamented as "a ridiculously low price" of $60,000. (In 1988, Dick saw the house listed for $350,000.) The buyers wanted to celebrate Christmas in their new home, which meant the Hennings had to leave their "happy house," as they called it, just before the holiday season. Dick and June moved temporarily into a one-bedroom apartment on Mercer Island, and June's mother went into a nursing home near the Northgate shopping mall. "I really hurt bad," Dick admitted, but he wasn't as angry at Boeing as he was at President Nixon for not helping the company with more government contracts. Like many Seattleites, he felt that Nixon had no sympathy for the people of Boeing or Seattle because the state of Washington had voted for Humphrey in the 1968 election. On February 1, 1971, Dick, June, and her mother moved permanently into a two-bedroom brick house in the Olympic Manor community on the northwest side of Seattle in sight of Puget Sound (where Dick still lived in the mid-1990s).

Dick was lucky to be getting a paycheck when so many others were being severed outright, and luckier still when, half a year after being cut loose, he found a unit in Boeing that needed someone with his background. He became a systems engineering manager in the AWACS airborne electronics program. The position was at a much lower level than the one he had left, and he had to take a jumbo pay cut of six thousand dollars, but Dick was filled with joy at working steadily again. He articulated his happiness: "It was a great relief to be back amongst my engineering buddies on a military project to defend the United States against Russian bombers. Life began to take on meaning once more. . . . We worked many long hours, sometimes even till midnight, and many Saturdays in love of our work. . . . There was meaning to my life once more." At the same time, the continuing layoffs and impermanence of life at Boeing terrified him: "I was very scared watching my friends leaving Boeing to search for work elsewhere. It was a nightmare!"

Part III

Winning the Pot

11 ‖ The Great Comeback

As terrible as Wilson's approach to saving Boeing was (and no other approach was obviously better), it worked. Boeing survived. Dropping employees and facilities stemmed the hemorrhaging of dollars and got Boeing marching a step ahead of its creditors. A small but steady flow of military and space-program orders kept cash flowing in. Remarkably, Boeing never had to report a net loss in any year in its annual report; the lowest profit was some ten million dollars. (The happy reports undoubtedly owed much to the ingenuity of Boeing's talented controller, Hal Haynes.)

In 1971, international airplane sales picked up somewhat as the rest of the world resumed the conversion to jets that had essentially been completed in the United States. The real turning point in Boeing's battle to regain its financial health occurred domestically, however. Out in the marketplace, a hole opened for a jetliner larger than the old 727 but smaller than the 707. It seemed a small opening, barely worth pursuing. Designing an entirely new model was out of the question—Boeing didn't have nearly enough money. Wilson looked at making a new derivative of the 727, but even that would be too costly. (Derivatives are wholesale improvements of models that don't go as far as designing entirely new models. The fuselage might be stretched to carry more passengers, for example, with bigger and more powerful engines added to increase speed and

317

range, and wings strengthened to carry the greater weight. The expense of designing derivatives is much less than the cost of developing an entirely new airplane.) Wilson chose the relatively cheap option of improving the 727-200 developed in 1968, a derivative that had flunked in the marketplace primarily because it couldn't go far enough—its range was even less than that of the original 727. Wilson told Jack Steiner, the father of the initial 727 and then running the operation that made 727s, to carry out the decision.

Pratt & Whitney agreed to upgrade and redesign the JT8D engine for the new airplane in return for a firm order, so Steiner ordered thirty of the multi-million-dollar engines on speculation. His design team then increased the range of the 727-200 by half as much again, increased the payload and speed, designed a nacelle that lowered engine noise, installed up-to-date instrumentation, modernized the interior to make it look like a wide-body, and made numerous other improvements—virtually creating a new derivative. After spending several million hard-to-come-by dollars on the project, Boeing first flew the new airplane, called the Advanced 727-200, in April 1971.

As Boeing salesmen marched out to sell the airplane, the company found that it had again misjudged the market—but, as if fate were trying to restore a balance, this time they had misjudged it on the low side. As the airplane was being developed, the airline business changed in directions that intensified the need for the model. Increasingly, passengers desired more frequent flights between cities, and thus the airlines needed aircraft of the Advanced 727-200 size to carry the same number of passengers per day on those routes. Airlines added more and more routes, most of them of the range that made the Advanced 727-200 ideal. The airlines snapped up the new airplanes as fast as Boeing could build them, and sales soared far past Boeing's modest targets. The airplane sold so well that the proceeds enabled Boeing to pay off its backbreaking debts and recuperate financially. (In retirement, Steiner emphasized how important the Advanced 727-200 had been to Boeing and him personally. "The best compliment ever paid me was by T, when he said in front of my peers, 'Steiner, I don't know whether you designed the [original] 727 or not, but I know you paid off our billion-dollar debt and we needed that paid off badly.'" Steiner stood with a visitor gazing out the picture window on the back of his large, luxurious house in an exclusive neighborhood on the eastern shore of Lake Washington. His yacht, on which he and his wife spent several months a year, was moored to his dock at the end of his expansive back lawn, and pitched and rolled slightly as swells passed beneath it on the windy day; they sail on Puget Sound, connected to Lake Washington by a lock. "The Advanced 727-200 got all this for Dorothy and me," Steiner said, sweeping his arm to include the yacht, the grounds, and the house. "It certainly wasn't paid for by my regular salary. It came from the generous stock options T gave me for paying off Boeing's debt." Interestingly, as great as Steiner was at leading aircraft development projects, he didn't impress Wilson's deputy, Wes Maulden, with his general management skills. In the early 1970s, Wilson put Steiner in charge of all aircraft programs save the 747. When Maulden complained, Wilson told Maulden to help Steiner succeed because he couldn't afford to lose such a talent to a competitor. If he had to choose between keeping either his closest adviser or the gifted jetliner creator, he declared forthrightly, he'd have to pick the creator.)

Another contribution to Boeing's get-well fund came from another unexpected source: the Douglas division of McDonnell Douglas. The 707 and the DC-8, the two old competitors, were losing money for their companies. In the depressed aircraft market, Boeing was producing only seven 707s a year and needed to make twelve a year to cover recurring production expenses. Wilson had decided to keep the production line for the aging airplane going in hopes that when good times returned the jetliner would live out the remainder of its model life and more than return the losses. Douglas chose the other option. In 1972, Douglas decided to cut its losses and kill the almost equally old DC-8; the first Douglas jetliner had never returned all the money that Douglas had put into it. Wilson was delighted. With the only direct competitor to the 707 gone, sales of the Boeing airplane increased immediately, and soon the pioneer jetliner was paying its way and then some. Boeing went on to sell eighty-one more of the cash-cow products at a large profit before shutting down the line. Douglas's critics point to this decision as one of the company's many management boners that furthered Boeing's ascendancy and Douglas's decline.

Not everything went Boeing's way at this time. Wilson himself stubbed his toe on another decision about an aircraft program. In 1973, hoping to extend the success of the Advanced 727-200, Wilson commissioned his engineers to design a bigger and more powerful derivative. United Airlines was keenly interested in the idea and worked closely with Boeing in drawing up specifications for the new airplane. Other airlines registered their desires for the new jetliner. The project looked like such a winner that Boeing touted the great promise of the upcoming airplane in its 1974 annual report. Then governments started to clamp down on jet noise, and this latest version of the 727 was too thunderous; the airlines lost interest. Boeing promised to get quieter engines, but, with future business conditions looking brighter and new technology becoming available, the airlines began to look for completely new models. Wilson aborted the airplane-to-be in 1975 and stoically wrote off the fifty million dollars Boeing had spent on it. Another setback came in 1976, when Boeing designed a tanker version of the 747 but lost out to Douglas in a hotly fought competition. (Boeing suspected that the Pentagon gave Douglas the award only because the other company was then in worse financial shape than Boeing.)

While insuring Boeing's immediate survival, and doing so without amputating any major organs (albeit with much bloodletting), Wilson went about correcting the company's deficiencies that had led to the crisis, getting Boeing healthy for the long term. An author, writing in 1970 about aircraft manufacturers, declared, "Military development methods appear to be so ingrained into the consciousness of the industry that it cannot change." Wilson determined to prove this thinking wrong for one company, at least, by making Boeing as efficient and productive as possible.

The airliner division, seat of the greatest problems, sought a major improvement in efficiency by sharply reducing the number of supervisory and staff employees; rearranging work areas and making procedural changes to increase productive time; overhauling production processes and, as Steiner pointed out, placing "thousands of changes into each assembly line"; modernizing computer systems; and opening up communications channels between engineering and manufacturing, insisting that engineers once again seek Boeing's pre–World War II goal of designing aircraft that could be produced inexpensively.

By these and other means, Boeing vastly improved a crude but reliable indicator of productivity in its industry: man-hours per pound of airplanes produced. The measurement for 727 production dropped from 2.6 man-hours per pound to just one man-hour per pound. When the figure reached "one," managers and supervisors held a party. Boeing could produce an airplane with 30 percent fewer people than required in the 1960s.

Wilson said he "felt good" about Boeing's "great progress" as early as 1970. The next year, somebody working for him calculated that if the airliner division had been as efficient in the 1960s as it was in 1971, early in Wilson's program, Boeing would have made half a billion dollars more each on the 707 and 727 programs. But Wilson kept the pressure on for even greater productivity. John Newhouse, who studied the aircraft industry at the beginning of the 1980s, declared, "By the mid-1970s, the big gap between Boeing's efficiency and everyone else's had developed." Still T kept pressing. In 1980, eleven thousand workers turned out seven 747s per month, compared to twenty-five thousand workers in 1969. "By [1978] Boeing was in a class by itself—much the most productive and successful of the world's aerospace companies and, indeed, one of the most efficient of all big manufacturing enterprises," Newhouse wrote. Like fire that hardens metal, the economic conflagration had strengthened Boeing's efficiency to a degree unprecedented in its history.

During the crisis, another step toward Boeing's rehabilitation may have been triggered or accelerated by a comment made by a member of Boeing's board of directors. George Weyerhaeuser picked up on the criticism made by fellow director Crawford Greenwalt about Boeing's careless approach to return on investment.

Weyerhaeuser told Wilson he'd never again approve a new airplane project unless Boeing had a plan that projected a decent ROI. In 1971, Wilson established a planning office and, with the aid of new computerized systems, developed the company's first ten-year business plan. He formalized management's approach to the business further by installing new cost-control systems.

Wilson never had a grand plan to orchestrate Boeing's comeback, but five elements of an ad hoc strategy evolved over the 1970s: first, slicing facilities, programs, and, above all, the payroll to stave off bankruptcy; second, boosting sales with the Advanced 727-200 to begin moving ahead again; third, making the company more efficient and rationalizing planning to make Boeing function better; fourth, improving sales by paying more attention to customers; and fifth, diversifying into nonaircraft businesses to buffer risks that were becoming too dangerous. At the same time, of course, Boeing had to continue to produce superior airplane models.

Wilson was shocked into the customer focus element during a trip that he and Tex Boullioun took to Europe in 1970 after the major European airlines had gotten their first 747s. Lufthansa executives lashed them verbally for hours about problems with Boeing airplanes, and particularly about the company's inattention and unresponsiveness to their needs. The airline executives chided Boeing for slipping so far behind the other manufacturers after being so good during the early 707 days. Wilson and Boullioun got no respite at their next stop, Air France. After essentially repeating the Germans' condemnations, the French emphasized their displeasure by icily canceling the dinner that had been arranged for executives of the two companies. The Boeing pair completed their hellish hat trick by getting the same kind of treatment from Alitalia.

Customer support at Boeing had a long history of ups and downs. Boeing had established a customer support function in 1936. After the war, however, arrogant treatment of purchasers had been one of reasons the Stratocruiser didn't sell better than it did. When Boeing's next airplane, the 707, came along, coddling of customers had been among the reasons for its success. After a chastened Wilson returned from Europe, he discovered that the customer support functions in the divisions had slipped to a low priority; if Boeing didn't think something was as important as a customer thought it was, which was often, the customer got put off. Wilson established a separate customer support division whose only priority was taking care of airplane buyers. (Boeing now has people stationed at every major airport in the world to give its airplanes immediate attention. When Boeing sells an aircraft, the customer support section of the sales contract is often one of the thickest parts. Overall, Boeing's customer support is considered the best in the industry.)

T couldn't expect any help in Boeing's hour of need from the business on which the company had grown big and ridden into the jet age—bombers and their refueling tankers. As foreseen in the early 1950s, guided missiles largely killed new bomber orders ten years later. Fortunately, however, Boeing had succeeded in the missile business and had gone on to become a major contractor in the space field. Reflecting the broadened mission, Bill Allen in 1961 had led the directors in dropping the word "Airplane" from the corporation's official name, the Boeing Airplane Company, making it simply the Boeing Company.

Boeing had beefed up the military side of its aerospace capabilities in 1960 when it acquired the Vertol helicopter corporation of suburban Philadelphia. Vertol, a leader in its field, made large "flying banana" helicopters with two overhead rotors, mainly for defense applications. In 1970, Boeing won its most important Pentagon contract in many years when it was awarded the AWACS—Airborne Warning and Control System—program based on 707s crammed with electronics gear.

Like Bill Boeing and Bill Allen, Wilson heard the siren song of diversification when the aircraft business seemed almost hopeless. He wanted to diversify more heavily than ever into businesses where Boeing could apply its management skills entirely outside its traditional lines. This move had begun in the 1960s to provide more growth than promised by the maturing airline market, when the idea that good managers can manage anything became popular with many companies. In the dark days of 1971, when anything looked better than passenger airplanes, Wilson went so far as to predict that by 1980 one-third of Boeing's products would be nonaerospace. He established the Office of Corporate Business Development to spearhead diversification. An annual report presented Wilson's grand vision of the company: "Our objective is to continue to be a broadbased company with primary emphasis on high technology transportation, missile, and space systems. Beyond that, our emphasis and interest are centered on computer services and engineering and construction activities, many of them directed at elements of the energy and environmental fields." Nontraditional projects Wilson took on included the following: building light railcars at the helicopter division for the Boston transit system; computerizing the control system of the Consolidated Edison electric company in New York City; forming a subsidiary, Boeing Computer Services, to provide information management for the general business community; and buying a 15 percent interest in the Peabody Coal Company. Wilson expected these ventures and others like them to cushion the inevitable drastic aerospace downturns in the future.

As Boeing was climbing out of the abyss, nothing signified the transition from the old Boeing to the new Boeing more than the retirement of Bill Allen and many of those who had worked with him. In September 1972, at the age of seventy-two, Allen retired as chairman of the board and turned his gavel over to Wilson. The event was largely ceremonial: Wilson had acted as top man since becoming CEO three years before. In his last act as chairman, however, Allen helped to create a situation that was unprecedented at Boeing and unusual for any corporation. He presided over the board's election of a new president to replace Wilson in that office whom Wilson didn't like, with whom he had no intention of working closely, and whom he didn't plan on allowing to succeed him. The newly elected president, who would also ascend to the board of directors, was none other than Mal Stamper, who had nearly taken over two years previously when Wilson was recovering from his heart attack. Stamper got the presidency with the same strong support he'd had from Allen and other board members in 1970. The thinking of the board hasn't been recorded. Possibly, however, the directors wanted to name a likely successor to Wilson as soon as possible because of Wilson's two heart attacks and the scare that the company had had after his second heart attack and four-month-long incapacitation. The real possibility of succeeding Wilson as CEO on his death from a third and fatal heart attack may have been the reason Stamper took a job that promised little but frustration for him while Wilson was in office. Wilson, moreover, with his health undoubtedly on his mind, had talked about serving only until he turned sixty in 1981, which—if he followed through—would clear the way for Stamper.

Mal Stamper, forty-seven, a green-eyed, dark-haired man, had features that made him stand out. One was a characteristic he shared with Bill Allen: a smooth voice. Stamper spoke with a deep, resonant, mellifluous tone that might have won him a career as a radio announcer. But many people said that his most impressive characteristic was his brilliant mind.

Wilson's attitude toward Stamper was partly due to a major mismatch in personalities, more glaring than the contrast between Wilson himself and Bill Allen, or between Allen and Wellwood Beall. Wilson was a country boy who, while in hotels on business trips, liked to put his bare feet up on a table as he chatted with colleagues. He was an unsophisticated leader in the style of Harry Truman or Lyndon Johnson. Stamper, on the other hand, was like Jack Kennedy: urbane, witty, and charming. Wilson still lived in Normandy Park, in a first-line supervisor's subdivision. His small ranch house was a block from a heavily trafficked road, and just a mile west of SeaTac. Stamper lived in a large house in the Highlands, the isolated little kingdom where Bill Boeing had lived and Bill Allen still lived. (Wilson had gotten angry when a board member suggested that he, too, move to the Highlands and get a residence more befitting Boeing's CEO. He had always said that, once his salary reached fifteen thousand dollars, he wasn't going to change his lifestyle—and he didn't.) Stamper was an accomplished artist whose abstract paintings sold for thousands of dollars. He was active on Seattle's cultural scene, and was frequently mentioned or pictured in the society pages.

Wilson had little interest in the arts or fashionable society; a colleague heard Wilson remark (unjustifiably, the colleague thought) that Stamper used the company to further his own social life rather than the other way around. Stamper had given up smoking and become a health enthusiast who liked to run in marathons, hike up mountains, and ski. Wilson had no special liking for fresh-air activities. In conversation, T was direct and to the point. Stamper was diffuse and loquacious, and chatted all around a subject; he did his thinking by talking to people. Wilson's demeanor was usually serious. Stamper wove humor throughout his conversations. In public, Wilson always dressed conservatively. Stamper was known to have taken an airplane trip wearing a sweat suit. Because of Stamper's humor and dress that was not always conservative, some people steeped in the Boeing culture regarded him as a clown. Stamper was nakedly ambitious in a culture that disdained the appearance of ambition. (The proper comment at an interview after being promoted to a high rank was something like "Aw, shucks, I was so completely surprised when they told me I'd been elected a vice president.") Wilson had grown up professionally at Boeing. Stamper had matured at GM. Stamper could not have won Wilson's admiration for the 747 program that he ran, whose devastating cost overrun left a mess that Wilson had to clean up. Wilson and Stamper were simply not simpatico.

Stamper was born on April 4, 1925, in Detroit. He entered the University of Michigan in 1943 and enrolled in the prelaw curriculum, but left to join the Navy at the height of World War II. The Navy sent him to the University of Richmond for two years and then, when tests showed an aptitude for electrical engineering, to the Georgia Institute of Technology. Solidly built, with the mesomorph's "no-neck" look, he played football at both schools and was a guard on the Georgia Tech team that went to the 1945 Orange Bowl. He wrote a column for Georgia Tech's student newspaper. Although he voted Republican, his views were so liberal for the time and place that the Ku Klux Klan tried to muzzle him. Stamper served out his career as a naval officer after graduation, and then went back to the University of Michigan to study law. Married with two children by that time, he dropped out to get a job. With only a semester to go, he intended to return for his degree but never did. He went to work for General Motors; career-minded and always looking ahead, he passed up a higher-paying job at Ford because the top positions at that company were reserved for Ford family members. He spent his entire GM career working with electrical products: AC spark plugs, Delco batteries, and missile electronics.

When President Truman tried to nationalize the steel industry, Stamper's conservative instincts impelled him to enter the Republican primary for congressman against a powerful incumbent. He lost, and gave up his political aspirations.

Stamper impressed the Navy with his executive skills on naval contracts to develop electronics for Polaris missiles. In 1962, when Bill Allen was looking for someone to head the buildup of Boeing's electronics capabilities to support initiatives in missile and rocket development, an admiral recommended Stamper. Allen made him an offer, and, after fourteen years with GM, Stamper moved to Seattle. He successfully launched Boeing into aerospace electronics, and then was assigned to the team bidding for the NASA contract to build the Manned Orbiting Laboratory. In 1965, while he was working on that competition (which Boeing ultimately lost to Douglas), Harold Geneen, the storied head of ITT, offered him a big electronics job at the conglomerate and an annual salary of one hundred thousand dollars. Stamper was then supporting a wife and six children on only twenty-eight thousand dollars. He accepted, and told his immediate boss at Boeing that he'd be leaving. News of the resignation quickly reached Allen and upset him. Unlike Wilson, Allen liked and respected Stamper, and found him completely simpatico. Socially and culturally, they were like brothers. Allen wanted to get Stamper into the top levels at Boeing and, eventually, maybe even the highest rank. He offered Stamper a vice presidency, his choice of assignments, and a raise to forty thousand dollars. (Scotsman Allen believed in keeping executive salaries low, including his own; Allen himself wasn't making much more than a hundred thousand dollars then.) He also dangled the prospects of bigger titles and money ahead. Stamper, who would have hated to leave the agreeable Seattle area anyway, decided to stay at Boeing and take the job of overhauling the gas turbine division. That was quickly followed by the 747 assignment and, later, the slot as general manager of the airliner division. In 1971, he had been named vice president of operations at corporate headquarters.

Colleagues describe Stamper as a generous man who gained satisfaction from acts of charity. Once, he had second thoughts about an overcoat he had bought. Instead of returning it, he drove around the city until he saw someone who looked needy and gave it to him. On Thanksgiving, the Stamper family would bake hams and pies, and distribute them to poor families.

Stamper got a kick out of practical jokes. While talking with another executive who had the office next door, he leaned back in his wooden chair and the leg broke. Somehow the now-useless chair inspired a trick on the two secretaries in the suite outside the office. The other executive flung open the door and ran out. Stamper came right behind him and heaved the chair in his direction, yelling "Get out and stay out, you son of a . . . !" He choked off his curses when he saw the women. The chair crashed to the floor and broke into several pieces as the other man fled the suite and disappeared; Stamper slammed his door shut. He let the secretaries whisper and wonder for five minutes before letting them in on the gag. An associate who knew him well described Stamper as a "boisterous, happy man" who enjoyed life. He'd need all his good humor in the years ahead serving a man who didn't want him.

Ed Wells, the brain behind all Boeing's technical programs, joined Allen in retirement in 1972 but remained active as a consultant and board member. His reasons for retiring early, at sixty-two, can only be guessed. The cancellation of the SST the year before and no prospect of major new development programs before his normal retirement age may have been factors, and he was reportedly in poor health. George Schairer also retired in the 1970s. (Bill Allen in retirement served as a consultant to Boeing, reporting to work every day at a headquarters office. He became forgetful, and his personality changed. One day, when he was eighty, Mef got a call from Wilson saying that Bill was behaving strangely and offending people in the executive dining room. They had to take him home. He was diagnosed as having Alzheimer's disease. The slow, sad disintegration that characterizes the grim affliction continued; he died at the age of eighty-five on October 29, 1985.)

The bad times in the aircraft industry went on and on during the 1970s. Just when it would seem that the industry was about to be resurrected, something would happen to knock it back down. The Arab oil embargo beginning in October 1973 sent the world into recession and delivered a one-two punch to the airline industry: Ticket sales were held down, and operating costs soared with the price of aviation fuel. Another international development affecting Boeing was the end of the Vietnam War and the period of détente with the Soviet Union that began in the mid-1970s. Although certainly the world benefited from peace and decreased tensions, Boeing and other manufacturers suffered when military sales, which had assumed new importance with commercial business so slow, dropped significantly. With the business dip in 1975, Boeing had to lay off production workers and engineers again to hang on to its gains.

(In the mid-1990s, a fifty-five-year-old engineer who had been shown the door in 1975 sat at a table in a noisy restaurant near Boeing's Renton offices, crowded with Boeing people, having lunch with a writer and telling his story. In 1975, he'd served the company for fifteen years. Like many engineers in all the layoffs, he felt betrayed. He had been called into his boss's office and handed his pink slip—in actuality a white release form. "I had assumed that I, and most other Boeing engineers, had an unspoken contract with the company: I work in a highly specialized job for you that leaves me with skills not marketable in many other places, and in return you find a way to keep me on for life. It turned out that Boeing never saw it that way. To them, I was no different than excess sheet metal in inventory, a cost to be eliminated." Having to support a wife and two-year-old boy, he collected unemployment compensation while looking for work. "I was one of few people standing in line at the unemployment office who had on a business suit. I thought, 'I don't belong here.'" He knew laid-off professional people who spurned unemployment checks, refusing to subject themselves to the indignity. He was out of work three months when he was lucky enough to land a job with an aerospace firm in Redmond at three-quarters of his Boeing salary. He kept up his so-called recall rights by sending Boeing a certified letter every three months indicating his availability to be rehired. After a year and half, when business picked up again, he was called back at his old salary, which was lower in real terms due to the high inflation rate. Afraid of getting a bad name at Boeing, he insisted on anonymity when he told his story.)

Diversification disappointed Wilson when it flopped miserably. The railcars derailed frequently on curves, and the doors often didn't work. The cars proved so technologically complex, moreover, that they were impossible for the Massachusetts Bay Transit Authority to maintain. The city of Boston successfully sued Boeing, which had to drop out of the market. Intractable contract problems over Consolidated Edison's computerized system forced Boeing into paying to get out of its commitment. Most of the other diversification attempts were equally disillusioning, for Boeing as well as the other aircraft companies that tried the same thing. The biggest stumbling blocks were the markets. The customers were usually businesses and unsophisticated municipalities that didn't act at all like the familiar airliner and military aircraft buyers. Cost was much more important than in the aircraft industry, and the customers didn't need or want the elaborate, expensive engineering and management attention that Boeing showered on the products as if they were high-technology airplanes. Boeing didn't know small but important marketing details—such as that longshoremen on the East Coast had to be paid off to "prevent damage" to railcars when they were shipped. Production techniques were dissimilar, moreover, and the new ventures never received the attention they needed, always taking second place to the aircraft business. Wilson said, one assumes half jokingly, that if the public had known about all the incompetence involved in the Boston railcar fiasco, Boeing's entire management team would have been fired. (An incident from the diversification days showed that, surprisingly for the CEO of a major corporation, Wilson was a poor negotiator, perhaps because he was so direct. Boeing's attorney during the dispute with Consolidated Edison said that he advised Wilson, preparing for negotiations with Con Ed's CEO, to offer to settle for twenty million dollars and go no higher than twenty-seven million. At the start of the discussion between the CEOs, Wilson blurted, "I've been told to offer you twenty million dollars, and my top number is twenty-seven million dollars." They settled immediately at twenty-seven million dollars.)

Wilson, never sentimental about losing propositions, got rid of the diversified dogs by the 1980s. He kept two diversifications that succeeded. Boeing Computer Services, while never a great money-maker, remained profitable enough that it's still in business today, although now it serves only government agencies and Boeing divisions. Frank Shrontz finally sold Boeing's interest in Peabody Coal Company at a handsome profit in 1990 to raise cash for jetliner development. (In retirement, Wilson lamented a particular short-fall in diversification. He revealed candidly that one of his greatest disappointments was blowing what he felt was a real chance to make Boeing the leader in guidance systems and other computer-related technologies, an area that McDonnell Douglas made pay off.)

Business only slowly returned to normal after the mid-1970s. It's hard to find a point where it could be said that Boeing had finally returned to health after the travail of the late 1960s and early and mid-'70s. But by the late 1970s Boeing was out of debt and financially healthy, the airline industry was back to normal, and orders were back to 1967 levels. Most important, Boeing had risen into a class by itself as the most productive aircraft manufacturer and the world's only profitable jetliner maker.

Wilson won awards and acclaim from the business world for saving Boeing from bankruptcy and forging it into the strongest aircraft manufacturer in the industry. *Financial World* magazine named him its man of the year in a 1979 cover story. *Time* magazine carried his picture on the cover of the April 7, 1980, issue and told the story of how he led Boeing's comeback in an article titled "The Engineer of Success." Wilson was praised for carrying through the deepest and most successful retrenchment in corporate history. He himself counts rescuing Boeing from the crunch as the achievement of which he's most proud, but he said he got no great feeling of satisfaction in doing it. Satisfaction, he declared, is what comes from winning a big order or major contract, not from laying people off.

Recently Wilson revealed that his life nearly ended just as he put Boeing back on the road to greatness. In an interview in the mid-1990s, he talked about having an angiogram to check on his heart in 1977. While he was undergoing the risky procedure, he experienced cardiac arrest. The doctors grabbed the paddles and jolted him back to life, just as they had after his 1970 heart attack. He recovered the same day, with no aftereffects other than temporary paddle burns on his chest.

Wilson's company, however, bore scars from its ordeal that would take a long time to disappear. Few of the laid-off employees returned. Many moved away or got other jobs that they stuck with; many engineers even got out of engineering entirely. Because of Boeing's newfound productivity, furthermore, it was a long time before Boeing got back up to 1967 employment levels. Some industry analysts argue that, since Boeing went for almost a decade with almost no hiring, a hole was created in its employee population. On top were the employees who had survived the layoffs, usually older (such as Dick Henning). At the bottom were the employees hired after the late 1970s. There were few employees in between. Years later, as a result, the normal, steady transitions in management were interrupted. When managers and supervisors retired, normally to be replaced by people from the middle of the age population, Boeing would have trouble finding seasoned replacements from within its own ranks. (Boeing disputes this analysis, positing that the age bubble was a function of birth rates and other demographic factors, and not the layoffs.)

In 1977, the most recent three-year contract with the Machinists' union ended, and a new contract had to be negotiated. Feelings of frustration and hostility built up over the twelve years—including the trying crunch—since the last strike had come to a head. Now that the company was economically sound again, the members were spoiling for another strike. Boeing learned (from its ordinary, legitimate contacts with the union) that the company could really do nothing to head off a strike: it was an emotional situation that defied logic. The workers wanted to walk out to show how they felt about all that had happened, and reason be damned. Union officials recognized this, and among themselves talked about a "therapeutic strike" to let off steam.

Despite the strike mood among the rank and file, relations between the local IAM and Boeing under the new leaders in both organizations were much better than they had been. There were people on each side who liked and respected one another. Wilson, a rough-hewn character and a SPEEA officer when he was a young engineer, had more empathy with union leaders than did Allen. On the other hand, Boeing officials had nothing but contempt for the leader of the IAM International in Washington, D.C., who was a self-proclaimed socialist named William Winpisinger. The nicest term Boeing people had for him was "jerk." The local IAM opinion of Winpisinger and his International crowd was much the same. The Seattle local was the biggest and richest IAM group in the country, and the Seattle officials resented being "pushed around," as they saw it, by an organization across the country that seemed interested mainly in the large treasury in Seattle.

No single issue or group of issues was at stake in 1977. The union asked for contract improvements over a wide range of the usual labor concerns, including wages, cost of living increases, retirement provisions, and health and welfare benefits. The strike began as anticipated on October 4 and lasted forty-five days, until November 17. Both sides were satisfied with the final agreement. The strike had hardly any effect on Boeing's resurgence. By late 1978, Boeing was more profitable than ever.

During the crisis and comeback, Boeing had been considering new aircraft ventures. Chastened by the lessons of the 747, they looked for partners to share the risk. For several reasons, Boeing struck out in new directions, looking not at home in the United States to form new relationships, but across the Atlantic to Europe.

=

Early in 1973, Dick Henning was assigned to manage a tour by a special aircraft. It was fitted out to demonstrate AWACS technology to NATO allies, who were potential customers. In Germany, an accident wrecked a ground-based radar installation that was part of the demonstration. New equipment was flown in from Seattle, and Dick led teams that worked twelve-hour shifts to repair the damage. They fixed the unit in three and a half days, in "a typical Boeing all-out effort," as he put it. The tour impressed the allies and left them eager to buy AWACS aircraft. "I felt down deep that I had earned the respect of my bosses and the Air Force, and my confidence was fully restored," Dick revealed. In high spirits and feeling more secure, he bought a new Cadillac Coupe de Ville.

In 1976, Dick was named AWACS test reliability chief for the long test-flight period, working at the main Boeing complex in south Seattle. He eloquently summarized his work day: "Morning management control meetings on events happening overnight were at seven A.M. I almost never left the office before six P.M. I usually drove home via the harbor freeway, and that gave me a chance to watch the cargo boats and to appreciate the beauty of Elliot Bay, Puget Sound, and the magnificent Olympic Mountains, especially at sunset. That easy ride home was like a drink of elixir after a difficult and demanding day." Despite the demands of his job, Dick took on off-hours responsibility in his neighborhood as chairman and president of the Olympic Manor Community Club. After the flight tests, he was carried over as production reliability chief. His fears of being laid off again vanished completely.

Dick, an ardent sports fan, was delighted when Seattle literally became a big-league city in the late 1970s, getting the Mariners baseball team and the Supersonics basketball team (to be followed by the Seahawks football team in 1984).

Dick was forced to confront the fact that he was getting old. He had to get dental plates. His biggest concern was the effect of the dentures on his work. "They affected my oral presentations substantially and that bothered me considerably," he moaned. He shouldn't have worried. In May 1979, the Aerospace Division honored Dick as Employee of the Month. His annual salary rose to forty thousand dollars.

Almost before Dick knew it, he was turning up the July page on his 1979 calender and staring at August. The time had come. The end. He had served Boeing for more than forty years and reached the age of sixty-four and one-half years. The Social Security Administration had advised him that he was already eligible for his maximum Social Security payout. With a total annual retirement income from all sources of forty-five thousand dollars—five thousand more than his current relatively low salary—it made sense to leave. (Dick was furious when the government's advice turned out to be mistaken: he would have gotten more Social Security had he stayed until age sixty-five.) But he felt let down by his retirement party: it was held at a bowling alley, and few of his old comrades from his SPEEA days came. ("Lots of people got better parties," he recalled years later, still hurt. "I wasn't happy!")

Dick said his only real regret about all those hardworking years is that he hadn't spent more time with his boy. Otherwise, he was gratified by his four decades with Boeing: "My greatest satisfaction in life has come from my career in engineering. I wish everyone could share the pride I feel in knowing that I served my country and my company well."

The Hennings had no yacht to sail in their golden years. On vacations, they had fished from a rowboat powered by a 7½-horsepower Ted Williams outboard motor—and a thief had stolen that shortly before Dick left Boeing. But they planned to splurge on a fun-filled kickoff to retirement: a seven-week tour of Europe and the Holy Land, when they would spend more time enjoying themselves together than ever before. Only a week after Dick's retirement party, June was felled by a slight stroke. While she was recuperating, her doctors noticed tremors in her right arm signaling the onset of Parkinson's disease. They had to call off their trip. Dick installed a telescope in front of the picture window in his living room so he could watch boats in Puget Sound, visible over the roofs of his neighbors, and settled down in his small house to begin his new job of caring for June and her mother.

The year before Dick retired, a quite different midwestern native started his job with Boeing. On March 13, 1978, former gas station attendant Bill Gray, twenty-nine years old and pleasant-faced—short and fat at five feet seven inches and 225 pounds—plodded into the company's cacophonous hammer shop on the Duwamish riverfront. Having no special trade, Bill would operate loud machinery that cut, ground, punched out, and polished parts for Boeing aircraft, including the device that gave the shop its name, a drop hammer that forged the aluminum ashtrays that fit into the armrests of passenger seats. Bill had held several jobs in his life. He had applied for this opening to make a little more money and work in a safer neighborhood, and because a friend of his was applying for a Boeing job. He had no idea how long he'd stay at the company.

William Joseph Gray was born at St. Joe's hospital in Milwaukee, Wisconsin, on September 22, 1949, the first child of William and Phyllis Marie Gray. His father sold lithographic services for a local firm, and his mother waited on tables at upscale clubs in the area. A few weeks later, Bill was baptized in the Roman Catholic Church. Two brothers, Paul and David, were born later. Bill grew up in the tense atmosphere of a rocky marriage, which climaxed in the trauma of his parents' divorce when he was nine years old.

Bill lived on the outskirts of the Milwaukee area, south of the city. Starting at age ten, he worked at part-time jobs as a farmhand and stable boy. He dropped out of high school in his junior year, along with most of his friends, as war raged in Vietnam and the draft raged at home. When he was a few days away from his eighteenth birthday and facing being inducted into the Army, Bill joined the Air Force. The service made him a maintenance specialist for Lockheed C-130 cargo airplanes, then shipped him overseas for three years to serve on Okinawa and, for brief periods, in Vietnam. Sorry that he hadn't graduated from high school, Bill applied himself to Air Force–sponsored correspondence classes and won his general equivalency diploma (GED).

Fired by ambition for more education and encouraged by the subsidy available under the GI Bill, he left the Air Force after four years and enrolled at the University of Wisconsin–Waukesha, near Milwaukee, to study journalism. He couldn't pass the required math course in his first semester, however, and his dream of a college degree was shattered. He had to leave the university and go to work, finding jobs with a landscaper, a mover, and—partially fulfilling his journalistic aims—with the *Milwaukee Journal,* where he served as a copy boy.

While at the Waukesha campus, Bill had edited the college newspaper. He started dating a cute girl on his staff, Linda Radtke, also of Milwaukee. In 1977, when he was twenty-eight and she nineteen, they got married in a civil ceremony (and again a little later in a Catholic church) over the objections of her parents. The newlyweds felt married life would be happier as far away from Milwaukee as possible. Linda left school, and she and Bill packed their belongings in a small trailer, hitching it up to a '74 Pontiac. With a thousand dollars in their pockets and hopes of enrolling in some college again, they headed for the West Coast and a city they'd heard nice things about: Seattle.

Arriving at Puget Sound, Bill and Linda bought a newspaper and scanned the "Apartments for Rent" section of the classifieds. They found a studio apartment in the Yeats Building on Lake Union—if you stuck your head out the window and looked in the right direction, you could see the water—and signed a monthly lease for $125 a month. Bill looked for a job and three days later was hired as an attendant at a Union 76 gas station in the rough Capitol Hill section, making $4.25 an hour.

A few months later, a man Bill worked with suggested that they both apply at Boeing. Bill was receptive. He'd heard that the company paid well, and he feared for his safety on Capitol Hill since having watched a gun battle across the street from the gas station. Bill and his friend went to the office of the Veterans Administration, which runs a jobs service, and were referred to two openings at Boeing. Bill and his buddy were both hired. Boeing gave him a bump in pay, to a base wage of $6.10 an hour.

Bill continued to work part-time pumping gas. Now that he was drawing two paychecks and making good money, he and Linda felt they could afford to rent a house. After six months on Lake Union, they spotted a good deal in Bothell, a town just northeast of Seattle. An ad asked only two hundred dollars a month for a big house on five acres, provided that the tenant take care of five horses quartered on the property. Bill knew horses from his boyhood experiences, so they went out one night after work and took the house, located on a hill at the edge of a small subdivision. A few days later their faces fell when, towing a U-Haul trailer, they saw their new home for the first time in daylight. Pieces of junk littered the ground all around the house. Resigning themselves to the decrepit appearance, the couple enjoyed all the room they now had. The dog they had recently bought had space to roam, and they added another dog and a cat.

Bill did well at work, quickly getting promotions, pay raises, and assignments that required responsibility. He rose to grade 4. The banging, clanking, and buzzing that filled the air in the hammer shop got on his nerves, however. A year after starting, he learned through a friend of an opening in the Resource Conservation Company (RCC), owned mostly by Boeing (one of Boeing's attempts at diversification) and located near the north end of Boeing Field. The company had a government contract to study a process for desalting water, and needed someone to operate and maintain the equipment. The job offered more opportunity for promotions. Bill applied and was delighted to get an offer for the position at his current pay grade. His supervisor at the hammer shop blocked his transfer, however, since he needed Bill. Disgusted, Bill told the RCC he couldn't make the move. Supervisors can't stop moves to higher-rated jobs, however, so the RCC raised its offer a pay grade. Jubilant, Bill started his new assignment in May 1979. He had to keep the pumps running, check for leaks, do simple tests on the water, and record data on the water and machinery. He had the most responsibility he'd had in any job, and was happier than ever. He rose to a grade 8, one of Boeing's highest pay levels.

Bill and Linda enjoyed life in Seattle. Bill liked hunting during the deer season, playing the horses at the Longacres track during the racing season, and picking out songs on the expensive Gibson acoustic guitar he had bought years before. He and Linda had fun camping in eastern Washington. Boeing followed the aerospace industry tradition of giving employees off the entire week between Christmas and New Year's day. Bill and Linda started the practice of adding vacation time to that holiday period and returning to Milwaukee for two weeks. The idea of going back to college faded away.

Bill and Linda's main problems came from the decaying old house they lived in. The bathroom fell apart, with the floor caving in and the toilet becoming hopelessly broken. Bill repaired the floor and replaced the toilet himself. When the landlord refused to reimburse them, they began looking at the classified ads again. They found a suitable place in North City, a couple of miles north of the Seattle city line, for $475 a month. They moved in late 1979. Only a few months later the furnace blew up, injuring no one but forcing them to move again quickly. There was a two-bedroom, one-bathroom rambler backing up to the Snohomish County line that was available to rent right away in the nearby neighborhood of Shoreline, in Saint Mark's parish, so they grabbed it. Bill guessed that 10 to 15 percent of the people in the neighborhood worked for Boeing.

A year later, the Gray household faced disaster of another sort. The government canceled Boeing's desalting project. The best job Bill ever had simply vanished. Having no more use for him, the Boeing-owned firm laid him off, getting rid of Bill along with the now-useless equipment. Demoralized, he began to look around for some kind of work to pay his bills.

12 || Double or Nothing

The 1970s introduced a major change to the character of the air-craft industry, an alteration whose effects are still being played out. Boeing and the U.S. government have yet to come to terms fully with the shift in the nature of the business. The causes of the flux were the emerging desirability of international affiliations in aircraft development programs, and the appearance of a strong competitor overseas. Worldwide aircraft sales have always been important, but significant international cooperation and competition were something new for the American industry.

Boeing's first confrontation with the newly ascendant foreign forces began in 1971, in the very pits of the Boeing depression and partly as a result of the factors that caused it. Wilson felt that the next all-new airplane model that the airlines would need in quantity would be at the opposite end of the spectrum from the 747—a short-haul aircraft rather than a long-haul one. (The Advanced 727-200 that he ordered into development at about the same time was an improved version but not a new model, and at first he didn't expect to sell many.) Because of anti-airport-noise regulations that had been passed by a society newly conscious about its environment, moreover, the new airplane would have quiet engines. The aircraft was designated the Quiet Short Haul Aircraft, or QSHA.

Wilson had decided to take a radical step: Instead of Boeing developing its next airplane all by itself with all the risks and costs that entailed, as it had done throughout its history, this time the company would go partners with another firm. Antitrust rules prohibited or severely restricted partnerships of American firms in such ventures, so Wilson looked abroad. He chose Aeritalia, the Italian aircraft manufacturer, to be Boeing's full partner in an arrangement by which design and production would be shared equally, and Aeritalia would pay generously for learning Boeing's design secrets. Aeritalia sent a large group of engineers to Seattle.

This move did several things for Boeing. It halved the company's development risk. (Of course, on the negative side, it also halved its expected profit.) It virtually guaranteed a sale to Alitalia, the Italian airline. Air traffic was growing faster overseas than in the United States, making the international market more important to Boeing, and governments (which own most of the world's airlines outside the United States) had begun to demand that aircraft manufacturers put some money back into the customers' countries as part of sales deals. It gave Boeing a footing in Europe that threatened to become protectionist; like other American firms, Boeing was faced with the probable formation of a European trading bloc that might raise barriers against companies that didn't contribute to local economies. The arrangement provided Boeing with access to development capital, which was hard to come by in the United States then; a major problem was that airlines were having hard times and couldn't afford heavy advance payments on new models. With Boeing's European connection, the money came from the Italian government through Aeritalia. The funds were most welcome then, when Boeing was in such a precarious financial position. Moreover, the deal helped Boeing to keep a design team together when there wasn't enough cash from other sources to do so.

Not long after the QSHA project began, Boeing showed its inexperience in foreign affairs and its lack of a feel for the subtleties of diplomacy. Wilson realized the QSHA would be too expensive to make, too fuel hungry, and not quiet enough. In his usual no-

nonsense way, he withdrew Boeing precipitously from the project and dumped the Italians. Boeing "decided not to build its half" of the QSHA, Wilson would say airily later. The Italians were furious, feeling they'd been used. Wilson admitted that the Italians "got very sore." Other European nations noted what happened, and the episode damaged Boeing's negotiating abilities with other potential foreign partners. Europeans had previously found Boeing patronizing when they dealt with the company. A Boeing official hadn't helped when, in commenting about the Italians, he said flippantly "We've got the smarts, they've got the money." Boeing had gained a reputation as an arrogant, condescending, and unreliable partner.

In the mid-1970s, Boeing began to think about successors to the aging 707 and 727. Airlines would have to replace most 707s by 1986 because of new international antinoise agreements. The 707 follow-on was designated the 7X7.

Wilson was rattled when Airbus Industrie, the upstart European firm, also announced its intent to build a new airplane for the 707 market, to be designated the A310. Airbus Industrie was a consortium founded in 1966 and largely owned with equal shares by two of Europe's aircraft manufacturing powerhouses, Aerospatiale of France and the German company known today as Deutsche Aerospace; CASA of Spain held a small interest. The combine had a French flavor: The French had pushed the consortium, it was headquartered in France, and the French were more equal than the Germans in the partnership. The name "Airbus Industrie" derived from the first model produced by the combine, the wide-bodied, medium-range A300, called an airbus, which had entered service in 1974. Sales of the A300 had been anemic and not a single one had been sold to a U.S. airline; Wilson had no reasons to think that Airbus Industrie would be more of a threat than any of the other little-respected European aircraft manufacturers in the jet age. Wilson couldn't totally ignore the possibility that the A310 might succeed, however. If it did catch on, there might not be room in the market for both a 7X7 and an A310; the competition could repeat the DC-10 and L-1011 clash that had devastated both McDonnell Douglas and Lockheed. A310 development, moreover, was a step by Airbus Industrie toward offering a family of models, the philosophy that had been so successful for Boeing. Wilson deemed it prudent to deny the European company any chance of becoming a real threat. He married this objective to his goal of finding a foreign mate or mates to help with development of new airplanes.

Boeing started batting its eyelashes at the French, meeting with Aerospatiale about the possibility of cooperating on the 7X7. Wilson wanted Aerospatiale to either collaborate with Boeing on its own, which would undermine Airbus Industrie, or persuade the other members of the consortium to join in 7X7 cooperative development, which would neutralize the threat. The French were looking for American partners anyway—they were talking with McDonnell Douglas, too—because they felt Airbus Industrie was stalled and were looking for options outside the combine. Wilson also offered Aerospatiale the opportunity to cooperate on the replacement airplane for the 727, designated the 7N7. Boeing and Aerospatiale even got to the point of signing a letter of intent.

Predictably, the deal fell through mainly because Boeing insisted on being the controlling partner—the heavily controlling partner. A Boeing executive had stated that it was a ground rule that Boeing will own 51 percent and will control any collaborative effort on a new Boeing airplane because otherwise "you get hung up on decisions and it costs you money." The proud French insisted on being equal if not the controlling partner.

While Boeing was courting the French and Airbus Industrie, the American company was also flirting with the British. From 1976 to 1978, Boeing held serious talks with British Aerospace (BAe), England's leading aircraft manufacturer, about BAe becoming its partner in developing the 7N7, which would be essentially the old 727 with just two engines, newly designed, and a new wing. BAe would take on the major job of designing and building the wing, which would embody the airplane's most advanced technology. This would give Boeing all the advantages of a European connection and at the same time would hold back BAe from joining Airbus Industrie, which was also romancing the British firm. The consortium lacked good wing-design capability, which was BAe's forte.

In favor of the partnership with Boeing were the majority of the British cabinet, British Airways, and Rolls-Royce. Against the partnership with Boeing and in favor of allying with Airbus Industrie was Britain's ambassador to France, who warned that BAe would be subservient to Boeing, becoming merely "hewers of wood and drawers of water" for the American company. (The debate brought out a penchant for poetic meter among the opponents. Others against the arrangement because it didn't allow BAe to do a significant amount of design work said that Boeing wanted the British to be nothing more than "benders of metal and drillers of holes.")

BAe itself was leaning away from Boeing and toward Airbus Industrie. One strike against Boeing was its bad reputation in Europe as a partner. BAe officials felt that their company would be dominated by Boeing and really be nothing but a glorified subcontractor rather than a genuine partner. Moreover, the arrangement would call for Boeing to pay BAe a fixed price for design and production of the wing, and the British company thought Boeing was offering not nearly enough to cover costs. Boeing argued that BAe's production costs would go down as they learned how to make the wing efficiently—called "going down the learning curve"—and BAe would wind up with an adequate profit; the English didn't believe it.

Britain's Prime Minister James Callaghan visited the United States in June 1978 and talked with Wilson and other Boeing executives about the proposed partnership. He left convinced that it was a bad deal for England and—among other reasons for distrusting Boeing—worried that the American company was after BAe's own renowned wing technology; he said later a "prowling" Boeing would have "sucked British Aerospace dry" of its technology.

BAe turned Boeing down that summer. (Years afterward, Tex Boullioun lamented the rejection, which he considered uncalled-for: "British Aerospace didn't trust me on the learning curve. They thought Boeing was taking advantage of them. Later on, they found out we'd been straightforward.") Being jilted was a disappointment—but a shock followed when BAe almost immediately joined Airbus Industrie. This linked four companies, including three of the strongest aircraft manufacturers in Europe, all supported by national treasuries so much wealthier than a private company's that they made Boeing's financial resources look like pocket change. Moreover, in combined assets and numbers of employees, the combination was roughly a quarter again larger than Boeing. The consortium was potentially the strongest competitor Boeing had ever had.

An electrifying marketing breakthrough transformed Airbus Industrie from a potential threat to a genuine contender for market share. Boeing had been trying to persuade Eastern, one of the largest U.S. carriers, to order 7N7s. Airbus Industrie had also been working hard on Eastern, trying to sell A300s. Boeing paid little attention to the Europeans' efforts, not believing that any airline in the United States would ever buy an A300, and for that matter not being terribly worried that any domestic airline would ever buy any airplane from Airbus Industrie.

But Eastern Airlines stunned Boeing and the whole American aircraft industry by ordering the A300s. The purchase was doubly surprising because Frank Borman, the former astronaut who headed Eastern, had thought the airplanes too big for his routes. It was soon revealed that Airbus Industrie had given him an unbeatable price and liberal financing. The clincher, however, had been a fantastic deal that Tex Boullioun would have been proud to pull off: Airbus Industrie would refund part of the purchase price if their A300s did prove too big, or even let the airline return the airplanes if they didn't live up to Airbus Industrie's promises. Borman, the former astronaut, revealed that the export financing provided by Airbus Industrie "subsidized this airline by more than $100 million." Referring to the French-dominated consortium, he told his employees, "If you don't kiss the French flag every time you see it, at least salute it."

Airbus was well on its way toward fulfilling its mission: to counter America's overwhelming domination of the aircraft industry. The Europeans bought 25 percent of all jetliners but made only 2 percent of them. They did not want to be economically subservient to the United States. The European mood was captured by a French Airbus Industrie chief executive who said, "If we don't have a place in high technology in Europe, we should be slaves to the

Americans and our children will be slaves. We have to sell. . . . We must fight, fight, and fight. . . ." (In the mid-1980s, a Boeing executive addressing a European audience disputed the legitimacy of the feeling that Europe needed a strong representative in the air-craft industry. "Every country does not have to build every prod-uct it consumes. You build good train systems and things like that in Europe and we do not," he said, unintentionally reinforcing Europe's view of Boeing as a corporate Ugly American.) Airbus Industrie had indeed fought, fought, fought, and had passed a watershed. The British had joined, strengthening the alliance immensely; the French, the leaders of the group, had reaffirmed their commitment; the icebreaking first sale had been made in America, the most important aircraft market; and the consortium had boldly launched a new airplane to compete head-on with Boeing.

T Wilson had more than Airbus to fret about in 1978. Douglas was planning to develop a new offering, designated the DC-11, which would compete with the 7N7. This put Wilson in a bind. If he launched the 7N7 first to head off Douglas and ignored the 7X7, he'd leave a wide opening for Airbus Industrie and its upcoming A310. On the other hand, if he went ahead with the 7X7 to counter the Europeans and postponed the 7N7, he'd leave Boeing open to attack from Douglas. He didn't have the European partner that he wanted for either craft. The market was ready for both airplanes. To develop both at the same time would take three billion dollars, nearly twice Boeing's net worth, and possibly, according to some analysts, as high as four billion dollars—or six billion, counting tool-ing costs. As Wilson explained later, however, he didn't agonize over the decision, any more than he had over the question of whether to lay off massive numbers of employees during the crunch. If you're in the airplane business, he commented philosophically, you design and build airplanes and, you hope, vanquish your competitors. He didn't see that he had much choice. Boeing had been resurrected and had accumulated a rich cash reserve. United, American, and Delta had agreed to be 7X7 launch customers; Eastern—even though it had ordered A300s—and British Airways had signed on as 7N7 launch customers. In spite of the unheard of risks, the lack of a partner to share them, and the suffering Boeing had endured with its last major development project, the 747, Wilson led the board of directors in launching the designs of both airplanes simultaneously. The 7X7 became the 767, and the 7N7 became the 757. They'd be Wilson's legacy to Boeing's family of products.

The 767 rolled out on August 4, 1981. Technically, its most distinguishing feature was its advanced wings: Thicker and extending farther out from the fuselage than previous jetliner wings, they cut the air more efficiently than their predecessors, provided more economical, less fuel-thirsty flight, and supported the weight of more passengers, cargo, or fuel. The maiden flight of the 767 took place less than two months later, on September 30. The landing gear wouldn't retract after takeoff, and the vacuum flushing system for the toilets sounded as if it were exploding when it was used, but otherwise the test went smoothly. The 767 entered service in September 1982.

On January 13, 1982, a little more than five months after the 767 made its debut, the 757 rolled out in a modern version of the traditional introduction of a new aircraft, featuring a discolike light show, classical music, and slides projected on a high screen. A huge curtain in the hangar was raised to reveal the 757 wreathed in swirls of artificial fog. This jetliner, too, sported an advanced wing and fuel-saving features. Because it featured a narrow, air-piercing fuselage like the original 727, the 757 was even more fuel efficient. Of the two new aircraft, the 757 was the least advanced technologically; Boeing couldn't afford the exorbitant cost of developing two highly advanced jetliners together. The 757 retained fewer features from its predecessor than planned, however, so it was really an entirely new model and not a derivative. The 757 first flew on February 19, 1982, a remarkable seven days ahead of schedule. It took several minutes to relight an engine after it had been deliberately shut down, but otherwise the test pilot found only minor bugs. The jetliner entered service, with Eastern, on January 1, 1983.

Having been designed during the "energy crisis" of the decade after the Arab oil embargo, the 757 and 767 were made with fuel efficiency as a top priority. Additionally, Boeing made the flight decks identical, and the flight characteristics of the jetliners are much alike, so that a pilot qualified to fly one of them was automatically qualified to fly the other.

The number of engines on the 767 had been chosen after a replay of the hot debate over the best number of engines for the 727. Most of the designers and most of Boeing's customers had favored three engines for their greater safety, or at least their reassuring appearance of greater safety. Ed Wells, Boeing's éminence grise, and George Schairer, on the other hand, decided that the time for two engines had arrived. The economies of the dual-engine arrangement had become more important than ever, the power and reliability of the engines made them safe, and rival Airbus Industrie was promoting the value of the two-engine configuration of its products. Boeing's designers worked on both two-engine and three-engine versions to hold the option open as long as they could, but Wells and Schairer wanted the two-engine model to receive highest priority. (Wilson characterized the choice to be made as a truly big decision, in contrast to his "no sweat" order to launch the two airplanes.) Tex Boullioun and Jack Steiner, who were then in charge of the development programs, still felt strongly that three engines would sell better, so they quietly reversed the priorities.

One day Wells—officially retired, but still active and powerful as a director and consultant—called Boullioun and Steiner to a meeting. They arrived at the conference room to find Schairer seated beside Wells. The meeting turned out to be not so much a conference as a kangaroo court. "I know what's going on," Wells began accusingly, and ordered them to change their priorities immediately. Steiner said he'd never seen Wells so angry. Schairer was also stern. Schairer's upper lip had a slight, perpetual curl on the right side, which made him look as if he were sneering when he talked and accentuated the menacing look he gave Steiner and Boullioun. "You guys screwed up. So cut it out," he warned. Steiner said he'd never been so uncomfortable in his working life. When the 767 rolled out, it had just two engines; the 767 inaugurated the era of long-range twin-engine airliners.

(Wells's choice of two engines for the 767 was his last major decision for Boeing. He gave up his consultancy in 1982, at the age of seventy-two. Four years later, he died of pancreatic cancer. He had been the major force behind the technical success of all Boeing's jetliners—indeed, of all Boeing's products since the B-17. Wilson, not given to exaggeration, affirmed, "Neither Allen nor I did one thing technically that Wells didn't approve of.")

Fellowship among engineers sometimes transcends business imperatives, and one of those incidents took place during development of the 767. Jack Steiner had taken one of Airbus's top engineers, of all people, on a tour of Everett, and broadly discussed Boeing's plans for the new jetliner. Even more remarkably, as the discussion continued later at Steiner's home, the European argued that it was foolish to design the airplane for three-man crews, as planned. He persuaded Steiner to go to a more economical two-man crew design. So, late in the game, not only the number of engines but also the planned crew complement dropped from three to two. The Air Line Pilots Association fought against certification of the small crews, as the group had been doing in the 737 controversy. The decision in favor of two-person crews by the Presidential Crew Complement Commission in July 1981 ended the opposition.

From scheduling and budgeting standpoints, the 757 and 767 projects were Boeing's best jetliner development programs. They were the first such programs to come in on schedule and on budget; in fact, they finished slightly early and under budget. Contrary to the experience of other programs, moreover, the twins performed better than planned. Boeing exhausted its funds in development, however, and had to borrow so heavily to pay early production costs that its bond rating slipped a notch.

Although Boeing never got the foreign partner it had once sought for its next development program, the company did take on its first major foreign subcontractors. Aeritalia and a group formed by three Japanese companies each manufactured 15 percent of the 767. The investments they made in expensive tooling significantly reduced the money that Boeing had to risk on the project.

Given the challenge by Airbus Industrie, Boeing had no choice but to sell its new products aggressively. Boeing came out swinging to beat back the new contender. After hard sales campaigns by both manufacturers, TWA told Airbus that the airline would buy A310s.

When Boeing learned this and was told that fuel economy had been the deciding factor, Tex Boullioun asked his engineers to compare projected fuel usages for the A310 and 767. (Neither airplane had flown yet.) The technical people told him that the 767 should beat the A310 by 4 or 5 percent. Tex told his people that their incentive pay rode on the accuracy of their assessment; they stood by it. Boullioun then offered TWA one of the daring bets that sometimes had to be offered to close big deals: If TWA bought the Boeing planes and they weren't at least 3 percent more fuel efficient than the Airbuses, then Boeing would pay TWA a million dollars per airplane. If the Boeing planes exhibited more than 3 percent greater fuel efficiency, then TWA would pay Boeing part of the savings. TWA took the bet, told Airbus "tough," and bought the American airplanes. Airbus officials fumed at what they considered a violation of a handshake agreement—not the first time Boeing had killed someone else's deal at the last minute—but neither Boeing nor TWA cared. Boeing's models turned out to be 5½ percent more fuel efficient than the Airbuses, and TWA paid off.

Wilson's fearless move in committing to two new airplanes at once cowed Douglas. Noting that the 757 would beat its DC-11 to market, Douglas backed off its plans to develop the alternative. In 1982, Airbus Industrie showed how strong and fierce it had grown by announcing it would fill the gap. The consortium declared that it would go after the 727 market by attacking the 757 with a new airplane, its first narrow-body, designated the A320.

Airbus kept coming on. In September of 1984 Pan Am—an airline that had never ordered a foreign-built airplane and that was close to Boeing—ordered a billion dollars' worth of Airbuses (two billion dollars, if options are counted) instead of American airplanes. It was one of the largest trade deals ever between the United States and Europe, and the money was flowing the wrong way. Two years later, Northwest Airlines agreed to buy up to one hundred A320s instead of Boeing's 737-400s. The dam had broken, and from then on—in the United States, Europe, everywhere—Boeing and Airbus Industrie would fight ferociously over every order.

Airbus was crafty as well as powerful. The firm had decided that it couldn't compete with Boeing on cost, and so decided to compete with the American company on technology: Airbus Industrie would try to make sure that all its airplanes would have more advanced technology than the competitive Boeing airplanes.

Ironically, Airbus was the first to commercialize some new technology that Boeing had developed. An Airbus official commented that the consortium sometimes copies Boeing to improve itself, since Boeing is so good at everything. The results of follow-through studies on SST technologies that NASA had funded at Boeing were publicly available, and the Europeans used them in developing the A310 and A320. Boeing had developed fully electronic flight controls, for example, and Airbus Industrie used this so-called fly-by-wire system in the A320 flight deck. Frank Borman of Eastern Airlines proclaimed the Airbus flight deck at least a generation ahead of what Boeing and others were offering.

According to Ian McIntyre, the British author who studied the Airbus-Boeing relationship, "Many of Airbus Industrie's technological claims are baloney—they sometimes steal credit from Boeing." An Airbus executive asserts, however, that Boeing, despite its putting-down of Airbus Industrie's originality, implicitly recognizes the Europeans' technological leadership: "They piss all over our innovations and then put them on their own planes."

The rise of Airbus as a formidable competitor coincided with the emergence of a new area of competition for aircraft manufacturers: financing terms for customers. Financing became more difficult for airlines for several reasons: the tremendous real increase in aircraft costs as they became more complex; in the United States, the increased risks because of airline deregulation that began in 1978; and the expanding market for aircraft among financially weaker airlines of the developing nations.

Airlines often found it more economical to lease aircraft instead of buying them. By 1991, half of all newly acquired aircraft were leased. As a result, one of the largest owners of aircraft was no airline but a financial institution—Citibank, which held title to about one hundred jetliners.

In considering aircraft purchases, airlines began to look hard at the financing deals and payment arrangements offered by the competing manufacturers; everything else being equal, the manufacturer offering the best financial package often won the order. In this respect, aircraft manufacturers began to wheel and deal like Chevrolet dealerships. Boeing, never slick in its marketing, was slow to catch on to the appeal of "low, low payments." The company eventually learned, however, that customers were becoming more interested in the business clauses of contracts than in the technical specifications. One of the most notable deals at Boeing involved accepting a billion dollars' worth of oil from Saudi Arabia in 1984 in payment for ten 747s. Boeing came to believe that offering a 2 percent interest advantage to customers sealed more deals than promising a 5 percent advantage in fuel efficiency.

Terms included such things as direct loans from the manufacturer's treasury and accepting "trade-ins" of used aircraft. This made aircraft manufacturing a chancier business and added to the risk of betting the company for U.S. manufacturers because they began to function as financial institutions without the safeguards of banks and investment houses. They didn't have large portfolios to diversify and hence lessen their financial risks, for example.

This trend gave Airbus Industrie a great advantage because the financing could be done by the treasuries of the countries joined in the consortium. The United States countered this to some extent, at least in dealings abroad, by the Export Import Bank. A federal institution begun during Roosevelt's New Deal in 1934, it encouraged exports by helping foreign customers of American businesses to finance purchases of U.S. products, providing better deals than the purchasers could get from private financing. When financing became so important to the aircraft industry, Boeing began to lean heavily on the ExIm, as it's known. So expensive are jetliners, and so great the need for ExIm assistance, that in 1981 $2.4 billion—almost half—of ExIm's $5 billion in loans went to finance purchases of Boeing aircraft.

This offended some people. Critics of the ExIm's expenditures derided the institution as "Boeing's bank." Opposed to subsidizing of private enterprise, the Reagan administration—although normally friendly to business—acted on its conservative principles and drastically cut back on ExIm's activities. The hobbling of ExIm made it more difficult for Boeing to fight Airbus Industrie in what had become Boeing's largest and fastest-growing market, the overseas arena. U.S. Senator John Heinz of Pennsylvania called this the economic equivalent of unilateral disarmament. Mal Stamper, telling *Business Week* magazine that the ExIm cuts "really got my dander up," urged Boeing's thirty-five hundred suppliers to complain to their congressmen.

Airbus exploited its advantages in financing. Its sale of nine A300s to a Japanese airline in 1980 reportedly hinged on a financial package more generous than the one Boeing offered. And financing was the key to Airbus's landmark 1978 sale to Eastern Airlines.

When Airbus became a major competitive threat to Boeing (and Douglas), its political, pricing, and financing advantages as a government-subsidized enterprise became a major concern to Boeing and the U.S. government. (Tex Boullioun always contended, however, that Airbus's emergence as a competitor didn't bother him in principle. He felt that the people and government of the United States wouldn't stand for one company to control more than 50 to 60 percent of a market, so it wouldn't be in Boeing's long-term interest to dominate the market completely. He said blithely that he was content to have half the market and let Douglas, Airbus, and any other interested company split the other half.)

Since governments of Airbus's partner companies run or heavily subsidize their airlines as well as their aircraft manufacturers, Airbus has an obvious political advantage in selling jetliners in those countries (although British Airways remained a staunch Boeing customer). For sales made in non-Airbus countries, however, politics seems to cut both ways. Some examples: In 1977, Western Airlines nearly bought ten Airbuses, but the deal was thwarted by a wave of anti-French feeling in the United States when the French released a PLO terrorist. In 1980, Boeing lost a string of orders in the Middle East largely because of the American government's pro- Israel policy. Boeing reportedly lobbied successfully for the powers in Washington, D.C., to block a currency transfer to Brazil that would have allowed that country to buy Airbuses. When the airline in Thailand was considering canceling an order for two

A300s in favor of 767s, Airbus reportedly threatened Thailand with cuts in the European import quota for tapioca, Thailand's second most important export. Airbus cried "Foul!" in 1994 when President Clinton personally intervened to persuade Saudi Arabia to order new jetliners from American companies, but Boeing maintains that Airbus itself was using all the political muscle at its command to win the orders. Each side alleges that the other uses the granting or threatened revocation of landing rights to force airlines to buy its airplanes.

At least before the Clinton administration, Boeing felt that the governments of Airbus's members helped the consortium much more than the U.S. government helped Boeing, although Boeing frequently asked for assistance. The U.S. government remained aloof partly for ideological reasons, not wanting to involve itself in the affairs of private enterprise, and partly because the United States is alone in having more than one jetliner manufacturer; the president can't help Boeing at the expense of Douglas. American policy appears to have changed with President Clinton and the late Commerce Secretary Ron Brown, who finessed the Boeing-Douglas rivalry by persuading Saudi Arabia to buy airplanes from both companies.

Of greater concern to Boeing than Airbus's political might is its government subsidies—anticompetitive subsidies, according to Boeing. Airbus has lost massive amounts of money, amounting to billions and billions of dollars. It's impossible to tell exactly how much Airbus has dropped; the consortium is organized under French law as a kind of joint venture that doesn't require financial disclosures. But Airbus officials admit the losses. Alan Boyd, then chairman of Airbus's North American operation, testified on June 23, 1987, to a congressional subcommittee: "My personal opinion is that the A300 program will never make a profit. Now I expect some derivative will show up to be profitable in the future. I question whether the A310 program will ever show a profit." An American aerospace executive has said of the A300, "My guess is that the Airbus consortium is selling a $40-million product for $25 million." Informed observers don't think that the A320 is profitable, either; they point to the several countries that turned down Airbus's invitation to participate in the A320, presumably because they couldn't see any money in the project. The U.S. Department of Commerce in 1987 commissioned an investigation of Airbus's profitability, known as the Gellman study. Initially suppressed for diplomatic reasons, the report was released in 1990. The study showed that Airbus had never earned its "cost of capital" (a measure of investment worth—projects whose profits promise to cover the cost of capital are worth investing in, while those that do not promise to return the cost are not financially worth the investment). The report calculated cumulative Airbus losses through the year 2000 of $30 billion in 1990 dollars. No truly private company could survive that ocean of red ink. Airbus, however, claims to have made money in 1990 and states that the consortium now makes more money annually than it spends; Airbus spokesmen say that subsidies are no longer significant.

The subsidies have paid for what are, compared to Boeing's operations of today, gross inefficiencies in management. Like Boeing's engineers before T Wilson, Airbus designers pay little attention to the cost of their creations. Because of European laws, Airbus has never laid off a worker, and so in down times has supported many more employees than needed. This makes the consortium reluctant to hire on the upswing, so in good times it has fewer workers than it needs. Since major decisions are made or heavily influenced by the committee of the consortium's four owners in four different countries, and manufacturing responsibilities are split among them, bureaucracy, red tape, and coordination difficulties make Airbus ponderous and slow to respond to problems or opportunities.

Mogens Peter Carl, a Dane who was Europe's chief negotiator in the 1988 talks with America on fair aircraft competition, advanced a curious argument. He held that Airbus's subsidies are fair because they simply compensate for the consortium's inefficiencies. He remarked in 1988: "What I don't like to have to say is that we have to subsidize because of our inefficient industrial structures. . . . But it's true. We are compensating for inefficiency. . . . If we are really compensating for inefficiency, our subsidies can't really be contributing to trade distortion."

Airbus asserts that subsidies have never been heavy, anyway. Boeing disagrees. The difference in views may lie in differing definitions of subsidy. Government "loans" that are never paid back could be counted as subsidies. Likewise, various kinds of grants, loan guarantees, and other financial assistance might be construed as subsidies under other names. Airbus charges that the U.S. government also subsidizes development at American aircraft companies indirectly through Pentagon, NASA, and FAA research contracts; Boeing points out that the dollar amounts involved are inconsequential compared to Airbus's estimated subsidies.

Boeing rages against the Airbus dole because a basic premise of a free market is that players who sell below cost (including the cost of capital) eventually go bankrupt. Airbus can sell its airplanes at losses that would eventually force a private firm like Boeing out of business. Competition from Airbus was a factor in Lockheed's pulling-out of the jetliner business in 1985, and the consortium is seriously threatening Douglas's jetliner business. Boeing doesn't want to be next.

One solution is for the U.S. government to subsidize Boeing. This, of course, runs counter to the American tradition of not subsidizing private enterprise. The Reagan administration felt so strongly about continuing this tradition that officials cut back not only on ExIm lending but also on the few existing subsidies for industry, such as the safe-harbor tax credits that helped aircraft manufacturers as well as other businesses. People have questioned whether the tradition is outdated, suggesting that the United States might at least subsidize a company when the size of the investment and risk for a worthwhile venture is beyond the capability of the private sector. The United States stands alone among countries in abstaining from subsidies. Noted MIT economist Lester Thurow wrote in 1992: "Can a commercial aircraft manufacturer survive without an interested government partner? No one knows for sure. America might run an experiment to see if Boeing can survive alone, but if the experiment turns out to be a failure and Boeing does not survive, what happens then?"

Another solution is to get Airbus to forgo subsidies. This is the approach much favored by Boeing, which doesn't want the government interference that would come packaged with government handouts. Having in mind Airbus's claim that it needed government subsidies to get off the ground as a price of entry into a mature industry, Dean Thornton said bluntly in February 1988, "Time for the kid to get off the tit and stand on its own legs."

The companies are wary of each other. An Airbus executive stated that his firm doesn't hire former Boeing executives because the consortium is afraid of spies. (Screwing up his face in obvious disdain, a Boeing spokesman declined comment.)

Mogens Peter Carl rated the conflict between the United States and Europe over aircraft as the issue that had more potential to damage European-American relations than any other: "If it were to develop into a trade war, the consequences would be more serious than in any other trade conflict we have ever known."

Complicating formulation of American policy on Airbus is that about 30 percent of the components for the consortium's airplanes are made in the United States, so naturally these component suppliers are in favor of anything that helps Airbus's business.

In 1992, the Congressional Research Service of the Library of Congress issued a tactfully worded report summing up this country's approach toward a policy for dealing with the competition from Airbus: "There has been considerable concern over the years that US policy toward Airbus Industrie has been somewhat waffling. Some of this is attributed to changes in overall US trade policy and some to the reluctance of the US makers to get involved in a trade dispute that might cause them to lose access to markets. An examination of the Airbus Industrie dispute can leave the reviewer with the sense that both government and industry, at least at times, lacked a clear vision of how they wanted the Airbus Industrie issue resolved." In the mid-1990s, the vision of neither government nor industry was much sharper.

Boeing's 757 and 767 didn't sell well in the early 1980s because of the competition from Airbus, a dip in the economy at the beginning of the decade, the reduction of the number of direct flights under airline deregulation (which worked against large airplanes), and the energy crisis fading away so that the fuel-saving feature of the jetliners became less of a selling point. The 757 had special problems. Because it was so closely modeled after the 727, many airlines thought it used tired technology; they were not impressed. During the evolution of the 757 design, moreover, the airplane grew so close in size to the 767 that potential customers for it often decided they might as well take the airplane with the more advanced technology, and bought the 767 instead. Frank Borman had pushed hard for the larger size; as Eastern was a launch customer, Boeing had listened—another example of the dangers of following suggestions from airlines too closely during development. Executives who developed the 757 regretted not having designed it differently, and thought about closing down production. T Wilson himself admitted, "It probably wasn't a very good decision" to make two airplanes of almost the same capacity. Boeing held tough, however, waiting for better sales conditions, and was vindicated in the late 1980s. The booming economy and strong demand for aircraft then saved the twins, which passed the break-even point, seized control of their markets, and began making money. Most satisfying to Wilson, the company even made sales to airlines—Air France and British Airways—in Airbus member countries.

Another aspect of the growing importance of internationalism in the aircraft industry of the late 1960s and early '70s is one that Boeing and other industry participants would like to forget. Fighting in the overseas marketplace became so cutthroat that it broke through ethical restraints and resulted in the industry's most notorious scandal.

The sensation began at Lockheed, with one of business history's most egregious clerical errors. A congressional committee had asked Lockheed to provide some innocuous information. The company's auditors sent a box of records—but they sent the wrong box. The committee's staff, in looking over the contents, saw that it was not what they had sought. What they found instead was explosive. The records documented large payments made under the table to garner sales in foreign countries. In July 1975, Lockheed admitted publicly to payoffs, including sums that went to the highest levels of the Japanese government to win an order for L-1011s over 747s and DC-10s. Although bribery of foreigners was not then illegal in itself, U.S. government agencies suspected that the payments had broken other laws governing tax deductions, full disclosure of information that could affect stock price, and the like. (In response to the Lockheed scandal, bribery abroad was made illegal by the Foreign Corrupt Practices Act of 1977.) The Internal Revenue Service, Securities and Exchange Commission, Federal Trade Commission, and Justice Department all launched investigations. Evidence soon surfaced that other aerospace companies had made improper payments. (When the SEC concluded its investigation, it had found questionable payments by 288 companies in many industries.)

On March 5, 1976, the SEC made the stunning revelation that even the "angel" of the aerospace industry—Boeing—had made questionable payments. Far from the Pacific Northwest, Boeing's overseas operatives seemed to have lost sight of the proclaimed stress on integrity back home. Boeing admitted to paying $70 million since 1970 to foreigners who helped with jetliner sales worth $5.5 billion. In "four or five instances," Boeing said, the recipients worked for foreign governments, although Boeing pointed out that none of the recipients could approve aircraft purchases. Boeing claimed that the fees were legitimate commissions and that it had broken no foreign laws. In September 1978, the SEC announced that it was formally charging Boeing with some forty improper payments in eighteen countries, totalling $52 million, including $27 million to foreign government officials. The charges were settled by a consent decree, in which Boeing agreed to accept the charges without admitting or denying impropriety, establish an international business policy to discourage improper payments, and appoint a committee of outside directors to investigate the company's foreign business practices and report the committee's findings to the SEC. On February 15, 1979, Boeing's committee reported to the SEC, "The Boeing company has made a complete disclosure of payments to foreign officials, and no further investigations are required."

Meanwhile, repercussions were felt in other countries. A high official for the Venezuelan government airline was arrested and confessed taking $500,000 from Boeing for a sale. In Egypt, a consultant to the national airline was jailed and admitted getting $150,000 in kickbacks from Boeing.

On June 30, 1982, the Justice Department, as a result of its separate inquiry, dealt Boeing the company's worst blow. In a plea bargain with the department, arranged with the help of famed criminal defense attorney Edward Bennett Williams, T Wilson took the stand in a Washington, D.C., courtroom that day. Speaking for Boeing, Wilson pleaded guilty to forty criminal counts of defrauding the Export Import Bank by concealing $7,380,000 in "irregular" payments, despite the company's denial to the SEC. The fees had been paid for help with sales of thirty-five jetliners in Spain, Lebanon, Honduras, and the Dominican Republic for $334 million. (To discourage its loans from financing bribes, the bank made companies sign statements to the effect that no kickbacks were built into the purchase price.) The big payoffs had been in Spain and Lebanon. Boeing had promised a Spanish sales agent $3.4 million to arrange the sale of a fleet of 727s to Iberia Airlines for $225 million. The government wouldn't complete the sale until Boeing provided assurances that no improper sales commissions had greased the deal. Boeing gave its word, then paid the agent a "termination fee" equal to the promised commission. To grease the sale in Lebanon, worth $101.4 million, Boeing had funneled $3.6 million into a Liechtenstein corporation. Boeing was assessed $400,000 in fines and $50,000 in costs. In return for plea bargaining by Boeing, the Justice Department ended its long investigation and declined to press charges against individual Boeing executives or other employees. Wilson always felt that neither he nor Boeing had done anything wrong, and had only reluctantly followed legal advice to plea-bargain. "I never felt like such a liar in my whole life as when I had to stand up in court and say I was guilty," he groaned to an associate.

Lockheed also plea-bargained and was fined $647,000; its transgressions had been the most severe of the three jetliner manufacturers, with high company officials directly involved in payments. "Mr. Mac" McDonnell, believing like Wilson that his company had done nothing wrong, refused on principle to plea-bargain about the charges against McDonnell Douglas. Because of his stubbornness, McDonnell Douglas paid the stiffest price: civil and criminal penalties of $1.2 million.

The American firms weren't the only ones involved in the corruption. The French government had hired at least one "consultant" to sell Airbus Industrie's products by whatever means he chose, keeping the government and the company it dominated clean—at least as to appearances. In 1989, it was alleged that Airbus Industrie and a joint venture of engine manufacturers had bribed eight officials in India to cancel a letter of intent to buy Boeing airplanes and instead to buy airbuses for $1.47 billion. In the post-Watergate years of the 1970s, however, the U.S. government's eagerness to condemn and punish its aerospace corporations worked to the advantage of Airbus Industrie. Foreign airline executives, approached by American investigators about their contacts with Boeing, were spooked from dealings with the Seattle company. The head of an airline in the Middle East said he'd do business with Boeing only if the Justice Department sent him a letter certifying that Boeing was clean.

The IRS found that all Boeing's deductions for sales expenses were legitimate. With all the money sloshing around, however, the suspicion was raised that some of it had washed back into the pockets of Boeing employees—that some of those who received kickbacks from Boeing were generous in their appreciation of Boeing employees who had set up the payments. Two Boeing workers whose personal financial records were subpoenaed resigned quietly.

Others besides Wilson still insist they did nothing wrong. An executive who had been with Boeing's international operations felt he was off the hook because he insulated himself from any wrongs by his method of working with agents: He retained them and told them not to talk with him again until they'd arranged the sale, and then he'd pay them a percentage. He believed he escaped responsibility for their actions since he knew nothing about their means of making the sale, and they used their own money in doing whatever they did. Casuistry such as this aside, Boeing's degree of guilt is a thorny question. Boeing asserts, with no evidence to the contrary, that none of its employees ever bribed an innocent person, placing payments more in the class of extortion than bribery. Baksheesh was expected; it's the way of doing business in many countries, and Boeing's competitors were assiduously greasing palms. As a Boeing marketing executive explained, "In some parts of the world, forget about the capabilities of the airplane. Forget about the price. It's whoever has the right consultant who's the most powerful." Richard Albrecht, a senior executive in Boeing's Commercial Airplane Group, isn't quite so cynical: "We have trouble selling because of the rules but, in most instances, a good product succeeds. There have certainly been exceptions—we've lost sales because of our unwillingness to bribe." The foreign bribery episode raised deep questions to which there are still no answers that bring general agreement: Are payments under the table to "consultants" and officials inherently wrong morally? If the alternatives are either to follow the prevailing practices or to lose sales, does an ethical company have any choice but to give up the business?

(In March 1977, the *Wall Street Journal* published an intriguing article that postulated an unusual angle to the bribery story. According to the newspaper, "Government investigators have strong indications that the CIA knew about and possibly encouraged the flow of under-the-table cash from leading American corporations to certain political figures abroad. The implication is that not all the money paid constituted commercial bribery; some was intended to buy intelligence information for the United States government or to reward pro-American politicians. . . . [Boeing] was funneling cash to political personalities whom the United States was eager to reward." The article noted that the State Department strongly supported Boeing's refusal to identify its consultants.)

Questions with no easy answers were to plague Boeing, not only in its dealings with foreign countries but also at home, as it tried to cope with the ethical quagmire in "the other Washington" on the East Coast.

13 ‖ D.C. Scandals

T Wilson, a controlled person, doesn't usually get agitated in conversation, but one subject sets fire to his voice and body language: the C-5, the huge cargo airplane Boeing wanted to develop for the Air Force in the 1960s, when it "got screwed" by the Pentagon. Boeing produced the 747 instead, and when the jumbo jet began flying commercially, it "turned out to be a hell of a lot better airplane than the C-5," according to Pan Am's chief engineer, John Borger. T tried to sell the Pentagon on the idea of buying only a limited number of C-5s and meeting the rest of the military's needs with 747s. He argued, and truly believed, that 747s could do most of what the C-5s could do but would be much cheaper, and that the mix of C-5s and 747s would accomplish all military purposes most economically. The Pentagon wouldn't buy the idea, so T let it rest.

After the fall of the shah in Iran, the Pentagon wanted to form a so-called Rapid Deployment Force to get troops and materiel quickly to the Middle East in case of war. The force would be based on a new kind of cargo plane with STOL—Short Take Off and Landing—characteristics so it could use almost any airstrip anywhere. Boeing, Lockheed, and McDonnell Douglas competed. In January 1981, the entrants submitted the usual gargantuan proposals, weighing in at nine tons. McDonnell Douglas won with its

C-17. T was disappointed but resigned to the decision. Lockheed was by no means resigned to a defeat, however. The company came right back with a proposal to develop modified C-5s cheaply and with a guarantee of no overrun charges or other unexpected costs; the C-5s would also be available much sooner than the C-17. Lockheed, typically, played a political card, pointing out that the company would shift 35 percent of the work from Marietta, Georgia, to California and save the jobs of many workers in Los Angeles who were on the failed L-1011 program, which was closing down; although Lockheed wasn't going bankrupt, in effect the company was nevertheless asking for another government bailout because of financial troubles caused mostly by the L-1011. To Wilson's astonishment, the Pentagon accepted the proposal, rescinded the award to McDonnell Douglas, and gave the contract to Lockheed. To mollify McDonnell Douglas, the Air Force bought forty-four more KC-10s (to be made in the politically important state of California) and increased production of McDonnell Douglas's F-15s. The only loser in the arrangement was Boeing.

Wilson was enraged on several counts. The deal made a mockery of the competition in which Boeing had invested expensive resources. And the reasoning that the Air Force accepted for buying C-5Bs, as they were called, applied even more strongly to the purchase of 747s. The jumbos could do a better job at less cost and be available even sooner than the C-5Bs. Wilson again argued to the Air Force that the combination of 747s and already-bought original C-5s, now called C-5As, was unbeatable. But the Pentagon said no deal—Lockheed would get the contract, and Boeing would get nothing. Wilson felt that politics and bureaucratic self-interest had prevailed; as Richard Stubbing, a former Pentagon budgetary official, commented, "Buying a commercial wide-body would put a whole Air Force bureaucracy out of business—the bureaucracy that controls the design, development, and procurement of special-purpose military airlift aircraft."

Traditionally, no matter how high-handed the Pentagon had been in making its awards, the losing contractor made no fuss, just backed away and licked its wounds. Wilson was fed up, however; no more Mr. Nice Guy for him, especially since development of the 757 and 767 was taking most of Boeing's cash, and jetliner orders were down in a poor airline economy. He considered the Pentagon's behavior such an outrage that he decided to go around the generals and present his case to Congress. As Clyde Skeen, then the company's senior vice president for defense, explained to *Business Week* magazine, "Normally, you don't hit one of your best customers right in the nose, but we're trying to solidify the military side of the house at a time when it's sorely needed."

The U.S. senators from Washington state, Scoop Jackson and Slade Gorton (who had replaced Warren Magnuson), presented Boeing's case to the Senate, which agreed with the company and voted to require the Pentagon to buy the 747s. A U.S. congressman from Washington state, Norm Dicks, whose district held large numbers of Boeing workers, presented the case to the House. Surprised by the Senate vote, the Pentagon, Lockheed, and the Georgia and California congressional delegations went all out to win the House. There ensued a political battle, which *Time* magazine called "one of the fiercest and, some say, most shameless lobbying battles Congress has seen in decades." Lockheed took out full-page ads presenting its case in the *Wall Street Journal* and *Washington Post*. T got a call from a Defense Department undersecretary threatening to cut funding of a Boeing military program if he didn't back off. He said the Air Force threatened to recompete contracts that Boeing had already won.

The House rejected Boeing's plea and voted to let the award to Lockheed stand. On August 18, 1982, the House-Senate conference committee upheld the House's vote. Lockheed had won. The Pentagon abruptly canceled a Boeing missile program, but T said the country was the big loser; he figured the Pentagon spent three billion dollars more at least in life-cycle costs for the C-5B and got less than if it had bought the 747s. His comment was typically pungent: "My blood boils on the C-5. . . . When the administration went back and bought more of those goddamn airplanes when our airplane carries more and carries it farther is absolutely atrocious. . . . The 747 was so much better than the C-5 that it's pitiful. That was the last time I cried at work."

Wilson's efforts on the C-5B weren't entirely wasted. Boeing's show of lobbying force earned the company the respect of the political and military communities, which appreciate the skillful use of force in the service of self-interest. The company had lived down the reputation it had gained after the SST affair as a political pushover and, far from disadvantaging itself at the Pentagon, actually gained ground there.

The next two years were relatively quiet for Wilson and Boeing. As 1986—the year of Wilson's sixty-fifth birthday—approached, however, Wilson faced one of his biggest decisions. No more ready to face retirement than Bill Allen, he told a colleague that the chairman of the organization committee of the board of directors "is on my ass, and we've got to do something to get lined up for a replacement for me." Ordinarily the line of succession would be clear. At Boeing, the president's position is considered the training ground for the person selected to be the next CEO. Mal Stamper should have been the CEO-elect. Allen and other members of the board of directors put him in the presidency with the intention of making him CEO. Wilson had always adamantly opposed Stamper succeeding him, however, and had let the board of directors know it. "I didn't hesitate to make my views known [to the board], even to the point where they became impatient with me," Wilson admitted. Wilson had little regard for his president. Attempting to establish more cordial relations, the recognized artist Stamper had tried to give one of his paintings to Wilson, who wouldn't take it. The chairman and president seldom spoke to one another. Over the years they had arrived at an accommodation where Wilson worked on the most important matters involving policy, strategy, high impact, and big bucks, and Stamper took care of the nitty-gritty details in the daily running of a large corporation. Wilson never gave Stamper critical assignments, but did give him responsibility for an area that Wilson seems to have cared about the least—employee motivation and welfare. Although, to be sure, Stamper would have preferred to share power, that was an area he liked.

Corporate executives with totally different personalities have worked well together even at Boeing: Wilson and Bill Allen are a prime example. Neither Wilson nor Stamper will dwell on the reasons they couldn't pull it off, but in their general comments both prominently mention different attitudes toward money. Wilson was tight with it. Stamper was free—Wilson would probably say "extravagant." "If T wanted exercise equipment, he'd go out and buy a couple of dumbbells for thirty bucks. I'd spend thousands on the top-of-the-line workout rig," Stamper observed. "I tried to humanize working conditions and spent money to do so. T wanted to guarantee jobs, and so cut to the bone," Stamper explained. Wilson declared flatly that "I had to lecture Stamper on money once." That lecture seems to have followed an incident where Stamper unintentionally embarrassed Boeing's senior management. About 1980, after a couple of years of sterling financial performance, Boeing's profits had turned down in a bad economy. Managers got only token raises and some senior managers took small cuts. Stamper exercised stock options and sold a large block of the stock, raising his total compensation to over a million dollars for that year. It became public knowledge and caused some grumbling among less well-to-do employees. Stamper compounded the problem when he spoke at a meeting of the Boeing Management Association. Trying to defuse the resentment about his income with typical Stamper humor, he laughed and quipped, "Turn up the lights. I want to let you all see a million-dollar guy." No one else laughed. Middle-level and low-level managers got the impression that the top level was living it up while they were sacrificing. To calm the troops, Wilson had to initiate a study of executive compensation and make some changes in the system.

On his ascension to the throne, Wilson had talked about retiring at sixty. When his heart held up and he didn't retire early (he said the board didn't want him to step down), Stamper's age became a consideration. Stamper would be only two months short of sixty-one when Wilson turned sixty-five. The board preferred to name a CEO who would serve longer than four years, and a few board members wanted a much younger man. Some Boeing executives think this was the deciding factor in changing the board's consensus on Stamper. At any rate, some time before 1985 the board scratched Stamper's name from the top of a list of half a dozen potential CEOs. Wilson broke the news to Stamper that his fellow board members no longer had him under consideration. Wilson gave Stamper credit for the way he took the news and comported himself afterward. "He did nothing to thwart anything. He was very supportive of the process—I'm sure disappointed, but quite supportive. I wouldn't have been surprised if he'd left. . . . He advised me on selection of a successor." (In 1996, asked to comment for publication on why he had agreed to serve as president under Wilson when it was obviously not a marriage made in heaven, Stamper denied that he and Wilson had a bad relationship: "I got along with T better than the world thinks. I liked him then and I like him now. I got along fine with him.")

Among the executives and board members who put up the names of candidates for CEO, there was some talk about going outside the company for a candidate, but early on Wilson and the board decided they had sufficient homegrown talent. Wilson would have the strongest voice in picking a successor. His own favorites had changed over the years as some prospects let him know they didn't want the job or fell short in some way, promising new faces emerged, and circumstances changed that favored one background over another. At one point Wilson liked an executive of the Boeing Vertol helicopter unit. As T put it in his inimitable way, however, the executive "didn't kick the smart engineers in the balls when they needed it." T dropped the man from consideration for lacking his own balls.

A senior executive urged that a very young man be put at the top of the list. His candidate was a fast-rising star who would be only forty-five in 1986. A well-liked and highly respected executive who had shown exceptional management skills, he was an engineer named Phil Condit. The board thought Condit too inexperienced, but would remember his name for future consideration.

The board decided to name Wilson's replacement to the presidency in 1985, give him a year of seasoning, and—assuming he worked out—make him CEO when Wilson retired the next year. They'd create the new position of vice chairman for Stamper to fill until he retired in 1990. The choice for the new president, who would also take a seat on the board, narrowed to two men, and it was virtually impossible to choose between them: Frank Shrontz, a lawyer, and Dean Thornton, an accountant. In some way, the board seemed to be seeking another Bill Allen: No matter which candidate they chose, the new chief would be a nonengineer from a Rocky Mountain state. In another remarkable coincidence (like Wilson's high school friendship with the future chairman of IBM), Shrontz and Thornton both grew up in Idaho and attended the state university at the same time; they had known each other there. In a kind of an interview process, Wilson had each of the two men make a half-dozen presentations to the board so the members would get to know them.

In January 1985, Wilson made his recommendation to the board: a difficult choice, but Shrontz. Shrontz, who had strong government experience in his résumé, said his Washington, D.C., background wasn't a factor, pointing out that he never worked on the military or government side of the company, but surely it didn't hurt; Wilson and the board were then trying to strengthen Boeing's contract business. The Washington connection may have been the tiebreaker between the two Idahoans. Thornton hated dealing with the government—"Those bloodsuckers," he called that crowd—and tried to avoid government projects. The board approved Wilson's selection. Thornton was made head of the Commercial Airplane Group, his greatest love, and his statement that he really wasn't disappointed in the outcome of the selection had the ring of truth. The announcement of all the job changes was made in February.

Shrontz, not a tall man, is the first Boeing chief since Bill Boeing always to be seen wearing glasses. Heavy-lidded eyes make him look, deceptively, tired and slow. Even with freshly pressed clothes, he somehow always seems rumpled. His words, pronounced deliberately and as if delivered through pursed lips, bespeak his Boise origin. His wife, Harriet, and he have three sons. His personality is unlike that of any previous Boeing chairmen or presidents, although closest to Bill Allen's. Associates describe him as always a gracious gentleman, trying not to offend, and more comfortable to talk with than Allen, whose formality sometimes unsettled people.

Like Allen, Shrontz is a good listener, mandatory for a non-technical person running an advanced technology corporation, and wants always to hear the truth, even if it goes against his opinions— he won't tolerate yes-men. He's even more reserved in his language than was Allen, for whom "damns" and "hells" spiced many a con-versation. Once a subordinate intended to give a humorous talk at a retirement party, in which he'd mention the honoree "peeing" after drinking freely at a bash. Shrontz asked him not to use that word because women would be present. In this old-fashioned sensitivity, he's at the opposite pole from Wilson and many other aerospace industry executives, who are often crude and profane. Mild-mannered and quiet, with a gentle humor, he's a man without edges, physically or temperamentally. In looks, speech, and manner he could be the slightly heavier brother of David Broder, the colum-nist and TV political analyst.

No one could reach his position without being titanium tough when the situation demanded it, but Shrontz asserted authority by exercising his brilliance, friendly way with people, and enormous capability rather than ruling through intimidation. People loved working for him, and he was loyal to those who helped him—or whom he served. Deane Cruze, a colleague and friend from Shrontz's Renton division days, marveled that Shrontz had lunch regularly with a former boss who was hard to get along with. Cruze pointed out that Shrontz differs from other Boeing executives in not reveling in "war" stories about funny and heroic events at the com-pany. "He lives in the present, and bases decisions on the present," Cruze observed. A knowledgeable sports fan, he especially enjoys the outdoor activities he pursued in Idaho, such as skiing and pheas-ant hunting, but once in the top executive ranks he could rarely find the time to get out to the mountains or woods. He attends musical and stage performances on Seattle's cultural scene when he can. Politically, he describes himself as a moderate conservative.

(One gray Seattle winter afternoon, as Shrontz was nearing retirement, a writer visited him at the penthouse condominium he had bought recently at the north end of Mercer Island, near the bridge to the city, after selling his spacious home on the other end of the island. Harriet was out shopping. Several times, Shrontz had to interrupt the questioning to answer phone calls from his daughter-in-law. She was worried about his twenty-two-month-old granddaughter, the pride of his life, who had an ear infection. The Shrontzes had offered to mind the child while his son and daughter-in-law went on a skiing vacation.

(That night, Frank, with Harriet seated beside him, drove their Ford Explorer through drizzle to the motel where the writer was staying in the decaying area south of the city near Boeing's facilities. The writer started to climb in back for the trip to dinner at a restaurant, but the seats had been folded to stow packages on a recent errand. "Oh my goodness, I'm sorry. I forgot about that!" Shrontz apologized as he got out and opened the other back door. Standing in the dark and getting wet in the cold rain, the chairman and chief executive officer of Boeing pulled and pushed the seat, but nothing happened. "I never could learn to work this thing," he grunted. A minute later, he did something right and was able to raise the seatback. The writer had known many high-level executives and believed he could spot one trying to project a phony image. He felt that Boeing's chairman, unlike a good number of his peers, didn't let his ego or concern for the bottom line or his career overwhelm his relationships.)

Shrontz was born in Boise on December 14, 1931. His last name comes from a long-ago German ancestor. When he was old enough, he worked summers in his father's small sporting goods store. He liked the job and decided to make business his career. Thinking ahead even then, he reasoned that a law degree would help him get ahead in trade, so he enrolled in the five-year LL.B. program at the University of Idaho, graduating in 1954. Shrontz married Harriet Houghton from Seattle, whom he had met at college, and then, having gone through Army ROTC, spent two years in the service. After his discharge, he got back on his career track by enrolling at the Harvard Business School, earning his M.B.A. in 1958. He found work in Indianapolis with Eli Lilly, the pharmaceutical company, but he and Harriet wanted to go back to the Northwest, an area they loved and where home and parents were. A friend from Harvard recommended that he try Boeing, and the company appealed to him. Boeing was prominent in the news in 1958, when the 707 went into service. In an M.B.A. class, Shrontz had studied a case history of the airlines' having to choose between the 707 and DC-8, and "was fascinated by the aircraft business." He successfully applied for a job negotiating sales contracts at Boeing and headed for Seattle after only a few months in Indianapolis.

The job proved a boon for a young man on the way up: Shrontz accompanied the head of the 707 program to sale closings and observed high-stakes deals being concluded. A singular chance came his way a few years later when he was assigned to make a presentation to persuade Bill Allen that legal risks made it imperative to spend millions of dollars on redesigning the thrust reversers for the 737. Shrontz poured everything he had into the pitch and so impressed Allen that his career caught fire. He attracted the attention of Wilson, who in 1969 gave him a sabbatical to pursue a year at Stanford University's business school, enriching the academic background he already had with his M.B.A. from Stanford's big East Coast rival. His next big break came in 1973, when the Pentagon asked Wilson if he could provide someone to fill an undersecretary position. He asked Shrontz, who accepted. Positions as undersecretaries of the Army and Air Force were both open, and initially Shrontz was headed for the Army slot because the Air Force job, while better suited to his background, would seem a conflict of interest. In the end, the Pentagon decided to risk taking some heat, and he was confirmed as Air Force undersecretary. When Donald Rumsfeld became defense secretary in 1975, he picked Shrontz to be assistant secretary of defense for installations and logistics. At the change of administrations after the 1976 elections, Shrontz had been at the Pentagon four years, when the average government tenure of business executives was eighteen months. He had sold his house in Seattle, and says he didn't expect to go back to Boeing.

United Technologies, General Dynamics, and Boeing all offered him prestigious jobs. The attachment he and Harriet had to the Northwest again came into play, so he heeded the call from Wilson to come back to Boeing as corporate vice president in charge of contract administration and planning. Less than two years later, Wilson put him in charge of Renton. (After he became Boeing's president, friends he had made at Renton would begin to assume key jobs in the company; in this respect, Shrontz's Renton assignment was like Wilson's Minuteman tour.) Again General Dynamics solicited him but, with the top job at Boeing in his sights, Shrontz refused even an interview. In 1981, Wilson further rounded out Shrontz's experience by making him vice president of sales and marketing. Early in 1984, Wilson told Tex Boullioun, who headed the airliner division, "I need your ass out of that job so I can try out Shrontz." Shrontz had to show he could handle the top divisional job at Boeing if only to demonstrate to the company's airline customers that he had mastered the business. He became president of the commercial operation in April, and Boullioun was promoted to the headquarters staff. Shrontz excelled at the job and relished it because, as he explained, "I liked seeing hardware come out instead of paper."

Shortly after Frank Shrontz was named Wilson's successor, the two men gave a joint interview to the *New York Times* in which they stated that one of their goals was to make Boeing the number one government contractor. This was really public affirmation of a policy of aggressively pursuing government business that Wilson had had under way for years. By the time of Shrontz's elevation, Boeing was already deeply involved in the ruthless world of Washington, D.C., where the only principles held sacred seem to be those of Machiavelli. Boeing's energetic efforts in Washington, begun long before Shrontz came to power, culminated in a series of scandals and bad publicity in the mid-1980s that dramatized the ethical quandaries that corporations and their employees can get into.

The incident that received the most publicity, and that's still referred to as one of the worst examples of government waste, was really the most innocuous on Boeing's part. The government had always issued detailed specifications for the materials it bought but had begun overspecifying. Agencies would specify their perceived needs in such minute detail that more and more items had to be specially manufactured for each contract. In many cases, suppliers couldn't even provide common parts such as nuts and bolts "off the shelf": they had to be custom-designed and custom-made, often at great expense. Orders continued to come in for such highly specified items as the pliers used to work on engines for military aircraft. The engine manufacturer provided the individualized item and Boeing passed along the cost—$675 a pair. In another example, the Air Force ordered three little plastic caps for the ends of the legs on a stool that airplane navigators stood on to use sextants. Boeing had to make them to stringent Air Force specs—for $907 each.

In 1985, the Tiffany pliers, stool caps, and myriad other items supplied by several manufacturers came to the attention of Congress and the media. A superexpensive, "gold plated" toilet seat put out by another company got most of the ridicule, but Boeing came in for its share of scorn and condemnation. Politicians and journalists framed the story as Boeing and other greedy firms fleecing the taxpayers. Ironically, even after all the bad publicity, Boeing had to turn down an Air Force order worth $6,750 for ten more pliers.

The other embarrassments were far more serious. One of them surfaced in 1984 when Informatics General, a small computer company in California, protested a contract awarded to Boeing by the National Park Service. The agency had put out for bid a $5.9-million contract to set up a desktop computer network at 112 parks. Boeing's Computer Services Division had won the competition, in which Informatics General was the only other entrant. The smaller company complained that Boeing had bid illegally since the aerospace giant had done more than allowable before the bid in advising the Park Service on the network. Boeing had acted as a consultant, helping plan the system and recommending the kind of contractor to hire. Informatics General also contended that Boeing had illegally used inside information in its bid.

The first 747 sits at the end of a runway of Boeing's Everett facility, also just completed and a sea of mud on a typical drizzly day. The 747 made its first commercial flight on January 21, 1970. *The Boeing Company Archives*

Hundreds of millions of dollars' worth of 747s are parked at the Everett plant, the largest factory in the world. Puget Sound is visible in the upper left. *The Boeing Company Archives*

Inside the cavernous Everett plant, listed in the *Guiness Book* for its size, the world's largest jetliners, 747s, are arrayed in various stages of construction. *The Boeing Company Archives*

The mockup—full scale model—of the supersonic transport, or SST, rests on supports in the Developmental Center near Plant II. Congress canceled critical government support of SST development in 1971. *The Boeing Company Archives*

Bob Withington, who headed Boeing's SST project, displays a model of the planned revolutionary jetliner. Withington also participated in the epic weekend design of the B-52. *The Boeing Company Archives*

T Wilson, who succeeded Bill Allen and headed Boeing as chief executive officer from April 1969 to April 1986, sprawls on an office couch. Wilson finished the 747 project, saved Boeing from potential bankruptcy, and produced the 757 and 767. *The Boeing Company Archives*

In April 1971, when unemployment and the economy reached Depression depths in Seattle, mostly due to Boeing's troubles, two residents put up this message. *The Boeing Company Archives*

Several members of the board of directors meet, probably in 1972, as Boeing was pulling back from near oblivion. Identifiable are controller Hal Haynes (extreme left), president Mal Stamper (left of Haynes), chairman T Wilson (at head of table), and retired chairman Bill Allen (second from right). *The Boeing Company Archives*

A 767, a large jetliner that replaced the 707 for non-jumbo loads, takes shape at Everett. The 767 entered service in September 1982. *The Boeing Company Archives*

A 757 lands at Boeing Field. The medium-sized airplane, which replaced the 727, entered service on January 1, 1983. *The Boeing Company Archives*

Mal Stamper, who led development of the 747 jumbo jet and construction of the giant plant at Everett. He became president in 1972 and vice chairman in 1985. He retired in 1990. *The Boeing Company Archives*

Dick Henning, an engineer who began his career with Boeing in 1939 and helped to found the union for engineers and technical workers. He retired in 1979. *The Boeing Company Archives*

Bill Gray, a millwright at the Everett plant, with his wife, Linda. A member of the Machinists' union, Bill started work at Boeing in 1978. *William Gray*

Frank Shrontz, due to retire after eight years as chairman at the end of 1996. Shrontz led Boeing to record profits and produced the 777 jetliner. *The Boeing Company*

Artist's rendering of the 7J7, a medium-sized "unducted fan" airliner that was to fly at near jet speed with unparalleled fuel efficiency. To be developed in partnership with a group of Japanese companies, it was canceled in 1987. *The Boeing Company Archives*

A crowd swarms around the large 777 during one of the rollout extravaganzas on April 8, 1994. Aimed at replacing the DC-10s and L-1011s, the jetliner made its first scheduled flight on June 7, 1995. (The chain hanging in front of the jetliner is attached to a curtain used in the staging.) *The Boeing Company*

Picketers cheer at a rally during the sixty-nine-day 1995 strike of the Machinists' union, Boeing's second-longest strike. The sign at the extreme right hints at the antagonism strikers feel toward fellow workers who cross picket lines. *District Lodge 751, IAM*

Phil Condit led the 777 project, was named president in 1992 and chief executive officer early in 1996, and is expected to succeed Shrontz as chairman at the end of 1996. *The Boeing Company*

Boeing withdrew its bid rather than respond to the protest. The federal government nevertheless suspended for a year all government contracts in which Boeing's Computer Services Division was involved, and initiated a criminal investigation. The suspension was devastating. The division provided services for most other Boeing groups, and the suspension resulted in a massive shutdown or slowdown of most of Boeing's government projects. The division fired two of the employees involved, disciplined nineteen others, and vigorously fought the suspension. Propitiated by the sacrifice of Boeing employees and astonished at the effects of its suspension—the feds hadn't realized the ramifications of blackballing one small division—the government lifted the suspension after only sixteen days. The criminal investigation went on for over five years and ended only after the statute of limitations ran out, so nobody went to trial.

The Park Service had invited the trouble. In deciding to install its network, the agency sought unsuccessfully to hire Boeing without going through competitive bidding because of Boeing's previous good work with another federal unit. The deputy inspector general admitted there was complicity by some Park Service employees in getting the contract for Boeing, but disclosed none was fired or disciplined because "arcane" federal personnel rules protected them from punishment.

The fired Boeing employees were Robert Gerard, head of Washington, D.C., operations for the Computer Services Division (who revealed he'd been making seventy-three thousand dollars a year in that job), and Willis Winder, the young salesman on the Park Service account. They tried to get their jobs back, claiming they were scapegoats. They admitted violating official policies that were on the books at Boeing, but charged that they were expected to follow diametrically opposed unofficial policies, and that their superiors knew what they were doing and indeed encouraged them to do it. Boeing denies this. Gerard and Winder also asserted that they were playing by the rules of the game as it was conducted in D.C. Implying that actions the government had indeed condoned or overlooked before this incident were now considered criminal, a senior vice president later observed, "We were moving into an era that I would call the criminalization of the procurement process." A high-ranking computer services official, who insisted on his innocence in the matter, related how a colleague in the company's aerospace division reacted. The aerospace executive criticized Computer Services for landing so hard on the involved employees because "that's the way everybody does business" in Washington, D.C. That comment was significant considering what happened later at the aerospace division.

Another momentous transition in power at Boeing took place quietly in Seattle during this period, in April 1986. Although he remained as chairman, Wilson gave up his CEO role and effectively handed over full control of the company to President Frank Shrontz. A company officer arranged a reception for Wilson in the boardroom to commemorate his years of leadership. When Wilson walked in, he was surprised to see all the officers at headquarters with their feet up on the big table, and wearing white hats, red bow ties with white polka dots, and large false noses—all looking like Wilson with his trademark features.

There was some irony in the next flap occurring shortly after Shrontz assumed his new role, for it involved Boeing employees who left temporarily to work for the government. Among such employees in the previous twenty years were three who had gone to the Pentagon and become director of research and development for strategic programs, an area vital to Boeing's interests, and then returned to the company in a classic "revolving door" scenario. The U.S. Department of Justice in 1986, spurred by results of an FBI investigation of a former Boeing executive, filed suit against Boeing and five employees. All the men had become high-ranking officials in the Department of Defense and the Navy, and the suit charged Boeing with giving them $40,000 to $132,000 in questionable severance pay in the years 1981–1982. Although Boeing didn't explicitly agree to rehire the men when they left the government, the Justice Department claimed that the sums were to make up for the loss of pay until the end of President Reagan's term when, the department surmised, Boeing expected the executives back. Boeing paperwork referred to the jobs as "assignments" and "tours," and internal memos about the men used phrases such as "will be helpful to us while he is in Washington" and "an asset to us in the NATO arena," seeming to indicate that the company considered the posts temporary duty in the service of Boeing. The company strengthened this suspicion by having billed the pay to overhead accounts for defense projects. (Boeing withdrew the billings when government auditors questioned them.) The suit was solely about the propriety of the payments; it did not allege that the employees had favored Boeing in their government positions. A lower court found Boeing guilty, but the U.S. Supreme Court later exonerated the company in a unanimous decision.

By far the episode most damaging to Boeing's treasury and the lives of the employees involved began early in 1978 in Washington, D.C., at cherry blossom time, the most glorious part of the year along the Potomac. Three men were having a fine lunch at an elegant restaurant in Georgetown called the Four Georges and discussing a position that Boeing wanted to create in the Washington office of its aerospace division. The diners were Ben Plymale, a Boeing vice president; a man on his staff; and Dick Fowler, who was within a week of retiring from his civilian job at the Pentagon at the age of fifty-two, after eighteen years of service with the Department of Defense and thirty-five years total with the federal government. Plymale wanted to hire Fowler for the new position. Although Fowler had only a high school education, he had climbed to the civil service GS-14 level, only two ranks below the senior executive level, and had received the Award for Meritorious Civilian Service, the Pentagon's top nonmilitary honor. As a program analyst in the Air Force Research and Development Office, he worked on budgets and plans for strategic weapons systems.

Plymale was trying to remedy a weakness that had developed in Boeing's government contract capabilities. About 30 percent of the company's revenues then came from defense. In the long-range business of aerospace, contractors had to prepare well in advance to meet the government's needs for aircraft, missiles, and the like. Plans had to be made, resources had to be allocated, and research had to be done in anticipation of future contract bids; companies that weren't ready didn't have time to develop new capabilities before the bidding deadline. Contractors had to know what kinds of products the military was planning to order, how much would be spent, and what the timetable was. The military thought that keeping abreast of developments was an important job of its suppliers. In the old days, Claire Egtvedt or Wellwood Beall or other senior Boeing executives—and their counterparts at other manufacturers— would get together with high-ranking generals to be briefed on the military's thinking. These informal sessions had ceased after World War II with the explosive growth in the size and complexity of the military, and growing national distrust of loose contacts between the services and corporations. The military still expected its suppliers to know what was going on but, in the view of the business world at least, didn't give them the necessary information. Companies had evolved intelligence operations to ferret out this information. They employed analysts who pored over government documents and produced forecasts of tomorrow's military orders. Many documents were on the public record, and others were formally made available to industry on a "need to know" basis. Still other documents, classified secret, were slipped to contractors by their contacts in the Pentagon. Boeing didn't have anybody with good contacts and was missing out on vital tips that its competitors were getting. Even when Boeing did find a source of Pentagon inside information, nobody in the company knew exactly what to ask for or how to interpret the data they got. Fowler understood that a Boeing vice president had invited him to an expensive lunch—certainly not the norm for job candidates at Fowler's level—because of his contacts.

Fowler had excellent document sources, the personable, friendly manner to make best use of them, and the experience, knowledge, and brains to produce intelligence of the highest quality. He and his Pentagon colleagues didn't think the kinds of information involved should be classified secret, and were convinced they were working in the country's interest by helping suppliers come up in timely fashion with the best products; there was no question (for Fowler or most other Pentagon employees, anyway) of payments or other forms of bribery. The documents didn't deal with national security matters such as diagrams of secret weapons. They concerned general ideas and administrative plans for making acquisitions. Fowler believed that overclassification was rampant (recognized as a serious problem and addressed by subsequent administrations), done mostly to keep grandstanding congressmen off the backs of the generals. He didn't consider acquiring secret documents to be illegal de facto because it was tolerated so extensively that in practice it was accepted as legal. Laws and regulations on the books that were breached regularly and with impunity by many people over a long period for good reason seemed not really laws and regulations at all. The document situation as industry's intelligence specialists saw it was like the highways Fowler drove to work every day. The speed limit was fifty-five miles per hour, but anyone who drove at that speed would soon be rear-ended. Most motorists drove at seventy miles per hour, each one breaking the law and subject to stiff penalties should a policeman choose to single him out. Everybody watched for police cars, ready to slow if one should appear. Likewise, the document flow was conducted clandestinely because of potential legal and political problems, with higher-ups at the Pentagon looking the other way. Fowler remembers Plymale assuring him that his sources would be nobody's business but his.

Before lunch was over, Plymale offered Fowler the job at $29,500 a year, and said he wanted him to start as soon as he left the Department of Defense. Fowler hesitated, mentioning a golfing vacation he'd planned at Myrtle Beach, South Carolina. Plymale, apparently not wanting to lose Fowler to a rival, told him to get on the payroll immediately anyway, take $400 for any job-related expenses he might incur, and go golfing as planned. Fowler filled out Boeing's official job application form on top of the Four Georges' fine white linen tablecloth.

Fowler was a rarity in the Washington, D.C., area—a resident who had been born there. He joined the Air Force after high school to defend civilization in World War II. A gunner in a B-29, he crashed during a training exercise and broke his neck, which kept him out of action. After the war, he got a job with Washington's major industry, the government; joined the American Legion, eventually serving as commander of his post; married his girlfriend, Muriel; had a son and daughter; and settled in the Washington suburb of Springfield, Virginia.

Back from golfing, he reported to the Boeing offices in the Rosslyn section of Arlington, Virginia, just over the Key Bridge from Washington. He quickly lined up a dozen key civilian and military contacts in the Pentagon to cooperate with him, including an assistant secretary of defense. He also built up contacts among his counterparts at other companies, including Lockheed, other aerospace companies, and most major manufacturers doing substantial business with the Department of Defense. Each person had his own special sources—Fowler in the Air Force, others in the Army and Navy—and Fowler and his confrères swapped documents "like trading cards," he said. Fowler was soon recognized by his allies as the best in the business. He got documents by the hundreds, including the Defense Department's five-year plan and three National Security Council documents signed by President Reagan or his national security adviser, which are among the most closely guarded documents in government; one was a Decision Directive intended exclusively for the secretaries of state and defense, and the chairman of the Joint Chiefs of Staff. Fowler related that Boeing officials would sometimes request specific documents, and he was usually able to get them.

Fowler's comrades at IBM and RCA wanted to show him that they were pretty good, too. They had gotten a wish list of projects that the Army had sent to the secretary of defense; Army intelligence had proven particularly difficult to obtain. The pair visited Fowler in his office and smugly displayed their prize. Fowler went to a cabinet and returned with a foot-high stack of Army documents. He pulled out a copy of the report his friends had brought and showed them the rest of the papers, all equally valuable. "I was astounded," the IBM man admitted.

Fowler passed important documents to appropriate people in Boeing, and periodically summarized the information he was getting for inclusion in weekly memos distributed by the D.C. office to almost three hundred Boeing employees. He sent many documents to a library of illegally obtained papers that Boeing had established five years before his arrival at the company's aerospace facilities in Kent, Washington. Fowler meticulously recorded the documents he received in an official log book that was examined every six months by inspectors from the Defense Criminal Investigative Service (DCIS). He took their acquiescence as confirmation that the Pentagon tacitly approved his activities. Fowler is sure that one reason his sources trusted him so completely was the careful way he handled the documents.

Late in 1983, the corporate intelligence community in Washington, D.C., was shaken by a misuse of its system. A consultant for Honeywell who was getting secret documents through the system was caught selling them. The DCIS could not overlook the flagrant violation and began questioning people about the traffic in secret papers. Since Fowler had never sold a report and never would, he didn't think he'd have any problems with the DCIS—even though the miscreant consultant's document had originated with him (which the DCIS didn't discover then). Undisturbed, Fowler never let up in his quest for documents. The government couldn't just drop the hot potato, however, and continued the investigation at a slow pace.

Fowler and others in Boeing were stunned in September 1985 when Bernie Zettl, a consultant for GTE who did that company's intelligence work at the Pentagon, was indicted for illegally acquiring secret documents—for doing nothing more than Fowler had been doing for seven and a half years. Hardly believing what was happening, Fowler stopped his pursuit of Pentagon secrets—after having acquired more than thirteen hundred documents—and switched to working full-time on the analysis of conventional data that had always been part of his job. The investigations lumbered relentlessly onward.

In November 1985, examiners stumbled onto a find at Boeing. An investigator examining Boeing's Huntsville, Alabama, aerospace facility found one of Fowler's secret documents. Descending on Boeing, the DCIS soon turned up fifty-eight other documents—helped by the logs Fowler had kept religiously. Investigators confronted Fowler with their findings and demanded to know where he had gotten the papers. He told them truthfully that they'd come from five of his Pentagon contacts. The investigators asked who they were. Fowler couldn't betray the people who had trusted him. He remembers the investigators telling him they were interested only in seeing that the leaks stopped, and promising that no one would be punished. Reassured, but still cautious, Fowler gave them the name of one man who had retired. Later, Fowler was flooded with remorse when he told the man that he had identified him and saw the look of devastation that came over his friend. The contact trusted the Pentagon less than did Fowler, and saw more clearly the legal problems and penalties he faced, the need to hire an attorney, the damage to his reputation. Fowler resolved never to reveal another source. Principles mattered to him. (He once had picketed an automobile dealership for two days when it wouldn't fix a problem with the car he'd bought for his teenage son.)

Although the possibility of being charged with a crime hung over Fowler, life went on. He continued to do good work for Boeing analyzing legally acquired documents. In June 1986, his division's marketing group honored his contributions by naming him co-employee of the quarter. In the same month, the government suspended his security clearance and began applying other pressures on him and the company to disclose the names of every contact who had ever provided a document. Boeing officials urged him to sing, apparently figuring that both he and the company would escape prosecution if they cooperated. His bosses pointed out that he was violating the provisions of the government's industrial security manual by not cooperating with the investigators. He refused, declaring that he would never again betray a trusting friend. The government, as Fowler discovered later, began secretly recording all the numbers he called from his home phone, hoping he'd ring his contacts.

Fowler took his two-week vacation late that summer, returning to his Rosslyn desk on Monday morning, September 8. His boss said he wanted to see him. When Fowler walked into his superior's office, he was introduced to a visitor from the personnel department in Seattle. His boss commended him on the good job he'd done but explained that Boeing faced suspension of all government contracts if the company continued to employ him. Therefore, the official said, he had no choice but to fire Fowler immediately. He stated, to Fowler's puzzlement, that the official reason for the dismissal was that Fowler had included classified data in the summaries he submitted for the weekly memo, which was distributed to many people who did not have clearance to receive the information. He ordered Fowler out by the end of the day. A guard was posted by the executive's office so that the fired employee couldn't retaliate. Fowler decided to leave right away and went to Boeing's local personnel office for processing out. He was told that his salary, then $57,200 annually, would stop that day and no benefits would be extended. A realist, knowing that Boeing could do nothing within reason to help him and could suffer substantial harm to its business by keeping him on, Fowler wrote on his termination form, "It has been a great 8.5 years working for this fine company." He was angry only at the abrupt and callous way he was cast out; oddly, the thing that upset him the most that awful day was that Boeing wouldn't let him take home the collection of coffee mugs he kept in his office.

Unemployable in his profession, as a sixty-year-old man dismissed for cause from a major corporation and facing felony charges, Fowler took various low-level jobs to make ends meet: salesman for a computer rental company, cashier in a clothing store, circular delivery man. He wasn't bitter, but his wife, Muriel, blamed Boeing for getting him in trouble and then throwing him to the wolves. "You got screwed, and you didn't even get a kiss!" she chided him.

The government's investigation went on at its glacial pace, with many people escaping the net as the statute of limitations ran out on various offenses. Career-minded officials salivated over reputations to be made if they could obtain convictions of high-profile defendants, however, and sped up their investigations when the political climate became favorable. The DCIS and the Justice Department teamed to run what they called "Operation Uncover," a name chosen to fit headlines. The *Wall Street Journal* termed the probe "one of the most sweeping white-collar criminal inquiries in years." Time ran out on Fowler. On Friday, August 25, 1989, a federal grand jury indicted him on thirty-nine counts. He pleaded "not guilty" to each of them. Twice, Fowler says, the government offered to plea-bargain with him in return for his naming sources. Although threatened with life in jail and fines exceeding all his assets, he spurned the offers.

The government was also prepared to indict Boeing as a corporation, but the company plea-bargained to avoid that fate. In an arrangement similar to what the government had worked out with GTE in 1985, Boeing would plead guilty to two felony counts of conveying government property without authority; this referred to two documents regarding future Pentagon programs. The company would pay fines and costs of $5.22 million. In return, the government would not press multiple fraud and conspiracy charges, and no current or former Boeing employees could be prosecuted— except Fowler. Boeing told the government that Fowler had acted alone and that really, despite the company's expedient guilty plea, no one else in the company knew what Fowler had been doing. (Later, some Boeing executives would confidentially admit the obvious—that managers in the aerospace division and some other segments of Boeing had known and approved Fowler's activities; like Fowler and all the others involved in the affair, they felt the document traffic wasn't actually illegal.)

On November 13, 1989, Boeing entered its guilty pleas through its attorneys at a pre-indictment hearing. Judge Thomas Ellis, making his own mark in the highly publicized case, declared indignantly that the penalty seemed light for a "very serious breach of security." The year before, Boeing had turned a profit of $614 million, so the fine was relatively small. The prosecutor explained that Boeing had cooperated fully in the probe. "What I'm looking for is a clear indication that the disposition reflects the damage done to the United States, and it reflects an awareness on the part of the Boeing Company of the gravity of it," Ellis blustered. For a while it looked as if he were going to reject the plea-bargained agreement. He finally accepted it, but then fumed about the absence of any Boeing executives in his courtroom. He said he was considering suspending the sentence until a Boeing official could appear before him. Instead, he demanded that Chairman Frank Shrontz write him a letter showing "the contrition any criminal defendant would express" in pleading guilty to felony charges. As ordered, Shrontz humbled himself and his company by sending Judge Ellis a page-and-a-half missive expressing his "deep regret and apology" for the company's involvement in secret document trafficking, and declaring that Boeing's senior management was "deeply distressed" over the episode. "I assure you that the kind of conduct to which we pleaded guilty is completely inconsistent with the ideals that I want all our employees to strive for and attain. . . . This unfortunate episode can serve as an object lesson of the kind of behavior that will not be tolerated," Shrontz stated. He said he was sorry for not having executive representation at the hearing. (Years later, Shrontz stated candidly for Boeing's official history, "In the time period when Fowler got involved, there is little doubt in my mind that it was generally accepted practice for companies in the defense business to have access to such things as program planning documents. . . . ")

Two days later, Boeing suffered what threatened to be the worst consequence of the documents incident. The government suspended all one hundred employees of the company's Washington-area office from working on any federal contracts indefinitely, and the Air Force proposed extending the ban to three years. The edict wouldn't lock Boeing entirely out of government work—employees in Seattle could handle Washington, D.C., affairs—but it would severely hamper Boeing's effectiveness. The employees were despondent because the Air Force made it difficult for them to find other jobs should Boeing have to lay them off: The service wrote to all the major manufacturers in the D.C. area and informed them that the ban applied to individual Boeing workers, who would be barred from contacts with the Pentagon no matter where they were employed. This punishment, too, proved not too severe when the government lifted the ban completely after three months.

Fowler's trial began December 4, 1989. He was represented by two attorneys chosen and paid for by Boeing (and whom Fowler feels served him fairly). With Boeing having pleaded guilty for harboring him, he didn't start with much of a case. Boeing employees and document traders at other firms, granted immunity from prosecution for testifying against Fowler, raised their right hands one after another and condemned him. Pentagon generals and former Deputy Secretary of Defense Frank Carlucci, their careers on the line, testified that they hadn't known about the release of secret documents and wouldn't have approved if they had known. Fowler's own logs tracking movement of documents through Boeing, which he kept conscientiously and openly for the government, were used to nail down the case against him. The prosecution concluded its case after a two-and-a-half-day parade of witnesses and records.

The defense came up—and it had no case. The only justification Fowler could present was that he was following common and accepted practice, and Judge Albert Bryan ruled that out, explaining, "Just because everybody does it is not a defense." Author Andy Pasztor described the obstacles that Fowler faced in the courtroom: "From the beginning, Judge Albert Bryan seemed sympathetic to the prosecution's arguments and sharply restricted the defense's maneuvering room. His comments and glowering looks indicated the odds were stacked in favor of [the prosecutor]." Fowler couldn't take the stand because he'd be ordered to name sources, and would be jailed for contempt of court when he refused. The defense rested its case after presenting only six witnesses over a mere hour and a half. After just two hours of deliberation, the jury announced its verdict—guilty on all counts: one count of conspiracy to defraud the government, eighteen counts of conveyance of government documents without authority, five counts of conversion of the documents to personal use, and fifteen counts of mail fraud. The judge sentenced Fowler to two years on each count, to be served concurrently, and fined him eleven hundred dollars. Muriel was taken from the courtroom in tears.

Patricia Garner, a juror, told a *Seattle Times* reporter that she thought Fowler was probably a scapegoat for the many people and companies who participated in the document traffic. "In my own opinion, going count by count, we had to find him guilty, but I also feel this is a widespread thing and I feel very badly he is the only one who will have to pay for it. I wonder myself if he wasn't a scapegoat. I think everybody felt badly. We basically felt he's a good man and felt it was too bad."

John Bray, one of Fowler's lawyers, observed that it was unfair that Fowler stood trial alone. He decried that Boeing had entered the documents in its log book while others who did the same work for other companies, named as unindicted co-conspirators and granted immunities "flowing like water" to testify for the prosecution, had admitted keeping secret books and burning the documents.

Fowler's nightmare got worse on Wednesday, January 10, 1990. The government hauled him before a grand jury investigating the Pentagon's role in the documents episode, gave him immunity from further prosecution, and commanded him to reveal the names of his sources. Remaining steadfast in his silence, he was handcuffed, shackled in leg irons, and led off to jail in Alexandria, Virginia, to remain there until the grand jury ended its term; his prison sentence on his convictions would begin after he left the Alexandria lockup. "If I talked, I wouldn't be able to face myself in the mirror," Fowler explained. He told *Seattle Times* newsman Duff Wilson that his family had reservations about his stand. "They'd have to. Like my daughter, Robyn Ann, at the beginning, the very beginning, said 'Dad, I'd rather have a snitch for a father than a jailbird.' And then she's turned completely around, and now she's saying 'My father's a hero.'"

Fowler told the reporter that his sources hadn't needed to beg him or even thank him for protecting them, and that he hadn't heard a word from any of them in nearly two years. "I don't care what they expect or don't expect," Fowler insisted. "I'm doing this out of my own—what do I say? Compassion? My own self-respect." He was sure his sources were "smart enough to just stay away and have no contact. I mean, these are not people who are inconsiderate, but they know enough to keep a respectful distance." A businessman who knew Fowler told Duff Wilson that, at a recent Christmas party, a group of Pentagon and industry people were talking about Fowler and agreed they had let him down. "Everybody in the industry is scared," he said. "What could we do? Speak up for Dick? If we did, we'd probably be targeted."

The chief of the DCIS investigation revealed that the government had a good idea who Fowler's sources were, but not enough to prosecute. "We need a little bit to put this thing over the edge, and Fowler could be that," he said. "We'll see how long he can sit in jail."

He could sit a long time. The grand jury lasted nine more months. Fowler left the Alexandria facility, had a seven-month "vacation" at home, and in early May 1991 entered the Petersburg, Virginia, correctional facility to begin his sentence; he was the only person in the whole affair ever to serve jail time. (GTE's Zettl was fined ten thousand dollars and sentenced to 150 hours of community service.)

Fowler was incarcerated in the prison's minimum security section. He was released after being confined for a year and a half. A few years later, chain smoking cigarettes and still looking haggard, Fowler discussed his ordeal with a visitor. He tries to accept life as it's dealt, and described life at Petersburg: "Not too bad—like being in the Army without weekend passes."

Boeing popped a "welcome home" surprise on Fowler shortly after he got out of jail. The company sent a letter dunning him for $780,056 to pay for the legal fees that the company had picked up for him. The letter explained that Boeing would not pay fees for a defendant found guilty because his conviction showed he "had reasonable cause to believe that his conduct was unlawful." The company never made another move to collect the absurd amount of money, and the notice seems to have been a pro forma action made for legal reasons. However well justified, nevertheless, it was another cruel twist of the knife in the back of the defenseless man who was taking the rap for the company.

One wonders if the government could have avoided inflicting misery on people—especially Fowler—and causing millions of dollars to be dropped on investigations, prosecutions, defenses, and fines if officials had simply called a meeting of representatives from industry and the Pentagon, announced steps they were taking to prevent document trafficking, and threatened severe retribution to anyone caught doing it.

Just before Fowler's trial, Mal Stamper had summarized Boeing's official position on the document situation for author Eugene Bauer: "What happened here is quite simple. We have 160,000 employees. We hired one fellow a number of years back, from the Air Force, and when he came, he kept his connection with the Air Force and brought documents with him, that he said everybody does. They were secret documents, of value to him, and he thought they would be of value to the company. It was, of course, illegal, immoral, and unethical. When we found out he was doing it, we fired him."

And the government imprisoned him for over two years, and took a significant part of his savings in fines, and ruined his life. And justice was done.

Government officials knew about and approved Boeing's actions in the cases of the ridiculously expensive items, the Park Service computers, and the classified Pentagon documents. The officials bought the pliers and computers, and handed over the documents and inside information about a competitor, in full knowledge of the questionable circumstances. The officials did what they did because they thought their actions would benefit the government; they weren't bribed. In the cases of the pliers and classified documents, Boeing's actions were unquestionably practices accepted by the Pentagon; some observers believe that even the Park Service contract maneuvers were accepted practice. The incidents raised profound questions about what's right and what's wrong with the actions of government, corporations, and individuals doing business inside the beltway.

The image of Boeing created by these stories didn't correspond to the image of the company in the minds of its employees. The belief in integrity—not just the appearance of integrity, or integrity assumed for public relations purposes—is a core element of the Boeing culture. Vice President Bob Withington's feeling about corporate ethics is typical. He was disgusted by the attitudes of people from other companies who were classmates of his during a short course at the Harvard Business School: "I was appalled at the unethical philosophy of the other students." The Boeing faith teaches that in the long run true integrity benefits the company; indeed, many employees attribute the company's remarkable success over the years to its generally honorable behavior. This is not to say there have never been sinners or heretics, even in the top ranks. Historically, however, unlike members of many other corporations and similar organizations, Boeing people would violate honor at the risk of the disapprobation of superiors, the disapproval of colleagues, and the resentment of underlings.

Nor did the scandals reveal the usual Boeing approach to getting government business or influencing the government. Somehow Boeing's culture was formed heavily from engineering attitudes, more so than other companies largely populated by engineers, even in the aerospace industry. Boeing's corporate personality reflects the personalities of the engineers who constitute most of the professional workforce and who, for the most part, run the company. Engineers work by indisputable mathematical and scientific principles, and tend to think that what they do is therefore indisputable. The influence of this attitude on Boeing's business practices cuts two ways. It's a factor in Boeing's reputation for arrogance; at least in the past, Boeing people have tended to think that their way was simply inarguable. But it also means that they tend to believe that their work speaks for itself and therefore doesn't need hard sell or political pressure. They're inclined to assume that other people behave as logically as engineers do, and as Boeing believes it does. This has given Boeing a reputation for naïveté in dealing with people. Scoop Jackson's staff used to tell a story about Boeing that may be apocryphal but captures the typical Boeing attitude exactly. It seems that, shortly after Boeing opened a plant near New Orleans, the company threw a large cocktail party and hired off-duty troopers to direct traffic. The troopers let Boeing know that it was traditional to give them the leftover liquor. The Boeing officials explained why that would be inappropriate: The troopers had agreed to a certain compensation determined to be fair by all parties involved, and therefore that's all they should or would get. There was a law in Louisiana that the speed limit on unmarked roads was 25 miles per hour. The next morning the signs had disappeared from the roads leading to the plant and troopers were giving employees tickets.

Boeing was also known to be halfhearted in its political contributing. Boeing had learned enough to know that the company should contribute to Washington's senators. Corporate contributions were limited by law, so every campaign season the company's Seattle area executives were expected to give something out of their salaries to Washington state's U.S. senators. But the company forgot the need for political support for its huge operation in Kansas. One year Senator Bob Dole of Kansas was battling for survival in a tight race and desperately needed funds. He got all of twenty-five dollars from the executives at the Wichita plant. A Boeing executive related, "We had one hell of a time with Bob Dole over the years recovering from that. He was mad, and every chance he'd get he'd sock it to us good. We finally recovered, but it took a while."

Nor did Boeing executives spend much time promoting the company's causes in Washington, D.C. T Wilson believes he might have helped Boeing's marketing efforts in Washington had he spent as much time pitching Boeing's products there as his counterparts at the competition: "I didn't go to the Pentagon as much as Tom Jones of Northrop or the Lockheed guy did. At Boeing, marketing [to the government] hasn't got the attention of the CEO that it does at other companies—it is a factor."

Boeing's small lobbying operation in Washington, D.C., reflects the company's engineering culture, and is run much like the company's highly professional lobbying group in Olympia. It's a low-key effort that relies heavily on providing legislators with good, solid information, forswearing razzle-dazzle, and maintaining good relationships based on trust. In a series that investigated Boeing's lobbying, the *Tacoma News Tribune* quoted U.S. Representative Les

AuCoin, an Oregon Democrat who often opposed Boeing: "It's about the classiest act in town. I only wish that the whole defense-industrial sector lobbied on the basis of facts, candor, and open-mindedness that the Boeing people do." Senator Ted Stevens of Alaska told the newspaper, "These are high-class people who do a high-class job."

Boeing doesn't ordinarily hire big-name influence peddlers, but it did in 1985, when the company felt that Douglas's DC-10 was about to beat out the 747 as the president's Air Force One because of politics rather than merit. Boeing paid $250,000 to President Reagan's former aide, Michael Deaver, to see that the White House selected its airplane based on what the company considered fair criteria. The details of what followed are unknown, but it was the 747 that moved into Air Force One's hangar at Andrews Air Force Base.

As Bill Allen had retired leaving Wilson the problem of dealing with Stamper as president, so Wilson retired leaving Shrontz the problem of dealing with Stamper as vice chairman. Shrontz and Stamper got along fine. Their fellow denizens in the jungle of corporate politics were amazed that Stamper not only displayed no bitterness but tried to help Shrontz as much as he could. He complicated the start of Shrontz's tenure, nevertheless, because he had four years to go as a highly paid executive with virtually nothing to do. Shrontz emphasized cost control, so Stamper's presence on the payroll threatened to be a major embarrassment. Shrontz's advisers urged him to buy Stamper out, and tried to get an idea from the vice chairman of the kind of severance package he'd accept. But Stamper didn't want to leave. He wanted something to do. He ended up in charge of alternative dispute resolution, a formal way of settling differences between companies out of court. He did a wonderful job and enjoyed it until he retired as an employee and board member in April 1990 at the age of sixty-five. He remained in Seattle and became deeply involved in a venture to improve literacy by publishing storybooks for children and distributing them free to schools.

The decade of the 1980s was a tumultuous time for Boeing, with towering peaks and abyssal valleys. The company's financial people experienced their highest highs, but people in other areas went through some of their lowest lows.

14 ‖ Big Bucks and Big Headaches

Boeing had been stunningly successful technically from World War II on, but only moderately successful financially. The company hadn't made as much profit as might have been expected of the market leader in the aircraft industry. In 1983, however, the financial data sections of Boeing's annual reports began to read as well as the pages describing airplane and aerospace programs. That year, a bad recession that had started in 1980 ended, interest rates sank way down from record high levels, and demand for aircraft picked up. The demand was partly fueled by low airfares as the impact of airline deregulation in 1978 kicked in, enticing thousands of people to fly. As the most productive aircraft manufacturer in the world, and creator of the world's only jetliner programs out of twenty-two up to that time that had earned in total more than they had cost—the 707 and the 727—Boeing was perfectly poised to take advantage of the airline recovery. Boeing's business surged, reaching levels the company hadn't seen since 1968; with business volume back as well as profitability, some business historians mark 1983 as the year that Boeing finally recovered completely from its near demise at the beginning of the 1970s.

The charts for most of Boeing's financial indicators—sales, earnings, backlog of orders, stock price, et cetera—headed sharply upward and kept on climbing. Business continued to grow steadily through the mid-1980s and then exploded in 1988. The boom started that spring with an order from United Airlines for 370 airplanes, including options, valued at $15.7 billion—the largest order in Boeing's history, about equal to the gross national product of the Republic of Singapore. Orders poured in for the next two years, stimulated partly by low fuel prices that made the airlines more profitable.

The business boom provided plenty of cash for Boeing to indulge itself. From 1988 to 1990, the company spent three billion dollars on new equipment and facilities. The company even shopped for a bauble that it never previously had the means for—a company to acquire. This led to the episode that Frank Shrontz later described as the greatest disappointment of his tenure. Boeing then had a complete family of jetliners in every size except very small; the company had no offerings in the commuter plane category. Starting with the Flying Fortress bomber, Boeing had made its reputation in both military and commercial airplanes with large aircraft. One incentive driving Boeing in this direction was that of "the larger the airplane, the larger the profit margin"; because certain design and manufacturing costs are about the same no matter what size the airplane, the profit increase on larger craft is even greater than the size increase—an airplane twice the size of another earns a profit more than twice that of the smaller airplane. The market for small commuter airplanes was expanding then, however, due to deregulation and the airlines' increasing dependence on hub-and-spoke routes, which relied on commuter jetliners to fly passengers to the hubs. The potential for a high sales volume made the total profit on the smaller airplanes begin to look attractive. By filling the gap at the lower end of Boeing's family, moreover, and offering a complete menu of sizes, Boeing would strengthen its appeal to customers as a "one-stop" shopping outlet for all airline aircraft needs.

Boeing had always dealt with trunk airlines, and the commuters really represented a new market. Rather than invest a bundle of money in a new design and try to break into the commuter market with Boeing's own model, Shrontz decided to buy an existing company that made commuter models. The de Havilland company of

Canada, a leading maker of commuter airplanes that had spun off from British de Havilland, was for sale.

De Havilland was available for a bargain price, and Boeing was fully aware of the reason: The company had serious deficiencies in plant operations—manufacturing was grossly inefficient—and relations between unions and management were terrible. Since Boeing was then far ahead of its competitors and flying high as the greatest commercial aircraft company the world had ever known, Shrontz felt that his managers could solve de Havilland's problems and make the Canadian company as good as Boeing. In January 1986, Shrontz shelled out the purchase price and took over de Havilland. With the hubris that so often accompanies a lofty position (and that got Boeing in trouble repeatedly in the jetliner era), Boeing hadn't studied the situation as carefully as it should have. The labor and production problems were worse than Shrontz had expected. Shrontz found, furthermore, that de Havilland's competitors were much more heavily subsidized by their governments than he had thought, making it virtually impossible for Boeing to charge a competitive price and make a profit. After trying for several years to turn de Havilland around and losing big money every year, Shrontz gave up. In 1992, he sold de Havilland to a Canadian conglomerate, racking up a total loss to Boeing in the hundreds of millions of dollars. Shrontz declared he'd not attempt to enter the commuter airplane business again without a partner to share the risks.

The year after Boeing had taken over de Havilland, Shrontz learned that Boeing's bulging treasury and flood of orders were a mixed blessing. On Monday, June 29, 1987, he was eating lunch in Boeing's classy management dining room when an aide interrupted him to deliver bad news. Although not totally unexpected, it still jolted him and destroyed his appetite for the remainder of the meal. This was the heyday of the hostile corporate takeover, and Shrontz had just learned that the dorsal fin of one of the biggest sharks was cutting the water fast and headed Boeing's way. T. Boone Pickens, chairman of Mesa Petroleum Corporation in Texas and an infamous takeover specialist, had just informed the Federal Trade Commission, as required by law, that he intended to acquire a large number of Boeing shares worth fifteen million dollars.

By a combination of good luck and smart planning, shortly before Boone's FTC notification Shrontz's staff had finished laying out a strategy to thwart a takeover attempt. The staff project had been kicked off two weeks previously at the behest of T Wilson, who was then nearing the end of his tenure as Boeing's chairman. Wilson was on the board of directors of Paccar, a Seattle-based specialty truck manufacturer. Paccar's executives had seen that their company was a good takeover target and had discussed their situation at a board meeting. Wilson realized then that Boeing might also attract sharks. (Wilson hated takeover raiders with a passion; talking about Pickens and his ilk got T as exercised as discussing the C-5.) Boeing had $3.27 billion in cash, a pension fund overfunded by $1.2 billion, loans it had made and could call in totaling nearly $1 billion, and a backlog of orders worth almost $30 billion. Long-term debt was insignificant, only $259 million, just 5 percent of total capital. Yet the price of Boeing stock was low, having declined 28 percent in the past year because of weak current earnings.

Assessing the situation, Shrontz understood that, although Boeing on the face of it seemed alluring takeover bait, a closer analysis showed several features undesirable to a raider. Airlines won't buy airplanes from an unstable company because they need long-term support; if Boeing were taken over, the company would likely lose all its business, and outstanding orders would be canceled. Boeing's military customers also need stability, and—unless the Reagan administration held to its policy of nonintervention in business affairs—would be expected to do everything in their power to fight a takeover of a critical supplier in the interest of national security; no unfriendly try for a large defense contractor had ever succeeded. Many of Boeing's facilities for making airplanes are so specialized that they'd be hard for a successful attacker using a leveraged buyout to sell off. And Boeing already had several so-called shark repellents in place, such as staggered terms for members of the board of directors that made it nearly impossible for a raider to replace the whole slate.

If Pickens really wanted to take over Boeing, it would be the first time he'd tried to acquire a company outside the petroleum industry. Mesa Petroleum was in financial trouble and desperately needed an infusion of cash. Wall Street experts were betting that Pickens just wanted to invest heavily in Boeing stock, drive up the price with a takeover pass, and dump the stock immediately for a quick profit. He had already been in and out of half a dozen nominal takeover attempts since January.

Despite the unlikely nature of the takeover bid, however, Shrontz couldn't take the slightest chance on losing the company: he had to assume that Pickens was serious. Furthermore, even a nonserious Pickens bid could put Boeing "into play," meaning that other sharks might sense the commotion and try to grab the prey for themselves. Pickens kept up his pursuit, becoming the single largest Boeing stockholder. When news about the takeover attempt hit the street, Boeing stock shot up from 47 to $53^6/_8$; on July 27 it was the most actively traded issue on the New York Stock Exchange. Shrontz retained a New York lawyer who specialized in takeovers.

Boeing's board of directors quickly approved the first element of the antitakeover strategy: adopting a "poison pill." If Pickens (or anyone else) acquired 15 percent of Boeing's stock, and the board declared that a coercive or unfair takeover was under way, the company could grant current stockholders rights to buy more stock cheaply. This would greatly expand the amount of Boeing stock in circulation and make it hard for Pickens to round up a controlling number of shares.

The next step was to ask the Washington state legislature for a law requiring the directors of an acquired company to wait five years before selling company assets, and prohibiting the firing of more than 5 percent of a company's workforce within five years of a merger; both provisions would further discourage buyouts. Shrontz himself helicoptered to Olympia to plead for a special session of the state legislature to take up the measure, which was granted (showing again the tremendous clout that Boeing has in the gray stone state house). District Lodge 751 of the Machinists' union, fearing loss of jobs, joined Boeing in heavily lobbying legislators to pass the bill. Pickens was silent throughout this maneuvering until, shortly before the vote, a Washington state senator reached him by phone. Pickens ridiculed Boeing's all-out campaign against him, saying "I'm like the little ant crawling up the leg of the big elephant with rape on his mind." The measure nevertheless easily passed into law on August 11. There was some doubt, however, whether a Washington state law could help Boeing, which was legally incorporated in Delaware.

It was Delaware that gave Boeing its strongest weapon against Pickens. A court had once issued a declaration that characterized Pickens in unfavorable terms. Always eager to strengthen its attraction to companies as the U.S. incorporation capital, Delaware passed a law that no one who had been legally so characterized could vote shares in a company incorporated in Delaware. Even if Pickens should acquire a majority of Boeing stock, this would stop him from doing anything with the company. Boeing denies originating this ploy, but certainly supported it.

There was no climax to the tense situation. The other shoe simply never dropped. Pickens turned his attention to Singer, another aerospace firm, and it was assumed he'd lost interest in Boeing. Shrontz learned later that Pickens had sold his shares, but the intentions of the Texan were never made clear. It's thought that he profited handsomely from a quick buy-and-sell of Boeing stock, but only he and Mesa know for sure.

Ironically, just when Boeing was at last about to achieve financial greatness, its shining technical side suffered severe setbacks in yet more of the misfortunes that plagued Frank Shrontz. The trouble started in the fall of 1985 when Shrontz was president but T Wilson was still CEO. Wilson launched design of a bigger, more powerful, and longer-ranged derivative of the 747. Incredibly, the program to make this plane, known as the 747-400, suffered a relapse of the kind of terrible problems that had plagued design and early production of the original 747 two decades before, although mercifully on a smaller scale.

Wilson began the program as a routine and relatively simple enhancement of Boeing's product line. At every step in development, however, airlines pleaded for newer technologies and more extensive modifications than planned. Long before, Wellwood Beall had commented on the frequent tendency to overdo aircraft development: "In a peculiar way, an airplane resembles a Christmas tree. The temptation is to keep hanging things on, changing things around." This time, the designers couldn't or wouldn't say "no" to the goodies that the airlines wanted, and the project got out of hand. Costs soared and schedules slipped. The 747-400 finally flew for the first time on April 29, 1988. About a third of the airplane—a huge chunk for a derivative—had been newly designed.

The design problems over, the production problems started. Essentially, the labor force couldn't handle the complex airplane that the 747-400 had become. The workers were inexperienced; over half of Boeing's total workforce had been with the company less than five years. Eugene Bauer, author of a history of Boeing, observed that the attitude of the workers was more casual than it had been historically, citing increased absenteeism and a "laissez-faire" attitude. A majority of the company's top four hundred executives were unseasoned, moreover. Managers in the middle-aged group that survived the layoffs of mostly younger people after the original 747 disaster began reaching retirement age in droves in the mid-1980s, and much younger, much less experienced people were taking their places.

Boeing had accepted many orders from eighteen different customers for the first year and had scheduled ambitious delivery dates. Hearkening back to the original 747 program, suppliers complicated the situation by late delivery of components. As on the original 747 project, managers were faced with either revising the schedule to make it more realistic or hoping against hope that they could make the schedule they'd started with. The managers chose hope over reality. The workers couldn't get the airplanes out on time. Boeing began missing promised delivery dates for the first time since the first 747s, falling as much as three months behind. Boeing tried to solve the problem by ordering employees at Everett to work overtime. As the problems worsened, so did the overtime, until employees were working long days every day, including weekends, for months on end; fifty- to sixty-hour weeks were common. The stress on employees and their families, and the resulting breakdown in morale, became a major problem itself. A worker griped to a reporter, "You're tired. There's no social life, no family. My wife would like to tell this place where to go."

The workforce problems afflicted all Boeing airplanes, not just the 747-400. Complaints began to come in from airlines about shoddy workmanship on their Boeing airplanes. In February 1988, the chief engineer for technical and quality services at British Airways angrily shot an extraordinary, blistering letter to Phil Condit, then executive vice president of the airliner division: "My quality inspectors can only properly inspect a very small proportion of each aircraft. They should never ever come across . . . missing fasteners, missing parts, cracks, bodged rivets, fasteners fitted the wrong way round. Yet we find instances of some of these on every aircraft. . . . All of these mistakes and the work that you have to carry out must be costing Boeing a king's ransom, and I cannot understand why you don't have a series of actions, starting with a training program, to really put quality back into your products within a definitive timescale, say a year. . . . [The situation] underscores our fears that the underlying reason for the Boeing Company's poor quality record is that the production work force are, in general, inadequately trained, possess a low level of basic working skills, and of paramount importance, seem oblivious that they are building aircraft where any mistake not properly corrected or hidden represents a direct compromise with safety." He said that some mistakes found on a 747 left "no doubt that the integrity of the aircraft structure had been compromised."

The very next month, the president of Japan Airlines got off a similarly fiery letter to Shrontz complaining about miswired fire extinguishing systems in the cargo holds of five 767s, and a faulty engine-overheating detector on a 747 flight deck. He demanded that Boeing make greater efforts to improve quality control.

The serious complaints mushroomed and resulted in one of the most humiliating moments in Boeing's proud history: In January 1989, the FAA issued a directive ordering special inspections of most Boeing jetliners produced since 1980 to look for defects that might affect safety. The recall netted ninety-five defective wiring and plumbing systems. In the four years ending in 1990, regulators fined Boeing at least fourteen times. A British Airways official commented that "Boeing has very, very, very big problems." Boeing took the unusual step of renting some seven hundred seasoned employees from Lockheed to work on the non-secret aspects of the airplanes until the company could get the problems under control.

In a *Business Week* magazine interview, Dean Thornton, president of the airliner division, made an admission of failure rare for a corporate spokesman, expressing Boeing's keen embarrassment over missed 747-400 delivery schedules and the quality mess: "We overcommitted. We violated a covenant with our customers, and I'm pretty damned ashamed of it."

The débâcle inflicted a serious political wound on one young Boeing executive: Phil Condit, who had been put up as a candidate for president before Wilson and the board chose Shrontz, and who had overall responsibility for the 747-400 program. When Shrontz had risen to chairman in January 1988, leaving the presidency vacant, he reportedly planned to promote Condit to that position soon. Aeronautical engineer Condit had become the chief technical adviser to lawyer Shrontz. The 747-400 tribulations made Condit's theretofore sterling qualifications suspect, however. Shrontz put Condit's elevation on hold until the star engineer could dispel the doubts that now surrounded him.

In 1988, Professor Doug Underwood of the School of Communications at the University of Washington wrote an article for the *Columbia Journalism Review* that teed off on Seattle newspaper coverage of the 747-400 problems and Boeing's other snags at the time. He criticized both the afternoon *Times* and the morning *P-I* (Seattle's nickname for the *Post-Intelligencer*) for chronically boosting the company and ignoring its mistakes and occasional wrongdoings. "Of the nearly 3,500 stories mentioning Boeing that appeared in the *Times* and *P-I* in 1986 and 1987, for example, no more than half a dozen could be considered local enterprise efforts that went beyond the usual flow of Boeing-is-booming reports. Even then, most of those enterprise articles . . . were one-shot pieces . . . which failed to lead to any deeper examination of the company's operations. . . . The shortcomings of that coverage might not be so troubling if the national press could be counted on to take up the slack. But, unfortunately, the national press also tends to give a Boeing story upbeat or superficial treatment."

As private entities, corporations legally don't have to reveal much about themselves: like individuals or families, they don't openly discuss "personal" matters. As the business editor of the *Times* told Underwood, "Hell, those are private corporations that don't have to tell you much, except for what they file with the SEC." Most companies make exceptions when they feel better understanding will help them, or silence will hurt. Some companies tell more than others, some—including Boeing—tell less, although (as this book attests) the company has been getting more responsive under Shrontz's policy of greater openness to the public. Reporters in the Puget Sound area (some of whom got more assertive in the 1990s) don't like Boeing because of its long record of "no comment" responses, unreturned phone calls, and runarounds they've experienced when the company believes—as it often has—that disclosure will result in compromising, misleading, or unfair coverage. From Boeing's perspective, Underwood's article witnessed the success, in the days of nonaggressive reporting at least, of the company's conservative information policy: coverage was fawning. Underwood clearly felt that society would be better off, however, if the business press were more aggressive. "If Boeing has come to symbolize the highest hopes of US industry, the daily reporting on the company symbolizes the need for newspapers to do a better job of monitoring what's really going on in US businesses that are being reshaped by growing profit pressures and tougher world competition," he concluded.

Boeing gradually worked itself out of the problems at its plants through special employee training and the normal efficiency improvements that come from the learning curve when producing a new airplane. The company was aided by being given breathing room from a timely but yet most unwelcome occurrence—related to the problem of overworking its labor force.

The timing of the severe demands for extra hours that Boeing made on its employees at Everett to speed up 747-400 production could hardly have been worse for the company. The mandates occurred near the end of the three-year cycle of the IAM contract. Negotiations for the new contract began as the resentment of the plant workers was at its peak. The labor relations aspects of the 747-400 program were no better managed than the rest of the project. An executive admitted later that, had he and other managers handled the grievances of Everett's workers more deftly, Boeing might have gotten the workers to identify more with the company and its problems. Management and labor might have worked shoulder to shoulder to turn the ill-starred program around, much as they had during the original 747 crisis in the late 1960s. Instead, an "us against them" mentality ruled both sides during the negotiations. Typical was the complaint expressed in a letter to the editor of the *Seattle Times* by one Leota More: "[Boeing's employees] are virtually slaves of a company that expects to drain off all their prime time and energy. Many are required to work 12 hours a day, seven days a week for prolonged periods. . . . In emergency situations, an employee should be willing to work extra hours to meet a deadline. The present legitimate complaint is that long hours on a long-term basis are built into production planning. When a company loses sight of the individual needs and rights of its employees, it is time for reform!" Boeing pointed out that the only alternative was to hire more people and then have layoffs when the problem was over.

The union insisted that Boeing end forced overtime and rely on volunteers to fill overtime needs. Boeing's negotiators retorted that voluntary overtime would never work but offered to reduce mandatory overtime. The plant workers also felt they weren't sharing in Boeing's prosperity. They saw TV news stories about the record orders and profits Boeing was raking in, but the union members hadn't had a general wage increase in six years. (They'd had bonuses and cost-of-living adjustments, but it seemed unfair to them that they'd had no true raises in that period.)

Boeing managers, not sensing the depth of discontentment or recognizing the other factors that favored a strike, naïvely expected a routine negotiation period and settlement. The many months of overtime had not only put the plant workers in an ugly mood, however, but had made being off work for a while on strike seem appealing, and the fat overtime paychecks had given them a rich strike fund. As contract deadline neared, the workers were fired up to fight. (Some insiders claim the IAM International in Washington, D.C., fanned the strike passions to show its muscle and solidify its membership.)

The contract ended at midnight October 3, and the workers promptly walked out. The strikers believed in their cause: only about one worker in twenty crossed the picket lines. (All Boeing's plant workers were union members, District 751 having won back the union shop in previous negotiations.) Late on a Saturday morning two weeks after the strike began, nationally prominent Democratic politician Jesse Jackson led two thousand strikers on a march from the IAM building to Boeing headquarters. His followers cheered loudest when he condemned Boeing for not sharing enough of its huge profits with workers. "If these workers are on management's hit list, everyone is in trouble," he bellowed.

The strikers had been out about five weeks when the federal mediator offered a proposal to both sides. (In negotiations between large corporations and large unions, mediators normally do little more than facilitate discussion. It's unusual for mediators to propose anything on their own. For political reasons, however, one side or the other, or sometimes both together, at times arrange secretly for mediators to announce seemingly independent suggestions that really come from the disputants. It's not clear if that happened in this case.) An official from the IAM International in Washington, D.C., tried to shoot the proposal down, grumbling that it didn't add more to the general wage increase. Both sides in Seattle liked the new proposal, however. The ideas the mediator put forth became the basis for an agreement that Boeing and the union both accepted. The strike ended on November 21, forty-eight days after it had begun and in time for all employees to enjoy the year-end holidays. Wages were essentially what Boeing had offered during negotiations. Mandatory overtime was still in place, but overtime rules were revised to the benefit of the workers.

Shortly after the strike had begun, negotiations opened with SPEEA, the engineers and technical employees' union. Since about 1970, SPEEA (which had long since represented only Boeing employees) had given up the pretense that it was only an association that acted as the bargaining agent for its members and not exactly a union. SPEEA now presented itself as a full-fledged union and used the term "union" in its contracts. The organization, however, still saw its role as one of partnership with Boeing to advance both the company and its engineering and technical employees at the same time. SPEEA didn't think of itself in any way as an enemy of management; indeed, most of its engineering members hoped to become managers. The group did not affiliate with the AFL-CIO. SPEEA's members included eighty-four hundred of the fifteen thousand engineers employed by Boeing, and eighty-five hundred of the thirteen thousand lower-level technical workers.

The people SPEEA represented had also worked long hours on the 747-400 project and had the same desires to share all the money that Boeing seemed to be rolling in. Boeing had offered the IAM bonuses in every year. But the company didn't offer the engineers bonuses in the second or third years. Those zeros in the package stunned the engineers. The engineers saw themselves working harder and harder for less and less. Dejected at what they thought was an exploitative and demeaning offer, and shocked by what they felt was a callous slamming of the door on what in Ed Wells's day had been a love affair between Boeing and themselves, the engineers rejected the contract. Having gone this far, however, the engineers weren't yet ready to go all the way and authorize a strike; they voted against that measure. Nevertheless, taken aback by this defiance from the engineers whose compliance they had taken for granted, the company immediately offered them bonuses in all years. Two months after their old contract expired, the engineers grudgingly accepted the revised offer.

Boeing had been hurt financially. The IAM strike sharply affected fourth-quarter sales and earnings, and the company's cash reserve. Boeing was trying to build up its cash to finance a new airplane model, and the strike greatly depleted this reserve. This discomfited Frank Shrontz, who was counting on the new jetliner to solidify Boeing's position in the industry and cut the legs from under Airbus Industrie.

=

On his second day looking for work in late 1980, Bill Gray learned of an opening for a millwright at Boeing's Everett plant. At Boeing, a millwright is a handyman who does odd jobs at a facility—erecting a partition, say, or moving heavy equipment, or posting company notices on bulletin boards. Bill drove up to the sprawling plant and applied. The man who would be his supervisor, a bearded, cigar-smoking former millwright, another midwesterner, interviewed him and offered him the job on the spot, but at a grade 4, steps below the level he had attained before being let go. Bill refused. The boss offered a grade higher. Bill turned that down, too. The boss presented a final offer two grades below that of Bill's last job. Sensing that he'd gotten his best deal, and recognizing that his loss in pay would be only a few cents an hour, Bill shook hands.

At first, Bill detected some resentment among his new coworkers over his high grade as a new millwright, but they soon accepted him. Bill found that he enjoyed the job and liked his supervisor.

Then Bill's life fell apart. Strains developed in his relationship with Linda. At work, Bill's group became overloaded, and he began working heavy overtime, including one stretch of eleven weeks with no days off. The stress on the job exacerbated the strains at home, which proved too much for Linda. She left Bill and returned to

Milwaukee. He was devastated. He sought the help of a counselor and began working things out with Linda long-distance. Six months later, she came back.

About that time, Bill got bad news at Everett. People were being transferred to other Seattle-area plants—known in Everett as "being sent south"—and Bill was tapped to go. He didn't like it, but, as the transfers were being done by seniority and therefore fairly in his eyes, he didn't protest. He was moved to Plant II in Seattle and then, after only a short while, to the close-by Development Center, which houses military projects. Bill had to pass a security clearance because the staff at the center was working on the secret B-2 Stealth bomber under a subcontract from Northrop. Beginning in 1983, he commuted to work in a new Chevy Blazer pickup truck.

In 1984, Bill's landlord notified him that the house he lived in was to be sold and could no longer be rented. Bill and Linda felt comfortable where they were and didn't want to move. Although the house needed extensive remodeling, they took one of life's big steps: They arranged a mortgage with the VA and bought the house themselves. Bill gave up his vacation time and took the equivalent in pay to take care of the closing costs on the house.

Problems on the job plagued Bill's time at the center. A forklift ran over the toes of his left foot. Despite the intense pain and severe bruising, Bill didn't want to seem a whiner and lose face in his macho work group, so he didn't report to the center's dispensary. The foot healed unaided, although the big toe hurt every so often, and the nail was permanently misshapen.

A welder saw Bill with a bucket labeled "paint thinner," pouring clear liquid from the bucket into a drain. The coworker reported Bill for violating a company rule that prohibited dumping thinner down a drain. Bill wrote a memo to the supervisor assigned to review the charge, explaining that he had used up the thinner, poured water into the empty bucket to rinse it out, and was seen pouring the water down the drain. The reviewer ruled against Bill, who was sentenced to a day off without pay. Bill felt that the outcome was predetermined because the complainant was a relative of the reviewer. Then, at the end of his shift one day, Bill did a favor for a coworker on the shift who wanted to sneak out of work early. Bill punched the time clock for him—and got caught, apparently reported by another coworker. He lost one more day's work.

The matter that bothered Bill the most, however, was that workers less senior—and, he felt, less competent—than he kept getting promoted ahead of him. He filed an official grievance, complaining that he was being passed over because of nepotism and workplace politics. He pleaded his case before a panel of five company representatives and three union representatives, who grilled him and then voted. The verdict: case not proven. Later, he filed another grievance, heard by four union people and three company people—and won his case. Five years after losing his grade 8 rating, he won it back. Fellow workers told Bill they respected him for "not taking any shit from anybody."

Bill and Linda had even more to celebrate in 1986. On September 26, Linda gave birth to their first child, a boy, whom they christened Michael, a name they picked simply because they liked it.

Bill's luck continued into 1987, when he got good news from Boeing: He was being "sent north"—transferred back to Everett. He worked happily there, even through the overtime connected with the 747-400 and quality problems, until October 3, 1989, when the working man's curse hit: the big strike of that year. He and Linda had enough saved to make out OK for a while, but after a few weeks Bill had to look for work. He landed a job as an equipment operator for a landscaping outfit in Bellevue, the satellite city across Lake Washington from Seattle. By the same charm that seems to prevent rain if a person troubles to carry an umbrella, the strike ended the day after Bill got his emergency job.

With life stable at home and work for several years, the Grays enlarged their family on, appropriately, Mother's Day, May 9, 1993, when Linda had a girl. They tried to think of the prettiest name and picked Melinda. The stability at work wasn't to last long, however. Bill himself and his union faced some of their toughest fights ahead.

15 ‖ Frank's Airplane

Throughout the 1980s, Wilson and then Shrontz were beset by uncertainties about Boeing's next entirely new airliner—how big it should be, when it should be introduced, to what extent Boeing should cooperate with the Japanese to produce the airplane, and whether it should be a radically new kind of propeller-driven airplane instead of a jet.

At first, Wilson decided to explore a 150-seat airplane tentatively designated the 7-7. Airbus Industrie's A320 was of this size; the 7-7 would be stronger than the 757 in competing with the A320. The airlines had been clamoring for 150-seaters, but Wilson wasn't sure his customers would back up their pleas with money when it came time to order. An airplane of that size would cannibalize orders for slightly larger 757s and slightly smaller 737s, moreover.

Wilson felt that the risks and financing needs involved in producing the new airplane were so great that he should again seek a partner abroad. Financing needs had intensified after deregulation of the airlines, which took place from 1978 to 1984, because American carriers, the usual source of launch customers for a new airliner, were no longer making enough money to help manufacturers pay for aircraft development. This time Wilson looked across the Pacific, to Japan. Boeing had explored a partnership with Japan before, in 1973. A Boeing analysis then had identified the Japanese as the best potential foreign partners. Boeing and a Japanese group had conducted a year-long study of the feasibility of jointly producing a new jetliner, which concluded that the project wasn't worth pursuing then. Now the Japanese were eager for a partnership, they were doing a superb job on the 767—better than Boeing's other subcontractors, and even better in some respects than Boeing itself—and an alliance with them would have strategic advantages. Airbus Industrie was romancing the Japanese, offering them membership in the consortium. Boeing could preempt the Europeans by tying up the Japanese on an American project. The Japanese were favorably disposed toward Boeing, whose winning methods they emulated. They disliked the heavy, long-term commitment that Airbus demanded. They favored an American link for several reasons, including their beliefs that Boeing was the stronger competitor and that Japan would benefit politically.

In March 1984, after several years of negotiations, Boeing signed a memorandum of understanding with the Japan Aircraft Development Corporation, outlining an agreement to produce a 150-seater as genuine partners. JADC included the prominent manufacturers Mitsubishi, Kawasaki, and Fuji, the same firms that were producing 767 components. The Japanese would finance 25 percent of the project, take a quarter of the profits (or losses), and be fully involved in development, marketing, finance, and product support. The togetherness would be a disruptive experience for Boeing, used to full control over an entire project and possessive about its design secrets, which it would have to share. The new partners expected the jetliner to enter service in 1990.

Less than a year after the endeavor began, in February 1985, Wilson reprised his performance of a decade before, when he had ditched the Italians and the joint QSHA project. This time he announced that sales prospects for the 7-7 were too dim to pursue, so Boeing would delay the project for two or three years—tantamount to killing it. The program had never been certain, so the end wasn't totally unexpected, but the Japanese—now wedded to nobody—were unhappy nonetheless.

Although Wilson had abandoned the 7-7 jetliner model, he hadn't forsaken the 150-seater. He thought an airplane based on a revolutionary technology might provide the economics necessary for an airliner of that size to succeed. He plunged into a race with Douglas to develop an unusual aircraft that Boeing called the UDF, for unducted fan. Its power plants would be essentially fan-jet engines with the fans not encased within the nacelle. Instead, the fans would be turned into large, curving propellers facing rearward, with tips swept back like jetliner wings. Each engine would turn two counterrotating propellers. Basically, UDF airliners would be turboprops that could fly close to pure jet speeds with super, cost-saving efficiency able to reduce fuel consumption by 20 percent. Thrifty use of fuel was key then, when the energy crisis was dictating many business decisions; people expected fuel to remain high in price and low in availability. Wilson chose GE to develop the engines.

Even though at that point Boeing's expenses exceeded its income for all the jetliners it had ever produced (because it had just begun to recover the billions invested in the 757 and 767), Wilson expected to lay down some four billion dollars more for the UDF. With Boeing still lacking a mate to beget the new airplane and share the cost, Wilson offered to get back together with the Japanese. In March 1986, Boeing and JADC signed a new memorandum of understanding for joint development of the UDF, provisionally designated the 7J7, the *J* standing for "Japan." Terms were much the same as for the 7-7. Wilson established a division within Boeing devoted to the 7J7, which was expected to enter service in 1992. Japanese engineers began moving to Seattle; at the peak of development, 250 of them were expected to transfer to the United States, with another 250 working on the project in Japan. Harvard Professor Robert Reich (who later became President Clinton's secretary of labor) criticized the program for handing over valuable technological know-how to a foreign power and strengthening a potential competitor. Other academics pointed out that, to the contrary, Japan was sharing its own expertise in composite materials and other technologies (not to mention its critical financial contributions), the Japanese were determined to ally with someone, Airbus Industrie was continuing to court them, and the threat from Japan to the American aircraft industry was debatable.

In mid-1987, little over a year after the agreement had been signed, Frank Shrontz, who had become CEO, made the kind of announcement that by then seemed almost inevitable for Boeing's international joint ventures: The company was putting the 7J7 project on hold (diplomatic language for getting out of the project) because airlines were no longer sure they needed an aircraft of that size, and development of the radical engine had hit snags. The market for the 7J7 had virtually disappeared, moreover, as fuel prices and availability had returned to normal. Douglas canceled its similar project. The one hundred Japanese engineers who had gone to Seattle by then packed up their calculators and drawing compasses and flew home. Shrontz tried not to think about the one hundred million dollars Boeing had dropped on the attempt.

Another major influence on Shrontz's decision to fold was surely the direction Boeing's competitors were taking. Airbus Industrie and Douglas had both announced they'd bring out new jetliner models at the other end of the spectrum from the 150–seater, in the range between the 767 and 747. This was the province of the DC-10 and L-1011. Neither was in production anymore, and those being flown by airlines were getting old. With airline traffic increasing at about 5 percent a year, and virtually no new airports being built, crowding on runways and in airways had continued to worsen. The squeeze was particularly acute on the Pacific Rim, whose major airports are restricted to a few megacities such as Tokyo and Singapore. These forces were increasing the need for fewer flights and therefore bigger airplanes. Airlines were adding long routes, moreover, but often the traffic wasn't high enough to support 747s. The market for the size just under jumbo had grown since Douglas and Lockheed had knocked each other out trying to serve it, so there would be a demand not only to replace DC-10s and L-1011s, but to buy additional craft, too.

Douglas was upgrading and updating its DC-10 to produce a new trijet designated the MD-11; the company had kept its DC-10 production line open by continuing to sell tanker and cargo versions. Airbus Industrie was taking a Boeinglike approach and developing two models for the market: the two-engine, medium-range A330 to carry some 335 passengers, and the four-engine, long-range A340, using basically the same airframe as the A330 but somewhat smaller, carrying some 295 passengers. Airbus Industrie believed that many airlines would prefer a four-engine airplane for routes over water. Even more than the 757 and 767, the A330 and A340 would have many features in common. These two aircraft fulfilled the strategy that Airbus had initiated in the early 1970s—to match Boeing in offering a large family of airplanes. Industry analyst David C. Mowery said that this "may be one of this consortium's most important strategic policy decisions."

One of Boeing's venerable competitors would not even consider entering the race. Lockheed's one attempt at a jetliner, the L-1011, having been a financial disaster, the company had announced in 1985 that the airliner business had grown too expensive and risky, and that it was bowing out to focus on military and government aerospace products. Lockheed's exit left Boeing, Douglas, and Airbus as the free world's only contenders in the market for large and medium-sized airliners.

Despite the logic behind a 300-seat jetliner and the commitments by Douglas and Airbus Industrie, Shrontz wasn't sure how big the demand would be. And he really didn't want to launch a jetliner of that size—it would cannibalize sales of his two biggest moneymakers, the 747 and 767. His concerns were much the same as those that had worried Wilson over the 150-seater. Much of the uncertainty was caused by deregulation of airlines in the United States. Many of Boeing's most important customers could no longer be sure what routes they'd be flying or how frequent flights would be in the future, so the manufacturers couldn't get a firm handle on what kinds of airplanes to make. Stopping the 7J7 saved money that might be used for a Boeing entry against the new Airbus and Douglas models, but Shrontz wouldn't spend the funds until he was convinced that a new big Boeing airplane would earn money for the company and not lose it. He'd be impossibly behind his competitors if he did nothing, however, so he had to get a program started that he could either scrap like the 7-7 and 7J7 or push forward depending on how the market developed.

At the end of 1987, T Wilson, then sixty-six years old, gave up his chairmanship and faded from the executive scene as quietly as Bill Allen had when he made way for Wilson. (Wilson would continue on the board of directors until he was seventy-two.) He and Grace planned to spend summers in Seattle and winters in a big home in Palm Springs, but (as he sighed to a visitor many years later) he would always miss his office on East Marginal Way across from Boeing Field. Returning to a hobby of his youth, Wilson set up a beehive in the yard of his Seattle home and placed two white plastic lawn chairs in front of it, so on nice days he and Grace could sip martinis and watch the worker bees go back and forth, back and forth.

In January 1988 the board installed Shrontz as chairman. They left the presidency vacant for the moment, the first time that office had deliberately not been filled since Bill Boeing's days, as they waited for Phil Condit to strengthen his credentials.

Unwanted pressures from some customers, stockholders, and others involved with Boeing were building for the new chairman to enter Boeing in the jetliner development race, to the extent that Frank Shrontz had to place a statement in the 1987 annual report that Boeing would likely *not* launch a jetliner in 1988 because the market wasn't ready. As Shrontz hesitated, however, Airbus and Douglas were carving up the market for themselves. Moving cautiously, he decided that the two-engine A330 offered the only real competition. Jet engines having become so powerful and efficient, he felt that the unfavorable economics of additional engines would take care of the three-engine MD-11 and the four-engine A340 for him. He decided to counter the Airbus twin-jet by spinning off a derivative of the 767, and not daring the risk and financial stress of a new aircraft program.

Phil Condit and other Boeing executives met in Chicago with Jim Guyette of United Airlines to see if United would be interested in a double-decker 767. Guyette said no, it couldn't compete with the new offerings from Douglas and Airbus. He urged them to launch a new model, and stated he'd like to work with them to develop the best jetliner of the new generation, one with incomparable airline appeal.

When Shrontz heard this, he realized he couldn't fight the inevitable—he'd have to go for a very big, very expensive, very risky new airplane. His engineers revived a three-hundred-seat idea studied about 1980 but dropped because the airlines then showed little interest. When Guyette got word of the decision, he called Dean Thornton at the Commercial Airplane Group, and arranged the flight to Seattle that cemented the cooperative relationship between United and Boeing in formulating the characteristics of the jetliner. Boeing's latest offspring would bear a preordained name: the 777.

In December 1989, Shrontz announced the 777 project to the world and began seeking orders; he wouldn't ask the board of directors to launch the project officially, however, until he had one hundred orders in hand. At the same time, he appointed Phil Condit, then executive vice president of the airliner division, as head of the 777 program. The selection of Condit gave the project a strong top man who could deal as easily and successfully with financiers in their Wall Street offices as with the engineers at their computer terminals and the Joe Six-Packs on the riveting guns. He understood pilots as a member of the fraternity, having won his flying license at the age of only eighteen. This was the chance for Condit, who had stubbed his toes on the 747-400 program, to prove himself worthy of being named president and heir apparent.

Jack Steiner is convinced that, with these announcements, McDonnell Douglas lost its main chance to knock out the 777. He reasoned that if the California company had decided before the end of 1989 to develop a twin-engine jetliner—instead of the trijet MD-11—to compete with the A330, Boeing would not have entered an overcrowded field, to avoid the fate that McDonnell Douglas and Lockheed had suffered in a small market for the similarly sized DC-10 and L-1011.

One of Condit's first steps was to push Boeing to the frontier of the jetliner design process, making it as efficient as modern technology allows. He threw out T squares, drafting tables, and other traditional engineering paraphernalia and practices—even blueprints. Engineers would work only with computers. From Dassault, the French military plane builder, Boeing had bought a multi-million-dollar program called CATIA, an acronym for Computer-graphics Aided Three-dimensional Interactive Application (pronounced "kuh-tee-uh"). Originally bought for the defunct 7J7, the ultrasophisticated software operates on a spectacular system that uses the world's largest cluster of mainframe computers, eight IBMs that radiate their power from an office in Bellevue, and the world's largest number of workstations—seventeen hundred terminals—connected to a single set of mainframes. Designers could immediately see how their creations looked in three dimensions, and how they fit with what every other designer was doing. No longer did the designers have to rely on a mock-up when their work was finished to discover in-compatibilities; if, say, an engineer tried to run a duct through an area where somebody had placed a beam that blocked the way, the computer screen would show the impasse immediately. If an engineer wasn't sure a maintenance person could squeeze into a tight space he'd designed, he could call up a figure of a man on the screen to see if he'd fit.

The 777 would be the first jetliner, Boeing claimed, to be designed entirely on computers. Because each designer could, in a way, comprehend the entire project through a computer, CATIA promised to eliminate the breakdowns in communications that had bedeviled the huge engineering teams employed to develop jetlin-ers. CATIA would return the advantages of pre–World War II days, when fewer than one hundred engineers, who tended to be engi-neering generalists, labored over the B-17 at the peak of design activity. Every member of the B-17 team had a good idea of what the other members were doing. Condit undoubtedly hoped to restore some of this intimacy to his legions of engineering specialists.

Communications obstacles had proliferated throughout the process of creating, making, and selling airplanes, and had become the greatest source of inefficiency. Designers were grouped by dis-ciplines, leading to problems like the electrical engineer's duct being blocked by the structural engineer's beam. Designers had little contact with manufacturing people, so often a blueprint would go to a plant and be met with the response "We can't make that" or "That's too expensive to make." Suppliers frequently complained about the same thing, and Condit listened hard because they had grown increasingly important as aircraft subsystems became more complex and specialized, and vendors made larger and larger portions of Boeing's products. Airlines, too, suffered from inadequate communications with manufacturers. When carriers got a new jetliner model, the typical first response was a barrage of complaints such as "That fuel inlet is too high for our airport trucks to reach" or "The bulbs in the passengers' overhead reading lights are so hard to get at that it takes more time and trouble to change them than it's worth."

Jim Guyette had tried to solve this problem for United Airlines when he butted into the early design process for the 777. Condit decided to expand airline participation, probably to avoid focusing too narrowly on United's particular circumstances, and so other customers wouldn't see the 777 as meant just for United and not them. (Exclusive arrangements such as Boeing had had with Pan Am wouldn't work because United didn't have the overpowering influence that Pan Am had had on sales to other airlines.) The airline advisers would also help to restore the links between Boeing's engineers and customers that had been severed when the airlines disbanded or cut back their technical staffs in cost-cutting moves after deregulation. Condit formed a consulting board of eight major airlines from around the world, which became known in Boeing as "the gang of eight." (Interestingly, two decades before the 777, British aviation experts Ronald Miller and David Sawers had co-written in their book: "The shrewd manufacturer will study the needs and likings of a worldwide sample of possible customers when preparing his design, but he will not follow the requirements of any one airline. The maker must combine knowledge of the market with knowledge of design, to produce an airplane that the airlines will wish they had thought of themselves.")

Taking on the airline advisers was a shrewd move from marketing as well as productivity viewpoints: these days a majority of aircraft sales are made to a few megacarriers, and Boeing has most of them as advisers. They should naturally be attracted to an airplane they were involved in designing (although they'd continue to be most heavily influenced by the best sales deal).

Condit saw that companies in other industries were solving communications problems similar to Boeing's by what they called "design/build" teams; GM had used the approach successfully in its Saturn division. Condit formed small teams each responsible for a certain section of the 777. The teams, described by one participant as like "little companies," were composed of not only engineers in various disciplines but also the people from Boeing's plants who would make the jetliner and—in a revolutionary departure for an almost insular company such as Boeing—representatives from major suppliers and airlines. A United Airlines engineer who participated in several design/build teams said that Boeing had been so secretive that everybody was uncomfortable and reserved in the first meetings: "It was as if I'd stepped into a ladies' locker room." Boeing representatives sitting down at meetings in supplier companies had the same uneasy experience. Participants report that everybody soon warmed up, however, and forgot the "foreigners" in their midst. Condit counted on CATIA and design/build teams to eliminate much costly redesign and give the 777 an edge over its competitors. Shrontz proclaimed that the 777 would be the most efficiently designed and manufactured aircraft ever built.

Phil Condit furthered togetherness among 777 workers by his own cozy style. A man who wears colorful sweaters instead of suit jackets at work, and likes to walk around with a coffee cup in hand, dropping by other offices to chat about business, Condit held a weekly "muffin meeting" of vice presidents every Tuesday morning. His wife Jan would bake muffins, and he'd pass them out to attendees as they hashed over problems and plans. His office was decorated with pictures taken by his mother, a noted professional photographer who had traveled around the world taking pictures of people in 140 countries. Keenly interested in what makes people tick, Condit hired an organizational psychologist to help him get the most out of his teams. Securities analyst Howard Rubell described Condit's two-sided personality: "Condit is a cross between a grizzly bear and a teddy bear. Good people skills, but furious in the marketplace."

Shrontz and Condit advanced the productivity of the design process by extending it from essentially just one airplane to include the whole family of derivative jetliners that would be based on the 777. They greatly expanded the idea of designing an airplane so it can be stretched into a derivative model. Boeing tried to anticipate all the derivatives that could clearly be foreseen, and design in the flexibility to effect the changes easily when they were required. This would make 777 derivatives, future "777 dash" airplanes, faster and cheaper to design than derivatives of previous models done from the ground up in reaction to changing needs. A member of Boeing's board of directors observed that Boeing "is not designing a model, they're designing a fleet." Condit prophesied that the 777 family would remain in production "easily" for fifty years.

Shrontz paid a call on the Japanese and asked if they'd like to try a close relationship one more time. The Japanese eagerly replied "yes." Boeing tentatively agreed with the JADC to cooperate on the 777 program under essentially the same understandings as for the 7-7 and the 7J7. The arrangement soon ran into trouble on both sides of the Pacific, however, for various economic, political, and business reasons. Boeing accumulated so much cash by its financial successes in the late 1980s, moreover, that it discovered it could fund the entire 777 project itself—it no longer badly needed a partner. When the time came to formalize the pact, each side wanted too many concessions from the other party. The agreement fell apart. The Japanese, without rancor, settled for the same kind of role they play as suppliers in the 767 program. A 777 manager flew frequently to Japan just to hold hands and strengthen the important relationship.

Shrontz's fears that there might not be enough demand for the 777 began to look well founded by mid-1990. He hadn't gotten the one hundred orders he'd set as his minimum before committing to an all-out effort on the project; in fact, he hadn't gotten any orders at all. The prospect of selling one hundred before commitment had practically vanished. Shrontz had to make up his mind whether to wait for his one hundred orders, go ahead anyway, or give up. The questionable market, blank early sales record, and late start argued for getting out of the project. Two circumstances favored proceeding, however.

One, Boeing had never been in a better financial position to develop a new model. In 1990, as airplanes ordered earlier were delivered and paid for, Boeing's financial numbers established company records. Boeing had never before excelled financially, and had often disappointed investors. No aircraft manufacturer had done much better; the returns from investments were seldom appropriate to the huge risks that characterize the business. In the late 1980s, however, Boeing performed sensationally not only for an aircraft manufacturer but for any kind of company—except for one measurement. The company continued to disappoint investors with the ratio many of them consider most important: return on equity (ROE), which shows how much profit a corporation makes for every dollar it has that belongs to stockholders. Even in the giddy 1980s, ROE was stuck at what investors consider the abysmal level of about 10 percent. Shrontz had set as his goal an incredible ROE of 20 percent for each of the next seven years beginning in 1990. ROE for the year was in fact headed toward a figure that not long before could only have been dreamed of: 21 percent. Having attained its technical goals in the commercial field with the best product line of any aircraft manufacturer and the largest share of the market, Boeing now achieved its financial goals with the best bottom line in the history of the business. By any reckoning, Boeing had joined the ranks of eminently successful corporations. With the company on a roll and management forecasting many prosperous years to come, Boeing declared a three-for-one stock split.

Boeing historically had little money of its own—equity capital—for development, and had to borrow heavily. The good times gave Shrontz access to plenty of cash for his first aircraft wager, if he cared to take it. What's more, Boeing wasn't taking as much financial risk with the 777 as it had done in the past, as for the 747. Then the company had more long-term debt and less cash, and was juggling the 747 with several other big projects. In the fall of 1990, Boeing had low long-term debt, only about 15 percent of capitalization, and enough cash on hand, $3.6 billion (despite the recent strike), with more coming in, that the company didn't have to borrow for development expenses. Development of the 777 was projected at about $4 billion. Plans for the 777 didn't call for great leaps in technology, moreover, so the technical risks would be low. Shrontz was the first Boeing CEO who could gamble comfortably—he wouldn't have to bet the company.

Another circumstance favoring a go-ahead for the 777 was the relentless strengthening of Airbus Industrie. The consortium was booking more orders in 1990 than the legendary ex-king of the aircraft industry, Douglas Aircraft. Airbus's offerings were outselling all Boeing's aircraft, too, except for the 747, a type that Airbus didn't make. Boeing's share of total new orders for the industry was dropping, and would end the year at 45 percent—the first time in decades that it had been below 50 percent. If Boeing didn't put up a competitor to Airbus's new jetliners, the company risked becoming an also-ran like Douglas.

Before rendering his verdict, Shrontz wanted to see what would happen at an unusual affair scheduled for Friday, October 12. United Airlines wanted to buy thirty-four jetliners. In what was probably the weirdest bargaining session ever in the aircraft industry, Jim Guyette of United summoned Boeing, Douglas, and Airbus Industrie, as well as all three engine makers, to a negotiating session at United's building in Elk Grove, outside Chicago. The companies occupied adjacent offices. Guyette and his staff called them one by one into his office, which the manufacturers nicknamed "the inquisition chamber," and recalled them time after time, trying to wring out everybody's best deal. Nothing had been settled by sunset, but Guyette decided to keep going until he'd selected an airplane and engine. The sun rose on Saturday, swung past noon, and set again.

Guyette had decided against Douglas but hadn't chosen between Boeing and Airbus. He called time-out for all the groggy participants to get some sleep, and drove back to his home north of Chicago. He woke up at dawn Sunday, unable to sleep with all that was on his mind. Gazing out over the lake in back of his house, he realized he'd prefer the 777, whose development was yet to be completed, over Airbus's completed airplane. United's chief financial officer was holding out for Airbus, however. Guyette figured he'd prevail with United's chairman if Boeing would give him an even larger say than United already had in the 777's final design and choice of suppliers. He yearned to eliminate totally the usual "new plane" glitches when United started flying its new jetliners. When he presented his proposal to Boeing later that morning, Boeing's negotiators had to get Condit to the meeting to cement the deal. Condit was with his daughter attending parents' weekend at Colgate University in New York, but his colleagues managed to reach him by phone. Used to corporate demands impinging on his personal life, he cut short his visit without hesitation and caught the next flight to Chicago. Guyette later remembered sweating that hectic weekend: "There was a great deal of tension. Jobs, careers, and companies were on the line."

When Condit arrived in Elk Grove, he met with Dick Albrecht, the executive vice president of the Commercial Airplane Group who had been leading the bargaining for Boeing, and Guyette. They agreed on objectives for their special relationship in foaling the 777, which Guyette wrote on a sheet of plain white paper: "In order to launch on time a truly great airplane, we have a responsibility to work together to design, produce, and introduce an airplane that exceeds the expectations of flight crews, cabin crews, and maintenance and support teams, and ultimately our passengers and shippers. From day one: Best dispatch reliability in the industry; greatest customer appeal in the industry; user friendly and everything works." All three men signed the document. Then they made mutual pledges for their companies in six areas: trust, cooperation, teamwork, listening, responsiveness, and quality. Guyette put these on paper, too, along with detailed descriptions of the purpose of each pledge, and again all three executives signed. These wedding vows closed the deal.

Guyette was sure that the order would make up Shrontz's mind for the 777 go-ahead—and it did. Boeing's chairman not only had his first 777 sale, a stronger marriage to United, and a definite program, he also had a motto for the 777 program. Soon emblazoned on signs, hats, T-shirts, and tote bags was WORKING TOGETHER, a phrase from the first sentence of the objectives. The motto came to symbolize the overall effort always to keep the various kinds of people involved in the program in touch with each other.

On October 29, 1990, the board of directors—with whom Shrontz had been consulting all along—formally gave its approval and the project was officially launched. The next day the company held a 777 launch party at lunchtime for its Seattle-area employees. A hangar at Boeing Field was decorated with red, white, and blue decorations. T-shirts and seat cushions imprinted with slogans were handed out. The party had a football-rally motif, and there were two large goalposts festooned with yellow balloons. A cheerleading squad from a Seattle-area high school led cheers. Two bands, including the marching band from the University of Washington, provided music. They played "Tequila" and paused when the audience usually shouts "tequila!"; these listeners yelled "CATIA!"

Considering how late Boeing was in launching the new airplane compared to its competitors, some observers felt that Boeing had grown too cautious. Douglas was about to deliver its first MD-11, and Airbus was promising deliveries in 1992 for the A340 and 1993 for the A330; Boeing couldn't deliver a 777 until 1995. In a speech to Boeing retirees not long after the 777 launch, legendary designer Jack Steiner, himself retired, gave the company a piece of his never-bashful mind: "I call Boeing today a reactionary bureaucracy. They do not lead, they react, and they're a bureaucracy." Shrontz replied to his critics that the delay simply enabled Boeing to let its competitors get locked into a design, so Boeing could develop an airplane that could beat them, as Douglas did to Boeing with the DC-3 and as Boeing itself did to its competitors with the 737. Condit, sounding alarmingly like Donald Douglas when he pooh-poohed the 707's early lead, said soothingly, "We haven't been first very often, but frequently we've been best." Both Shrontz and Condit genuinely believed that their airplane sported such better features and performed so much better, that it would lick its rivals and avoid the unhappy fate of the look-and-fly-alike DC-10 and L-1011 when they fought for the same market. Enthusiastic now that the 777 was committed, Boeing spokesmen told the press that they thought the company would sell one thousand of the jetliners, and expected the model to be Boeing's most profitable ever.

Shrontz ordered that the already-huge facilities at Everett be enlarged to handle 777 production, and planned to spend $1.5 billion on the addition. Then he ran into galling hitches in his attempt to produce the 777 cheaply. The city of Everett made the company pay almost $50 million to build roads that could handle the increased traffic and to improve other aspects of Everett's infrastructure. Shrontz felt this was unfair in view of the economic benefits created by the expansion, especially since other localities, far from taxing the creation of new business, actually offer companies tax breaks to relocate or expand there. Shrontz also complained about the long bureaucratic delays in the environmental assessment process that seriously (and expensively) delayed Boeing's construction schedule. He let it be known that in the future, rather than expand or build new facilities in the Puget Sound region, Boeing might undertake construction in a more accommodating place. Given Boeing's serious looks at California in the past, the strong desire of Kansas to get more of Boeing's action, and the company's current stress on the economics of its business, this seems no idle threat.

The major new technologies in the 777 involved the controls and cockpit displays, which had been made all-electronic and heavily computerized; greater use of composite materials; and the wing. Boeing claimed that the wing, unusually long and thin, would be the most efficient wing ever designed, and would help the airplane to reach a speed about twenty miles per hour faster than any other jetliner. It's strong enough to support greatly enlarged derivatives; an American Airlines vice president observed, "They've got enough wing on that airplane to lift New York."

For passengers, Boeing made the fuselage five inches wider than any competitive airplane, expecting that the airlines would use the extra room for passenger comfort rather than cramming in more seats, and redesigned the overhead bins to leave more headroom. As an option for airlines to offer customers, Boeing designed a combined video and computer system that features a monitor on the seat back in front of each passenger for such activities as watching movies, playing computer games, and shopping by computer. The system is so powerful that it represents 40 percent of all the aircraft's computer capacity.

The airline "gang of eight" advisers looked at fifteen hundred design features and changed three hundred of them (including making it easy for flight attendants to change bulbs in reading lights). Gang members suggested the swing-down overhead bins that would become a big selling point to airlines and their passengers.

The three major jet engine manufacturers developed the largest and most powerful engines ever built for an airplane—almost double the previous thrust record. The engines became the center of a controversy. For the 777 to be profitable, Boeing had to be able to sell it for use on overseas flights. Yet the FAA had a standard rule that would not allow an airplane with only two engines to fly routes that took it more than an hour from an airport where it could make an emergency landing in case of engine trouble. Airlines that flew overseas routes would not buy the 777 if faced with this restriction. The FAA would make an exception, called Extended Twin-engine Operations, or ETOPS, after new engines had proved themselves in commercial service for two years. The two-year wait could prove devastating to the 777 program. Boeing therefore began lobbying to get ETOPS, allowing the 777 the three-hour margin it took to cross the Atlantic, before the jetliner even entered service. Boeing wanted to substitute exhaustive ground-testing and test-flying of the engine for in-service experience. Boeing counted on getting early ETOPS, taking a small technical risk that the 777 might not be able to pass the ground and flight tests, and an enormous political risk that early ETOPS might not be granted for any number of nontechnical reasons.

Pratt installed a test engine on a 747. On the third flight, the engine surged—backfired—twice, spewing fire and smoke. Pratt had to redesign the compressor, the heart of the engine—a major setback. Author Karl Sabbagh reported, "People at Pratt were leaving meetings and vomiting in wastebaskets."

Shrontz said that all in all the 777 would be the world's most technologically advanced jetliner, and analysts agreed. Convinced that the airlines value reliability more than fancy technology, however, Boeing devoted much of the development effort to making the new product virtually trouble-free.

The 777 development program continued smoothly, with no major complications. Halfway through it, the board of directors determined that Phil Condit had proved his fitness for the presidency. In August 1992, the board elected him president and welcomed him to membership on the board as one of its own.

Phil Condit, a thick-featured man who, like Shrontz, wears glasses, was born in Berkeley, California, on August 2, 1941. His father, descended from French Huguenots who had settled in England, was a chemist for Standard Oil of California. His family moved to Lafayette, east of Berkeley, where he grew up as an only child. Under the guidance of his father, a Scoutmaster, the precocious Condit became an Eagle Scout at the age of only 12½ years, when many of his friends were still struggling to achieve first class. Fascinated by aviation, he wallpapered his bedroom with a route map he had gotten from Pan Am. His father took him for walks in the Sierra Nevadas, inculcating Condit with a love for mountains and hiking. He was elected student body president in high school.

After graduation as an A student, he enrolled at the University of California at Riverside to study physics. Deciding to become an engineer, he transferred after his freshman year to the University of California at Berkeley to major in mechanical engineering. He earned his B.S. in 1963, and planned to go to Cornell to get an M.S. in aeronautical engineering. Before he committed himself, the chairman of the rival department at Princeton called and sold him on going there. The Princeton faculty urged him to get a Ph.D., but the department chairman advised him he'd be happier as a working engineer at Boeing with his M.S.

Condit interviewed with Boeing, as well as Lockheed and McDonnell Douglas. Boeing's two rivals offered him jobs right away, but he heard nothing from Seattle. He had decided to take the Lockheed job when Boeing came through. He started in 1965 at Langley Field in Virginia, working on a test program that Boeing was conducting with NASA. He rose fast in the company, and spent a year at MIT as a Sloan fellow studying management in 1974. He became a vice president in 1983, taking charge of the 757 division, and, six months later, was named head of the entire Renton division. He was appointed executive vice president of the Commercial Airplane Group in 1986. Unlike Wilson and Shrontz, who had had strong backgrounds in government or government contract projects, Condit had spent his entire career on the commercial side, which seemed to say that, in choosing him as Shrontz's likely successor, the board considered that side of the company more important or in need of more attention.

The new president was married to Jan, his third wife, and had two daughters. They live by a river in North Bend, out I-90 about thirty-five miles east of Seattle at the foot of the Cascades. Chez Condit is an immense, multi-million-dollar mansion situated out of sight from the road on a sprawling estate. ("Ostentatious," one of Condit's few detractors sneered.) Like Bill Allen, he likes to do business entertaining and hold meetings at home, but on a scale unmatched by anything in the Highlands. The "great room" in his house can hold six hundred people. Ever the engineer, he built a computerized miniature railroad that runs through the house delivering drinks to guests. He exercises by splitting wood on his grounds for his fireplaces, as well as playing fiercely competitive racquetball and squash at a gym. He doesn't spend as much time as he'd like in his manse, traveling frequently. When he's not out of town, he leaves by six most mornings, driving himself to work like his predecessors, and usually stays late for customer dinners or business functions.

He enjoys the Seattle lifestyle, which he characterizes as doing things with friends. Seattleites tend to make their friends through their leisure activities, he notes, unlike people in other places such as Wichita, who find friends in their neighborhoods. Condit appreciates opera and likes to sing himself in what a friend rates as a "great" voice.

He can't stand by while there's work to be done, and has been known to help arrange chairs in meeting rooms where he was to be the featured speaker. When he and Jan spend time at the bed and breakfast inn that she owns in California, Condit dons old clothes and does odd jobs around the place; guests have mistaken him for a hired hand.

People who know Condit typically describe him as a "people person." Asked to explain that trendy phrase, they generally go on to say, in one form or another, that he's interested in people, likes them, understands them, empathizes with them, and treats them with consideration to a greater degree than some who previously held his job. Yet, a friend pointed out, he doesn't need company around to be happy, and often requires time by himself.

Condit seems to learn best by listening to people, and an associate claims he has a "photographic memory" for what he's heard. This is appropriate for the leader of Boeing, because the company has what Don Krebs, Condit's organizational psychologist, classifies as a tribal culture. He explained that this means Boeing maintains its culture partly through executives and other employees telling one another stories about Boeing's people, often featuring great personalities of Boeing's past. In conversation, Condit will tell a story to make a point. He's developed a ritual around this aspect of Boeing's culture. Periodically, he invites groups of managers to his house who have never been there. They sit around a fireplace, and each one tells a story about a good episode at Boeing. Then each person takes pencil and paper, writes a story about a bad episode, and throws the paper on the fire. Finally, they write stories they'd like people to tell about Boeing in the future, and keep the papers— some managers carry them around in their wallets ever after.

He enjoys acting as a guide and teacher for his subordinates. His leadership style is to draw people out, to lead by example and indirection rather than explicit command.

Condit would rather work in groups than alone and foresees tasks at Boeing being handled increasingly by teams instead of individuals. He bemoans the lack of teamwork in Congress, exemplified by the budget impasse that shut down the federal government (not a political judgment—he labels himself neither liberal nor conservative, but "gray" philosophically). He's said to feel uncomfortable with controversy, and some subordinates are wary of presenting controversial opinions or bringing conflicts to his attention. There are colleagues who worry that unanimity and consensus may please Condit too much, although he gets high marks from observers in almost all other areas of management.

The 777 rolled out at Everett on April 9, 1994, bearing a "sticker" price of $120 million. The term "rollout" had become a misnomer, because Boeing—now as savvy as anyone about promotion—instead made the event a grand unveiling, literally a Hollywood extravaganza, arranged by Dick Clark Corporate Productions, Incorporated. The festivities started the night before, with a dance in the hangar housing the 777 for customers and other VIPs. About dawn the next morning, in the semidarkened hangar at Everett, a crowd of fourteen thousand employees stood before a huge curtain decorated with the faces of people from around the world. As a recording of Frank Sinatra singing "Come Fly with Me" played through loudspeakers, lights slowly came up behind the translucent curtain and revealed the shiny new 777, its red, white, and blue coat of paint sparkling under the lights. Onlookers could be seen wiping tears from their eyes. The curtain lifted, and staff members with light-sticks in their hands, moving their arms like airport attendants guiding an airplane into a gate at night, motioned the people to come see the new jetliner. The mob moved under and around the airplane, gawking and taking it all in. The performance was repeated several times throughout the day for different groups of employees, who had tickets for specific shows.

Though not quite as big as its older sister, the 747, the latest member of the family was nevertheless a huge airplane. The horizontal part of its tail (the stabilizer) was the size of a 737's wing, and the engines were as big around as a 737's fuselage. Each engine generated around eighty thousand pounds of thrust—more powerful than the rocket that lifted off with the first American astronaut.

The 777 flew for the first time on Sunday, June 13, 1994. Explosive charges were placed on four windows on the right side, so in an acute emergency the glass could be blown out to decompress the cabin instantly, allowing the crew to open the doors and parachute to safety. Just before departure, in the usual test-flight ritual, crew members filled out insurance forms. With Seattle's KOMO-TV telecasting the event live, the jetliner took off into the usual overcast skies at 11:45 A.M. As Shrontz's great hope in the competition between new-generation aircraft shot skyward, he and other Boeing executives slapped each other on the back and hugged their wives.

As chief test pilot John Cashman raised the landing gear after taking off, he felt an abnormal vibration; nothing to worry about, but one of the observations he had to make a note of that working Sabbath. (It was later found to be a minor design problem that had to be reworked.) He flew the new airplane uneventfully for nearly four hours, changing his planned flight course only to avoid clouds — the Associated Press reported Cashman as saying the worst problem he met was "Washington's lousy weather"—and landing smoothly, relieved that no windows had to be blown out. In a post-flight debriefing, sounding like a new car buyer after taking his automobile out for its first spin, Cashman talked about little things such as the brakes making a grinding sound after landing.

United Airlines continued its intimate involvement with the development by participating in flight testing, the first time the airline had ever been invited to take part in this last stage of development.

Fortune magazine estimated that the total cost to develop the 777 had been a mind-boggling $5.5 billion. Break-in costs associated with the CATIA computer system that were much higher than anticipated jacked up the cost considerably. Interest costs seem to have been higher than expected, as Shrontz had less cash to work with and had to borrow more than planned because airlines were suffering financially, couldn't make fat preliminary payments, and asked Boeing to extend credit. Shrontz, while he couldn't be surprised at a budget overrun in the aircraft development game, had had to put more money in the pot than he'd hoped.

United planned to make the first scheduled flight on June 7, 1995, from London to Washington, D.C. Engine testing for early ETOPS from the FAA that would allow the 777 to fly that route so soon had gone well, and Boeing and Pratt thought they had proved conclusively that the engines were worthy of a favorable ruling. Ten days before the flight date, however, the FAA still had not granted the necessary permission. The FAA was taking no chances of mishandling this political hot potato, of being damned if they gave permission and engine failure killed a planeload of passengers, and damned if they didn't give permission and undermined a key company in the U.S. economy. If permission were not granted in a few days, the flight would have to be called off. If permission were not granted for the usual two years, airlines wouldn't buy many more 777s, and Boeing and Shrontz would be in deep yogurt again. Fortunately for the companies, the mountain of test data convinced the FAA of the engine's safety. Permission came through on May 30, and the inaugural flight took place as planned. *Business Week* magazine reported that this victory for Condit's 777 program "bolsters Condit's chance of succeeding CEO Frank Shrontz [who was nearing retirement age] by year end."

United—and Boeing—were delighted that passengers took to the roominess, quiet, and other cabin amenities of the 777, and began to request 777 bookings. United ticket agents found it convenient to keep special cards by their computer terminals listing all 777 flights.

That was the best news for Shrontz as his 777 salesmen fanned out around the globe. The rest of the news stunk. Boeing executives lament that recessions in the airline industry can be predicted by noting when Boeing plans to bring out a new jetliner model. In a scenario eerily similar to that exactly twenty years before, growth of passenger traffic slowed well below expectations at the end of the 1980s. Traffic shrank in 1991, the first year in the jet age in which world airline passenger traffic declined from the previous year. A recession gripped the airline industry, so that when Boeing tried to sell the 777 to other customers, the airlines had less need of new airplanes and less money to spend on them than when the 777 project had started. Unlike the similar circumstances of the early 747 days, however, Boeing was strong financially and could wait out the downturn—if it didn't go on too long.

That proviso began to concern Shrontz as the airline recession deepened into a depression. Deregulation of the airline industry was the root of the problems. Under regulation, generous fares had been set by the FAA, and airlines couldn't compete on price. All had to charge the same fares for the same service, and no airline could advertise that it flew cheaper from New York to Los Angeles than its competitors, for example. Under deregulation, passengers flocked to lower-cost flights, and price competition proved vital to success. U.S. carriers had been fully deregulated by 1984, when the fare-setting Civil Aeronautics Board passed out of existence; European countries also began to deregulate. Inexperienced at operating in an unfettered market, the airlines let costs get out of control, and engaged in suicidal fare wars. From 1990 to 1992, American carriers lost ten billion dollars, which wiped out all the profits they had ever made as a group since they started business. By 1995, all the world's airlines had lost a total of fifteen billion dollars. Airlines couldn't even find enough passengers for many of the aircraft they already had; by the mid-1990s, some one thousand jetliners were in mothballs and parked in long rows in western deserts.

Boeing's customers had never been worse off. Seeing what was happening in 1991, Boeing joined the airlines in conducting a world-wide advertising campaign to persuade people to fly more. That may have stemmed some red ink, but not enough to help Pan Am and Eastern, which went bankrupt that year. In 1994, sounding much like T Wilson during the post-747 trough, Shrontz told an interviewer: "My goal is to come through the downturn and still be willing to make investments for the long-term future, even though the money is tough to come by."

Signs of a slow recovery emerged late in 1994, and the next year airlines began reporting profits for the first time since 1989. By 1996, the upswing seemed to be well under way. Boeing managed to do more than keep its corporate head out of the water. Shrontz had been able to keep his long-term projects going. The same bad economic forces had also affected Airbus and Douglas, moreover, so Boeing didn't lose ground. Better, it gained ground on its competitors because the 777 proved the most popular by far of the new-generation offerings. Such orders as were available in the early 1990s usually went Boeing's way, and the trend accelerated as the airlines regained their health. Boeing's future looked better than ever.

As important as the 777 was to Boeing's future, Shrontz considered another initiative he took in nontechnical areas to be even more key.

=

Bill Gray thrilled with pride when he saw the 777 roll out, knowing that he had played a role in creating it. (Coincidentally, his younger brother in Milwaukee also had a role. He owned a machine shop and turned out parts for 777 galleys.) Bill wanted to do a good job and be even more important to Boeing—perhaps even become a supervisor, if he could somehow get around the politics that he felt went against him. The work that had given him the most satisfaction was the desalting project, where he had the most responsibility and control. He tried to assume more responsibility and control as a millwright, criticizing what he saw as poor work and management practices, and suggesting what he felt were better ways. His supervisors, however, seem to have regarded him as an irritant.

Bill remembers one incident in particular. At a quality circle meeting in 1993, he suggested that aerostands for upcoming 777 production be ordered early. Aerostands are tall, combination ladders and work platforms on wheels custom-made for working on airplanes. The company took his suggestion, and he was assigned to inspect the expensive structures when they arrived from the manufacturer. He felt that there wasn't enough slant to the ladders, making them too steep to carry tools safely up the rungs. He rejected the stands. The company flew him to Indiana to show the manufacturer exactly how much incline the ladders should have. The stands were redone, but they still didn't suit him. The stands went back and forth several times between Washington state and Indiana for reworking until Bill was satisfied. Bill says that Boeing's costs for the repetitive shipments and modifications were large, and fccls that management was "steamed" at him for causing so much trouble and expense.

Another incident happened when a supervisor addressed a group of millwrights and made what Bill considered uncalled-for comments about the union and an engineer who was in legal trouble. Bill wrote a letter to the human resources department objecting to the comments.

As Bill tells the story, the supervisor began making disparaging remarks about his obesity. Diabetes he had developed intensified his natural tendency to put on weight, and he admits grazing too much at the many snack bars scattered throughout the huge Everett plant. He had ballooned to 321 pounds, then dropped to 300, where he stabilized. In the summer of 1995, talking with the supervisor, Bill pointed out something he considered a poor work practice, adding, "They don't do things like that in the Air Force." The supervisor shot back, "The Air Force has regulations about being overweight, too." The supervisor made an official note for the record that he considered Bill too heavy to perform his job satisfactorily. Fearing for his employment, Bill consulted a lawyer, who assured him that he was not so overweight that he could legally be fired.

Later that summer, the supervisor approached Bill and handed him a memo. Bill looked at it and blanched. The document said that the company was transferring him to Auburn, nearly fifty miles from his house and on the other side of Seattle. The commute would be ghastly, but he didn't want to uproot his family and move—buy a new house, put Michael in a new school, leave friends and a familiar neighborhood they liked. The dislocation would be awful for each member of his family, and Boeing wasn't offering a promotion or pay increase to make it worth their while; by accepting, Bill got to keep his job, that's all. He believed that being fourth in seniority in his group should have protected him from such a wrenching order, and was sure he was being singled out by Everett management in retribution for his dissidence, probably in hopes that he'd quit. Bill informed his superiors that he was being treated by a doctor for sleep apnea, a condition that had been diagnosed nine years previously, and that he was in danger of falling asleep at the wheel if he had to drive at least seventy-five minutes each way during the rush hours.

The company didn't relent, so Bill began making the long hauls morning and evening. He also went immediately to a union representative to fight the reassignment, but was told nothing could be done. Bill went back to his lawyer, who began a legal battle for his return to Everett. When the traffic or weather was especially bad, the commute took as long as two hours one way. Everett was only twenty minutes away from his house. The Auburn assignment reduced his free time at home every workday by a couple of hours, and became a major hardship when Linda started having seizures. She had fallen on her head when she was fifteen and developed epilepsy. Her doctor put her on new medication in the summer of 1995, and she was undergoing a period of adjustment while experimenting with the best dosage. During one bad seizure, Linda injured her right shoulder so severely that she required repeated treatments by an orthopedic surgeon. Bill took two leaves of absence, seven days and twelve days, to care for her and the kids.

After two months of the gruesome commute and twenty-five hundred dollars in attorney's fees for the legal wrangling to end it, Bill won his fight: Boeing transferred him back to Everett.

Bill had barely finished fighting his individual battle with Boeing when he was caught up in a landmark union confrontation with the company.

16 ‖ Revolution and Turmoil

At the same time that Boeing was designing its new jetliner, Frank Shrontz was designing a new Boeing. Just as T Wilson is proudest of saving Boeing after the great crisis at the beginning of the 1970s, Shrontz is proudest of saving Boeing from another crisis—the one he's sure would happen if he didn't prevent it. He recognized that the business environment had evolved, and his company had to change with it to stay on top—indeed, to survive. The terms of competition had changed markedly since the beginning of the jetliner era. Then manufacturers had tried to win sales mainly by producing airplanes that flew faster and more economically than those of their rivals. Shrontz believed that the chief selling point in the 1990s and beyond would be low lifetime cost, led by affordable prices for jetliners. Several circumstances brought this transformation about. For one thing, aeronautical technology had matured to the point that the performance and efficiency of competing airplanes now differed little, thus bringing price differences into sharper relief.

A couple of factors tended to drive up the cost of jetliners and drive down the ability of airlines to pay for them. Each new generation of airplanes was technically more sophisticated than the last, and the increase in cost to pay for the new technology exceeded inflation. Modern airplanes were pushing the limits of the airlines' ability to buy them. At the same time, deregulation was forcing airlines to be more cost-conscious. Aircraft manufacturers would have to compete heavily on price, not only against the costs of each others' new models but against the airlines' low costs of keeping their geriatric models up in the air.

Shrontz was convinced that Boeing had to overhaul all its operations; in the business-world lingo of the 1990s, Boeing had to reinvent itself. Although Boeing was the most productive company in its industry, earning profits of about 20 percent on jetliners whose development costs had been written off, it was only average among all industries. A study had shown that the company's inefficient methods had wasted a sickening $3.5 billion in 1987 alone. (Many employees ate lunch at the Lazy Bee restaurant in Renton, and thought the old name still appropriate.) The pioneer in streamlining airplanes in the 1930s, Boeing would now have to streamline its functions to make all of them as inexpensive as possible—especially factory work, the biggest money drain. Low-cost operations would translate into cost-competitive products. Companies that had failed to adapt to changing circumstances in recent years had been seriously weakened or killed—GM, IBM, Sears, Pan Am, and Eastern, for example. "I want to avoid disappearance from the Fortune 500 list [of America's biggest companies]," Phil Condit asserted. It would be a wrenching experience, but Boeing would either go through it or face the prospect of joining such onetime major rivals as the Thomas-Morse Aircraft Company in oblivion.

If Boeing should allow itself to get old and arthritic, moreover, there were carnivores circling the marketplace to fear. Like many executives in the 1980s, Shrontz and other senior managers at Boeing had been alarmed by the Japanese takeover of a large share of the automobile industry's market; the fact that American makers of transportation vehicles had been hit so hard struck especially close to home. As one of the executives confessed, they were afraid that they'd wake up one day and find their markets taken away by "the Toyota Airplane Company, or something like that."

Like T Wilson solving his productivity problem twenty years before by emulating the "ink and ice water" man he was afraid would take over, Shrontz and Condit confronted their challenge by emulating Toyota. Impressed by the account of Toyota in the book about the automotive industry titled *The Machine That Changed the World,* Condit made that company the model for the changes he had to effect as Boeing's president.

Executives of most other large companies in the same situation waited until there was an immediate threat before they instituted large-scale changes; no other company, Shrontz believed, had revolutionized itself without duress. He, on the other hand, remembered how devastating the early 1970s had been because Boeing hadn't changed on time. As an institution, Boeing hadn't learned all it should have from that débâcle, and during the 1980s began making many of the same mistakes again. When Shrontz realized this, he decided he had to act before the problems got out of hand and not afterward. Dean Thornton pointed out, however, that acting early made Shrontz's job tougher: there was no crisis to rally the troops, so breaking through Boeing's bureaucratic inertia would be all the harder.

Shrontz and Condit were convinced that, like Toyota and the other world-beating Japanese companies, Boeing had to involve its workers in identifying and carrying out the needed changes. The top executives knew that such a revolution would be harder at Boeing than at many other companies. Partly because Boeing's organization and culture had been formed in close alliance with the defense industry, the company had always been a top-down, rigid organization run by almost military procedures. Underlings unquestioningly followed orders from their bosses and, in essence, spoke only when spoken to. As one Boeing executive put it, "Openness, candidness, trust, and communication has not been the Boeing way." The executive, who quit a company with more progressive policies to work for Boeing, recounted his interview with T Wilson: "He asked me why I was willing to leave a company with great personnel practices and come to Boeing, which didn't treat anybody worth a damn." In the jargon of academic management experts, Boeing was a strong "Theory X" organization—authoritative as opposed to participative.

The military style didn't fit the wide-body era, whose liberated employees had a different attitude toward work than their parents— not as grateful for the job, less fervent in their devotion to Boeing (they didn't "bleed Boeing blue," as the saying in Seattle goes, referring to the color of the company's promotional material), and more concerned with having enough time to fulfill personal and family interests. A Boeing executive expressed understanding of the new breed: "It's a different loyalty. . . . We've got to earn those people's respect, and we haven't done that by treating them the way we've treated them. And once we get their respect, we'll have their loyalty."

Shrontz sent one hundred top managers to Japan in 1990 to see the results of that country's renowned methods and learn how to adapt the methods to Boeing. He also sent teams around the world to learn the secrets of success from the best companies in many industries.

Shrontz took some innovative steps in his campaign for change. He hired, for a new full-time position, a man whose specialty was helping companies change their corporate cultures. And in a unique move to promote Boeing's values and foster a sense of belonging among employees, Shrontz commissioned veteran aviation writer Robert J. Serling to write the history of Boeing. The book emphasized yarns such as the heroic design of the B-52 over a weekend in the Dayton hotel room, and anecdotes about the company's senior executives and colorful characters. Boeing distributed the thick volume free to all employees and retirees. (Although Boeing paid for the manuscript and vetted it, the text nowhere states this. St. Martin's Press published it in 1992 as a regular book, titled *Legend and Legacy*, and it was reviewed like an independently written work in major publications.)

To prepare employees for the convulsive changes, Boeing showed them a videotape of what would happen if they maintained the status quo: A Seattle anchorman led off the presentation with a mock lead-in to a newscast announcing that Boeing was closing all its plants and offices because it had been driven out of business.

In theory, employees should have rejoiced that Boeing was freeing them from old restraints and empowering them to do better, more satisfying work. In actuality, however, fear and apprehension permeated the workforce, especially among older employees who had experienced the unfeeling irrationality of bureaucracies. Some managers were afraid of being double-crossed—of being forced to form quality circles (employee discussion groups) and then penalized if the groups didn't tell higher executives what they wanted to hear. The fearful managers manipulated the groups, having them meet repeatedly on problems until they came up with solutions that the managers thought their own bosses desired. Some other managers, perceiving correctly that the new approach would end many managerial jobs, ignored the changes when they could and pursued them half-heartedly when they couldn't. People even distrusted the technologies adopted to improve productivity. An old engineering manager made the designers in his group do old-style engineering drawings besides the computerized renderings they did on CATIA. When CATIA showed a problem that the drawings didn't, he ignored it—causing unnecessary delay and expense in a portion of the 777 project.

As a huge corporation, conservative by virtue of a business where safety is utmost—and more conservative than most in its class—Boeing was naturally slow to change. One of the most dramatic demonstrations of Boeing's deep-seated troubles and the time that it would take to overcome them occurred in 1994, when Vice President Grace Robertson resigned "in frustration because of bureaucratic impediments to improving efficiency," according to a reporter who interviewed her. The story was told over water coolers at Boeing of an enraged Robertson slamming her work badge on the table at a meeting, shrieking "I quit!" and stalking out. The president of Boeing's Commercial Airplane Group remarked to his employees in a bulletin, "It is unfortunate that Grace's frustration with the time it takes to implement change, and with the bureaucratic obstacles that can get in the way, led to her resignation." Gossip spread, using the *b* word to describe Robertson, that the company was better off without her—leaving listeners to wonder whether that was indeed true or was a reflection of an endemic male chauvinism that had helped to drive her out. Another Boeing executive explained that women have only recently joined the engineering "club" in significant numbers, so there are few highly placed women in companies dominated by engineers, like Boeing. Because women are unusual in the upper ranks, some people who work with female executives at Boeing perceive them as risks to be avoided, he mused. "Grace Robertson was told to make changes in the way Boeing works and got some resistance from the traditional engineering fraternity. I think that is the source of most of the frustration. Management didn't give her proper support," he admitted. Robertson, a forty-one-year-old avionics engineer and career Boeing employee, would say nothing beyond her brief initial statement. Three months after walking out on Boeing, she became a vice president at Douglas.

Employee expectations were often too high: Quality circle members felt frustrated when they weren't given all the power they had anticipated, and when many of their suggestions were turned down or put on long timetables. Lifting the lid on employees long repressed also produced the paradoxical phenomenon that often occurs when repressed races or ethnic groups are given their freedom: Instead of generating happiness, the new openness unloosed emotions of anger and discontent.

Shrontz felt that he and other managers hadn't done a good job of guiding the transition. "There's much rank & file resentment that management is not up to the task. We have not performed well at changing, and have not communicated well," he confessed to an interviewer.

It was in this simmering witches' brew of bad feelings that two significant labor negotiations took place. The first was in 1992 with SPEEA, whose contract ended December 7. (Boeing had had no trouble signing a new contract with the IAM that October.) A cost-of-living adjustment (COLA) for technical employees, equaling what the IAM had won in 1989, was highest on SPEEA's agenda. These workers have earned associate degrees, or nontechnical college degrees, and help engineers or do other technical work. They constituted close to half the membership of SPEEA, which bargained separately for their contract. Over the past year, SPEEA had lobbied and demonstrated for COLA, its most visible plug being a section of seats at home games of the Seattle Mariners major-league baseball team, designated the "SPEEA strike zone" and decorated with signs promoting COLA. When Boeing made it clear during negotiations that the company was against COLA as strongly as the union was for it, SPEEA employed informational picketing, its members marching in front of Boeing plants and offices carrying placards with messages such as WE WANT COLA. Boeing was unmoved, but presented a contract proposal that was otherwise generous. SPEEA's negotiators, knowing Boeing's adamance against COLA and understanding that realistically COLA had no chance, decided to recommend accepting the contract.

On November 3, SPEEA held a rally in the cavernous Kingdome to present the proposal and recommendations to its members. Many of the nine thousand engineers and technical workers who attended arrived carrying their COLA placards. The members were handed summaries of Boeing's proposal as they filed in. For the first time, many of them learned there was no COLA in the proposed contract. Mumbling against the contract got louder and louder as the seats filled, then quieted when the meeting started. Charlie Bofferding, SPEEA's lead negotiator and executive director (the hired administrative head), formally presented the contract and his recommendation to sign. As he spoke, his audience began to boo. Then chants of "We want COLA" welled up from the assembly. Someone tore a COLA picketing sign off its stick and hurled the stick like a spear toward the speaker. Others did the same, and Bofferding had to dodge a barrage of wooden spears. His seven-year-old daughter, there to see Daddy at work, screamed in terror at the assault on her father. When the fusillade stopped, leaving Bofferding unharmed, he had to tell the enraged throng that Boeing wasn't offering any general wage increases to the engineers, either. He had to go on to say that individual bonuses, although large and given every year, would be partly tied to performance appraisals by supervisors and therefore, his listeners knew, subject to favoritism. It seemed to those in the Kingdome seats that the IAM was again getting a much better deal than they were. As a SPEEA engineer later told a reporter, "The IAM gets a 12 percent bonus, but Boeing only offers us 6 percent? That's ridiculous. Shop people deserve more than we do?" Bofferding got thunderous applause and cheers when he announced that SPEEA's leadership council, the elected representatives of the membership, recommended rejecting the proposal. The members began stomping their feet and chanting "Strike, strike, strike!"

In balloting by mail that ended December 7, engineers and technical workers overwhelmingly turned down the despised contracts. At a meeting between negotiators for Boeing and SPEEA the next day, the Boeing representatives declared that negotiations were legally at an impasse. Labor law allowed Boeing, by formally making this declaration, to impose its contracts on the employees; SPEEA's only recourse was to file an appeal with the National Labor Relations Board asserting that there was no impasse, which the union did. At least until the appeal could be resolved late in January, Boeing could implement its contracts. The company did put key portions into effect, minus provisions that would help the union, such as automatic payroll deduction of dues. Holding the position that the matter was thereby settled, Boeing refused to meet further with SPEEA.

On their ballots, the members had authorized SPEEA to call a strike. With the holidays coming up, however, SPEEA bided its time and encouraged members only to write letters to Boeing's top management and wear black armbands at work. Activity picked up at lunchtime on January 7, when thousands of SPEEA members picketed all Boeing plants with placards carrying messages such as CAN WE TALK? and BACK TO THE TABLE. When Boeing continued refusing to talk with union representatives, SPEEA organized a one-day strike as a show of force. The big question was how many of Boeing's normally nonmilitant engineers and technical workers would honor the strike. Boeing seems to have expected only a minority to stay away from work, and only active SPEEA members at that; SPEEA hoped to turn out a large majority.

At 5:30 A.M., Tuesday, January 19, 1993, Boeing's engineers and technical workers began the first strike of professionals in the company's history, and one of the few in the history of any large corporation. Many picketed and many more stayed home. Ominously for Boeing, many of the absentees were not dues-paying SPEEA members.

Everybody returned to work the next day. Boeing pointedly refused to tell reporters how many engineers and technical people had been absent. Jubilant SPEEA officials, on the other hand, gladly gave reporters their estimate that 70 percent of all of Boeing's engineers and technical workers, SPEEA members and nonmembers alike, had taken part in the strike; SPEEA later revised the figure upward, stating that Boeing had admitted to 80 percent absenteeism of its engineering and technical personnel that day.

SPEEA polled its members by phone to gauge the degree of sympathy for a major strike, and found that most members were not in favor of a longer walkout. Having made its point and demonstrated both the depth and breadth of discontent with Boeing among all the company's engineers and technical workers, SPEEA recommended, and its members agreed, that the union should sign the contracts. The entire agreements could then be put into effect, ending the battle with the company; if necessary, the war could be resumed at the next negotiating period.

SPEEA's members were not pleased with the union, however. Angry that their representatives for the second time had failed to stop objectionable contracts, and putting some of the blame for the broken relationship with the company on SPEEA, many disillusioned engineers and technical workers quit the organization. After the strike, membership plunged from 60 percent of represented employees to 25 percent.

Even before the strike, District Lodge 751 of the IAM, on the prowl again, had tried to exploit the free-floating anger by circulating petitions among engineers and technical workers to make 751 their bargaining agent instead of SPEEA. Despite token efforts at cooperation, the IAM and SPEEA had never gotten along well. The IAM, even after nearly half a century of SPEEA's existence, still wanted to take over SPEEA's membership, or at least the technical worker segment, and occasionally tried a raid. Bill Johnson, District 751 president, contended that many technical workers wanted to affiliate with the IAM because they'd fallen behind in wages. "We had a real pissing match with SPEEA," he admitted. The IAM petition didn't garner enough signatures, however. Johnson aborted the recruitment drive partly, he explained, because his sounding of his members showed resentment of technical employees for getting all the benefits of IAM strikes in the past without missing any paydays themselves.

Boeing insists that the contracts were far superior to any other in the industry, and were among the best any company in any industry had offered for years. SPEEA's staff analysis showed the same thing. Boeing thought itself especially munificent considering that business was slowing and the company was slashing costs wherever it could. Showing a typical Boeing failing, however, the company missed the sensibilities involved. The emotionally charged, outright rejection of the contract, especially by so many highly intelligent, educated, analytical, and restrained engineers, seemed less an expression of logic than of strong feelings against Boeing. The one-day symbolic walkout by the large majority of Boeing's engineers added to the impression that they were seething with resentment against the company. SPEEA members felt that Boeing favored IAM members over them, and neither respected them nor cared much about them. Seeing the enormous amounts of money that Boeing was then pouring into new facilities and equipment, and the vigor with which management was trying to meet its ambitious financial goals, the members felt that the company was getting the money partly at the expense of its employees. Charlie Bofferding, the outgoing young engineer who heads SPEEA, charged in a perceptive analysis, reflecting a changing mood throughout the company, that Boeing was losing consideration for its employees: "Boeing seems to be insuring shareholder return with minor consideration for employee participation in the advances. Employee wages and benefits are being treated as an expense to be minimized. Careers are being turned into jobs."

The employees' attitude toward Boeing was also partly due to the age bubble in the company's management that followed the massive layoffs twenty years before. As older, experienced managers were replaced by much younger, much less experienced people, resentment began to grow among the older employees about the attitudes of the new crop of supervisors. Mature plant workers bridled at "kids" telling them in detail how to do jobs they knew how to perform better than their stripling bosses. A retired engineer expressed bitterness about his last years at Boeing. He sneered at all the "Harvard M.B.A. types," recalling one galling incident where one of these young "assholes" patronizingly lectured his group on the need to consider aircraft safety in their work—the basic principle of the aircraft engineering profession, well known and rigorously followed by every member of the group.

Boeing's own periodic employee surveys showed that most engineers and technical workers were dissatisfied with the company. Because a highly motivated technical force is such a vital part of Boeing's success, understanding and properly addressing these workers' concerns constituted a serious problem for Shrontz whether the beliefs behind them were true or not. Boeing's best engineers could leave, and the best of the new engineering graduates might not consider Boeing. Establishing a solution as one of his highest priorities, Shrontz set a goal of moving Boeing into the top quarter of all companies for employee satisfaction.

Another negotiation cycle came up in 1995; Boeing's three-year contract with the Machinists' union ended on October 3. In spring, preparing for talks with the company, the union polled its members about their concerns. The survey showed that the issue that most angered plant workers was their feeling that Boeing was double-crossing them. Through training programs, they learned the company's new, more productive way of doing business; they actively participated in quality circles; and they cooperated with management, "working together" in striving for higher levels of efficiency. The employees thought they'd been promised greater job security for their efforts. Since 1989, however, Boeing had been laying off its people by the thousands every year. The company attributed the dismissals mainly to the downturn in the airline industry, which substantially dried up orders for new airplanes; the end of the cold war, which greatly turned down the flow of defense money; and the winding-down of 777 development. The workers had always accepted layoffs caused by such economic ups and downs: they understood that was the nature of the work when they hired in.

They became convinced, however, that the flood of layoffs concealed betrayal. They thought that Boeing was inducing them to work themselves out of jobs—that as soon as they became so efficient that two persons could do the jobs formerly done by three persons, say, Boeing would lay off the third person. As a worker told a reporter, "They said, 'Help us, and we'll help you,' and instead they shafted us."

Boeing was taking jobs away from its own workers, furthermore, and giving the jobs to others—subcontractors in this country or abroad—who were willing to work for much less. Boeing was quite open about the practice. The company announced in mid-July that it intended to increase work farmed out to subcontractors from 48 percent of aircraft components to 52 percent. Some of the work that Boeing subcontracts is in "tit for tat" arrangements with foreign buyers who place orders with the understanding that Boeing will place some manufacturing in their countries. District 751 President Bill Johnson contended, however, that most of the additional sub-contracting would be not to further sales but to save on labor costs. Not long before negotiations began, for example, Boeing had discontinued its operation to make insulation blankets, which are stuffed in the space between the cabin walls and the fuselage. The company had contracted with a Mexican firm that could make the blankets for fifty million dollars less in a deal unrelated to aircraft sales.

Bill Gray had worried about his position for years as he watched the jobs of millwrights and other crafts being taken over by contractors. He maintained fiercely that any savings to the company weren't worth what he judged to be the poor workmanship of the outsiders.

A Boeing spokesperson replied to the union's calls for job security with a statement that the company repeated many times afterward in one form or another: "If customers can afford the products and continue to purchase them, that's the only thing we can call job security." In other words, job security comes from making airplanes affordable, which means lowering costs, which to most workers means sacrificing their jobs. The Boeing spokesman seemed to be saying that the only way to secure jobs was to sacrifice them— a corporate spin on the military declaration that the only way to save a town is to destroy it.

Bill Gray had sensed for more than a year that the two sides were headed toward a strike, partly because workers came to believe they were being played for suckers. "We feel we've been duped. Boeing has meetings to make you feel part of the company, and then you find out you're not." He also resented being put through what he considered time-wasting training programs on the global forces affecting the company's business; he'd have much preferred advanced lessons on such topics as making repairs to facilities and equipment. And he was convinced that managers he dealt with were neither as competent nor as dedicated to good work as they used to be. As he saw it, bureaucratic wheel-spinning, workplace politics, and favoritism had taken over Boeing's plants in recent years. "There's so much waste and inefficiency. If I took Shrontz on a tour, I could show him how to save millions," he averred.

Negotiations, under way informally for many weeks, began their final leg on Thursday, September 21, at the Red Lion Inn near SeaTac airport. Boeing's negotiators shook hands with counterparts from a weakened union. At the end of 1993, longtime District 751 President Tom Baker had been sentenced to a year in prison for embezzling thousands of dollars from the union. Bill Johnson, who has the looks and easy, almost diffident manner of an ordinary Joe drinking beer at a tavern, succeeded Baker but had worked with him, and so was suspect in the minds of many union members. The severe job cuts over the past six years had chopped the state's IAM membership from 40,000 to 23,500, sapping the union's strength. Boeing knew that the workers were unhappy with their union, and Johnson was sure that the company thought the workers who had survived felt lucky to have jobs and would roll over for the company's proposals. Boeing clearly had to cut its costs to compete with Airbus Industries and survive, moreover. The company seemed to have totally discounted its employees' feelings about the issues, and naïvely expected them to go along with cutting labor costs. Johnson thought these calculations emboldened the company to press hard for its workforce to make financial sacrifices and forgo significant increases in compensation.

Boeing lacked the sensitivity to be aware of how employees would react to that move at that time. Just two months previously—and only two days before Boeing had announced its intentions to increase sub-contracting—Frank Shrontz and four other top executives had been awarded multimillion-dollar stock options as bonuses for the company's good performance. The awards, established by the board of directors in 1993, were made automatically according to a for-mula based on high stock prices and the time they were maintained.

The word coming out of the meetings seemed to confirm sus-picions that Boeing was knifing its employees in the back. The com-pany wanted to take back the free medical insurance (one of the most generous plans in the country, worth six thousand dollars per year for the average worker) that the union had won in previous nego-tiations, make the workers—including recent retirees—pay for part of the premiums, and increase the deductibles.

This attempt to reduce the workers' gains instead of increas-ing them, in the face of the colossal executive bonuses, was like pouring fuel on the employees' smoldering anger. The union mem-bers thought it made a mockery of the 777 project's "Working Together" theme. "Our members went crazy. The execs were get-ting all the gravy," Johnson related. Sounding wounded, he com-mented, "We look at the compensation package of Frank Shrontz and we're not outraged by it. But what we are upset about is that we're not sharing in Boeing's success." The workers felt they deserved a reward, too, and certainly not a cut. They were in a mood to deliver a good punch in the nose to management.

On Friday, September 30, Boeing's team put a complete con-tract proposal on the table, with the degraded benefits, and bonuses and pay increases much lower than those provided by the existing contract. District 751 officials called the offer "totally unacceptable." On Monday night, Boeing laid its final, only slightly improved offer on the table.

On Tuesday, employees marched at Everett, Renton, and Auburn, shouting defiance. Referring to "World Class Competitiveness," Boeing's rubric for its program to re-engineer the corporation, several people carried signs emblazoned WORLD CLASS, MY ASS. In some locations, they hammered in unison for five minutes every hour, chanting "Strike! Strike! Frank got the gold and we got the shaft!" The union recommended that workers vote "no" to the contract and "yes" to a strike.

Boeing sent a letter to each union employee, signed by Shrontz and Condit. It summarized what Boeing had been trying to drum into its workers in recent years:

> . . . As you consider the offer, recognize that all of us at Boeing are standing at the cross roads. . . . Airbus has accomplished what it set out to do: capture market share, develop a family of airplanes, and become a formidable competitor.
>
> The nature of the defense business has changed dramatically, with declining budgets and the consolidation of competitors. Our customers—airlines and governments alike—tell us our products simply cost too much.
>
> We need to take decisive action to control our own destiny. If we don't, our competitors will control it for us.
>
> We believe that the proposed new contract recognizes both the realities of today's business situation and your efforts to keep the company competitive.

The union replied caustically:

> . . . Normally we would not take the time to respond; however, with the strike imminent we believe that we will have enough time to spare.
>
> . . . We feel compelled to ask: Does your recent pay raise and bonus recognize both the realities of today's business situation and your effort to keep the company competitive?

We would also like to ask you if you think it is fair to have Boeing's Most Valued Asset, the Boeing employees (so we are told), accept what would amount to a cut in pay while the top executives receive their million-dollar salaries and bonuses.

In past contract years, you have asked us to sacrifice for the good of the company. In return, you accepted pay raises that could have paid for the annual incomes for several employees—maybe for a few you laid off.

How do you expect us to feel now that you have asked us once again that we sacrifice for the good of the company? . . . You are not merely asking us to make a sacrifice, you are asking us to be the sacrifice.

Sincerely,

Boeing's most valued asset: the Boeing employees.

On Thursday, the union (having agreed to work on a contract extension for two days) set up polling places near each plant, and workers voted on the contract and strike just as if they were casting ballots in a political election. A simple majority would approve or reject the contract, but a strike needed a two-thirds majority. Bill Gray felt that Boeing's terms were tolerable and not worth striking over, so he voted to accept the contract. He believed, however, that if there were to be a strike, it should have the strongest possible support among union members, so he voted to sanction any walkout.

At 9:15 P.M., Bill was watching channel 7 when a news flash appeared: 76 percent of the workers had rejected the contract, and 78 percent had voted to walk out—they'd strike at midnight.

Milt Grover, a sharp former factory hand who worked himself up to Boeing vice president and chief labor negotiator, later summarized the causes of the strike. "The layoff situation is what made the workers angry. It's been going on for five years, and fear is prevalent," he observed. He explained that Boeing's decision to increase subcontracting—although "not a lot of instances"—and the campaign of the Machinists' International in Washington, D.C., against foreign subcontracting combined to fan the anger and fear. Finally,

"Our desire to modify the health care plan played a part. It almost made the strike inevitable." Grover downplayed the role of the fat executive bonuses: "The bonuses were not that important. The timing was unfortunate, but as an issue it was a red herring."

Prudent workers cut spending to the bone. Just the chance of a long strike meant that many of the hardships of an extended paycheck drought began immediately: Families had to drop cable TV and on-line computing services (a surprising number had home computers), tell the children they couldn't take piano or gymnastics lessons, put off the purchase of new clothes. Bill Gray dropped plans to buy a new pickup truck.

Bill normally thinks of himself as a Boeing man first and a union member second. He turned completely around when the strike began (one reason unions favor periodic walkouts), but was nevertheless astonished at the breadth and depth of support for the strike among his coworkers. The solidarity with fellow Machinists helped to sustain him as the strike began. The prospect of being off work awhile wasn't all bad, either. Bill looked forward to deer hunting and getting "rainy day" jobs done around the house.

Linda had none of these consolations and was most unhappy. She and Bill figured they could last a month before they'd need to take out a loan against their savings. They'd have trouble paying Michael's parochial school tuition of $1,800 a year, and making their loan company and credit union installments. Medical benefits would cease at the end of October, and they'd have to pay $750 a month for a plan that would keep up the coverage they'd had. If the strike should go on for months, they'd have to worry about meeting their mortgage payments, and might have to sell their house.

Bill got out of bed at 2 A.M. on Saturday, the second day of the strike, and drove to the Airport Road gate at Everett in the dark for his first picket duty. His turn wouldn't come until 4 A.M., but he wanted to hang out with the guys and chat awhile first. When it was time, he picked up a sign that read ON STRIKE AT BOEING in big letters, with a sticker that said NO TAKEAWAYS, and began parading for four hours with a dozen other strikers in his group.

On Wednesday, the union organized a mass march from the union hall to the company's headquarters. One striker waved a sign that said FRANK—YOU HAVE YOURS. WHERE'S OURS? Others brandished similar sentiments. Someone led the chant, "Spank Frank Shrontz!" Bill Johnson and George Kourpias, head of the Machinists' International, both gave rousing speeches.

(Later, Johnson explained the importance of the strike in the national labor picture. He declared that, because District 751 was the IAM's largest unit, Kourpias was "looking to us to set the stage for further industry negotiations." The IAM would be holding contract talks with several of the largest aerospace firms in 1996. "We planned with the national IAM for eighteen months. They provided major resources for us. When we saw Boeing balking during negotiations, Kourpias backed us up." Labor experts also speculated that the national IAM wanted to shore up its power within the combined Machinists', Auto Workers', and Steel Workers' union that was scheduled to be formed, and that John Sweeney, newly elected head of the AFL-CIO, had to show his strength.)

On October 23, SPEEA began negotiations on its contracts for engineers and technical workers, which ended December 1. (Understandings that Boeing worked out with SPEEA on some issues would become the basis for arrangements with the IAM.)

Bill drove to Tyee High School on Saturday to pick up a check for one hundred dollars from the union. He and the other picketers could get the checks every Saturday from then until the end of the strike, unless it went over six months and exhausted the fund.

By mid-November, the Grays were almost out of cash. Down to their last six hundred dollars of spending money, they were putting off paying bills. Bill could get cash from the company instead of the 40 hours of paid vacation he had coming (out of the 120 hours he earned every year), but didn't want to give up his holidays. They did give up plans to fly to Milwaukee for their annual Christmas vacation, however, as well as thoughts of buying a new rug and couch. Bill applied for a large loan against his retirement account.

On November 15, Bill went to the bank to cash his latest strike check, and saw that he wasn't the only one feeling the pinch. As he described the scene, "Lots of people were there holding stacks of savings bonds in their arms to cash in—from the savings bond plan at work. One guy had a stack a foot tall." He went from the bank to the loan company to get more money to pay his bills.

The director of a Seattle-area coalition of food banks announced that the charity's stocks were low because Boeing workers who normally contributed heavily to the banks were instead drawing from them. The union began a charity drive to raise money for the children of strikers.

The biggest story on the business pages of the nation's newspapers on November 16 was a Boeing piece. The company was reported to be holding talks with McDonnell Douglas about buying all or part of its longtime rival. Jokes spread through the picket lines that the new company would be called "McBoeing." A labor expert volunteered that the news helped the strikers because it showed that, if Boeing had all the money to buy a huge business, it had plenty to spend on its employees. Neither company would confirm the talks and, although analysts thought the report well-founded, the excitement died down and nothing happened.

Boeing and the union made no substantive move toward a settlement in six weeks of striking. Negotiators finally got together for serious bargaining on Saturday, November 18, at a location kept secret to remove the pressures and leaks that press coverage brings about.

Big news broke with the dawn on Sunday: After twenty straight hours of negotiations, the sides had agreed to a contract. As a Boeing spokesman described the agreement, "The basic wage offer remains unchanged from the October 2 proposal. . . . [although] it does look like the company gave a little" on nonwage issues. The union issued a brief, bland statement, recommending the settlement but not sounding enthusiastic. (Indeed, unannounced to the public, union officials didn't like the contract, but thought their members were ready to settle, and considered Boeing's offer the best they could get then. They might have tendered the contract to the members for a vote without a recommendation, but Boeing wouldn't settle unless the union recommended the pact.)

As Sunday wore on and strikers got word of the agreement's provisions, union officials began to act strangely. They issued another, lengthy statement almost apologizing to members for the poor settlement. Bill Johnson recorded a new message for the union hot line, downplaying his recommendation of the morning and stressing that accepting the contract—thus ending the strike—was really up to the workers themselves.

Bill Gray saw what was going on when he tuned into TV news coverage of the agreement that evening. He described to a telephone caller what he was watching: "There's a mob of angry people at the union hall. I've never seen people so angry at the union. They're shaking their fists at Bill Johnson. . . . There's a picket line on the TV now. People are ripping up copies of the contracts. They're burning the contracts in the burn barrel."

As soon as union officials had announced the settlement and gotten first reactions, they realized they hadn't grasped how strongly their members felt about what they were striking for. The strikers hadn't given up paychecks for a month and a half to get token concessions and be told "that's the best we can do." What's more, based on their experience in the last strike and the spectacular bonuses being given to Boeing executives, the workers had assumed—incorrectly—that the settlement would include a larger bonus than first offered to help compensate for wages lost during the walkout. The strikers were furious with Boeing for not granting more, and with the union for caving in.

Members voted on Tuesday. In an incredibly unlucky turn of events for Boeing, that very day the top executive bonus formula automatically triggered another outpouring of over three million dollars into the personal bank accounts of Frank Shrontz and four of his colleagues. (Relating the entire story of the executive bonus farce afterward to a visitor, Bill Johnson and an assistant broke up laughing. A securities analyst asserted that a smart management and board of directors should have foreseen the possibility and consequences of an automatic bonus scheme being activated during labor negotiations—not to mention that giving fabulous awards to executives while asking blue-collar workers to sacrifice was questionable to begin with.)

Bill Gray drove to the abandoned tavern in Everett that served as his polling place. Hundreds of workers were milling around, their looks and voices betraying anger and resentment. Some held up signs protesting the contract terms, a typical message reading 47 DAYS FOR WHAT? Although Bill sympathized with the general mood, he'd had enough. If the strike went on much longer, he and Linda would see their savings disappearing, and their future and that of their children daily getting grimmer. But he couldn't bring himself to vote for the contract. He left his ballot blank and attached a note to the union leaders: "You can vote what you want." Even fuming as his coworkers were, he thought they, too, were ready to give up rather than prolong their ordeal.

Bill was watching the 6:30 P.M. local news on TV when the channel cut to the union hall for a live announcement. Bill Johnson stood before screaming Machinists, who were raising clenched fists and yelling "No givebacks, no way!" He waited for silence, then spoke briefly: "We just finished the tally moments ago. And we still have a labor dispute going on." Two of every three voters had elected to turn down Boeing's offer.

The results stunned Boeing executives. Like union officials, they'd figured that strike fever was spent, especially with Thanksgiving on Thursday, and Christmas decorations and music at the malls reminding the pickets that the year's biggest, most expensive holiday was little more than a month away. The company had expected its employees to return to work Wednesday, so they could get the next two days off as paid holidays.

Bill had mixed feelings about the outcome, but Linda was definitely glum. She put her own plan into action, making arrangements to become an Avon lady. Bill admitted somewhat sheepishly that he "wasn't too aggressive about part-time job hunting."

At least two Boeing supervisors sent the people in their work crews twenty-dollar bills to pay for Thanksgiving turkeys. Bill and Linda had their feast on Thursday and another thanksgiving of sorts the next day. The loan against Bill's retirement account was approved, yielding nine thousand dollars. They fervently hoped they wouldn't go through it all.

On Wednesday, December 6, negotiators went back to the bargaining table at an "undisclosed" location. (Those who had to be informed discovered they were at the Port Ludlow Resort & Conference Center on the Olympic Peninsula.)

Reporters found out that, the day after the last vote had shocked both the company and the union, Frank Shrontz and George Kourpias spoke by phone for twenty minutes. (Each of the power-conscious leaders later claimed that the other placed the call.) Shrontz revealed to a writer afterward that Kourpias "told me that if I would do some things, he could get a unanimous recommendation to accept the contract—otherwise, there would be no recommendation. The changes he suggested didn't seem major. I talked with our people, and they agreed. We were both concerned that if it went on, it would be more difficult to settle, and there'd be resentment." Shrontz divulged that several times he'd gone to picket lines and talked with strikers personally, and took calls at home from some of them. (He's listed in the phone book.) He believed this gave him good insights about how they thought and felt, and what they were going through. "A strike tears at you," he allowed. Three other phone conversations between Shrontz and Kourpias followed over the next two weeks. Bill Johnson later explained the import of the phone talks: "They were able to do the thing that 'card playing' negotiations couldn't." As in politics, a summit meeting, even by wire, could accomplish what was impossible for professional negotiators. (Of importance to Phil Condit's future, he wasn't responsible for negotiations: Boeing's labor relations people reported directly to Shrontz.)

Other factors must also have influenced Shrontz, especially pressures from his customers, the airlines. United and Southwest had already canceled future flights because delivery of the new jetliners they'd been counting on had been postponed, and more revenue-losing cancellations were possible. Other airlines that needed airplanes soon threatened to buy Airbuses. Shrontz also had to worry about suppliers. Boeing had kept supplies from most vendors coming so as not to disrupt the pipelines, but costly inventory was piling up. In one case where Boeing had to slow down subcontracted work, Northrop Grumman was forced to furlough 6,450 workers as a result.

As Bill Gray was preparing to leave for Saint Mark's Church to work as a bid recorder at a parish auction on Friday, December 8, he was intrigued to learn that Everett management had told employees not to report to work that weekend. As he sized up the situation, "Usually people work on weekends. This shows they have a secret agreement already. This stops people from looking through computers for scabs." Since many scabs had avoided identification, strikers were trying to find them out before the walkout ended by having contacts inside the plants from other unions tap into the computers, and print and smuggle out lists of employees reporting to work. Bill recognized the possibility of extenuating circumstances, and didn't hate scabs, as some strikers did. But he resented their going to work, getting as much overtime as they wanted, "making lots of money" while his family and the families of other loyal unionists suffered, and then in time sitting back and enjoying all the benefits won by the sacrifices of him and the others. Picketers were supposed to identify fellow workers crossing the lines and report them on standard union forms, scary in their bureaucratized efficiency. The orange 8½-by-11 sheets were headed PROCEDURE TO VERIFY SCAB CROSSING on one side. The reverse side, titled 1995 VERIFIED SCAB, had spaces for names and testimony of three witnesses under the subheading WITNESS VERIFICATION OF CROSSING THE LINE BY THE ABOVE-LISTED SCAB.

Unknown to Bill and the rest of the public, the negotiators isolated at the Port Ludlow Resort hadn't finished but were making rapid progress. At 11 A.M. Monday, however, they deadlocked on the wording of four sentences concerning the key issues of subcontracting and job security. A union spokesman later divulged, "The company still wouldn't budge. So we said we would take the offer back to the membership with a recommendation that they reject it, and if need be we would hold this strike together until well into January."

Shrontz and Kourpias had pledged to talk if their negotiators stalemated on an issue. Kourpias called Shrontz to report there'd be no deal unless Boeing strengthened the job security language. Nineteen minutes later, the negotiators reconvened, made a few changes in the disputed sentences, and signed off on them.

At 1:30 P.M., the negotiators left Port Ludlow and returned to Seattle. That night Boeing and the union announced they had agreed to a tentative contract.

"We hope [strikers] understand that this proposal represents the limits of a prudent contract," Shrontz commented. Indeed, he had made major concessions in all key areas. Boeing would actually pay workers to join a health maintenance organization, and suspend employees' payments to the most popular medical plan; observers agreed that new, complex job-security provisions were the best in the industry; and the company doubled the bonus it would pay workers in the first year of the contract, to 10 percent of wages. Raises and cost-of-living adjustments, although essentially unchanged from the original offer, would lift the average wages for Machinists to over twenty-three dollars an hour, highest in the industry. (Bill Gray made almost exactly the average wage. With overtime pay and bonuses, his yearly income would approach sixty thousand dollars.)

Union officials gleefully termed the agreement a "slam dunk" win on every important issue and gave it strong support. Analysts pointed out, however, that it didn't go much further than the company might have gone initially in better-managed negotiations. ("The strike was unnecessary," one of them insisted.) Health care costs were so expensive that even paying employees to switch to a cheaper plan would save Boeing money in the long run. The job security language allowed the company enough wiggle room that it wasn't significantly weakened against its competitors. Boeing preferred paying bonuses instead of higher base wage increases because, year after year, the arithmetic of bonuses allowed the company to pay out less in total than it would in bigger raises. Also, the new agreement changed contract negotiations from three-year to four-year cycles, giving Boeing longer periods of labor peace and stability.

The strikers were relieved—they liked the proposal. On Wednesday, as Bill Gray passed the plant gates on his way to vote "yes" to the contract, he noted, in an almost melancholy mood, the lifelessness of the former picket sites: empty chairs, cold burn barrels, unburned logs. That night, Bill Johnson stepped onto the stage of a packed auditorium at the union hall, an architecturally interesting building not far from Boeing's headquarters that's stylized as a Boeing plant. Johnson was delighted to hear cheers instead of the boos he'd attracted the last time. Shouting to make himself heard by a boisterous crowd, he intoned a command that set his listeners to frenzied celebrating, even though it was symbolic for his members having jumped the gun: "Will someone inform the picket captains to pull the pickets? This strike is over!" To no one's surprise, the workers had overwhelmingly ratified the contract, with 87 percent expressing approval. The happiest he'd been in a long time, Bill Gray immediately bought airline tickets to Milwaukee for each member of his family so that they could spend Christmas week "back home," and started thinking about a new truck (later buying a three-quarter-ton Chevy four-wheel-drive with an extended cab).

Early Thursday morning, December 14, Bill left for work, rueful that Linda, probably like most wives of the recent stay-at-homes, seemed a little too glad to kiss him good-bye. After being away from his job for sixty-nine days—a walkout second in length at Boeing only to the monumental 1948 strike—Bill rejoined his millwright crew at Everett, once again bustling at the task of making jetliners. "It was a strange day," Bill reported. Chairs had been set up in his work area, and coffee and donuts had been put out. Supervisors and higher executives spoke at an hour-long welcome-back ceremony. They interspersed their pleasantries and bromides with a repeated warning: "You'll be fired if you harass scabs." Boeing said that 10 percent of Machinists had crossed the lines, although the union claimed that was an overstatement.

The company could do nothing about ostracism, however. No one talked to the scabs or voluntarily had anything to do with them. Bill risked being branded a "scab lover" by acting not friendly but only civil to the outcasts.

Bill felt better about the company and his job than he had felt after the last strike, which had left lingering dissatisfactions, and thought the feeling was general. Sales of Boeing paraphernalia at employee stores seemed to confirm this. There was a run on caps, T-shirts, mugs, and the like with the name BOEING displayed prominently on them as employees rushed to reassociate themselves with the company that, when all was said and done, they were proud to work for. Commenting on the special relationship between Boeing and its people, Bill Johnson pointed out that most unions the size of his District 751 would process three or four thousand grievances against the employer every year—he had to contend with only around fifty a year.

SPEEA's two bargaining units had worked on contract extensions until the IAM settled, and then—with Boeing having no stomach for another labor confrontation—agreed by votes of 80 percent to similarly generous terms. SPEEA and IAM had worked closely during the negotiations, and in the afterglow of their victories seemed to have grown fond of one another and ready to march into tomorrow together.

Economists reported that the strike had had little effect on the economy of the Seattle area, evidence that the diversification of recent years had softened Boeing's financial impact on the city.

At a poststrike press conference, Shrontz contended that Boeing's biggest mistake leading to the strike, whose correction would become a high priority, had been a failure to communicate successfully with employees about the costs of doing business in the mid-1990s. In subsequent statements about managing the workforce for the future, he stressed the emphasis Boeing would put on not hiring so many people as its fortunes improved, so the company wouldn't have to lay off so many when business declined.

Shrontz talked about what the company planned—not what he himself would do. His time was almost up.

17 ‖ Widening the Lead

O n the unusually bright February afternoon of Monday, February 26, 1996, reporters and news cameramen from around the Seattle area gathered in the office building that was serving as Boeing's headquarters. Fittingly, given the nature of the announcement that was to be made that day, the news people had to walk past the wrecking crew that was making rubble of the company's antique headquarters building next door. The old was making way for the new.

Frank Shrontz walked up to a podium and, without preliminaries, announced that, on his recommendation, the board of directors had named Phil Condit to be Boeing's next chief executive officer, effective on the day of the annual meeting, April 29. Shrontz said that he planned to continue as chairman only until the end of the year, when he would turn sixty-five years old, and would then retire from the company and the board.

Bill Allen and T Wilson had remained on the board until they were seventy-two, but Shrontz's associates said he had felt inhibited when Wilson had hung on, and wanted to give Condit total freedom. He said he had no retirement plans, but friends said he'd probably spend a lot of time at his vacation house on Puget Sound's Vaughn Bay southwest of Seattle.

With the 777 flying, the pace of aviation technology slowing as it matures, and no pressing need for another new model, Condit will likely be Boeing's first CEO not to roll out a new aircraft during his tenure. "By the time I retire in 11 years, probably no new airplane will have been developed," he told an interviewer. Design of two new jetliner models may begin under him, however: a small airplane of fewer than one hundred seats, and a supersonic jetliner. He will probably also stretch the 747 into a larger, major derivative, and there's a small chance he may build a new superjumbo model.

Boeing is talking with several Asian countries about developing the small jetliner in partnership. The supersonic aircraft would have to overcome economic and environmental objections to the old Supersonic Transport; it would probably cost around twenty billion dollars to develop. The supersonic passenger airplane, and any attempt at a superjumbo, would likely also be undertaken with partners.

Condit is convinced that, despite the abortions of all Boeing's previous attempts at partnerships to develop jetliners, an alliance involving sharing of equity and control is inevitable. Observers think a marriage with a Japanese group most likely. Although Condit can't ignore the possibility of Japan learning the business and then going out on its own, experts tend to discount the threat, mainly because the risks are much greater than the Japanese have encountered in any other industry they've entered.

Boeing's future looks increasingly international all around, with more and more foreign customers, competitors, partners, and suppliers. Because of the growth of airlines in other parts of the world, only 30 percent of Boeing's sales in the mid-1990s come from U.S. airlines. Most forecasters agree that the overseas market will continue to expand faster than the domestic market, with new opportunities opening up in the former iron curtain countries, and the greatest growth happening in Asia and the Pacific Rim. Condit expects to be trading punches with Airbus in all the markets throughout his term. At home, Boeing's competition these days is weak. The company's only American rival, McDonnell Douglas, continues to hang on, denying reports that it's near death, but many observers wonder how long it can survive.

Phil Condit and other Boeing executives who want to continue the company's success, and outsiders who want to copy it, would all like to answer a question that's proven imponderable: What's the secret to Boeing's success?

Condit and his colleagues also want to identify and fix the company's flaws. People within and without Boeing are more agreed on the company's biggest flaw then they are about the basis of its success. The widely recognized failing: Boeing's arrogance in treating the people it deals with. As Jim Guyette of United Airlines put it, referring to Henry Ford's notorious, haughty comment that his customers could have any color car they wanted as long as it was black, "A Boeing flaw has been any color as long as it's black. For a long time, their attitude was 'We understand airplanes—you fly them.'" Shrontz has made overcoming the weakness a priority, and Guyette hails Boeing's handling of the 777 program as a turning point. While Boeing has been trying to correct its high-handed treatment of employees, its recent labor problems show that it has yet to develop the necessary empathy.

Phil Condit is working hard to eliminate another defect that he feels is primary. "Boeing's main flaw is that it's capable of growing a bureaucracy," he asserted. Some others, in positions to be less tactful in public utterances than Condit, declare that Boeing has already become a hidebound bureaucracy.

Suggested reasons for Boeing's success range from the character and culture of the company, through fortunate circumstances, to pure luck. Boeing has undeniably been lucky. In many ways, it seems no better than its rivals. Analyzing why Boeing has fared better than its competitors can seem like assessing the superiority of the winner and the inferiority of the loser in a basketball game where a shot at the buzzer wins the contest 100–99. On the other hand, observers argue that Boeing's string of victories is due to more than just chance. A few key ideas come up repeatedly in discussions of the topic; the answer may be a combination of factors.

One of the most frequently mentioned ingredients of Boeing's success is the company's desirable location in Seattle, which helps to recruit and keep good people. Furthermore, Boeing's isolation up in the Pacific Northwest discourages its employees from the job-hopping among aerospace companies that's routine in Los Angeles, the center of the industry.

Boeing's flexibility in the higher management levels is often cited as a key to its success. Although bureaucracies are often rigid and conformist, and ruled through mean office politics, present and retired Boeing executives adamantly assert that their company is different. They insist that the focus on what's good for the company is sharper at Boeing than at other corporations, and that the chilling phrase "That's just not the way things are done around here" and the knife in the back are used less often at Boeing than elsewhere. Boeing, they claim, tolerates dissent and idiosyncrasy, and discourages political infighting, to an unusual degree. The irrepressible Jack Steiner—he of the 737 lobbying plot and the 767 three-engine conspiracy—might have been fired several times from other companies.

Some people say that Boeing succeeds because it generally keeps its eye on the customer more intently than competitors do, providing better and more varied products and service for the money, and allowing and encouraging its engineers to do top-quality work.

Many Boeing veterans trace the company's success not to any fundamental characteristics that business schools could describe in management classes, but rather to getting the right people—or, perhaps, by making itself attractive to the top people. There's no doubt that Boeing has had some outstanding individuals. Repeatedly, executives and retirees note the management brilliance of Allen and Wilson, and the technical genius of Wells and Schairer. Boeing has always been able to find top talent to fill its ranks, partly because of the self-perpetuating aspect of excellence: once a company exhibits superiority, it attracts the best job candidates.

Condit and others believe that Boeing's heroes play a large role in a strong, unifying culture that helps to explain the company's endurance. The stories that are told about these idols often point up their devotion and integrity, and encourage other employees to be like them.

Some people add tall, white-haired, aloof Hal Haynes, the chief financial officer for Allen and Wilson, to the list of Boeing's immortals. The terms "ultraconservative" and "superconservative" come up regularly in discussions of his style of money management. He husbanded Boeing's financial resources, which were often strained to the limit, and did the best with what he had. Especially considering that financial mismanagement has been a leading cause of failure in the aircraft industry, Haynes did a superb job. In line with the business-school dictum that a company's total risk, financial and operational, shouldn't exceed some established level, Haynes's financial conservatism allowed Allen and Wilson more leeway to take risks with development projects that CEOs at rival companies couldn't afford. Haynes's protégés have continued his approach since he retired.

For a company to win the jackpot, the necessary adjunct to financial conservatism is operating daring when risks seem manageable. When Haynes reigned, his policies cut the equally conservative Allen enough slack that the old Scotsman became, as Mal Stamper put it, "a Las Vegas gambler when it came to product." Joe Sutter, developer of the 747, asserted that Douglas, by contrast, has been too afraid of risk to win at the jetliner game. As he put it in typical aerospace industry phraseology, "Douglas never really had the balls to get in."

Boeing historians Drs. Paul Spitzer and Charles Bright and others who have studied the company give credit for its achievements to the continuing influence of the founder, Bill Boeing. In contrast to most other aircraft industry pioneers, he was primarily a businessman—a successful one—and not basically a flier. He established his company on a solid business foundation. Unlike many others who failed, Boeing ran his company and made his major decisions in a businesslike way, influenced but not driven by the romanticism of early aviation. He taught his managers this approach by his example and imbued them with his sense of integrity. He strove to build the reputation for trustworthiness, in both ethics and product quality, that characterizes his company still—not perfectly, to be sure, but certainly as an ideal.

Although Bill Boeing didn't grow up in a small town, he—like the fathers of many great American corporations—instilled in his company the values of turn-of-the-century, small-town America, principally the Calvinist work ethic, frugality, conservatism, and middle-class respectability. (On the downside, these Yankee virtues have been accompanied by small-town smugness.) The Boeing company has been essentially a gigantic version of one of the businesses lining Sinclair Lewis's Main Street.

Bill Boeing further helped his company when he let it go early on and passed on nothing of the corporation to his family. Management had to answer to a broad spectrum of stockholders, which encouraged continuation of the businesslike approach.

To one who has been looking closely at Boeing for several years, it seems not a paragon of all a corporation might be (he knows no companies that even come close), but a firm whose strong points have generally been stronger than those of its rivals and whose weak points have not been as weak. In talking with Boeing employees, however, one senses an implied belief in the organizational equivalent of a soul that *is* such a paragon, an almost spiritual Boeing apart from the corporate body that happens to exist at any moment. While sometimes cursing certain people in charge of the company or a department ("sonofabitches," Dick Henning always calls them), the employees paradoxically express their pride in Boeing and their commitment to it, seeming to mean this immortal Boeing. Senior executives appear to be influenced (but not always compelled) in their practical decisions by a feeling for what the ideal Boeing would do—like a conscience guiding individual moral behavior. This near-religious aspect of Boeing—certainly not shared by Airbus—may be as important as any factor in explaining why it has been so blessed.

The student of Boeing hopes that the company will find a way to develop the High Speed Civil Transport, the politically correct new name for the controversial jetliner that used to be called the Supersonic Transport, or SST. It's aimed mostly at flights between countries separated by the vast Pacific, and would slash travel times between, for example, Los Angeles and Tokyo or Sydney. Like subsonic jetliners that shrank the Atlantic, supersonic jetliners would make a lake out of the Pacific. With subsonic jetliner technology having matured, this project would mark a return to the romantic days of aviation, when the quest for speed drove the pioneers. The student believes that this project would solve many of Boeing's workforce problems (at least for the long duration of development), because in the past daring, exciting projects have motivated and unified employees in a way that no other industry can know. Phil Condit has spoken of the excitement of meeting the mid-1990s challenge of improving manufacturing processes, and he's right, but even toothpaste makers can claim that. There's nothing like a dramatic aircraft development program to bring new life to an aircraft company. One yearns to see Boeing betting the company at least one more time, advancing simultaneously our technology-based society and one of the world's premier corporations.

Frank Shrontz recognizes the attraction of inspiring work. As he prepared to leave his office at the company's nerve center, having passed control to Condit, he was asked why a person should work for Boeing. He answered, "Because of the challenges, the dynamic business, the big decisions. And we'll last a long time."

Acknowledgments

I am indebted to several people for launching this book, and wish to give them prominent thanks:

Russell Galen, my literary agent, who suggested that I apply my background in business and technology to writing the story of the people behind the Boeing Company and its "sexy" airplanes. He started me on a fascinating adventure that covered many years and miles, introduced me to scores of interesting, likable people and the lovely city of Seattle, and made me several new friends.

Morgan Entrekin, head of Atlantic Monthly Press, who took a Boeinglike business gamble in contracting for this book and staking me when I had no assurance that people in the company would talk to me. May he reap Boeinglike rewards.

Harold Carr, Boeing's vice president for public relations and advertising, who took the kind of gamble normally associated with his company's line executives. Boeing has a reputation, earned in years not long past, for not cooperating with writers. In addition to mining libraries, I planned to get my information from Boeing's competitors, customers, unions, government regulators, suppliers, "deep throats," and reporters who cover the company (and I did so). Having spent most of my career in public relations, however, I knew that the first principle in the field is to cooperate with a writer when you know that publication is inevitable and other sources may not be sympathetic. A friend introduced me, publisher's contract in hand, to public relations people he knew at a Boeing division— and they refused cooperation. I learned later they represented the old Boeing staff philosophy: When challenged, hunker in foxholes and do nothing, hoping to survive. I approached Harold and argued that if Boeing was as good as it claimed, then cooperation with an impartial writer would help the company, despite embarrassments likely to come to light in the investigation of any corporation. In fact, I contended, an account of a basically praiseworthy company would impress readers by mentioning the expected faults and mistakes, thereby demonstrating lack of bias; I was sure that the "Nice Nelly" publications that Boeing had issued or sponsored molded few opinions, especially in these cynical times. Harold, influenced by Chairman Frank Shrontz's policy of greater candor, agreed. He opened Boeing to me, scheduling interviews with every current and retired executive I wanted to see, allowing me to use the company's archives, even arranging to get me copies of unarchived minutes of critical meetings of the board of directors. He never refused a request (and I never wasted my breath on solicitations no company could honor). I hope Harold finds his trust in my integrity well-placed; so as not to spoil my story, I leave it to my readers to judge for themselves whether he won his bet that Boeing would emerge better off from even-handed reportage than had he not cooperated.

Two men were singularly helpful to my project. I extend my gratitude to a pair of remarkable people, Dick Henning and Bill Gray, for sharing with me and my readers, sometimes in intimate detail, the stories of their lives and careers with Boeing.

I want to especially recognize people who played key roles in my research:

Paul Binder, Harold Carr's lieutenant, and his staff, notably Sherry Nebel, who helped me with interviews and date gathering.

The staff of Boeing's Historical Archives, Tom Lubbesmeyer particularly, for being so accommodating in gathering documents for me.

Elizabeth Furlow, records collection manager at Seattle's Museum of Flight, for allowing me access to the collection after a budget cutback closed it to outside researchers.

Mrs. William M. ("Mef") Allen, who generously allowed me to copy and use her late husband's diary.

I appreciate the special help of two men: my friend in the business, Marty Kraegel, who vouched for my trustworthiness; and Brindu Giridharadas, who gave me insights into the Boeing story, showed me around the neighborhood where I stayed in Seattle, and introduced me to the Green River walking trail that I came to love.

I thank the many people who gave me their time for interviews—some brief, and some repeated, long, and exhaustive. Four were security analysts who made room in hectic schedules for in-depth talks: Peter Jacobs, Howard Rubell, Bob Toomey, and William Whitlow. Several wish to be anonymous. Others willing to be identified include Byron Acohido, Richard Albrecht, Peter Aseritis, Daryl Banks, Eugene Bauer, Larry Bishop, Ted Boehme, Charles Bofferding, Tex Boullioun, Alan Boyd, Charles Bright, Bob Brown, Peter Callahan, Ed Carrig, Lawrence Clarkson, Bud Coffey, Phil Condit, Deane Cruze, Wolfgang Demisch, Jim Devaney, Bob Fecht, Richard Fowler, Mary Wells Geer, Jim Gepford, Boyd Givan, Linda Gray, Milton Grover, James Guyette, John Hayhurst, Ted Heka-thorn, Glenn Huffschmidt, Robert Hunt, Bill Johnson, Gary King, Don Krebs, Polly Lane, George Martin, Doug May, Gordon McKinzie, Lowell Mickelwait, Bill Olson, Ben Partlow, Merle Peak, Dan Pinick, David Postman, David Price, David Provan, Bill Richards, Robert Rosati, Lisle Rose, George Schairer, Terry Sell, Frank Shrontz, Paul Spitzer, Paul Sporleder, Mal Stamper, Jack Steiner, Joe Sutter, Dean Thornton, Gail Torgeson, Laurie Wells Tull, Dean Wilkinson, Howard Wilson, T Wilson, Bob Withington, Ron Woodard, and, in a general discussion, members of the "Old Farts" retired Boeing engineers lunch gang.

My interviews with current and former Boeing executives delighted me for several reasons. They were almost all friendly, pleasant people, not always the case with managers who have fought their way up the corporate ladder. They enjoyed being interviewed, their pride in their own achievements and that of their company evident as they reminisced. (One elderly retiree thanked me for coming, explaining that his daughter had recently died and our exchange had been a tonic for his depression.) And they were amazingly frank for corporate veterans, apparently feeling, as I was sure Harold Carr did, that Boeing was so great that criticism and admission of errors wouldn't shake it.

Three experts provided invaluable help by reviewing the manuscript: Dr. Charles D. Bright, retired associate professor of history at Southwestern College in Kansas, author of the definitive history of the jet aircraft industry, *The Jetmakers*, and a former fighter pilot, who is writing a history of Boeing; Dr. Paul G. Spitzer, former corporate historian and archivist at Boeing; and Commander Harvard C. Huber, U.S.N. (retired), a former engineer and pilot (and my father-in-law, who, with his wife, Betty, put me up during my research trips to Washington, D.C.). I made the final decisions on disputed points, and any errors are mine.

Staffs at several places helped me: the libraries of Bon Air, Chesterfield County, Midlothian, Museum of History and Industry in Seattle, Richmond, Smithsonian Air and Space Museum, University of Richmond, University of Washington, and Virginia Commonwealth University; the office of Representative Tom Bliley, which aided me in using the Library of Congress; and the Continental Court Motel, which helped to make my visits pleasant and productive.

I appreciate the hospitality of Mensa of Western Washington and the East Side Writers' Group, which assisted me in making independent contacts with Boeing employees.

Only an author's family can appreciate the many sacrifices that writing a book entails. For her patience, love, and support, I owe more than I can express to my wife, Carol.

Bibliography

BOOKS AND BOOKLETS
Works Devoted to Boeing

Bauer, Eugene E. *Boeing in Peace and War*. Enumclaw, Wash.: TABA Publishing, 1991.

Boeing Company. *A Brief History of the Boeing Company*. Seattle: Boeing Company, 1994.

————. *Bill Allen: A Personal Portrait*. Seattle: Boeing Company, 1990.

————. *The Boeing Logbook, 1916–1991*. Seattle: Boeing Company, 1991.

————. *Flight Path: A History of the Boeing Company*. Seattle: Boeing Company, 1991.

————. *Year by Year: 75 Years of Boeing History, 1916–1991*. Seattle: Boeing Company, 1991.

Cleveland, Carl M. *Boeing Trivia*. Seattle: CMC Books, 1989.

Cook, William H. *The Road to the 707*. Bellevue, Wash.: TYC Publishing Company, 1991.

Geer, Mary Wells. *Boeing's Ed Wells*. Seattle: University of Washington Press, 1992.

Henning, Richard A. *The Green-Eyed Engineer*. Seattle: Emerald City Graphics, Inc., 1988.

Irving, Clive. *Wide-Body: The Triumph of the 747*. New York: William Morrow and Company, 1993.

Johnston, A. M. Tex. *Tex Johnston, Jet-Age Test Pilot*. Washington, D.C.: Smithsonian Institution Press, 1991.

Kuter, Laurence S. *The Great Gamble: The Boeing 747*. University, Ala.: University of Alabama Press, 1973.

Mansfield, Harold. *Billion Dollar Battle*. New York: David McKay Company, Inc., 1965.

————. *Vision: A Saga of the Sky*. New York: Madison Publishing Associates, 1950. Rev. ed., New York: Duell, Sloan, and Pearce, 1966.

McCann, John. *Blood in the Water*. Seattle: District Lodge 751, IAM&AW, 1989.

Montle, L. K., and J. E. Steiner. *Post World War II Commercial Transport Design History*. Seattle: Boeing Company, 1981.

Renton Division of the Boeing Company. *How to Build an Airplane*. Seattle: Renton Division of the Boeing Company, 1991.

Sabbagh, Karl. *Twenty-First Century Jet: The Making and Marketing of the Boeing 777*. New York: Scribner, 1996.

Serling, Robert J. *Legend and Legacy: The Story of Boeing and Its People*. New York: St. Martin's Press, 1992.

Steiner, John E., et al. *Case Study in Aircraft Design: The Boeing 727*. Washington, D.C.: American Institute of Aeronautics and Astronautics, 1978.

Steiner, John E. *Jet Aviation Development: One Company's Perspective*. Washington, D.C.: Smithsonian Institution Press, 1979.

Van der Linden, F. Robert. *The Boeing 247: The First Modern Airliner*. Seattle: University of Washington Press, 1991.

Other Books

Ames, Mary E. *Outcome Uncertain: Science and the Political Process*. Washington, D.C.: Communications Press, Inc., 1978.

Bender, Marilyn, and Selig Altschul. *The Chosen Instrument*. New York: Simon & Schuster, 1982.

Biddle, Wayne. *Barons of the Sky*. New York: Simon & Schuster, 1991.

Bilstein, Roger E. *Flight in America*. Rev. Ed. Baltimore: Johns Hopkins University Press, 1994.

Bluestone, Barry, Peter Jordan, and Mark Sullivan. *Aircraft Industry Dynamics: An Analysis of Competition, Capital, and Labor*. Boston: Auburn House Publishing Company, 1981.

Bright, Charles D. *The Jet Makers: The Aerospace Industry from 1945 to 1972*. Lawrence, Kans.: Regents Press of Kansas, 1978.

Brooks, Peter W. *The Modern Airliner: Its Origin and Development*. London, England: Putnam & Co. Ltd., 1961. Reissued in 1982 with an additional chapter and revised bibliography and indexing by Sunflower University Press, Manhattan, Kans.

Contractor, Farok J., and Peter Lorange. *Cooperative Strategies in International Business*. Lexington, Mass.: D. C. Heath and Company, 1988.

Daley, Robert. *An American Saga*. New York: Random House, 1980.

Gandt, Robert. *Skygods*. New York: William Morrow and Company, Inc., 1995.

Hayward, Keith. *International Collaboration in Civil Aerospace*. London: Frances Pinter (Publishers), 1986.

Hochmuth, Milton S. "Aerospace." In *Big Business and the State: Changing Relations in Western Europe,* edited by Raymond Vernon. Cambridge, Mass.: Harvard University Press, 1974.

Hochmuth, Milton S., and William Davidson, eds. *Revitalizing American Industry: Lessons from Our Competitors*. Cambridge, Mass.: Ballinger Publishing Company, 1985.

Horwitch, Mel. *Clipped Wings: The American SST Conflict*. Cambridge, Mass.: MIT Press, 1982.

Jacoby, Neil H., Peter Nehemkis, and Richard Eells. *Bribery and Extortion in World Business*. New York: Macmillan Publishing Co., Inc., 1977.

Jones, Nard. *Seattle*. Garden City, N.Y.: Doubleday & Co., 1972.

McIntyre, Ian. *Dogfight: The Transatlantic Battle over Airbus*. Westport, Conn.: Praeger Publishers, 1992.

Middleton, Don. *Civil Aviation: A Design History*. Shepperton, England: Ian Allen, Ltd., 1986.

Miller, Ronald, and David Sawers. *The Technical Development of Modern Aviation*. New York: Praeger Publishers, 1970.

Mowery, David C. *Alliance Politics and Economics: Multinational Joint Ventures in Commercial Aircraft*. Cambridge, Mass.: Ballinger Publishing Company, 1987.

Mowery, David C., and Nathan Rosenberg. "The Commercial Aircraft Industry." In *Government and Technical Progress: A Cross-Industry Analysis,* edited by Richard R. Nelson. New York: Pergamon Press, 1982.

Nayler, J. L., and E. Ower. *Aviation: Its Technical Development*. Philadelphia: Dufour Editions, 1965.

Nelson, Gerald B. *Seattle: The Life and Times of an American City*. New York: Alfred A. Knopf, 1977.

Newhouse, John. *The Sporty Game*. New York: Alfred A. Knopf, 1982.

Ognibene, Peter J. *Scoop: The Life and Politics of Henry M. Jackson*. New York: Stein and Day, 1975.

Ott, James, and Raymond E. Neidl. *Airline Odyssey*. New York: McGraw-Hill, Inc., 1995.

Pasztor, Andy. *When the Pentagon Was for Sale*. New York: Scribner, 1995.

Perlman, Mark. *The Machinists: A New Study in American Trade Unionism*. Cambridge, Mass.: Harvard University Press, 1961.

Peterson, Barbara Sturken, and James Glab. *Rapid Descent*. New York: Simon & Schuster, 1994.

Phillips, Almarin. *Technology and Market Structure: A Study of the Aircraft Industry*. Lexington, Mass.: Lexington Books, 1971.

Prochnau, William W., and Richard W. Larsen. *A Certain Democrat: Senator Henry M. Jackson*. Englewood Cliffs, N.J.: Prentice-Hall, Inc.

Rae, John B. *Climb to Greatness: The American Aircraft Industry, 1920–1960*. Cambridge, Mass.: MIT Press, 1968.

Rice, Berkeley. *The C-5A Scandal*. Boston: Houghton Mifflin Company, 1971.

Rodden, Robert G. *The Fighting Machinists: A Century of Struggle*. Washington, D.C.: Kelly Press, n.d. [appears to be 1980s].

Sale, Roger. *Seattle: Past to Present*. Seattle: University of Washington Press, 1976.

Sampson, Anthony. *The Arms Bazaar: From Lebanon to Lockheed*. New York: Viking Press, 1977.

———. *Empires of the Sky: The Politics, Contests, and Cartels of World Airlines*. New York: Random House, 1984.

Sherry, Michael S. *The Rise of American Air Power: The Creation of Armageddon*. New Haven, Conn.: Yale University Press, 1987.

Simonson, Gene Roger, ed. *The History of the American Aircraft Industry: An Anthology*. Cambridge, Mass.: MIT Press, 1968.

Smith, Henry Ladd. *Airways: The History of Commercial Aviation in the United States*. New York: Alfred A. Knopf, 1942.

Stekler, Herman O. *The Structure and Performance of the Aerospace Industry*. Berkeley, Calif.: University of California Press, 1965.

Stubbing, Richard A., and Richard A. Mendel. *The Defense Game*. New York: Harper & Row, 1986.

Thurow, Lester. *Head to Head: The Coming Economic Battle among Japan, Europe and America*. New York: William Morrow & Co., Inc., 1992.

Todd, Daniel, and Jamie Simpson. *The World Aircraft Industry*. Dover, Mass.: Auburn House Publishing Company, 1986.

Vander Meulen, Jacob A. *The Politics of Aircraft: Building an American Military Industry*. Lawrence, Kans.: University Press of Kansas, 1991.

Wyckoff, D. Daryl, and David H. Meister. *The Domestic Airline Industry*. Lexington, Mass.: D. C. Heath and Company, 1977.

MAGAZINE AND JOURNAL ARTICLES

"A Study in Contrasts." *Nation* (3 Feb. 1962).

"Accelerating the Jet Age." *Nation's Business* (Aug. 1967).

Banks, Howard. "Boeing by Default?" *Forbes* (31 Oct. 1988).

———. "Moment of Truth." *Fortune* (22 May 1995).

————."Running Ahead, but Running Scared." *Forbes* (13 May 1991).

Beall, Wellwood E. "No U.S. Jet Transports—Why?" *Boeing Magazine* (Sept. 1949).

"Boeing." *Newsweek* (12 May 1934).

"Boeing, Airbus Brace for Fight over Wide-Body Twin Market." *Aviation Week & Space Technology* (22 Jan. 1990).

"Boeing: An Industry unto Itself." *Financial World* (15 Dec. 1978).

"Boeing at 50." *Time* (29 July 1966).

"Boeing: Back on Course." *Financial World* (18 Jan. 1994).

"Boeing Booms Again." *Business Week* (29 Sept. 1951).

"Boeing Chief Foresees Service, Price as Transport Market Drivers." *Aviation Week & Space Technology* (16 Dec. 1985).

"Boeing Conquers the Skies." *Dun's Review* (Dec. 1978).

"Boeing: Is the 'Lazy B' a Bad Rap?" *Fortune* (25 Jan. 1993).

"Boeing Pays Off—and Later Pays Up." *Newsweek* (16 July 1982).

"Boeing Places Its Supersonic Bet." *Forbes* (24 Dec. 1966).

"Boeing Rolls Out Its 757 Twinjet." *Aviation Week & Space Technology* (18 Jan. 1982).

"Boeing's Birthday." *Newsweek* (25 July 1966).

"Boeing's Bombers." *Fortune* (Sept. 1951).

"Boeing's Future Changes to Cloudy." *Business Week* (28 Mar. 1970).

"Boeing's New Beauties Are a Tough Sale." *Fortune* (18 Oct. 1982).

"Boeing's Ordeal with the SST." *Fortune* (Oct. 1968).

"Boeing: Slimming Down an Aerospace Giant." *Business Week* (1 Apr. 1972).

"Boeing Spreads Its Wings." *Newsweek* (28 Aug. 1972).

"Boeing, the Jumbo Exception." *Atlantic* (Apr. 1976).

"Boeing Transport Activities Reorganized under Stamper." *Aviation Week & Space Technology* (5 May 1969).

"Boeing Tries to Maneuver Out of Downdraft." *Business Week* (26 Apr. 1982).

"Boeing Turns to Germans for More of Its Bread and Butter." *Business Week* (23 Sept. 1985).

"Boeing Will Continue Renegotiation Duel." *Aviation Week & Space Technology* (24 Dec. 1956).

"Boeing Wins $700-Million Tanker Award." *Aviation Week & Space Technology* (7 Mar. 1955).

"Bombers by Beall." *Fortune* (Oct. 1944).

"Braniff 707 May Have Attempted Low-Speed Exercise before Crash." *Aviation Week & Space Technology* (26 Oct. 1959).

"Brass Tacks for the Investor." *Barron's* (7 Feb. 1938).

"Bright Smiles, Sweaty Palms." *Business Week* (1 Feb. 1988).

"Can the Northwest Rise Again?" *Economist* (17 July 1982).

Chandler, Jerome Greer. "Just Maybe—a Truly Great Airplane." *Travel & Leisure* (Feb. 1993).

Clifford, Mark. "Stormy Weather." *Financial World* (3–16 Apr. 1985).

"Cloudy in Seattle." *Fortune* (8 Feb. 1993).

Cook, William J. "Building the Biggest Jets." *U.S. News & World Report* (18 Nov. 1991).

"Copilot Inattention, Autopilot Blamed in Uncontrolled 707 Dive." *Aviation Week & Space Technology* (9 Nov. 1959).

"Costly Problems of Success." *Economist* (8 Aug. 1981).

"Delight on the Duwamish." *Time* (1 Mar. 1937).

"Deus Ex Machina." *Economist* (9 Nov. 1991).

Dornheim, Michael A. "Computerized Design System Allows Boeing to Skip Building 777 Mockup." *Aviation Week & Space Technology* (3 June 1991).

———."777 Twinjet Will Grow to Replace 747–200." *Aviation Week & Space Technology* (3 June 1991).

Dubaski, Jagannath. "Boeing in a Stall." *Financial World* (2 June 1987).

"FAA Emphasizes Training Need after Boeing 727 Accident Talks." *Aviation Week & Space Technology* (21 Feb. 1966).

"Fasten Your Seat Belts." *Forbes* (26 Nov. 1979).

"First American Jet Airliner." *Newsweek* (8 Mar. 1954).

"First Boeing 767 Transport Rolls Out on Schedule." *Aviation Week & Space Technology* (10 Aug. 1981).

"From Understudy to Top Dog." *Forbes* (1 July 1970).

"Gamble in the Sky." *Time* (19 July 1954).

Gizzardi, Walter. "U.S. Business Hall of Fame: T. A. Wilson." *Fortune* (13 Mar. 1989).

Hage, David. "A Wing and a Prayer." *U.S. News & World Report* (18 Nov. 1991).

"Headwinds for Boeing." *Forbes* (1 Sept. 1960).

Herrera, Philip. "Magalopolis Comes to the Northwest." *Fortune* (Dec. 1967).

"Hey, Get Your Chin Off Your Chest." *Forbes* (15 May 1971).

"How to Win by Losing." *Forbes* (15 June 1971).

"How GM Won the High-Tech Prize." *Fortune* (8 July 1985).

"Hysteria Triumphs." *Economist* (21 Apr. 1990).

"Impact of Boeing Profit Ruling Weighed." *Aviation Week & Space Technology* (22 Jan. 1962).

"Is Boone Bluffing?" *Business Week* (10 Aug. 1987).

Johnson, Michael. "Tex Boullioun Looks Back at Boeing's Rough Ride to the Top." *International Financial Management* (Nov. 1984).

"Johnson of Boeing." *Fortune* (Aug. 1940).

"Justice Dept. Brings Suit against Boeing, Its Employees for Conflict of Interest." *Aviation Week & Space Technology* (28 July 1986).

Kraar, Louis. "Boeing Takes a Bold Plunge to Keep Flying High." *Fortune* (25 Sept. 1978).

Labick, Kenneth. "Boeing Battles to Stay on Top." *Fortune* (28 Sept. 1987).

"Magnificent Flying Machines." *Time* (16 June 1986).

Main, Jeremy. "Betting on the 21st Century Jet." *Fortune* (20 Apr. 1992).

Markoff, John. "Boeing: One That Won." *Saturday Review* (7 July 1979).

"Masters of the Air." *Time* (7 Apr. 1980).

McLenahan, John S. "Boeing's Turbulence." *Industry Week* (3 Apr. 1989).

Mecklin, John M. "Why Boeing Is Missing the Bus." *Fortune* (1 June 1968).

Merwin, John. "The Boeing Bonanza." *Forbes* (5 Feb. 1979).

"Mesa Purchase of Boeing Stock Highlights Industry Pressures." *Aviation Week & Space Technology* (3 Aug. 1987).

Nevans, Ronald. "T. Wilson of Boeing." *Financial World* (15 Mar. 1979).

"New Intermediate Bomber." *Time* (4 Aug. 1952).

O'Lone, Richard G. "Pan Am Pushed Aircraft Builders to Advance Transport State of the Art." *Aviation Week & Space Technology* (16–23 Dec. 1991).

————. "777 Revolutionizes Boeing Aircraft Development Process." *Aviation Week & Space Technology* (3 June 1991).

"Outcast into Hero." *Time* (10 Aug. 1942).

"Pan Am 707 Dives 29,000 Feet." *Aviation Week & Space Technology* (2 Mar. 1959).

"Passenger Jets?" *Business Week* (8 Oct. 1949).

"People." *Fortune* (Oct. 1952).

"Phil Johnson." *Time* (25 Sept. 1944).

Proctor, Paul. "Boeing Meets Competition with 'Six-Month Airplane.'" *Aviation Week & Space Technology* (22 Nov. 1993).

"Quality Assurance Role Was Factor in United's 777 Launch Order." *Aviation Week & Space Technology* (29 Oct. 1990).

Ramirez, Anthony. "Boeing's Happy, Harrowing Times." *Fortune* (17 July 1989).

————. "Cool, Calm, and Lawyerly." *Fortune* (3 Aug. 1987).

Rappleye, Willard C., Jr. "Last of the Titans." *Financial World* (20 Aug. 1991).

"Recorder Checked for Crash Clues." *Aviation Week & Space Technology* (24 Aug. 1959).

"Restless in Seattle." *Barron's* (26 July 1993).

Schroeder, Michael. "It's Fat and Snazzy—and Worth Billions to Boeing." *Business Week* (29 Oct. 1990).

"Schools, Housing Feel Boeing Pinch." *Aviation Week & Space Technology* (6 July 1970).

Sekigawa, Eiichiro, and Michael Mecham. "Japan Shelves YS-X Launch." *Aviation Week & Space Technology* (18 Sept. 1995).

"707 Drops Engine in Test Flight." *Aviation Week & Space Technology* (2 Mar. 1959).

Shaw, Maria. "Frank Shrontz." *Business Week* (14 Apr. 1989).

———."Trying Times at Boeing." *Business Week* (13 Mar. 1989).

"Soaring Boeing Stock under a Cloud." *Business Week* (2 Feb. 1966).

Spadaro, Frank. "Transatlantic Perspective." *Design Quarterly* (Winter 1992).

Steiner, John E. "How Decisions Are Made: Major Considerations for Aircraft Programs." *The Bridge* (National Academy of Engineering magazine) (Winter 1982–1983).

Stix, Gary. "Plane Geometry." *Scientific American* (Mar. 1991).

"Stop, Thief!" *Time* (16 Sept. 1949).

"T. Wilson of Boeing." *Financial World* (15 Mar. 1981).

"Taking Off." *Financial World* (9 Nov. 1993).

Taylor, Alex, III. "Boeing: Sleepy in Seattle." *Fortune* (7 Aug. 1995).

"The Case against the Supersonic Transport." *Harper's Magazine* (July 1966).

"The Corporate Elite." *Business Week* (11 Oct. 1993).

"The Engineer of Success." *Time* (7 Apr. 1980).

"The Higher the Flight, the Farther to Fall." *Economist* (3 May 1986).

"The Selling of the 707." *Fortune* (Oct. 1957).

Tregaskis, Richard. "Boeing's $15–Million Gamble." *Collier's* (19 Mar. 1954).

Tully, Shawn. "Can Boeing Reinvent Itself?" *Fortune* (8 Mar. 1993).

———."The Value Sell at $115 Million." *Fortune* (Autumn/Winter 1993 special issue).

———."Why to Go for Stretched Targets." *Fortune* (14 Nov. 1994).

"Turbulent Fight for the C-5B." *Time* (2 Aug. 1982).

"Turbulent Fortunes." *Maclean's* (13 Mar. 1989).

"U.S. Jetliner Outlook is Bleak." *Aviation Week & Space Technology* (8 Aug. 1949).

"Uncommon Agreement." *Economist* (2 Oct. 1982).

Underwood, Doug. "The Boeing Story and the Hometown Press." *Columbia Journalism Review* (Nov.-Dec. 1988).

"United Aircraft." *Newsweek* (22 July 1933).

"When Boeing Gets into the Streetcar Business." *Business Week* (12 Sept. 1977).

White, W. L. "Out of the Doghouse." *Saturday Evening Post* (15 Nov. 1941).

"Why Boeing's Hard Line Didn't Pay Off." *Business Week* (4 Dec. 1989).

"Will Boeing's Tails Turn White?" *Economist* (13 Apr. 1991).

"William E. Boeing." *Scientific American* (Mar. 1929).

Wilhelm, Steve. "Boeing: Clear Skies All Around." *Puget Sound Business Journal* (23 Apr. 1980).

Wrubel, Robert. "The Last Titan." *Financial World* (8 Dec. 1992).

Yang, Dori Jones. "Boeing Knocks Down the Wall between the Dreamers and the Doers." *Business Week* (28 Oct. 1991).

———. "How Boeing Does It." *Business Week* (9 July 1990).

Yang, Dori Jones, and Andrea Rothman. "Reinventing Boeing." *Business Week* (1 Mar. 1993).

THESES AND REPORTS

Bofferding, Charles. "Financial Review of the Boeing Company from a Union's Perspective Covering 1988 through 1992." Master's thesis, University of Washington, 1993.

Calkins, K. L. "An Analysis of Labor Relations News Coverage in the Boeing Company Paper and the Union Paper during the Strike of 1948." Master's thesis, University of Washington, 1968.

Erickson, Rodney Allen. "The 'Lead Firm' Concept and Regional Economic Growth: An Analysis of Boeing Expansion, 1963–1968." Ph.D. diss., University of Washington, 1973.

Mahoney, Dan. "Talking Paper III on Agency Fee." Seattle: Seattle Professional Engineering Employees Association, Sept. 1995.

Pascall & Glenn. "The Boeing Company Economic Impact Study." Consultant's report on study sponsored by the Boeing Company. Seattle: Perkins Columbia, Inc., Sept. 1989.

Shin, Tai S. "A Financial Analysis of the Airframe-Turned-Aerospace Industry." Ph.D. diss., University of Illinois, 1969.

Simonson, Gene Roger. "Economics of the Aircraft Industry." Ph.D. diss., University of Washington, 1959.

NEWSPAPERS

Numerous articles in the *Chicago Herald and Examiner, Everett Daily Herald, New York Times, Seattle Post-Intelligencer, Seattle Times, Tacoma News Tribune, Wall Street Journal, Wichita Eagle.*

SPEECHES AND PRESENTATIONS

McKinzie, Gordon. "'Working Together' and the Boeing 777—a Recipe for Reliability." Paper presented at the Association for Manufacturing Excellence. Atlanta, Ga., n.d.

Schairer, George S. "The Role of Competition in Aeronautics." Wilbur and Orville Wright Memorial Lecture of the Royal Aeronautical Society, London, England, 5 Dec. 1968.

————."The Engineering Revolution Leading to the Boeing 707." Paper presented at the Seventh Annual Applied Aerodynamics Conference of the American Institute of Aerodynamics and Astronautics, Seattle, 31 July–2 Aug., 1989.

Steiner, John E. "Aircraft Program Guidelines: Their Application to New Developments." Paper presented at the Twenty-fifth Annual Conference on Aviation and Astronautics, Tel Aviv, Israel, 23 Feb. 1983.

————. Paper presented at Boeing retirees' meeting, Bellevue, Wash. 11 May 1991.

————."Problems and Challenges: A Path to the Future." Paper presented to the Royal Aeronautical Society, London, England, 10 Oct. 1974.

Sutter, Joseph F. Paper presented to the Aerotech Conference of the Society of Automotive Engineers, n.p., 1 Oct. 1990.

————. Museum of Flight lecture, Seattle, 6 June 1991.

————."The Changing Scene in the U.S. Air Transportation System." Paper presented to the Wings Club, New York, 1986.

————."The 747 Skies." Paper presented to the Conference of the American Institute of Aeronautics and Astronautics, Washington, D.C., 1993.

Wells, Edward C. "Aerospace Engineering 1917–1974." Paper presented to the Wings Club, New York, 1974.

DIARY

Allen, William M. Diary (3 Jan. 1944 to 15 Feb. 1978). Owned by Mrs. Allen.

SOURCES AT BOEING'S ARCHIVES
Film Clips

Allen, William M. Employee films collected on videotape, Seattle, n.d.

Interview Transcripts

Bale, Dan. Interviewer unidentified, n.p., n.d.

Pennell, Maynard. Interviewer unidentified, Seattle, n.d.

Schairer, George. Interviewed by Paul Spitzer, Seattle, 25 Feb. 1983.

Interviewed by Harold Mansfield for his official Boeing history, *Vision:* William Allen, Wellwood Beall, Ralph Bell, William Boeing, Claire Egtvedt, Archie Logan, Edward Wells.

Interviewed by Robert J. Serling and others for Serling's official Boeing history, *Legend and Legacy:* Dick Albrecht, Mrs. William T. Allen, Bob

Bateman, Doug Beighle, Marjorie Blair, John Borger, Tex Boullioun, Wally Buckley, George Burton, Art Carter, Bill Clark, Bud Coffey, Phil Condit, Bill Cook, Bob Craig, Deane Cruze, Frank Del Giudice, Carl Dillon, Bob Dryden, Harry Goldie, Alvin Heitman, Ken Holtby, Lowell Houtchens, Bud Hurst, Tex Johnston, Gary Jusela, Bayne Lamb, Russ Light, Robin Little, Stan Little, Richard Loesch, Art Lowell, Sam Lowry, Kenneth Luplow, George Martin, Edith Martin, Lowell Mickelwait, Boris Mishel, George Nible, Dave Olson, Maynard Pennell, Bob Perdue, Dave Peterson, Dan Pinick, David Provan, Tom Riedinger, Rusty Roetman, George Schairer, Clyde Skeen, Otis Smith, Don Smith, Mal Stamper, Jack Steiner, Joe Sutter, John Swihart, Dick Taylor, Bob Tharrington, Harley Thorson, Dean Thornton, Jerry Tobias, Sof Torget, Guy Townsend, Frank Verginia, Lew Wallick, Bert Welliver, George Weyerhaeuser, Ben Wheat, Clancy Wilde, T Wilson, Bob Withington, Ron Woodard, Brien Wygle, Bob Wylie.

Letters of Intent
Connelly, J. B. Letter to Pan American World Airways, Inc., Seattle, 28 Oct. 1965.
Connelly, J. B. Letter to Juan Trippe, chairman and CEO, Pan American World Airways, Inc., Seattle, 17 Dec. 1965.

Minutes of Meetings of Boeing's Board of Directors
22 Apr. 1958; 1 Aug. 1960; 31 Oct. 1960; 9 Nov. 1964; 28 Feb. 1966; 25 July 1966.

Videotaped Interviews
Pennell, Maynard. Interviewed by Donald A. Schmekel, Seattle, 6 Feb. 1988.
Schairer, George. Interviewed by Bill Hamilton, Seattle, 3 Jan. 1986.
Stamper, Malcolm. Interviewed by Donald A. Schmekel, Seattle, n.d.
Surviving participants in "hotel room" design of B-52. Interviewed by Lloyd Goodmanson, Seattle, n.d.
Wells, Edward. Interviewed by Donald A. Schmekel, Seattle, n.d.
Wells, Edward. Interviewer unidentified, Seattle, n.d.
Wilson, T. Interviewed by Donald A. Schmekel, Seattle, 1 Mar. 1985.

MISCELLANEOUS MATERIAL
"Aerospace Industries Association." Packet of information about the industry. Washington, D.C.: Aerospace Industries Association of America, 1994.

Allen, William M. Scrapbooks of newspaper clippings about Allen and Boeing, with some letters and memorabilia, (1947–1981), Seattle, library of the Museum of Flight.

Allen, William M. Transcript of interview by Carl Cleveland, Seattle, library of the Museum of Flight, n.d. [but noted as after Allen's retirement].

Boeing Company. Annual reports, Seattle, 1934–1995.

Johnson, Philip G. Scrapbooks of newspaper clippings about Johnson and Boeing, covering period of Johnson's career, Seattle, library of the Museum of History & Industry.

"Seattle—King County." Packet of promotional literature. Seattle: Seattle–King County Convention and Visitors Bureau, 1995.

Van Voorhis, Jerry. "Decision-Making in the Airframe Industry: Boeing's Reconversion after V-J Day." Comment draft for the summer seminar of the NASA Historical Office, Washington, September 1971. Washington, D.C., library of the Smithsonian Institution's Air and Space Museum, Boeing folder.

Index